# Introduction to Design Education

This practical, engaging book offers design educators a comprehensive, hands-on introduction to design education and pedagogy in higher education. Featuring instructional strategies and case studies from diverse design disciplines, including fashion design, architecture, and industrial design, from both the US and abroad, award-winning author Steven Faerm contextualizes design pedagogy with student development—a critical component to fostering successful teaching, optimal learning, and student success in this ever-evolving industry. Features include the following:

- Advanced pedagogical methods and strategies to improve design students' learning, holistic development, and design school experience.
- Insights into the changing nature of the design industries and future challenges faced by design educators within higher education, and how design programs can be strengthened to better respond to these challenges.
- A range of practical, flexible teaching methods and pedagogical techniques that design educators can easily adapt to their own settings.
- Diverse international case studies and interviews with thought leaders in design, design education, and higher education.

Written by a leading educator in fashion design, Faerm offers educators, school leaders, and administrators the context and skills to understand the evolving nature of the design industry and design education, and to improve design students' learning and design school experience.

**Steven Faerm** is an Associate Professor of Fashion at Parsons School of Design. A Parsons alumnus and Designer of the Year Nominee, he has been teaching for over twenty years and is the author of *Fashion Design Course: Principles, Practices, and Techniques* (3rd edition, 2022) and *Creating a Successful Fashion Collection* (2012). His work has been translated into nine languages and his scholarly research has been published in leading academic journals and other publications.

# Introduction to Design Education

Theory, Research, and Practical Applications for Educators

Steven Faerm

NEW YORK AND LONDON

Cover image: Nathalie du Pasquier, *Cut out*, 2015

First published 2023
by Routledge
605 Third Avenue, New York, NY 10158

and by Routledge
4 Park Square, Milton Park, Abingdon, Oxon, OX14 4RN

*Routledge is an imprint of the Taylor & Francis Group, an informa business*

© 2023 Steven Faerm

The right of Steven Faerm to be identified as author of this work has been asserted in accordance with sections 77 and 78 of the Copyright, Designs and Patents Act 1988.

All rights reserved. No part of this book may be reprinted or reproduced or utilised in any form or by any electronic, mechanical, or other means, now known or hereafter invented, including photocopying and recording, or in any information storage or retrieval system, without permission in writing from the publishers.

*Trademark notice*: Product or corporate names may be trademarks or registered trademarks, and are used only for identification and explanation without intent to infringe.

ISBN: 978-0-367-50230-0 (hbk)
ISBN: 978-0-367-50007-8 (pbk)
ISBN: 978-1-003-04916-6 (ebk)

DOI: 10.4324/9781003049166

Typeset in Sabon
by KnowledgeWorks Global Ltd.

To Kelly

# Contents

*List of Figures and Tables*   x
*About the Author*   xii
*Contributors*   xiii
*Acknowledgments*   xvii
*Preface*   xviii

SECTION I
**Design Industries**   1

1 Introduction to Design Industries: Growth, Responsibility, and Uncertainty   3
2 A Study of the Fashion Industry as a Model of Widespread Systemic Change   11
3 The New Design Entrepreneurs   27
4 The Future of the Design Industries   44
   INTERVIEW WITH MATTHEW KRESSY

SECTION II
**Design Education**   53

5 Introduction to Design Education: The Historical and Contemporary Contexts of US Higher Education   55
6 The Design School Experience   68

viii  *Contents*

7 Speculations on the Future Design School Structure    78
BENJAMIN STOPHER AND TOBIAS REVELL

8 The Future of Design Education    85
INTERVIEW WITH TIM MARSHALL

9 Global Directions: Unique Approaches
to Design Education    93
VERÓNICA FIORINI, SUSAN ORR, BENJAMIN STOPHER,
ARTURO TEDESCHI, AND CHRISTINE TSUI

SECTION III
Design Pedagogy    115

10 Introduction to Design Pedagogy    117

11 Young Adult Development    124

12 Students' Transition from High School
to Design School    140

13 Developing Competent Pedagogy:
A Web of Practices    152

SECTION IV
Design Classrooms    185

14 Introduction to Design Classrooms: A Workbook
of Effective and Strategic Teaching Methods for
Design Educators    187

15 A Practical Guide to Teaching the New Design
Undergraduates    192

16 Teaching as Performance    206

17 Classroom Dynamics: Trust and Conflict    217

18 Motivation and Design Students    229

19 The Inclusive Design Classroom    243

20 Designing the Learning Experience:
The Syllabus    253

| | |
|---|---|
| 21 Assessment as Learning<br>MARIAH DOREN | 267 |
| 22 Faculty Mentorship | 277 |
| Conclusion | 290 |
| *Index* | 293 |

# List of Figures and Tables

**Figures**

| | | |
|---|---|---|
| 1.1 | A lab technician tests nanofibers on an electrospinning machine | 8 |
| 2.1 | A garment sweatshop in 1905 | 13 |
| 2.2 | Number of employees in the US apparel manufacturing industry, 1990–2019 (in 1,000s) | 15 |
| 2.3 | Clothing and clothing accessories store sales in the US, 1992–2019 (in billion USD) | 19 |
| 3.1 | Maslow's Hierarchy of Needs | 32 |
| 3.2 | Mycelium "leather" is a bio-based sustainable and bio-degradable material made of mushroom spores and plant fibers | 35 |
| 3.3 | Designer Kenneth Cole's "Tied with Pride" advertising campaign is one of many the company has developed to support social issues | 37 |
| 5.1 | Number of US degree-granting postsecondary institutions and their total fall enrollment, 1974–2020 | 58 |
| 5.2 | Average undergraduate tuition and fees and room and board rates charged for full-time students in degree-granting postsecondary institutions, 1969–2020 (in constant 2019/2020 USD) | 59 |
| 6.1 | The Bauhaus at Dessau | 71 |
| 6.2 | Gropius' curriculum schema displaying students' sequence of learning, from the outer ring (the *Vorkurs*) to the centralized areas of disciplinary study | 73 |
| 9.1 | The Fiat 500 (1957) | 102 |
| 9.2 | Prototype for a solar balloon that floats above a city by day and lights its streets by night | 110 |
| 10.1 | The studio critique | 121 |
| 11.1 | Emotional well-being, by hours per week using social media (% indicating "frequently") | 129 |
| 11.2 | Percentage of twelfth-grade students who have a driver's license, who have ever tried alcohol, and who have a paid job, 1989–2020 | 134 |

12.1   Perry's Scheme of Intellectual and Ethical Development   142
13.1   The studio classroom   154
14.1   The Pedagogical Ecosystem   189
16.1   Interpersonal distances   214
16.2   Seating positions   215
18.1   Flow model   230
18.2   The Zone of Proximal Development   232
21.1   Bloom's Taxonomy Pyramid   272
22.1   The Model of Effective Mentoring   279

## Tables

9.1   The four phases of growth in the Chinese design industries   99
9.2   Public and private design schools in Italy   105
12.1   Initiatives to support design students' transition into design school   149
15.1   Practical teaching strategies for the new generation of design school undergraduates   193
22.1   Examples of specific responsibilities and activities commonly practiced in faculty mentorship   281

# About the Author

**Steven Faerm** is an Associate Professor of Fashion at Parsons School of Design. A Parsons alumnus and Designer of the Year nominee, he began teaching at Parsons in 1998 while simultaneously working as a professional fashion designer and illustrator. He has been recognized for his teaching by receiving both his University's "Distinguished Teaching Award" and his School's "Faculty Award."

Steven has taught and lectured at over 40 institutions on five continents for students spanning all educational levels, from pre-college- to undergraduate- to graduate-level and beyond. He has created college- and pre-college programs and workshops at Parsons and other leading international institutions, and has served on academic advisory boards for numerous colleges of art and design. He is the author of *Fashion Design Course: Principles Practices, and Techniques* and *Creating a Successful Fashion Collection: Everything You Need to Develop a Great Line and Portfolio*, and his scholarship has been widely featured in academic journals. His research examines design education, teaching and learning, young adult development, and the complex connections between these subject areas.

Steven holds a BFA from Parsons School of Design, an MSEd from Bank Street College of Education, and an EdM from Harvard University.

www.StevenFaerm.com

# Contributors

**Katherine C. Boles** taught at the Harvard Graduate School of Education for twenty-five years, serving as a Senior Lecturer on Education and Director of the Learning and Teaching Master's Program. She retired in 2018. A classroom teacher for over twenty years before teaching at Harvard, Boles, along with her colleague, Vivian Troen, has written and taught about school reform, teacher education, and new forms of teacher leadership. Boles is co-author with Vivian Troen of *Who's Teaching Your Children: Why the Teaching Crisis Is Worse Than You Think and What Can Be Done About It*; *The Power of Teacher Teams: With Cases, Analyses, and Strategies for Success*; and *The Power of Teacher Rounds: A Guide for Facilitators, Principals, and Department Chairs*. Boles wishes to thank Barney Brawer, Nneamaka Eziukwu, Amy Kiser-Schemper, Katherine Merseth, Barbara Neufeld, Rulan Tangen, Vivian Troen, and Michael Sy Uy for their gracious and invaluable assistance with this essay.

**Mariah Doren** has a Doctorate in College Teaching of Art and Design from Columbia University, an MFA in Photography from Pratt Institute, and a BA in Growth and Structure of Cities from Bryn Mawr College. She is Director of Academic Programs, Continuing Education, at Rhode Island School of Design. Her work is a mix of studio practice, writing, and teaching, carefully woven and intermixed such that each component feeds and supports the others. Mariah has a studio practice based on photography that includes collage work combining printmaking, drawing, and photographs included in exhibitions at the Monmouth Museum, New Britain Museum of American Art, and Northern Kentucky University. Mariah's writing centers on teaching: projects include a book titled *Do We Have to Call It Critique? Reimagining the Tradition: More Inclusive, More Fulfilling, and Maybe a Little more Fun* (Intellect Press) and articles include "Working Collaboratively-Teaching Collaboration" in *Transformations: The Journal of Inclusive Scholarship and Pedagogy*.

**Verónica Fiorini** is an Associate Professor of Accessories design in the Fashion and Industrial Design Program at the University of Buenos Aires (UBA), Argentina. She began teaching at UBA in 1999 and served as Coordinator of the Fashion and Textiles Design Program between 2001 and 2006. Her research centers on the intersections between design education, innovation, identity, and the communication of design. She is the co-author of "Fashion Collection as a Discourse" in *Thinking About Design* (Ediciones Infinito, 2021). Her research has also been featured in the academic journal Cuadernos de Estudios en Diseño y Comunicación (Cuaderno 53, 64, and 78), a collaborative publication between the University of Palermo, Buenos Aires, and Parsons School of Design, New York.

**Matthew Kressy** is the founding Director of the MIT Integrated Design & Management (IDM) master's degree program and founding Trustee of the New England Innovation Academy, the first middle and high school that prepares innovators to shape the world through human-centered design. He is an expert in product design and development. As an entrepreneur and founder of Designturn, he has designed, invented, engineered, and manufactured products for startups, Fortune 500 companies, and everything in between. Kressy believes in interdisciplinary, design-driven product development derived from deep user research, creative concept generation, and rapid prototyping. He is passionate about teaching this approach to the design process. Since 1999, Kressy has co-taught collaborative courses in product design and development at top design and business schools, including the MIT Sloan School of Management, the Rhode Island School of Design (RISD), and Harvard Business School. As IDM director, Kressy leads curriculum development and co-teaches the track's primary and required courses. He holds a BFA in Industrial Design from RISD.

**Tim Marshall** is the Deputy Vice-Chancellor, Design and Social Context, and Vice-President at the Royal Melbourne Institute of Technology University. Prior, Tim spent sixteen years at The New School in New York City, first as Dean of Parsons School of Design (2006–2009) and then as Provost and Executive Vice President of Academic Affairs at The New School (2009–2016). As Parsons' Dean, he led a major restructuring based on a visionary academic plan that established the formation of five thematic schools and a more integrated and comprehensive suite of undergraduate and graduate degrees. As Provost, he championed innovative approaches to curricula development and pedagogy, including work in creating a trans-disciplinary approach to the integration of design studies with the humanistic disciplines of the liberal arts, social sciences, and performing arts. Prior to moving to the US, Tim spent ten years in academic roles at the University of Western Sydney, predominantly in the School of Design.

**Susan Orr** is the Pro-Vice-Chancellor: Education at De Montfort University. Previously, she was a Pro-Vice-Chancellor at York St John University. Before her PVC roles, Susan was the Dean of Learning & Teaching Enhancement at the University of the Arts (UAL) in London, UK, a post she held for seven years. In this role, she led the University's Teaching and Learning Strategy. Susan chairs the European League of Institutes of the Arts' Teachers Academy and has published extensively on creative education. Susan co-authored the book *Art and Design Pedagogy in Higher Education: Knowledge, Values and Ambiguity in the Creative Curriculum* and she edits the international journal *Art, Design and Communication in Higher Education*.

**Tobias Revell** is a digital artist and designer from London. He is the Design Futures Lead at Arup Foresight, co-founder of design research consultancy Strange Telemetry, and approximately 47.6% of the research and curatorial project Haunted Machines. He lectures and exhibits internationally on design, technology, imagination, and speculation, and works with clients to imagine alternative futures.

**Benjamin Stopher** is the founding Dean of the UAL Creative Computing Institute, University of the Arts, London, UK. His research interests center on the intersection of design and computation and he is the co-author of the book *Design and Digital Interfaces: Designing with Aesthetic and Ethical Awareness*.

**Arturo Tedeschi** is an architect and computational design specialist with more than ten years of experience in the avant-garde segment of architecture and industrial design. He works as a consultant for leading companies, providing services and training related to algorithmic modeling, complex geometry, digital fabrication, and data-driven design. He is the author of the books *Parametric Architecture with Grasshopper* and *AAD Algorithms-Aided Design*. He taught and was an invited speaker at the Architectural Association School (London), Politecnico di Milano, IUAV (Venice), The University of Sydney, Dubai Institute of Design and Innovation, University of Edinburgh, and Universidad Europea (Madrid). His personal work has been featured in international magazines and exhibited worldwide. He has collaborated with major architecture and design firms, including Zaha Hadid Architects and Ross Lovegrove Studio. info@arturotedeschi.com

**Christine Tsui** is a researcher, commentator, writer, and consultant. With nearly fifteen years of professional experience in the fashion industry, Tsui has worked in operations, sales, retailing, product management, and general management. Her clients have included Nike and Li &

Fung Group, and she has been widely interviewed by the leading fashion/financial media in China. Her scholarly work includes a comparative study between Western and Chinese fashion systems that was conducted when she was a Fulbright Scholar at Parsons School of Design. Tsui's publications include *China Fashion: Conversations with Designers* (Bloomsbury, 2009; Hong Kong University Press, 2013; China Textile Press, 2014), *Work Book for Fashion Buyers* (China Textile Press, 2011; 3rd edition, 2020), and *Advanced Buying and Merchandising* (2020). Tsui has also contributed to *The Encyclopedia of Asian Dress* (2020) and is a section editor of *Economics and Business of Routledge Encyclopedia of Chinese Studies* (forthcoming). Dr. Tsui earned her MA from London College of Fashion and her PhD from The University of Hong Kong.

# Acknowledgments

I give profuse thanks to Simon Jacobs, Senior Editor at Routledge. His warm support and confidence in this book and my abilities, from the very beginning, have been a vivid beacon for me throughout the project. I'm extremely appreciative for being given the opportunity to share my ideas that aim to strengthen design education.

I offer endless gratitude to Kelly Quinn for her outstanding help in editing this manuscript during its development. Her ability to deftly polish and strengthen each chapter's numerous iterations, all while helping to elevate and amplify key ideas, is a very special gift. Our partnership and collaborative processes were profoundly rewarding and inspiring.

I am forever grateful to my "dream mentor" Dr. Katherine Boles. It is through her teaching and our rewarding friendship that has grown over the years that I came to understand what qualifies as a Master Educator. Katherine embodies this awesome role in every conceivable way. It is from her, and the many other faculty members and classmates I met at Harvard, that I learned more deeply what the goals and responsibilities of higher education must always be for our students, faculty, and future world.

I'm honored to feature in this book the remarkable contributions of Katherine Boles, Mariah Doren, Verónica Fiorini, Matthew Kressy, Tim Marshall, Susan Orr, Tobias Revell, Benjamin Stopher, Arturo Tedeschi, and Christine Tsui. Their formidable insights are invaluable to this book, and they will undoubtedly benefit readers and the field. To my research assistants Cheryl, May, and Weijing, I am indebted. Their enthusiasm, curiosity, and perseverance during many sleepless nights contributed greatly to this endeavor.

Finally, I thank my parents, whose great esteem for and prioritization of education sparked in me a lifelong passion for learning, educating students, and working with fellow educators.

# Preface

"Don't worry, you'll figure it out."

In the late 1990s, when I first entered the design classroom as an educator, my hiring director assured me I'd soon "figure out" how to teach. Like many of us, I had vast professional experiences as a designer, so it was assumed I could teach design. With little ceremony, I was placed in a classroom with essentially no pedagogical training or any professorial insight into student development. Through trial and error, course after course, and semester after semester, I was left to "figure it out."

What is "good teaching?" Over two decades after teaching that first course, I still don't have a precise definition of what "teaching" is; rather, as the adage goes, "The more you know, the more you know you *don't* know." My decades of experience working with thousands of students from across academic levels, holding diverse roles in academic leadership and advisorship positions, lecturing across five continents at over forty institutions, completing two advanced degrees in education—and then making sense of it all—has made me think more critically about what constitutes "great teaching" and what being an "educator" *really* means.

The meanings of these terms are far more complex than I ever imagined prior to setting out on my journey as a design educator. My experiences and reflections on this journey have awakened me to the fact that we, as design educators, must give far greater priority to advancing and strengthening our teaching practices than we have before. There is just too much at stake if we don't. Thus, I ardently hope that *Introduction to Design Education: Theory, Research, and Practical Applications for Educators* provides design educators with the knowledge, insights, and skills they need to advance their pedagogical practices.

This book, the first of its kind, provides readers—including design educators, directors, and scholars—with an understanding of the shifting design industries as well as how and why design education in the US is responding. Through the presentation of extensive research, theory, and practical instructional strategies, the text contextualizes design pedagogy with student development. I strongly believe this contextualization is a critical component of fostering successful teaching, optimal learning, and student success.

Design education in the US is responding to the dramatically changing design industries by evolving curricula. Traditionally, these curricula have emphasized vocational skills, but they are now being replaced with those that prioritize the development of students' conceptual thinking, interdisciplinarity, and innovative design processes. Program structures, coursework, and degree offerings are being reimagined to meet the new demands of an increasingly tenuous, accelerated industry so that graduates and young professionals may flourish as their professional design practices and their design thinking evolve.

Concurrently, a new student population is entering design school campuses. This growing population of design undergraduates—the largest *ever*—exhibits markedly different learning styles, personal and professional goals, views of higher education, and developmental needs than the preceding cohorts. Their unique attributes, coupled with the shifts in design industries and education, make it essential for educators to advance and strategize their pedagogy so that their design students, institutions, alumni, and industries can flourish.

For many US design educators, these sudden and ever-increasing shifts have been challenging. Often with little or no support for faculty development from their institutions, they must self-create new teaching methods and strategies that address both the widespread institutional changes and the unique attributes of the new student generation. These design teachers, typically trained as design practitioners and not as educators, are asked to rewrite long-standing mission statements, curricula, syllabi, and design briefs to meet the new requirements. This book provides teachers and others with the guidance they need to work successfully with this particular demographic.

With US higher education's increasing prioritization of student retention, colleges and universities must aggressively focus on faculty development so their faculty may better support these students and thus improve retention rates. Design students are at particularly higher risk when it comes to retention, with many dropping out of college. By some statistics, approximately 40% of art and design students drop out of college, and, among the general undergraduate population in the US, fewer than half graduate within six years.

Research shows the impact high-quality teaching makes on students' well-being and academic success. For example, students who receive three ineffective teachers in a row may achieve at levels that are as much as 50 percentile points lower than students who receive three highly effective teachers in a row. This book presents contemporary research in design education, student development, and pedagogy to contextualize these challenges and provide readers with practical solutions for their students and institutions.

Moreover, the spikes of enrollment in design programs will prompt design schools to hire more design educators, many of whom will be new to the teaching profession. These faculty will need additional pedagogical support due to the reasons outlined above *and* due to the hiring process itself: my professional observations and experiences show that design educators are typically hired for their design experience, not their teaching experience. In the hiring process, school leadership assesses the candidate's design experience and upon hire, places the beginner teacher in a classroom without any (or remarkably limited) form of pedagogical training or support. Consequently, these teachers must experiment with teaching methods through "trial and error," learn as they go, and ultimately "sink or swim" at their students' and institutions' expense.

Although the examination of the design Academy in this book is articulated from a US-centric perspective, I strongly believe that the key dynamics impacting US design higher education are affecting teachers and students in *all* parts of the world, from student retention to student mental health. These dynamics, along with the many others presented throughout this book, will require international design educators and institutions to evolve and adopt new practices.

It is my sincere desire that this book helps prioritize and advance design pedagogy across design schools and, in doing so, reaches beyond design school classroom walls.

## The Structure of This Book

This book contains four sections:

**Section I: Design Industries** examines how and why the US design industries are experiencing unprecedented shifts. These changes are subsequently radicalizing the traditional role of the designer, emergent business models and strategies, consumer behavior, and even the very aims and purposes of design. This section intertwines historical and contemporary contexts with speculations about the likely future of the US design industries. It looks at the changes that will directly impact the ways design schools educate and prepare future students.

In **Section II: Design Education**, US design education is contextualized by first summarizing how the nation's Academy formed into its present model. Chapters in this section discuss the broader, holistic landscape and circumstances of US higher education along with the more nuanced approaches that are specific to design higher education. Following these discussions, theories are articulated with regard to the tenuous futures of both the design Academy and the design classroom experience. This section concludes with descriptions of unique approaches to design education practiced in Argentina, China, Italy, and the UK, all of which have the potential to educate and advance US design programs and educators.

Section III: Design Pedagogy focuses on design pedagogy through diverse lenses. Chapters discuss a range of topics that include the distinct elements of design pedagogy; the nuances of the emergent generation of undergraduates; the cognitive and emotional developmental needs of design students; the newly expanded role of the design educator; methods to employ strategically and successfully diverse pedagogical methods in the design classroom; the adoption of a critically reflective teaching practice to strengthen teaching quality; and the key attributes commonly found among highly effective educators.

Section IV: Design Classrooms, which builds upon the previous three sections, offers a wide variety of research-based pedagogical techniques that will support design educators in the evolving design classroom. Chapters in this section present and examine a broad swath of key concepts, including teaching strategies that target the key attributes and learning styles of the emergent design student generation; interpersonal methods that build trust and manage conflict effectively; guides to crafting well-designed syllabi; practices that foster dynamic pedagogy and class sessions; techniques that bolster student motivation and subsequent success; and ways to cultivate an inclusive learning environment. When synthesized together and utilized in the classroom, these pedagogical techniques can help engender an optimal student experience.

Steven Faerm<br>
June 2022<br>
New York City

# Section I
# Design Industries

# 1 Introduction to Design Industries
## Growth, Responsibility, and Uncertainty

John Dewey (1916/2008), the venerated education reformer and philosopher, famously observed, "we live not in a settled and finished world, but in one which is going on and where our main task is prospective" (p. 134). It is precisely this sentiment that has long governed the direction of the design industries—in the past, in the present, and, most importantly, in the *future*. In no other time in recent history has there been a greater urgency for the design industries to understand and address the interconnectedness of our complex social, economic, political, and natural systems (Davis, 2018a). It is vital that designers and their practices demonstrate contextual intelligence if they are to engage successfully and strategically with informed iterative speculations about our future design industries—and the wider systems they affect (Davis, 2018c).

### The Growing Design Industries

Annually, the US arts industries, which contain the design industries as a subset, contribute approximately $763.3 billion US to the US economy, employ nearly 4.9 million workers, and, in 2015, exported $20 billion US more than was imported into the US (National Endowment for the Arts [NEA], 2018a). Their economic growth frequently surpasses the national average of 2.4%; for instance, between 2014 and 2015, it was 4.9% in inflation-adjusted dollars (NEA, 2018a). Within this sector's growth, the nation's design industries exhibit markedly strong economic performance, especially in particular design disciplines and US states. For example, in 2015:

- graphic design in Illinois grew 69% above the national rate (adding $589.5 million US to the state's revenues);
- architectural design services in Massachusetts grew 73% greater than the national rate (adding $804.6 million US to Massachusetts' economy);

DOI: 10.4324/9781003049166-2

- industrial design in Michigan grew nine times the national rate (adding $429 million US to Michigan's coffers); and
- jewelry manufacturing in Rhode Island grew thirty-three times the national rate (adding $224 million US to the state's economy) (NEA, 2018a, 2018b).

More recently, between 2017 and 2019, the value added to GDP from arts and cultural production increased at a pace of 3%—faster than the overall growth rate of the US economy that was 2.5% for the same time period, and, in 2019, arts and cultural goods and services produced in the US added 4.3% to GDP (NEA, 2021; The World Bank, 2022). The US arts and design industries are so important to the US economy they have generated a widening trade surplus that has increased ten-fold from 2006 to 2019, totaling more than $33 billion US today (NEA, 2021).

Accordingly, employment has risen in many of the US design industries. For example, between 1999 and 2020, there was an increase of graphic designers (up 68%), interior designers (up 100%), set and exhibit designers (up 32%), commercial and industrial designers (up 22%), landscape architects (up 50%), fashion designers (up 119%), and art directors (up 113%) (US Bureau of Labor Statistics [USBLS], 2021a).

Contributing to this growth is the rapid surge of non-design industry companies that are now hiring designers in order to integrate "design thinking" into their organizations. These companies recognize the unique ways of thinking and problem-solving that designers possess; companies are leveraging these designers to innovate new approaches to staid corporate systems and customer experiences. For instance, at IBM, there are more than 2,500 user-experience (UX) designers and researchers embedded across the organization's nearly sixty global studios (IBM, 2022; Miller, 2019). Other companies are following suit due, in part, to the emergent consumer generation's demands for more personalized, customized products and experiences across all aspects of their lives—both in-person and online (see Chapter 3).

Subsequently, there has been a pronounced shift in the hiring ratios of designers-to-developers: between 2012 and 2017, the average increase in designer-to-developer ratio grew 2.5 times, with notable changes occurring at LinkedIn (from 1:11 to 1:8), Dropbox (from 1:10 to 1:6), Atlassian (from 1:25 to 1:9), and IBM (from 1:72 to 1:8) (DeAmicis, 2019). In fact, research shows the general demand in the US economy for employees trained in design and emerging technologies grew 250% in just ten years (2009–2019) (Kett, 2019). Rosanne Somerson, President Emerita of the Rhode Island School of Design (RISD), has spoken publicly about this growing proliferation of designers across diverse corporate sectors. For example, while RISD's annual career day always draws the standard design companies seeking new hires (e.g. architects, graphic designers, and interior designers), over the last several years, the scope of attendees has been expanding to include employers from venture capital firms, the insurance, finance, and healthcare industries, and other sectors that "want the creativity of people that can spot trends, that can think about what's coming, what's important, what's well designed," and can "conceive ideas for new things that aren't evident" (Somerson, as quoted in Vartanian, 2019, n.p.).

The future bodes well for many employees in the diverse design industries. Between 2020 and 2030, total US employment is projected to grow by 7.7% (USBLS, 2021b). (This percentage reflects recovery growth from the low 2020 base-year employment following the emergence of COVID-19 in 2019.) The design industries are anticipated to experience varying levels of economic growth during this ten-year period. Job growth is predicted for architects (3%), graphic designers (3%), industrial designers (6%), set and exhibit designers (9%), art directors (11%), and web developers and digital designers (13%) (USBLS, 2021b).

## A Bigger Role and Responsibility

The ever-growing scale and ubiquity of design and the design industries in nearly every area of our lives require that corporations and their designers assume far greater responsibilities than ever before for the impact of their products and services on numerous areas, including the environment and critical social issues. One factor that impacts this significantly is the fact that there is rapidly increasing adoption of designers in non-traditional "design" environments, such as companies that offer technologies across vertical markets—as seen above with enterprises such as IBM. These roles require additional levels of interdisciplinary understanding of design and society. Fortunately, in the US, there is a growing number of designers who increasingly engage in inter-, multi-, and trans-disciplinary practices.

While designers of the 20th century primarily focused on object-driven outcomes (e.g. those that improved products and environments), designers of the 21st century will be focused on knowledge- and service-driven outcomes. This shift in focus has consequently "spawned audience-centered theories of interpretation; raised concern for how complex information systems are planned, produced, and distributed; and highlighted the social, political, and economic consequences of design" (Davis, 2018b, p. 4).

As a result, the design industry has expanded its foci from the technical skills of "drafting" and "styling" to include strategic skills such as "design strategy/thinking" and "problem-solving." Although the demand for "traditional" designers is constant within the design industries, "[our] society today demands a new generation of designers who can design not only products and communications, but systems for living as well" (Muratovski, 2016, p. 19). This transformation—from an industrialized system that is concerned with commerce ("product creation") to one that also acknowledges its place in and responsibility to a more complex and challenged world ("process creation")—requires designers to assume a bigger role and more responsibility in our global society (Muratovski, 2016). Design practitioners must now ask more meaningful and probative questions about their respective industries, their work, and their customers.

It is through this heightened awareness and engagement in systems construction that designers can understand better that every single decision they and/or their corporations make has consequences. As Chochinov (2007) incisively notes, "We have to remember that…design equals mass production, and that every move, every decision, every curve we specify is multiplied—sometimes by the thousands and often by the millions. And that every one of those everys has a price. We think that we're in the artifact business, but we're not; we're in the consequence business" (n.p.). These consequences are vast and include sustainable sourcing and manufacturing, ecosafe disposal methods, attention to biodiversity and ecology, and social responsibility. Additionally, as applications and implementations of automation and robotization increase across industries, designers must also consider the ramifications of adopting these technologies throughout global systems—and the impact these systems will have on people's livelihoods.

For some designers, these responsibilities may seem daunting at first. Yet each obstacle can be mitigated or eliminated if, at the educational level, design teachers work hard to lead students to understanding and contemplating the esoteric potentials, opportunities, and obligations of design, rather than merely teaching the pragmatic process of churning out more and more "pretty things" (Chochinov, 2007). As design educators and as design professionals, everything we choose to discuss, espouse, spotlight, advance, and ultimately produce brings us that much closer to or farther from a sustainable and symbiotic world.

## Systems-Oriented Design

What, then, is the raison d'être of the design industries in the years ahead? Numerous scholars (e.g. Davis, 2018c; Dubberly, 2008) assert the design industries must assume an advanced role—as a sort of "systems steward." In this role, designers are afforded the necessary time and support to analyze a system's patterns and apply theories of change at the advent of every new venture, no matter its scale. This "systems-before-artifacts" design process affords ample benefits, including a more sustainable practice whereby every element of the design system is quantified—"metrics before magic"—prior to proposals being approved for advancement (Chochinov, 2007). Naturally, this underscores the imperative of interdisciplinary design practice. When designers eschew siloed approaches and build connections across relevant but diverse practices, they ensure design initiatives address what previously had been unforeseen psychological, ecological, social, or other challenges and consequences—within both the system and the final product. By reorienting the designer's focus, the design industries can now recognize the difference between systems-oriented work and simply producing "stuff."

Accordingly, this systems-oriented design process radically alters the traditional designer-consumer relationship. In that relationship, the traditional designer-auteur works independently and creates saleable products for a passive, receptive audience. By prioritizing systems *first*—which includes considering all constituents involved throughout the development of the product, from start to finish—the traditional product-oriented framework that is top-down, planned, rigid, sequential, and "expert-driven" is replaced by a service-oriented framework that is more organic, adaptable, and is co-created with customers and members of the supply chain (Dubberly, 2008; Evenson, 2006). In systems-first design, the designer is the facilitator, and the customer is a contributor. The designer-collaborator designs *with* rather than *for* people (Davis, 2018b). When developing systems-oriented frameworks, designers must ask themselves, "How can I increase my consumer's engagement as a partner, as a stakeholder, across all areas of a product's planning, development, experience, and subsequent evolution?" As a result of this shift in focus toward viewing the consumer as a collaborator, an ongoing feedback loop emerges between designers and consumers, one that allows a brand to gain greater meaning and an industry to gain greater relevance.

## A Great Uncertainty

Over a decade ago, Linda Darling-Hammond (2010), Professor of Education Emeritus at the Stanford Graduate School of Education, noted the top ten in-demand jobs projected for 2010 did not exist in 2004. Shortly before 2004, in the span of just three years (1999–2002), "[t]he amount of new information produced nearly equaled the amount produced in the entire history of the world previously" (Varian & Lyman, 2003, as cited in Darling-Hammond, 2010, p 4). In today's world, advanced technology and information resources have enabled an even greater acceleration of information creation and consumption, which is subsequently opening up opportunities for new job functions and careers in our society, both now and in the future. Design teachers must therefore "prepare students to work at jobs that do not yet exist, creating ideas and solutions for products and problems that have not yet been identified, using technologies that have not yet been invented" (Darling-Hammond, 2010, p. 2). Ultimately, the only certainty—in design industries and education alike—is uncertainty.

8  Design Industries

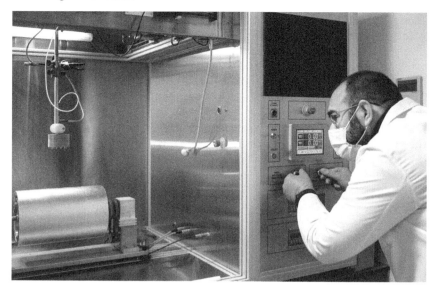

*Figure 1.1* A lab technician tests nanofibers on an electrospinning machine.
Source: MAOIKO/Shutterstock.com.

While the rapid growth of information and advancements in technology will impact all industries, in many ways the US design industries will experience higher levels of acceleration and uncertainty than other industries (Figure 1.1). The quickening lifecycles of designed products and services, spikes in global competition, growing urgency for sustainable practice and attendant policies, and an emerging consumer generation that increasingly demands change across corporate and federal sectors are just some of the factors that will amplify the speed of these changes (Davis, 2018c). Resultantly, the designer's core attributes of nimbleness, versatility, responsive, and flexibility must remain at the center of their practice; we do not yet know what the needed technical skillsets and creative practices will be in the years ahead. Additionally, we do not know how the design industries themselves will evolve. This uncertainty will drive not only the aforementioned attributes of the designer, but also how they should approach each venture—namely, how they conceive of, hone, and ultimately present their designs to the market. Rather than completing a design until it is nearly "perfect"—which is the traditional approach—designers should, as Meredith Davis (2018b, 2018c) argues, adopt an ability to recognize when the effort input is surpassing the benefit to be gained. They must develop an attitude that enables them to stop short of perfection and adopt a "good enough for now" attitude, since new versions quickly replace preceding products and services. It is the uncertainty and volatility of the design marketplace, the expansiveness of designers' roles and responsibilities, and the unrelenting acceleration of technology and information that will chart the course for the 21st century's design industries.

## Section I: Design Industries

This section examines the past, present, and future states of the design industries that, in turn, directly impact the evolution of US design education. The following chapters discuss:

- the systemic changes occurring in the US design industries and marketplace as seen through the lens of the nation's fashion industry;
- the evolving role of the design entrepreneur, people's changing relationships with design and associated consumer behaviors, and a model for advanced changes in what the new role of the "designer" looks like; and
- key qualitative assessments into the future design industries and how these sectors may best prepare themselves and grow successfully.

Together, these chapters establish a foundation for understanding how and why US design education is undergoing an evolution, a topic that is fully discussed in Section II. This development in academia is largely attributed to the design industries' unprecedented acceleration, growth, and ever-expanding scope in shaping our world, a world that is growing more fragile and in dire need of innovative designers who operate beyond the conventional modus operandi to solve the seemingly impossible and insurmountable problems we as a society face, both today and tomorrow.

In 1969, the acclaimed designer Charles Eames was asked, "What are the boundaries of design?" In response, he famously quipped, "What are the boundaries of problems?" Today, the question of boundaries is more salient than ever before. The boundaries of the design industries and their workforces will become more porous, with more designers following careers that differ from the "traditional" design career track. In turn, the design industries will continue to exert strong influences on the future direction of US design education. It is by examining and contextualizing these complex shifts and speculations of the design industries that we, as design educators, can strengthen our Academy's programs, curricula, and pedagogy in order to prepare students for success in the evolving design practices.

## References

Chochinov, A. (2007, April 6). 1000 words: A manifesto for sustainability in design. *Core 77*. https://www.core77.com/posts/40586/1000-Words-A-Manifesto-for-Sustainability-in-Design

Darling-Hammond, L. (2010). *The flat world and education: How America's commitment to equity will determine our future*. Teachers College Press.

Davis, M. (2018a). Design futures trends: Core values matter. *AIGA*. https://www.aiga.org/sites/default/files/2021-02/Core%20Values%20Matter.pdf

Davis, M. (2018b). Design futures trends: Introduction. *AIGA*. https://www.aiga.org/sites/default/files/2021-02/introduction-to-design-futures.pdf

Davis, M. (2018c). Design futures trends: Resilient organizations. *AIGA*. https://www.aiga.org/sites/default/files/2021-02/Resilient%20Organizations.pdf

DeAmicis, C. (2019, December 16). The decade of design: How the last 10 years transformed design's role in tech. *Figma*. https://www.figma.com/blog/the-rise-of-ux-ui-design-a-decade-in-reflection/

Dewey, J. (2008). *Democracy and education*. Wilder Publications. (Original work published 1916).

Dubberly, H. (2008). Design in the age of biology. *Interactions*. http://www.dubberly.com/wp-content/uploads/2008/09/ddo_article_ageofbiology.pdf

Evenson, S. (2006, September). *Experience strategy: product/service systems* [Presentation]. CMU's Emergence Conference, Detroit.

IBM. (2022). *IBM: IBM iX*. https://www.ibm.com/services/ibmix

Kett, R. (2019, June 25). College of Engineering and College of Environmental Design launch new Master of Design program. *University of California, Berkeley*. https://engineering.berkeley.edu/news/2019/06/college-of-engineering-and-college-of-environmental-design-launch-new-master-of-design-program/

Miller, M. (2019, October 21). Are traditional design degrees still relevant? *Fast Company*. https://www.fastcompany.com/90419644/are-traditional-design-degrees-still-relevant?partner=rss&utm_source=rss&utm_medium=feed&utm_campaign=rss+fastcompany&utm_content=rss?cid=search

Muratovski, G. (2016). *Research for designers*. SAGE.

National Endowment for the Arts (NEA). (2018a). *The arts contribute more than $760 billion to the U.S. economy*. https://www.arts.gov/about/news/2018/arts-contribute-more-760-billion-us-economy

National Endowment for the Arts (NEA). (2018b). *Arts and cultural production satellite account: State highlights*. https://www.arts.gov/sites/default/files/BEA_2018_State_Highlights5.pdf

National Endowment for the Arts (NEA). (2021). *The U.S. arts and cultural production satellite account: 1998–2019*. https://www.arts.gov/impact/research/arts-data-profile-series/adp-28

The World Bank. (2022). *GDP growth (annual %) – United States*. https://data.worldbank.org/indicator/NY.GDP.MKTP.KD.ZG?locations=US

US Bureau of Labor Statistics (USBLS). (2021a). Occupational employment and wage statistics. *US Department of Labor*. https://www.bls.gov/oes/tables.htm

US Bureau of Labor Statistics (USBLS). (2021b). Occupational outlook handbook. *US Department of Labor*. https://www.bls.gov/ooh/arts-and-design/home.htm

Varian, H., & Lyman, P. (2003). How much information? *University of California, Berkeley*. https://groups.ischool.berkeley.edu/archive/how-much-info-2003/index.htm

Vartanian, H. (2019, November 21). The realities facing art schools today: A conversation with RISD President Rosanne Somerson [Audio podcast]. *Hyperallergic*. https://hyperallergic.com/529483/president-rosanne-somerson-risd/

# 2 A Study of the Fashion Industry as a Model of Widespread Systemic Change

## Introduction

Over the last century, the American design industries have undergone radical changes. Local manufacturing-focused design practices have been transformed into highly globalized systems that prioritize "design thinking" for its innovation. Offering more than mere products, today's American designers—including those in packaging, furniture, textile, graphic, and industrial design—engage across design platforms that incorporate diverse systems, technologies, and user experiences. As the US design industries evolve due to these widespread changes, it is useful for us to approach the nation's fashion industry as a case study to understand the multinational dynamics and events that have shaped and changed US design industries across all media. In doing so, we will gain an understanding of how and why design education has responded to these shifts while enabling speculations into the future of the design industries and design education.

The histories of the nation's fashion design industry and fashion design education are intrinsically intertwined. At the turn of the 20th century, the nascent US apparel industry was rooted in manufacturing, which grew steadily in the US in the first seventy years of that century. By 1973, New York City's garment manufacturing industry employed 400,000 people at its peak (Karimzadeh, 2013). However, due to factors that include reduced importation tariffs with other nations, rising manufacturing costs in the US, and increased access to expanding international garment factories, the US manufacturing aspect of this industry was largely displaced overseas by the end of the 20th century. As manufacturing was phased out of the US, the design aspect of fashion, rather than the manufacturing aspect, became the focus of the US fashion industry. With New York City as its epicenter, this industry has evolved over the past four decades by focusing on new, high-value endeavors that focus on design, research and development, technology, marketing, entertainment, and other creative practices. Fashion design education has responded by placing greater emphasis now on conceptual thinking,

DOI: 10.4324/9781003049166-3

design innovation, and interdisciplinary practice than it ever did in the 20th century.

The futures of both the fashion design industry and fashion design education will continue to be closely intertwined, with each sector informing, advancing, and challenging one another. The past two decades have been hallmarked by growing concerns around sustainability in an economy that is becoming increasingly "disposable." Additional issues around environmental degradation and ethical labor practices compound the untenable position of historical fashion design practices. To address these and other concerns, national and international initiatives are growing. These efforts aim to elevate consumers' awareness of these issues, promote legislation, sustain fragile resources, reshore/nearshore US manufacturing, and more. As one of the world's largest industries, the direction the fashion industry takes on these issues will play a significant role in our planet's future. Subsequently, design education must understand this unique industry's past, the trends shaping its present, and future critical issues it may face so that it can play a positive role in our holistic futures.

## The Rise of the US Apparel Industry

The mass production of apparel in the US emerged at the beginning of the 20th century. The invention of the sewing machine in the mid-1800s and the introduction of a standardized body-size measurement system necessitated by the demand for Civil War military uniforms gave rise to industrialized production and consumers' reliance on ready-made, fashionable clothing. After 1900, the number of US garment makers increased dramatically, particularly in New York City, where the number of women's apparel companies grew 246% (from 1,850 to 6,392) between 1900 and 1917 (Selekman et al., 1925) (Figure 2.1). It was during this time that factory owners, located in the Lower East Side, began to relocate to Seventh Avenue between 30th and 42nd Streets, where they established larger production centers. By 1920, the vast influx of large-scaled apparel manufacturers in that location led the US to become the major producer of clothing for American women.

Although New York City's early 20th century fashion industry flourished, the city itself was not recognized as a design center. Historically, Paris was seen as the pinnacle of fashion creation; by 1925, there were approximately 300,000 couturiers in France (Wolf, 2017). To acquire designs, American manufacturers commonly paid fees to attended seasonal Paris shows and receive the rights to adapt the haute couture (made-to-measure) garments into inexpensive (mass-producible) versions. American manufacturers often promoted their laudable adapting skills and, in the case of the Simon Crawford Company, "displayed in their store window an original Drecoll imported gown costing $485,

*Figure 2.1* A garment sweatshop in 1905.

Source: Chicago Sun-Times/Chicago Daily News collection/Chicago History Museum/Getty Images.

reproduced in every detail by their dressmakers for sale at $24.75"—a retail price reduction of 95% (Marcketti & Parsons, 2007, p. 4). For decades, New York City's industry focused on producing affordable fashions; one 1940s stylist noted the city's manufacturers were "not so interested in making something good, as in making it cheap—and cheaper" (Rantisi, 2004, p. 96). These practices continued until WWII when the Nazi's occupation of Paris isolated the city's fashion industry.

Following the war, New York City became an international fashion capitol due, in part, to Manhattan's rising status as a cultural center and hotspot for high society (Municipal Art Society of New York [MASNY], 2011). Although Parisian couturiers remained authorities of "high" fashion, a growing number of entrepreneurial American "ready-to-wear" fashion designers emerged during the 1950s and 1960s. These designers targeted American women's growing need for fashionable clothing that did not require custom-fittings and addressed their more active lifestyles. New York designers, including Claire McCardell, Bonnie Cashin, and Norman Norell, drew global attention for their comfortable, uncomplicated designs, which became a hallmark of American fashion for decades to come. Igniting designers' success were the nation's growing middle class, rising wages that strengthened consumers' purchasing power, and escalating apparel sales. Resultantly, the US fashion industry's workforce doubled between the 1950s and 1973 (Karimzadeh, 2013).

## Offshore Manufacturing and Apparel Importation

The US fashion industry's exponential growth during the second half of the 20th century concurrently experienced increases in globally outsourced garment manufacturing and importation. The mass outsourcing of apparel began in earnest when, during the 1950s, the US "directly subsidized the building and re-building of modern textile and apparel industries in [countries, such as] Singapore, the Philippines, and India" (Rosen, 2002, p. 47). By 1960, Taiwan, Hong Kong, Pakistan, India, and the Philippines had established highly productive apparel manufacturing complexes that were well prepared to become large-scale suppliers (Rosen, 2002). Moreover, reduced import tariffs led outsourced apparel to compete directly with higher priced American-made garments. Later, additional legislation increased offshore manufacturing and importation, particularly with the North American Free Trade Agreement (NAFTA) in 1994 and the Agreement on Textiles and Clothing (ATC) in 1995. NAFTA reduced or eliminated barriers to trade and investment among the US, Canada, and Mexico, thus enabling non-US goods (made by a cheaper workforce) to compete with American-made goods. Between 1994 and 2000, Mexico's exportation of textiles and apparel to the US increased 335%, from approximately $2.4 million US to nearly $10.2 million US (World Integrated Trade Solution [WITS], 2020). The ATC further impacted US manufacturing through its four-stage plan that increased import limits from 16% in 1995 to no limits by 2005. In 2020, NAFTA was rescinded by the participating nations and replaced with the United States-Mexico-Canada Agreement (USMCA).

Federal legislation, coupled with escalating labor costs in the US that increased manufacturing costs, devastated America's apparel manufacturing infrastructure and workforce. Between 1960 and 2015, the amount of American-made clothing purchased domestically dropped from 95% to 3% (Morgan, 2015). In just twenty-nine years (1990–2019), the sector's workforce dropped by approximately 89%—while globally, apparel and textile jobs spiked from 34.2 million to 58.8 million (Thomas, 2019; US Bureau of Labor Statistics [USBLS], 2021) (Figure 2.2). For their goods to remain competitive, apparel manufacturers have shifted production from the US (where factory workers make around $1,600 US a month) to more affordable nations such as Bangladesh ($95 US a month) and China ($326 US a month) (McCarthy, 2019).

The resultant increase of apparel importation into the US is equally unprecedented. Apparel importation reached new heights during the

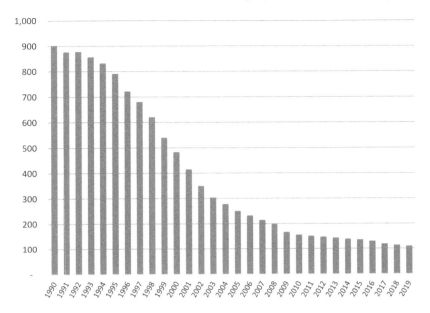

*Figure 2.2* Number of employees in the US apparel manufacturing industry, 1990–2019 (in 1,000s).

Source: USBLS, 2021.

presidency of Ronald Reagan, when, between 1981 and 1988, the value of imported apparel nearly tripled from $7.7 billion US to $22.4 billion US (Rosen, 2002). Throughout the proceeding decades, companies continued to outsource their manufacturing—particularly to China, where, from 2000 to 2018, textiles and apparel exported to the US increased 430% (WITS, 2020). By 2018, Chinese-manufactured products accounted for over one-third of all US apparel imports (WITS, 2020). Apparel importation is so high in the US that today, approximately 97% of clothes sold nationally are imported, making the US the global leader of imported textile apparel articles (Reagan, 2018). The exorbitantly high levels of reliance on foreign manufacturing continue to contribute to the nation's trade deficit of $80.2 billion US as of November 2021 (US Census Bureau [USCB], 2022).

### Reshoring and Nearshoring Apparel Manufacturing

Against this backdrop of the tradition of offshoring, there are indications the fashion industry may increase "reshoring" (return manufacturing to the US) and/or "nearshoring" (moving physical production geographically closer to the US). Researchers speculate this shift will occur due to several reasons. The first reason is the escalating manufacturing costs in most of the top twenty-five exporting countries. Once considered inexpensive manufacturing locations, the cost of operations within those countries has become comparable to those in the US. For instance, in recent history, labor costs in China were "one-tenth of those in the US; today, they are about one-third. Across Asia, labor costs are increasing more than the rest of the world and in some markets the gap to offshore labor costs has even disappeared …" (Andersson et al., 2018, p. 10).

The second reason is geographic proximity to the US. Closer geographic proximity reduces the typical shipping time to the US of thirty-days from Asia to approximately two days from Central America (Andersson et al., 2018). The reduction in duration and costs enables fashion companies to respond faster to trends while simultaneously testing and scaling styles. This helps reduce the physical waste that results from unpopular, unsold merchandise. Additional environmental sustainability is promoted through this improved proximity; environmental damage from shipping is reduced as the accompanying carbon footprint is reduced. Given consumers' growing concerns over sustainability—more than 50% report they would choose a more sustainable brand over non-sustainable alternatives—fashion companies are progressively including sustainability as an integral part of their businesses and brands (Andersson et al., 2018; Martinez-Pardo et al., 2020).

The recent rise of geopolitical tensions may also encourage reshoring/nearshoring activities due to volatile trade agreements and duties—both of which factor heavily into the costs of materials and manufacturing. Rather than relying on offshore production, US-based designers may scrutinize the economic differences among offshoring, reshoring, and nearshoring in order to determine which model yields the best financial outcome. These decisions will be increasingly influenced by emergent technologies and automated machinery. For example, automated garment assembly via "sewbots" (robotic sewing machines) will offset higher labor costs and increase productivity, thus making nearshoring/reshoring a more compelling economic model. The future growth of automation is a certainty: 82% of surveyed fashion professionals believe simple garments will be fully automated by 2025 (Andersson et al., 2018).

Support for reshoring apparel manufacturing has gained momentum, particularly since the "Save the Garment Center" campaign was founded in 2008. This ongoing campaign raises awareness of New York City's dwindling manufacturing facilities. Proponents cite the Center's historic significance, opportunities for employment growth, and its benefit to fashion designers who need rapid turnaround of their prototypes and immediate input from production and manufacturing teams (MASNY, 2011). The location is also "a critical resource for emerging designers who cannot afford to export production and rely on their interactions with manufacturers to shape the product" (MASNY, 2011, p. 48). The area's resources equally benefit the small- and mid-scale fashion companies that are often unable to meet the high production minimums required by overseas factories. These local fashion companies rely heavily on the approximately 164 facilities in New York City that specialize in sewn goods (e.g. cutting, sample making, and pattern making)—a subset of the city's 1,500 garment manufacturing firms (Council of Fashion Designers of America [CFDA], n.d.; New York Economic Development Corporation [NYCEDC], 2017).

The industry has received additional support through an unparalleled $51.3 million US support package from the New York City Economic Development Corporation, in collaboration with the Council of Fashion Designers of America (CFDA). Announced in 2017, this ten-year support package is designed to help stabilize and strengthen the City's garment manufacturing industry. It includes grants for investment in advanced technology to improve competitiveness globally, workforce development, overall business development, and relocation assistance to help companies from the Garment Center move to Sunset Park in Brooklyn (NYCEDC, 2017). Furthermore, The Fashion Manufacturing Initiative, a $14 million US partnership, offers New York City-based contract manufacturing facilities grants to grow their businesses.

These and other initiatives are helping transform the US fashion industry. Between 2010 and 2017, apparel became the third-largest reshoring industry in the US manufacturing sector, with nearly 600 companies and 40,000 jobs returning to the US (Reshoring Initiative, 2019). In 2016, American workers produced 10% of the nation's fashion goods—a considerable leap from 3% in 2013, at a compound annual growth rate (CAGR) of 49% (Thomas, 2019). In a recent survey, 60% of apparel procurement executives expect that over 20% of their sourcing volume will be from nearshore facilities by 2025. The same survey revealed 63% of respondents believe that by 2025, fabric production will likely move to nearshore manufacturing options to support regional supply chains better (Andersson et al., 2018).

## The Contemporary US Fashion Industry

Amid these developments, the US fashion industry remains an international leader. The industry contributes to the national economy and specific sectors that include finance, marketing, advertising, entertainment, photography, education, and tourism. In 2017 alone, New York City's fashion industry employed approximately 4.6% of the city's private-sector workforce and generated more than $11 billion in wages and $3.2 billion in tax revenue (Joint Economic Committee [JEC], 2019).

The industry's semiannual New York Fashion Week (NYFW) is a particularly important event that both promotes design innovation and creates opportunities for substantial economic development. Attracting more than 230,000 attendees annually, NYFW generates over $530 million US per year in direct visitor spending, leading to a total economic impact of nearly $900 million US (CFDA, 2016). In fact, among the fashion weeks of the international fashion capitals of Paris, Milan, London, and New York City, NYFW accounts for more than half of the total number of shows presented and generates more income than the other three cities' fashion weeks combined (JEC, 2019).

Fashion design has become an especially strong focus for artistic and economic growth. Between 1999 and 2019, there was a 129.5% increase (9,600–22,030) of fashion designers in the US, with the highest density of 8,460 fashion designers (38% of all US designers) working in New York City (USBLS, 2020). Additional key areas of the workforce are located in Los Angeles, San Francisco, and Portland, Oregon. These cities have the next-highest densities to New York City of approximately 6,010, 510, and 490 fashion designers each, respectively (USBLS, 2020).

## *The Imperative of a Sustainable Fashion Practice*

The fashion industry's growth and the extreme levels of demand from consumers for rapid apparel production and consumption have resulted in substantial environmental damage. The industry's growth has been particularly high in "fast fashion," an apparel sector that prioritizes making fashion trends quickly and inexpensively for consumers. This category of companies includes such international mass-retailers as Hennes & Mauritz (H&M), Zara, and Uniqlo. The sector's accelerated growth is evidenced by the nearly 4,400 stores H&M opened globally between 2000 and 2019 and the over 6,300 stores the Inditex Group (which contains Zara) opened globally during the same period (H&M, 2020; Inditex, 2020).

To fill their stores and ensure they meet consumers' demands, fashion companies worldwide currently manufacture an unprecedented amounts of goods. Between 2000 and 2014, the number of garments produced globally doubled from 50 billion to 100 billion annually (Thomas, 2019). Recently, Americans' apparel consumption reached an all-time high, with clothing and clothing accessories store sales leaping by more than 123% from 1992 to 2019 (USCB, 2021) (Figure 2.3). This rapidly increasing rate of consumption leads some to speculate that, "If the global population swells to 8.5 billion by 2030, and GDP per capita rises by 2% in developed nations and 4% in developing economies each of those intervening years…and we don't change our consumption habits, we will buy 63% more fashion—from 62 million tons to 102 million tons [per year]" (Kerr & Landry, 2017, as cited in Thomas, 2019, p. 3).

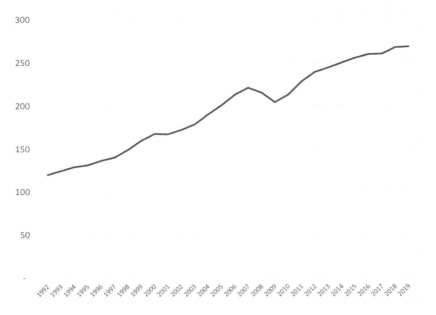

*Figure 2.3* Clothing and clothing accessories store sales in the US, 1992–2019 (in billion USD).

Source: USCB, 2021.

The accelerated growth of fast fashion has led the sector to develop new systems that offer unparalleled levels of speed and scale. For instance, Zara employs 300 designers, develops 24,000 products each year, and produces approximately 450 million items for 2,264 stores in ninety-six countries annually (Hanbury, 2018; Inditex, n.d.; Lee, 2019; Thomas, 2019). Zara's supply chain is so well organized that it typically takes only three weeks from initial product concept to in-store product launch, thus allowing the brand to deliver new styles twice per week (Inditex, n.d.). The H&M Group (consisting of eight brands) operates 5,076 stores in seventy-four countries and employees over 120,000 people (H&M, 2020). In 2019 alone, the Group opened a gross total of 281 new stores (net new 108) (H&M, 2020).

These increased rates of apparel consumption have led to significant environmental damage. Currently, the world consumes 400% more garments on an annual basis than it did just two decades ago (Morgan, 2015). Consumers keep these garments roughly half as long as they did fifteen years ago—typically wearing a garment seven or eight times before it is discarded (Remy et al., 2016). In the US, clothes are only worn for one quarter of the amount of times of the global average, and the national rate of garment discard has doubled in the past twenty years, from 7 million to 14 million tons per year (Ellen MacArthur Foundation [EMF], 2017; Wicker, 2016, as cited in Thomas, 2019, p. 7). Beyond the material waste lies tremendous financial loss: globally, consumers miss out on $460 billion US worth of product each year due to the apparel they prematurely discard (EMF, 2017). Ultimately, three-fifths of all produced apparel is lost to incinerators or landfills, with less than 1% of material recycled into new clothing (Remy et al., 2016; EMF, 2017).

Not surprisingly, these and other fashion industry practices are causing unrelenting environmental damage by putting increasing pressure on natural resources, polluting the environment, and disrupting the global ecosystem. These practices include cotton production that requires exorbitant amounts of water; if fashion manufacturing maintains its current pace and demand for cotton products, the demand for water will surpass global supply by 40% by 2030 (Kerr & Landry, 2017, cited by Thomas, 2019, p. 71). Additionally, a recent study found that greenhouse gas emissions from textile production surpassed all greenhouse emissions produced by international flights and global maritime shipping combined (International Energy Agency, 2016). Some estimates anticipate that by 2050, the fashion industry alone will be responsible for approximately one-fourth of the earth's total climate cost (Amed et al., 2017).

## A Future Paradigm

Efforts to address the fashion industry's unsustainable practices are escalating across diverse platforms. For instance, The United Nations' Alliance for Sustainable Fashion was launched in 2019. Later in that year, more than 7.6 million people participated in the worldwide 2019 Global Climate Strike (Amed et al., 2019). Initiatives like these are significantly raising awareness about sustainability: for example, internet searches for "sustainable fashion" tripled between 2016 and 2019 (Berg et al., 2019). In a recent survey, fashion professionals cited sustainability as both the biggest challenge facing their industry and the biggest opportunity (Amed et al., 2019). Of those surveyed, 78% of sourcing managers agreed sustainability will be a "somewhat likely" or "highly likely" key purchasing factor for mass-market consumers by 2025 (Amed et al., 2018). Consumers—such as Millennial (born between the early 1980s and mid-1990s) and Generation Z (born between the mid-1990s and early 2010s) shoppers—increasingly scrutinize their brands' integrity, social engagement, and environmental impact. Over 70% of both generations make purchases based on personal, social, and environmental values, with 45% of Generation Z shoppers researching background information before making purchases (Amed et al., 2018; First Insight, 2020).

Concurrently, companies are increasingly addressing issues relating to ethical manufacturing, sustainability, environmental wellness, and brand transparency. Of course, some fashion brands have maintained a sustainable ethos from their beginnings. The US-based brand Alabama Chanin, launched by Natalie Chanin in 2000, exemplifies sustainable practice through the use of local manufacturing, organic cotton, and repurposed/reclaimed materials. Among certain fast fashion companies, sustainability efforts have been more recent and evolutionary. For instance, by 2025, H&M's plastic packaging will be reusable, recyclable, or compostable; by 2030, all their products will be made from recycled or other sustainably sourced materials; and by 2040, the company will be "climate positive" by developing sustainable ways to make, transport, and package its products (H&M, 2020). Zara has pledged to use 100% sustainable fabrics by 2025, and Adidas has committed to only using recycled plastic in footwear by 2024 (Conlon, 2019; Cooper, 2018). The future expansion of sustainability is suggested by the 67% of sourcing executives who believe the use of sustainable materials will be important for their companies (Amed et al., 2019).

Sustainable initiatives are also developing in laboratories. Bio-fabricated and reengineered materials include threads created from discarded coffee grounds, lotus stems, milk, and algae, along with "leathers" made from mushrooms, collagen proteins, tea leaves, and apple waste. Material waste is also being used to develop both molecularly engineered fibers made from discarded clothing and regenerated nylon made from discarded industrial plastics. Scientists are even experimenting with growing near-complete items without the need for factory assembly. The environmental benefits of these materials (in particular their biodegradability) include the ability to make or grow the precise amount of material needed, thus eliminating waste.

Additionally, digital technology is spawning "smart textiles" that connect users with web applications, change color, guard against radiation, release medications, kill bacteria, and conduct electricity. Developments have been swift: in just five years (2012–2017) the revenues in the smart textile industry grew at a CAGR of 20%, from $700 million US to $1.76 billion US (QYResearch, 2017, as cited in International Labour Organization, 2019, p. 5). Between 2018 and 2025, the smart textile industry is expected to increase 30% every year, for a total increase of 525.78%, from $878.9 million US to $5.5 billion US (Grand View Research, 2019).

Innovations in manufacturing technologies enhance sustainability. For example, the Jeanologia manufacturing company uses a range of tools that support environmental wellness. These include using lasers, rather than water and chemicals, to treat and distress denim; "e-flow" technology that treats fabric and saves up to 95% of water, 40% of energy, and 90% of chemicals typically used in manufacturing; and "G2" technology, which is the first ozone treatment for continuous fabric and provides savings in water, energy, and chemicals that are similar to those found with "e-flow" technology. Jeanologia's services make a significant impact on both the fashion industry and the environment: its technologies are used to make 35% of the five billion jeans annually produced worldwide (Jeanologia, 2020).

Waste reduction is also found in the growing accessibility to technologies such as body scanning, made-to-order apparel, and 3D printing. Body scanning technology utilized for the apparel industry gained significant attention when, in 2005, Levi's adopted the Intellifit System of electronic body scanners at the retail level to produce made-to-measure jeans for individual customers. More recently, Adidas launched a temporary pop-up store in Berlin that provided customers with 3D body scans to create sweaters that were ready within four hours. Similarly, the company Unmade produces on-demand knitwear that can be delivered in mere days rather than the weeks it used to take to fulfill such orders. This technology leads many to speculate clothing sizes eventually will become obsolete, particularly given the accessibility of body scanners in smartphone technology. Combined with the increasing accessibility of 3D printing due to its decreasing costs, future apparel production may be as simple as customers scanning their personal measurements, purchasing a link for the desired garment, and printing it themselves at home (Thomas, 2019). The impact on sustainability is high: deadstock from untested, unsold merchandise is eliminated; textile waste from cutting patterns from yardage is decreased; and the impact of these new technologies and reshoring/nearshoring options means a mitigation of environmental harm that has previously arisen due to manufacturing and the supply chain. Moreover, the addition of design customization and personalization may increase garments' lifespans due to the heightened emotional connection consumers will have toward their "co-designed" purchases (see Chapter 3 for more detail).

Automated sewing machines ("sewbots") will further support on-demand and made-to-measure apparel. Akin to the expansive growth of robotic technologies that transformed automotive assembly lines and now perform surgeries, the increase of sewbots will decrease the requirement for human labor, increase efficiency, and possibly help reshore US apparel manufacturing (Thomas, 2019). Proponents of sewbots anticipate an uptick of purchasing of products that have the "Made in the USA" label (albeit by sewbots) and are produced by companies that have reduced their carbon footprints, decreased volumes of unsold goods, and the more competitive costs of merchandise. Opponents cite the possible explosion in volume of products produced and the accompanying costs to the environment due to that volume of production. For example, a sewbot in the US can produce as many shirts per hour as approximately seventeen human beings can, and at a cost of approximately $0.33 US each—a cost so low that most low-labor-cost countries cannot compete

(Bain, 2017). Concerns for the destabilization of human welfare owing to automated sewing technologies must also be considered, given vast populations of garment workers will lose their jobs as these technologies become increasingly ubiquitous.

## Conclusion

The widespread systemic changes occurring across US design industries are exemplified by those that have occurred in the nation's fashion industry. As a manufacturing-turned-design leader, the US fashion industry will continue to drive innovation for knowledge-based economies. The fashion industry's trajectory has deeply informed and helped shape fashion design education. As discussed in Chapter 6, the design school's former curricular emphases that prioritized the process of making in response to the nation's manufacturing industries' demand for labor have given way to sophisticated pedagogies that increasingly prioritize innovation, conceptual thinking, interdisciplinary practice, sustainability, inclusivity, societal impacts, and more. This shift, which started in the industry, is leading design schools to alter design educational aims in order to better prepare students so they may address successfully the design industries' challenges of the future. Indeed, the design industries'—and particularly the fashion industry's—future "self-disruption," facilitated by design school graduates, will play a crucial role in impacting our planet's long-term future.

## References

Amed, I., Andersson, J., Berg, A., Drageset, M., Hedrich, S., & Kappelmark, S. (2017). The state of fashion 2018: Renewed optimism for the fashion industry. *McKinsey & Company and Business of Fashion.* https://www.mckinsey.com/industries/retail/our-insights/renewed-optimism-for-the-fashion-industry

Amed, I., Balchandani, A., Beltrami, M., Berg, A., Hedrich, S., & Rölkens, F. (2018). The state of fashion 2019: A year of awakening. *McKinsey & Company and Business of Fashion.* https://www.mckinsey.com/industries/retail/our-insights/the-state-of-fashion-2019-a-year-of-awakening

Amed, I., Balchandani, A., Berg, A., Hedrich, S., Poojara, S., & Rölkens, F. (2019). The state of fashion 2020: Navigating uncertainty. *McKinsey & Company and Business of Fashion.* https://www.mckinsey.com/industries/retail/our-insights/the-state-of-fashion-2020-navigating-uncertainty#

Andersson, J., Berg, A., Hedrich, S., & Magnus, K. (2018). Is apparel manufacturing coming home? *McKinsey & Company.* https://www.mckinsey.com/industries/retail/our-insights/is-apparel-manufacturing-coming-home

Bain, M. (2017, August 30). A new t-shirt sewing robot can make as many shirts per hour as 17 factory workers. *Quartz.* https://qz.com/1064679/a-new-t-shirt-sewing-robot-can-make-as-many-shirts-per-hour-as-17-factory-workers/

Berg, A., Hedrich, S., Ibanez, P., Kappelmark, S., & Magnus, K. (2019). Fashion's new must have: Sustainable sourcing at scale. *McKinsey & Company*. https://www.mckinsey.com/industries/retail/our-insights/fashions-new-must-have-sustainable-sourcing-at-scale

Conlon, S. (2019, July 17). Zara clothes to be made from 1005 sustainable fabrics by 2025. *The Guardian*. https://www.theguardian.com/fashion/2019/jul/17/zara-collections-to-be-made-from-100-sustainable-fabrics

Cooper, K. (2018, July 31). Fast fashion: Inside the fight to end the silence on waste. *BBC*. https://www.bbc.com/news/world-44968561

Council of Fashion Designers of America (CFDA). (n.d.). *Resources*. https://cfda.com/resources

Council of Fashion Designers of America (CFDA). (2016, February 10). *NYFW memo from the CFDA*. https://cfda.com/news/nyfw-memo-from-the-cfda

Ellen MacArthur Foundation (EMF). (2017). *A new textiles economy: Redesigning fashion's future*. https://www.ellenmacarthurfoundation.org/assets/downloads/publications/A-New-Textiles-Economy_Full-Report_Updated_1-12-17.pdf

First Insight. (2020). *The state of consumer spending: Gen Z shoppers demand sustainable retail*. https://www.firstinsight.com/white-papers-posts/gen-z-shoppers-demand-sustainability

Grand View Research. (2019). *Smart textile market size worth $5.55 billion by 2025*. https://www.grandviewresearch.com/press-release/global-smart-textiles-industry

Hanbury, M. (2018, November 11). These are the tricks that Zara uses to figure out the styles you want before you even do. *Business Insider*. https://www.businessinsider.com/zara-design-process-beats-trends-2018-11

Hennes & Mauritz (H&M). (2020). *Reports and presentations*. https://hmgroup.com/investors/reports.html

Inditex. (n.d.). *Corporate home page*. https://www.inditex.com/about-us/inditex-around-the-world#continent/000

Inditex. (2020). *Annual reports*. https://www.inditex.com/investors/investor-relations/annual-reports

International Energy Agency. (2016). *Energy, climate change & environment: 2016 insights*. https://www.iea.org/reports/energy-climate-change-and-environment-2016-insights

International Labour Organization. (2019, February 6). *The future of work in textile, clothing, leather and footwear*. https://www.ilo.org/sector/Resources/publications/WCMS_669355/lang–en/index.htm

Jeanologia. (2020). *Products*. https://www.jeanologia.com/products/

Joint Economic Committee (JEC). (2019). *The economic impact of the fashion industry*. https://www.jec.senate.gov/public/_cache/files/39201d61-aec8-4458-80e8-2fe26ee8a31e/economic-impact-of-the-fashion-industry.pdf

Karimzadeh, M. (2013, October). Ralph Lauren boots N.Y. manufacturing initiative. *WWD, 206*(84), 1.

Kerr, J., & Landry, J. (2017). The pulse of the global fashion industry. *Global Fashion Agenda*. https://www.globalfashionagenda.com/publications-and-policy/pulse-of-the-industry/

Lee, H. (2019, December 10). How extreme agility put Zara ahead in fast fashion. *Financial Times*. https://www.ft.com/content/3f581046-cd7c-11e9-b018-ca4456540ea6

Marcketti, S., & Parsons, J. (2007, January). American fashions for American women: Early twentieth century efforts to develop an American fashion identity. *Dress, 34*(1), 79–95.

Martinez-Pardo, C., Seara, J., Razvi, A., & Kibbey, J. (2020, April 20). Weaving a better future: Rebuilding a more sustainable fashion industry after COVID-19. *Sustainable Apparel Coalition.* https://apparelcoalition.org/wp-content/uploads/2020/04/Weaving-a-Better-Future-Covid-19-BCG-SAC-Higg-Co-Report.pdf

McCarthy, N. (2019, May 7). Where pay is lowest for cheap clothing production. *Statista.* https://www-statista-com.libproxy.newschool.edu/chart/17903/monthly-minimum-wage-in-the-global-garment-industry/

Morgan, A. (Director) (2015). *The true cost [Film].* Untold Creative.

Municipal Art Society of New York (MASNY). (2011, October). *Fashioning the future: NYC's Garment District.* https://www.mas.org/wp-content/uploads/2018/01/fashioning-the-future-report.pdf

New York City Economic Development Corporation (NYCEDC). (2017). *NYCED announces $51M support package for NYC garment manufacturing industry.* https://edc.nyc/press-release/nycedc-announces-51m-support-package-nyc-garment-manufacturing-industry-collaboration

QYResearch (2017). *Global smart fabrics and textiles industry 2017 market research report.* https://www.hexareports.com/report/global-smart-fabrics-and-textiles-industry-2017

Rantisi, N. (2004). The ascendance of New York fashion. *International Journal of Urban and Regional Research, 28*(1), 86–106.

Reagan, C. (2018, April 9). You're already paying tariffs on clothing and shoes, and have been for almost 90 years. *CNBC.* https://www.cnbc.com/2018/04/06/americans-are-already-paying-tariffs-on-clothing-and-shoes.html

Remy, N., Speelman, E., & Swartz, S. (2016, October 20). Style that's sustainable: A new fast-fashion formula. *McKinsey Insights.* https://www.mckinsey.com/business-functions/sustainability/our-insights/style-thats-sustainable-a-new-fast-fashion-formula#

Reshoring Initiative. (2019). *Reshoring initiative 2018 data report.* https://reshorenow.org/?pageLink=blog-detail&blogLink=reshoring-initiative-2018-data-report

Rosen, E. (2002). *Making sweatshops: The globalization of the U.S. apparel industry.* University of California Press.

Selekman, B., Walter, H., & Couper, W. (1925). *The clothing and textile industries in New York and its environs.* Regional Plan of New York and Its Environs.

Thomas, D. (2019). *Fashionopolis: The price of fast fashion & the future of clothes.* Penguin Press.

US Bureau of Labor Statistics (USBLS). (2020). *Occupational employment statistics.* https://www.bls.gov/oes/tables.htm

US Bureau of Labor Statistics (USBLS). (2021). *Industries at a glance: Apparel manufacturing.* https://www.bls.gov/iag/tgs/iag315.htm

US Census Bureau (USCB). (2021, January 28). *Annual retail trade survey: 2019, sales (1992–2019).* https://www.census.gov/data/tables/2019/econ/arts/annual-report.html

US Census Bureau (USCB). (2022, January 6). *Monthly U.S. international trade in goods and services, November 2021.* https://www.census.gov/foreign-trade/Press-Release/current_press_release/ft900.pdf

Wicker, A. (2016, September 1). Fast fashion is creating an environmental crisis. *Newsweek*. https://www.newsweek.com/2016/09/09/old-clothes-fashion-waste-crisis-494824.html

Wolf, E. (2017, February). A conversation with fashion's biggest homme d'affaires: Didier Grumbach. *1 Granary*, *4*, 579–584.

World Integrated Trade Solution (WITS). (2020). *World textiles and clothing exports by country and region 2018*. https://wits.worldbank.org/CountryProfile/en/Country/WLD/Year/2018/TradeFlow/Export/Partner/all/Product/50-63_TextCloth

# 3 The New Design Entrepreneurs

## Introduction

As the contemporary design marketplace reaches unprecedented levels of abundance, saturation, and consumption, consumers' needs and desires for design move well beyond the material realm. No longer is object creation, which offers traditional forms of value (e.g. material worth, aesthetics, and function), the sole goal of designers. Now, their creations must carry an "emotional value" that targets consumers' unique practical *and* emotional needs. Subsequently, the traditional role of the designer is no longer relevant or sustainable.

This new form of design practice requires the designer's long-held position in the creative economies to shift. The conventional notion of the "designer-as-auteur" whose personal proclivities and dictates are blindly followed by devotees has become obsolete. It has been replaced by designers who, through their use of new design and research processes grounded in the social sciences, craft emotionally compelling products that provide "emotional value" to their customers (Faerm, 2021). By doing so, the designer transforms the creative process itself; rather than creating design from myopic, personal biases, the designer must begin their work by rigorously researching their consumers' psychographics and emotional needs. This research grounds and substantiates all proceeding stages of design development—from concept to final product to marketing presentation format—and, consequently, enables designers to accurately identify, create, and deliver the "emotional value" increasingly sought by consumers. Designs become more meaningful and desirable to consumers who, due to this heightened "emotional value" and sentiment, may cherish and retain the products longer, thus contributing to global sustainability. Moreover, this approach to the creative process enables designers to stand out in the oversaturated marketplace and businesses to increase consumer loyalty and resultant sales by offering only those products that are truly desired by their target audience.

Presented in three parts, this chapter examines the emerging new role of the design entrepreneur: namely, the "Designer-As-Social Scientist."

DOI: 10.4324/9781003049166-4

In this chapter, historical, contemporary, and speculative lenses are used to examine the key reasons why and how the designer's role has advanced into one that crafts strategic, emotionally compelling narratives and products for evolving marketplaces and consumer needs. "Part 1: A History of 'Stuff'" discusses society's altered relationship to and perception of design beginning in the early 2000s. It was during this formative period that mass attention to design grew exponentially in both the media and design retail marketplaces—thus spawning radically new consumer attitudes toward design and the designers themselves. Building on this historical overview, "Part 2: An Emerging Paradigm in the Design Industries" explicates the psychosocial reasons behind contemporary consumers' needs for heightened "emotional value" in designed objects, systems, and experiences. Particular focus is given to the emergent generation's values, beliefs, and consumer behaviors that help shape their unique perceptions of and distinct needs for emotional value in design. Accordingly, these new consumer attributes are directly impacting the role of the future design entrepreneur. "Part 3: Implications for Design Practice and Design Education: The 'Designer-As-Social Scientist'" proposes methods for how designers and educators can respond to these shifts within their respective sectors. Collectively, these three parts provide readers with a better understanding of the evolving design industries and thus how design students can be best prepared for professional success.

## Part 1: A History of "Stuff"

### *Our Emerging Obsession with Design*

Design has become a near-obsession and a dominant force permeating nearly every facet of our daily lives. At the turn of the 21st century, consumers' growing interests in "high" design became especially piqued; the growing attention to design in the media and the greater accessibility to internationally esteemed designers' creations via mass retailers emerged with considerable fanfare. One formative event occurred in 1999 when the acclaimed architect Michael Graves was commissioned by mass-market retailer Target to design a range of over 2,000 household objects that included outdoor patio sets, tea kettles, clocks, and ice cream scoopers—many of which achieved remarkably high volume in sales. Other mass retailers followed with great fervor and success, including H&M, whose partnerships with over twenty design luminaries since 2004—including Karl Lagerfeld, Versace, and Lanvin—have received high media attention and customer demand, resulting in high financial returns. Consumers' demand for these "high-design" collaborations can be extreme: when Target introduced its housewares collaboration with Missoni in 2011, its website crashed soon after the products went live online due to the extraordinary volume of website traffic driven by interest in the collection. The massification of "high" design has become so prevalent and revered in contemporary culture that a simple wastebasket—namely, the "Garbo" produced by Umbra—is featured in the permanent collection of the Museum of Modern Art in New York City (Volf, 2016).

This pervasive interest in design has led many other mass industries and traditional institutions to respond to their audiences' increasing interest in all things "designed." The television industry was among the first to capitalize on their viewers' heightened interests in design by creating a wide variety of design-focused television programing. These programs feature competitions across design disciplines, including *Top Design* for interior design, *Blown Away* for glass blowing, *Ellen's Next Great Designer* for furniture design, *Full Bloom* for floral design, and *Project Runway* for fashion design. Viewers learn about the contestants' personal histories, creative processes, and professional pursuits. This presentation enables design to extend its value beyond its traditional attributes of function and aesthetics. Viewers form emotional "bonds" with contestants over the course of the competition and resultantly associate those positive emotions with the design that is produced. As a result of these programs, an enhanced, deeper relationship forms between people and design to the point where the value of "stuff" moves beyond its mere utilitarian attributes and acquires valuable intangible meanings and emotional responses by viewers.

The sudden explosion of enthusiasm for design has led it to be featured in sectors that historically did not spotlight design—such as fine art museums. At Boston's Museum of Fine Arts (MFAB), The Department of Textiles and Fashion Arts held just six exhibitions in seven years between 1997 and 2004. Yet, in a later seven-year period, between 2012 and 2019, the number of exhibitions spiked 183% to seventeen exhibitions (Museum of Fine Arts, Boston [MFAB], 2019). The Metropolitan Museum of Art's (MMA) exhibition "Heavenly Bodies: Fashion and the Catholic Imagination," a display of religious and non-secular-inspired fashion, attracted more than 1.65 million visitors, making it the most visited exhibit in the museum's 150-year history (Metropolitan Museum of Art [MMA], n.d.). The exhibition's unique "conversation" between tangible objects and intangible beliefs and feelings underscored design's ability to surpass mere aesthetics and functionality and deliver emotional fulfillment to broad audiences. The substantial growth and popularity of museum exhibitions that feature design further illustrate society's changing relationship with and feelings toward design.

## *Consumption and Production in the Design Marketplace*

The 21st century consumers' zealousness for design has fostered unprecedented rates of consumption and production of designed objects. In the US, these rates are especially high; the average household final consumption expenditure—the market value of all goods and services purchased by households—has risen 329% in just three decades (1988–2018) and has grown by nearly 2,700% since 1970 (Index Mundi, 2019). The typical American will consume fifty-three times more goods and services than someone from China, and although Americans account for only 5% of the world's population, they create half of the globe's solid waste, consume one-third of the world's paper products, and use a quarter of the earth's oil (Scheer & Moss, 2012). If all nations used resources at same rate as the US, the human race would need approximately five planets equivalent to the Earth to sustain itself (Global Footprint Network, 2021).

Levels of production and consumption are particularly egregious in the "fast fashion" sector of the apparel industry. The H&M Group, for instance, has perfected an efficient "sketch-to-floor" production cycle that takes just two weeks and sells an estimated three billion pieces of clothing annually (Paton & Maheshwari, 2019; Peterson, 2019). Automated manufacturing is helping propel this acceleration: machinery can make running-shoe uppers twenty times faster than humans, bathmats every twenty seconds, and T-shirts every five seconds (Thomas, 2019). Automation drives this accelerated production timeline, which yields extremely high volumes of low-cost goods. For example, the number of garments produced between 2000 and 2016 doubled and exceeded 100 billion for the first time in 2014 (Remy et al., 2016). This mass-production approach also neglects customization and personalization in design. Instead, these companies develop uniformity in design, regardless of socio-political or regional differences among their customers; they showcase the same products in Seattle as they do in Shanghai. This approach to "global economies of scale" propagates homogeneous design that, in turn, fails to address fully consumers' specific physical and emotional needs.

This constant stream of mass-market "high design" that entices consumers to buy things more often creates unprecedented levels of consumption. These levels are remarkably steep among Americans, who purchase nearly five-times more items of clothing now annually than they did in 1980 (Thomas, 2019). Accordingly, rates of disposal have risen, too. On average, a garment is worn just seven times before being discarded, and for every five garments produced, the equivalent of three end up in a landfill or incinerated each year (Remy et al., 2016; Thomas, 2019). In 2018 alone, consumers discarded approximately 11.3 million tons of textiles into landfills—an increase of 387% since 1980 (US Environmental Protection Agency, 2021).

Within this lifecycle, design moves between a state of usefulness and a state of garbage at hyper-speed; this rapid lifecycle decreases the sentimental value placed on items by consumers. In this mindset, clothing simply becomes "stuff" or a "thing" with no meaning. Designed products become mere objects that provide an immediate sense of reward through the act of selecting, purchasing, and owning them. For a brief moment in time, buyers experience instant gratification by owning the designed item before they quickly come down from the "buying high" that drives this consumer behavior. Once they come down from the high, buyers again quickly reenter the market in a circular quest for emotional fulfillment through designed "stuff."

## Part 2: An Emerging Paradigm in the Design Industries

### Our Evolving Relationship with Design: "Emotional Value"

Consumers' excessive demands for high design and the resultant surge of production and consumption of such products have created an oversaturated marketplace. This oversaturation creates an environment of overabundance for consumers, who then may feel inundated and overwhelmed with choices. For most first-world consumers, their basic needs are not only met but, rather, far surpassed.

To succeed in the emerging global design marketplace, designer entrepreneurs must differentiate their offerings in ways that go beyond the standard attributes of design (aesthetics and function) through the new attribute of "emotional value." Author Daniel Pink, who has contextualized this marketplace and the ways consumers will relate to and engage with design in the near future, states: "[a]s more of our basic needs are met, we increasingly expect sophisticated experiences that are emotionally satisfying and meaningful. These experiences will not be simple products. They will be complex combinations of products, services, spaces, and information. They will be the ways we get educated, the ways we are entertained, the ways we stay healthy, the ways we share and communicate" (Pink, 2005, p. 46).

Pink's assertion aligns with the pyramidal framework of Maslow's Hierarchy of Needs (1943) (Figure 3.1). In today's overabundant world, consumers climb the hierarchical pyramid from the lower levels (where basic necessities such as food, shelter, and safety are located) toward its peak (where they are able to fulfill their higher level needs for esteem, creativity, and self-actualization). This progression changes how consumers relate to design as their engagement with a product is no longer driven by need, which is low in Maslow's Hierarchy but, rather, by the desire for emotional fulfillment, which is at the pinnacle of the Hierarchy. This fulfillment is achieved as a result of the designer's uniquely compelling narratives and design processes, which manifest in the objects and/or systems directly. Of course, this does not mean that design's core goal can (or should) be overlooked: it still must work and elevate aesthetics. What it does mean, however, is that design's emotional value is what consumers now seek. As a result, crafting a compelling emotional value must be a driving force behind all stages of the design process moving forward.

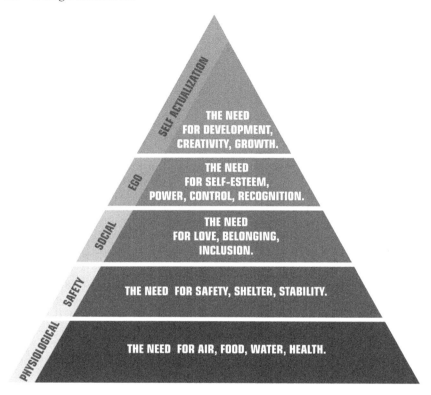

*Figure 3.1* Maslow's Hierarchy of Needs.
Source: Shutterstock.com.

Emotional value can be instilled in design many ways. Personalization and customization are particularly advantageous approaches for the emergent generation of shoppers "who no longer respond to being treated solely as consumers and, instead, seek to occupy the role of brand collaborators" (Lonergan, 2020, p. 110). Increasingly, design companies are responding by offering consumers co-design opportunities. For example, Nike and Coach allow shoppers to choose colorways, materials, and other design elements that personalize certain "standard" products. The Lego Group engages consumers in toy design creation on a dedicated innovation platform. Benchmade Modern and Inside Weather invite customers to design their own furniture.

Customizable services are expected to become so ubiquitous that researchers predict retailers will feature "smart" mirrors in dressing rooms that will scan the shopper's face and body to make specific recommendations about size and styles (Rohrbaugh, 2019). It is through these personalized and customized design options that consumers' high-level needs are being met—with substantial sales success for the designers. Consumers of these products feel more strongly connected to personalized or customized items and their brands; they are connected to them more deeply, as they perceive these products as more meaningful representations of their personal identities. These design services, and the resultant deeper emotional connections they promote between consumers and products, can also increase a product's lifespan, thus offering the significant benefit of being more sustainable—an attribute that is increasingly in demand by today's consumer.

In a survey of over 1,000 people, researchers found that 80% of respondents stated they are more likely to patronize a company if it offers personalized experiences (Epsilon, 2018). Additionally, 87% of respondents want more meaningful relationships with brands, which further emphasizes the critical role emotion plays in our evolving design industries (Schwarz, 2020). Successful design entrepreneurs must therefore ensure they creatively develop designs and experiences that strategically deliver emotional fulfillment through participatory relationships between their target audiences and their products.

## *The Emerging Consumer Generation*

Today's design undergraduates are part of the most populous generation to date in the world. They are often known as "Generation Z," and their members were born between 1997 and 2012 (June, 2021). Representing 40% of the world's consumers, this generation has nearly $150 billion US in purchasing power that will greatly impact how the design industries evolve (Amed et al., 2019). It is therefore incumbent upon designers to understand how these consumers' values, attributes, and behaviors are markedly different from previous generations.

While a growing body of research literature reveals extensive shared interests and associated consumer behaviors that are common to this generation, this chapter examines three specific themes that are especially important to this cohort and thus salient to the future of design entrepreneurship: Sustainability, Corporate Transparency, and Social Justice. Together, these themes illustrate the ways in which this generation consumes goods and services as a way to express their values and beliefs for a better world and, in doing so, will evolve the purpose of design and the role of the design entrepreneur.

## *Sustainability and Corporate Transparency*

Sustainability and corporate transparency have gained widespread attention following a stream of recent infamous corporate catastrophes. These events include the Rana Plaza garment factory collapse in Bangladesh that resulted in 1,134 deaths and over 2,500 injuries, abundant allegations of forced labor in design manufacturing, and Burberry's incineration of 28.6 million pounds of unsold goods (Paton, 2018; Thomas, 2019). As the media further exposes the design industries' nefarious acts (e.g. manufacturing sweatshops, worker abuses, and ecological disasters), more consumers are scrutinizing their purchases to ensure ethical and sustainable practices have been followed. This scrutiny is especially high among teens and young adults: 45% of them always research for background information before buying, and 75% consider a trusted brand to be an important purchasing factor (Amed et al., 2019; Granskog et al., 2020).

Sustainability is an especially widespread value among the emergent generation: 94% believe companies have a responsibility to address environmental and social issues, and 92% would switch brands to one associated with a good cause, given comparable cost and quality (Cone Communications, 2017). Additional data reveal:

- 67% consider the use of sustainable materials to be an important purchasing factor;
- 60% went out of their way to recycle and purchase products in environmentally friendly packaging;
- 66% are willing to pay more for sustainable goods; and
- 60% of online shoppers state they would be willing to pay more for delivery if $CO_2$-neutral shipping was guaranteed (Amed et al., 2019; Kirienko & Schreiber, 2021).

This generation of consumers' intensifying demand for sustainable practices has prompted corporations to respond through diverse initiatives that promote environmental wellness (Figure 3.2). For instance, Pandora, the world's largest jewelry brand, sources 71% of its silver and gold from recycled sources and aims to reach 100% recycled sources before 2030 (Pandora, 2020). Michelin developed a new tire that is 3D-printed from biodegradable materials, designed to prevent blowouts, and allows for simple repair. IKEA purchased a forest to safeguard the property and its ecosystems from development. AIR-INK collects $CO_2$ emissions from automobiles and distills it into a carbon pigment that can be used to make ink. In the resale marketplace, companies like The RealReal and Vestiaire Collective offer previously owned luxury goods that range from housewares to artwork to apparel.

The growing popularity of renovation and "do-it-yourself" (DIY) craft projects (such as refurbishing or upgrading used furniture) among these consumers is further evidence of their commitment to sustainability; these projects lengthen a product's lifespan, promote new skillsets and self-sufficiency among consumers, and afford personalization for greater emotional fulfillment. Accordingly, brands are shifting consumers' perceptions of their purchases from being things that are disposable

*Figure 3.2* Mycelium "leather" is a bio-based sustainable and bio-degradable material made of mushroom spores and plant fibers.

Source: Yulia Panova/Shutterstock.com.

to things that need greater care and are more durable. Examples of this ethos in practice abound, including Eileen Fisher's Renew program that collects gently used Eileen Fisher items and either refurbishes them or recycles the materials to make new designs. Patagonia's Common Threads Initiative promises the company will make long-lasting products, help customers make repairs, and offer credit toward future purchases when customers perform trade-ins. In turn, Patagonia asks its shoppers to buy only what is needed, to make repairs to currently owned merchandise (rather than buying a new replacement), and subsequently keep goods out of landfills and incinerators. This unique approach—one in which Patagonia promises to adhere to set principles and the buyer commits to acting ethically—creates and cultivates a partnership between the company and its consumers that subsequently enhances the emotional value of their products.

Sustainability and traceability are also gaining greater prioritization in the international public sectors. The United Nations Sustainable Development Goals (SDGs) were established in 2015 and are comprised of seventeen interdependent goals that function as the main framework for putting sustainability strategies into action. The SDGs are intended to be achieved by 2030, and they include: responsible consumption and production; clean water and sanitation; affordable and clean energy; gender equality; and climate action. Another global initiative is The Fashion Pact (TFP). Launched in 2019, the Pact unites over sixty leading apparel and textile companies from fourteen countries—together representing more than 200 brands that comprise one-third of the fashion industry—that have committed "to a common core of ambitious quantified environmental objectives focusing on three themes: climate, biodiversity, and oceans" (The Fashion Pact [TFP], 2020, p. 1).

International public partnerships like these are a significant advancement in formal worldwide policy. They also bolster the rise of unification efforts occurring in private industry. For example, a survey of sixty-four sourcing executives from the apparel industry who are responsible for a total sourcing value of over $100 billion US revealed that 65% expect their companies to achieve full traceability of products from fiber to store by 2025, and the majority aspire to source at least half of their products with sustainable materials (Berg et al., 2019).

Corporate transparency is also increasingly sought by consumers, particularly following the outbreak of COVID-19 that amplified public awareness for and scrutiny of global supply chains. In response, growing numbers of corporations are providing information to consumers about their products' supply chains and/or ecological impact. The retailer Reformation, for instance, measures the environmental impact of every garment it sells and discloses the results to customers. Its "RefScale" methodology tracks amounts of carbon dioxide emitted, gallons of water used in production, and pounds of waste generated by their products. Other design companies, like Arket, disclose each product's country of origin, factory names and addresses, and numbers of factory employees. Consumers can then make more informed decisions and, if the brand's practices meet their needs for sustainability and ethical practice, become more loyal toward that brand.

*Social Justice*

The emergent generation is highly attuned to issues of inclusion, diversity, social equity, and human rights (see Chapter 11). Design brands are actively addressing these issues both to offer their support for these causes and to connect more meaningfully with consumers. Such corporate initiatives can include unique consumer experiences, philanthropic partnerships, and advertising campaigns. For example, to offer a unique consumer experience, the footwear brand Toms distributed virtual reality headsets to 100 of their locations, allowing customers to virtually travel to Peru to see the impact of their "One for One" local giving initiative in that country. Moore (2020) notes, "As you walk through the village with locals smiling and waving at you, it is impossible not to feel warmed by the friendly atmosphere. Not only did this retail experience improve awareness of their social corporate responsibility and promote their giving campaign, it also gave customers an unforgettable and immersive experience they were unlikely to forget" (n.p.).

Since 2005, Gucci has donated more than $20 million US to UNICEF's work, focusing on the Schools for Africa program, which

*The New Design Entrepreneurs* 37

*Figure 3.3* Designer Kenneth Cole's "Tied with Pride" advertising campaign is one of many the company has developed to support social issues.

Source: Leonard Zhukovsky/Shutterstock.com.

gives disadvantaged children in Africa access to high quality education (UNICEF, 2021). In 2013, Warby Parker partnered with DonorsChoose. org, an organization that helps US public school teachers crowdsource materials and experiences for their classrooms. Designers, too, are publicizing their own *personal* values, beliefs, and stances on social issues. This is evidenced in designers' advocacy for gun control (e.g. Levi's, Gucci, and Toms), encouragement of political action (e.g. Nike, Under Armour, and Uber), and support for the LGBTQIA+ community (e.g. Target, Apple, H&M, and Kenneth Cole) (Figure 3.3). Socially oriented initiatives like these enable brands to engage with the global community well beyond conventional sales transactions and simultaneously imbue their products with a newer form of emotional value.

Corporate initiatives are playing a greater role in swaying consumers' behaviors. A survey of 2,000 Americans revealed 76% of respondents cited a company's responsible and fair behavior when buying materials, products, or services it uses as a deciding factor in their consumer buying decisions (Edelman, 2019). Two-thirds of global consumers say they would switch, avoid, or boycott brands based on their stance on controversial issues (Amed et al., 2019). And, in a sample size of 16,000 people spanning eight global markets, 72% said the ability of a brand's values matching theirs is a deciding factor when shopping (Edelman, 2019). Consumers' positive responses to these socially minded collaborations can be notable, as seen when Balenciaga supported the United Nation's World Food Program and various store managers reported shoppers expressing it was the first time in their life they had donated to an organization (Amed et al., 2019).

The emergent consumer generation is "looking beyond tangible products and actually trying to understand what it is that makes the company tick. What's its mission? What's its purpose? And what is it actually trying to build for us as a society?" (Rahilly et al., 2020, n.p.). Accordingly, a brand's *practices*—and not merely the physical products they offer—factor heavily into this demographic's purchasing decisions and brand loyalties.

## Part 3: Implications for Design Practice and Design Education: The "Designer-As-Social Scientist"

The factors discussed above have sparked the imperative for a new framework of design practice and role of the designer, namely that of the "Designer-As-Social Scientist." As emphasized by Cédric Charbit, Chief Executive of Balenciaga, "A product can no longer be only and purely craftsmanship plus creativity and heritage: we need to add values and emotion to it. Products need to be meaningful" (Amed et al., 2019, p. 48).

To succeed in this new role, designers must employ an understanding of advanced research methodologies historically found in the social sciences, not design. Through the synthesis of pragmatic social science methodologies with artistic creative design, a new framework is emerging, one that designers need in order to understand the complexity of people, cultures, and belief systems that exist in the designer's target market, which may well be far outside of the designer's own myopic world view. This new design framework will serve as the foundation upon which designers must establish future design proposals and products. Design initiatives that were previously formed by personal preferences and speculations about consumer wants are being replaced by initiatives that have objective research at their foundation, research that leads to the analysis that determines exactly what their target audiences truly want and emotionally desire.

Accordingly, the very design process itself is in a state of flux. Designers, before entering each creative venture—from the designing of tangible objects and retail spaces to the intangible experiences and systems that engage consumers—must begin the design process first by developing questions that will help ground the research process and answer:

- "How does my customer wish to feel in six or twelve months from now?";
- "What will be my customer's emotional needs?";

- "How can my designed objects(s) and/or experience(s) provide consumers with the identified emotional fulfillment they seek?"; and
- "How can these objects and/or experiences provide consumers with long-term gratification?"

This research framework will then be populated with data derived from primary research with consumers and be used to guide designers in determining which attributes their products and services will have. By "designing emotion" based on factual data, designers can craft products and services with strong narratives and emotional content. Designing emotion directly influences what kind of design designers make, for whom they make it, what its aesthetics and emotional value will be, and the design's ultimate end-use (Faerm, 2021).

This process upends the traditional creator-consumer hierarchy, one in which the designer-auteur espouses personal proclivities and dictates of design through their work that are then followed blindly by devotees, It enables a model to emerge, one wherein brands devise more strategic, uniquely compelling narratives that also directly fulfill the specific emotional needs of the designer's target consumer. This research framework and attendant design processes will provide the essential foundation required to target successfully the emergent consumer population—which is one that increasingly expects brands to develop unique products that represent the *consumer's* sense of style, self-image, beliefs, and values.

## *Impact on Educators*

For teachers, this shift in the designer's role creates an existential dilemma: how can design education train future designers to design emotion? Design has always questioned how to improve society. But the growing need to design emotion that can support people's sense of well-being is especially warranted given the escalating, unprecedented emotional health crisis among today's emergent generation (see Chapter 11 for full discussion). Design students need to be prepared for this new role of "Designer-As-Social Scientist" so they may be better equipped creatively to improve people's well-being, communities, and our world as a whole. The issues design students (and future professionals) *choose* to address, *how* they are addressed, and how students are *taught* to design emotion must be at the forefront of academic discourse and subsequent planning. After all, design schools play a vital role in helping create the future world and thus need to adopt new curricular priorities that ensure design pedagogy becomes more *issues* driven, and founded in data, rather than a pedagogy that centers on the designer as omnipotent auteur.

This directive in design education opens up extensive opportunities to innovate curricula. For instance, new courses and projects could ask students to develop things such as systems-based partnerships and co-design initiatives for their target audience, subsequently promoting conceptual collaborations, design personalization, and more meaningful emotional value in design. The teaching of sustainability could include students researching resource consumption, supply chain traceability and mapping, and responsible sourcing for their creations. Additionally, a product-specific label—something akin to a nutrition label on food—that explicitly states the materials used to create the product, the environmental effects of its production, and the local/global community impact of the product could be created and thus prompt students to adopt this practice as professionals.

Sustainability is further supported through virtual sampling, which will become widely adopted and made normative practice to benefit our students' professional development. In the design world's apparel sector alone, the amount of companies that will use virtual sampling for product development is predicted to spike by 309% between 2019 and 2025 (from 11% to 46%, respectively) and will likely increase further after 2025 (Berg et al., 2019). Other issues-driven curricula can teach students about the potential roles their work can play in supporting critical issues, such as social justice. Projects, courses, and even new design programs that focus on political action, international affairs, governmental initiatives, social equality, and design law are just some areas that will, through our students and alumni, create a more anthropocentric design industry in which the "Designer-As-Social Scientist" plays a central role in guiding a critical component of humankind's advancement.

## Conclusion

Design entrepreneurship is undergoing radical changes. While the traditional values of aesthetics and function remain essential components of design, a product's ability to deliver emotional value to the user must increasingly become the focus for designers if they are to attract buyers and sustain consumer loyalty. Several factors have contributed to this growing imperative. These include the mass obsession with "high" design; the oversaturated marketplace in which designers struggle to stand out and capture consumers' attention; and excessive rates of consumption fueled by affordable "high design" and consumers' use of it for emotional fulfillment.

The factors that are creating an increasing demand for emotional value in design will also lead to the creation of a new role for the design entrepreneur, namely that of the "Designer-As-Social Scientist." No longer confined to the creation of objects that are simply aesthetically pleasing, this new role will require designers to understand better the psychosocial needs and wants of their customers so they may craft well-targeted *emotionally* compelling designs that deliver greater overall value to the customer than ever before. In this role, designers will pivot from the myopic design process to one that takes a much broader view of the actual emotional needs of their audience, a view that is based in social sciences research practices that reveal how and where the consumers' future emotional needs are headed. Rather than designing from personal proclivities and unproved assumptions, future designers will look to data to answer such critical question as: "What type of narrative will emotionally resonate in my targeted audience?", and "How can I apply this to my designs and the design process as a whole?", and "How can my emotionally-led design process contribute to sustainability?" It therefore behooves future design entrepreneurs to develop data-driven detailed understandings about the emergent generation's values, beliefs, and emotional needs, all of which increasingly influence consumers' preferences. These include consumers' growing demands for designers and brands to adopt and promote sustainable practices, corporate transparency, social justice, and similar initiatives that engender issues-driven design.

In many ways, design is a service to customers. When designers' work becomes informed by the emotional needs of its audience, designers will respond by crafting more enduring designs. The distinctions between creators and analyzers—or, designers and social scientists—will blur as everyone engaged in the process of defining, planning, and designing products and systems will be instrumental in the future of design. It is by doing so that the designer and design industry will remain successful and sustainable.

*A version of this chapter was first published in Fashion, Style & Popular Culture, Vol. 8, No. 4.*

## References

Amed, I., Andersson, J., Balchandani, A., Beltrami, M., Berg, A., Hedrich, S., Kim, D., Rölkens, F., & Young, R. (2019). The State of fashion 2019. *McKinsey & Company*. https://www.mckinsey.com/~/media/McKinsey/Industries/Retail/Our%20Insights/The%20State%20of%20Fashion%202019%20A%20year%20of%20awakening/The-State-of-Fashion-2019-final.ashx

Berg, A., Hedrich, S., Ibanez, P., Kappelmark, S., Magnus, K.-H., & Seeger, M. (2019). Fashion's new must-have: Sustainable sourcing at scale. *McKinsey & Company*. https://www.mckinsey.com/~/media/mckinsey/industries/retail/our%20insights/fashions%20new%20must%20have%20sustainable%20sourcing%20at%20scale/fashions-new-must-have-sustainable-sourcing-at-scale-vf.pdf

Cone Communications. (2017). *2017 Cone Gen Z CSR study: How to speak Z.* http://www.conecomm.com/2017-cone-gen-z-csr-study-pdf

Edelman. (2019). *2019 Edelman trust barometer: In brands we trust?* https://www.edelman.com/sites/g/files/aatuss191/files/2019-06/2019_edelman_trust_barometer_special_report_in_brands_we_trust.pdf

Epsilon. (2018, January 9). *New Epsilon research indicates 80% of consumers are more likely to make a purchase when brands offer personalized experiences.* https://www.epsilon.com/us/about-us/pressroom/new-epsilon-research-indicates-80-of-consumers-are-more-likely-to-make-a-purchase-when-brands-offer-personalized-experiences

Faerm, S. (2021). Evolving "places": The paradigmatic shift in the role of the fashion designer. *Fashion, Style & Popular Culture, 8*(4), 399–417.

Global Footprint Network. (2021). *Media backgrounder.* https://www.footprintnetwork.org/content/images/uploads/Media_Backgrounder_GFN.pdf

Granskog, A., Lee, L., Magnus, K.-H., & Sawers, C. (2020, July 17) Survey: Consumer sentiment on sustainability in fashion. *McKinsey & Company.* https://www.mckinsey.com/industries/retail/our-insights/survey-consumer-sentiment-on-sustainability-in-fashion#

Index Mundi. (2019). *World–household final consumption expenditure.* https://www.indexmundi.com/facts/world/household-final-consumption-expenditure

June, S. (2021, July 10). Could Gen Z free the world from email? *The New York Times.* https://www.nytimes.com/2021/07/10/business/gen-z-email.html

Kirienko, E., & Schreiber, L. (2021). *Sustainable consumption in the United States of America 2021 report.* Statista.

Lonergan, P. (2020). Co-creative storytelling. In E. Huggard, & J. Cope (Eds.), *Communicating fashion brands: Theoretical and practical perspectives* (pp. 110–121). Routledge.

Maslow, A. (1943). A theory of human motivation. *Psychological Review, 50*(4), 370–396.

Metropolitan Museum of Art (MMA). (n.d.). *The Costume Institute.* https://www.metmuseum.org/about-the-met/curatorial-departments/the-costume-institute

Moore, N. (2020, February 18). 9 case studies that prove experiential retail is in the future. *Storefront.* https://www.thestorefront.com/mag/7-case-studies-prove-experiential-retail-future/

Museum of Fine Arts, Boston (MFAB). (2019). *Past exhibitions.* https://www.mfa.org/exhibitions/past

Pandora. (2020, June 2). *All Pandora jewelry to be made from recycled silver and gold.* https://pandoragroup.com/investor/news-and-reports/press-releases/newsdetail?id=23761

Paton, E. (2018, September 6). Burberry to stop burning clothing and other goods it can't sell. *The New York Times.* https://www.nytimes.com/2018/09/06/business/burberry-burning-unsold-stock.html

Paton, E., & Maheshwari, S. (2019, December 18). H&M's different kind of clickbait. *The New York Times.* https://www.nytimes.com/2019/12/18/fashion/hms-supply-chain-transparency.html

Peterson, H. (2019, September 12). How H&M churns out new styles in just 2 weeks. *Business Insider.* https://www.businessinsider.com/hm-produces-new-fashions-in-two-weeks-2014-9

Pink, D. (2005). *A whole new mind: Why right-brainers will rule the future.* Riverhead Books.

Rahilly, L., Finneman, B., & Spagnuolo, E. (2020, August 4). Meet Generation Z: Shaping the future of shopping. *McKinsey & Company.* https://www.mckinsey.com/industries/consumer-packaged-goods/our-insights/meet-generation-z-shaping-the-future-of-shopping

Remy, N., Speelman, E., & Swartz, S. (2016, October 20). Style that's sustainable: A new fast-fashion formula. *McKinsey & Company.* https://www.mckinsey.com/business-functions/sustainability/our-insights/style-thats-sustainable-a-new-fast-fashion-formula#

Rohrbaugh, L. (2019, December 16). The retail store of the future. *Total Retail*. https://www.mytotalretail.com/article/the-retail-store-of-the-future/

Scheer, R., & Moss, D. (2012, September 14). Use it and lose it: The outsize effect of U.S. consumption on the environment. *Scientific American*. http://www.scientificamerican.com/article/american-consumption-habits/

Schwarz, R. (2020, March 24). The power of consumer collaboration. *Forbes*. https://www.forbes.com/sites/forbescommunicationscouncil/2020/03/24/the-power-of-consumer-collaboration/?sh=15dd60234c17

The Fashion Pact (TFP). (2020, October 12). *About*. https://thefashionpact.org/?lang=en

Thomas, D. (2019). *Fashionopolis: The price of fast fashion & the future of clothes*. Penguin.

UNICEF. (2021). *Gucci and UNICEF USA's partnership to save and protect children*. https://www.unicefusa.org/supporters/organizations/companies/our-corporate-partners/gucci

US Environmental Protection Agency. (2021). *Textiles: Material-specific data*. https://www.epa.gov/facts-and-figures-about-materials-waste-and-recycling/textiles-material-specific-data

Volf, M. (2016, January 19). Karim Rashid's Garbo at 20: Does it still hold up? *Metropolis Magazine*. https://metropolismag.com/projects/karim-rashids-garbo-20/

# 4 The Future of the Design Industries

Interview with Matthew Kressy, founding Director of the Integrated Design & Management Program, Massachusetts Institute of Technology

## Introduction

The future of the US design industries is more uncertain than ever before. The industries' evolving characteristics and roles, the ways designed products and systems will respond to and affect people's lives, and the growing necessity of Human Centered Design (HCD) across all design practices are central considerations among designers and educators. Designers and educators alike must focus on these considerations if the US design industries are to advance strategically and successfully, both domestically and globally. This chapter presents an interview with Matthew Kressy, founding Director of the Integrated Design & Management (IDM) Program at the Massachusetts Institute of Technology (MIT). Within the discussion, Kressy identifies and discusses several key factors that have the potential to guide and shape the future US design industries in a positive way. It is essential that design educators identify these factors and use them to improve their incorporation of critical elements of technology into their pedagogical practice. By doing this, educators contribute to their design institutions, enabling those institutions to continue to evolve their programs' curricula to better support students' professional preparation.

## Interview

STEVEN FAERM: *What attributes or characteristics make the US design industries so distinct from and admired by other global design leaders? Will these evolve in the near future? If so, in what ways?*

MATT KRESSY: There are certain factors that I think put us in a very strong position in terms of design. One is that, until recently, the US has been the leading consumer market on the planet. As [US-based] designers, we happen to be located in that market, we are a part of that market, and we have access to that market. So, we understand what users and consumers desire, and we understand their problems.

DOI: 10.4324/9781003049166-5

## The Future of the Design Industries 45

Being so close to our market, we intuitively pick up on things through osmosis—movies, music, what people are wearing, to name a few—and we have access to that before those designers located elsewhere. A designer in China, who might be extremely talented but a little disconnected from the US market, didn't grow up immersed in all these subtle emotional trends. It's not a part of their fiber, which I think makes it difficult for them to design products that would strongly resonate or be on the cutting edge in our market.

Also, I think our culture is also really great for designers. We are a country that celebrates freedom—freedom of thought and freedom of expression. Not all cultures do that. In fact, some of them quietly—and some not so quietly—discourage people from thinking freely and independently, and from expressing themselves. In the US, we are able to express ourselves not just as designers but as individuals in terms of our gender, sexual preferences, and political preferences. We're able to express ourselves without worrying too much that we're going to get hurt in some way or held back. That makes a great designer—someone who can think freely, who doesn't feel encumbered, who can really explore the creative space that's out there and uncover every stone that might have a little feature, or nuance, or solution, or beauty. That's hard for others to do.

The last thing is that we have great design schools. I think that creates a design culture that we have here, in which designers like and support each other as best they can.

However, I think the design industry will change. Recently, China overtook the US as the largest consumer market. So, similar to those designers in China that were disconnected from our markets and trends, designers from the US are disconnected from theirs. If I'm asked to design products for the Chinese market, I'd say, "Let's find a Chinese designer who lives in China and grew up with Chinese pop culture, someone who understands everything about the psychological things that happen when you grow up in that area." This means we might see more specialization; maybe designers will design for specific regions or markets. It definitely will impact sustainability and the health of the Earth.

SF: *How/Where will design enter our future lives in ways/areas we haven't yet seen or experienced?*
MK: We are seeing a greater role for design in business, or in the business operations of organizations. There are more people with design sensibilities in leadership roles or decision-making roles in businesses. Design skills—such as design thinking, processes, and methods—are not only great at creating product and experiences, but also great at creating organizations and business models.

Secondly, I believe that if we were to teach HCD [Human Centered Design] more widely, it would improve our own abilities to be thoughtful and empathetic citizens. Some of the projects I'm working on include a K-12 school that will make HCD "front-and-center," and this will make that whole process of [HCD] thinking habitual for students. This will lead to better citizens because now, instead of making assumptions about what other people are thinking and feeling, people will know from HCD that you shouldn't make those assumptions ever. You should talk to those people and understand what they are saying to the point that you feel their pain, that you feel their joy. When you get to that point where you are feeling empathy for those people, you have an understanding that allows you to make better decisions and form better ideas, strategies, and opinions.

I hope that eventually, every child in this country is introduced to HCD at some point because they become our next generation of leaders in businesses and politics. In the future, everyone who is running for Senate, or the presidency, will have had HCD [experience] and this means, hopefully, we have people in leadership that have a new kind of sensibility about making decisions.

SF: *Your IDM program at MIT considers "love" as a metric when reviewing applicants' materials. Can you discuss how and why this is an important attribute for future design leaders?*

MK: Our admissions process connects with the idea of looking at character above skills—not on par with skills, but giving it priority. If someone is deficient in some skills, we can probably teach those skills. Yet, if someone is deficient in some character, that's very hard to teach. For example, you can't have them up-to-speed on how to be a nurturing collaborator. You can't change that in a person in a week, but I sure can teach someone how to sketch perspective or use Arduino in a week.

I believe character is the predictor of someone's success. How much passion do they have? What's their drive? How much integrity do they have? How true are they to their own unique purpose? And of course, how much compassion and love do they have? When you have all of these characteristics, plus some skills, you have a very powerful collaborator or person to go out into the world. The converse of that is you have lots of skills but no character. That's great for the Industrial Age, because we can stick you in a gray cubicle and you can do technical drawings all day long for whatever we're making.

SF: *What emerging needs will consumers and society have from design?*

MK: My sense is that we're all kind of "teched-out." I think we're all really tired of our monitor not working with our laptop, of our iPhone not syncing, of our Wi-Fi not connecting, of our username and password management. I think we're all feeling that we're spending too much time maintaining this technology infrastructure, and we're desiring more time to sit in the woods under some trees or having a dinner with each other. It's about having more human experiences. So, I think the role of design will be to make technology disappear—to keep the functional benefits, but without this immersion in the details.

This would mean simplifying user interfaces and user experiences by giving up some crazy functionality that are outliers for more robust systems. I think AR [augmented reality], and machine learning in particular, will play a big role in a lot of this. Since designers are really needed in how machines learn—because how machines learn will dictate how they create an experience for us—it's a big opportunity for designers to inject themselves into that process and get involved. It's only a matter of time. I think the more we're saturated with technology, the closer we get to a tipping point where we think, "OK, enough!" A new design ethos will be born, where less is more and less technology is better. Everyone will be chasing that design objective.

Also, design will be more included in government, hopefully. From town planners and how they design roads for cyclists and pedestrians, to the Registry of Motor Vehicles and the experience of renewing [a driver's] license, getting a license plate, or registering cars. These are notoriously awful experiences. Why? Because designers weren't involved. Then, hopefully, that will lead to national leaders bringing design vision and integrity into policy-making, with a design practice that advocates for the needs and emotions of other people.

SF: *With the increasing simplification of technology, AR, and machine learning, will consumer services and attendant experiences become more "frictionless?"*

MK: Regarding the idea of "frictionless service," I think how you define "frictionless" is very important. Some people might define frictionless as the absence of human involvement. Others would define it as the shortest amount of time, or as achieving the best results, or as the most pleasurable experience. There are probably more ways of defining it, or a combination of all of those things, but that needs to be carefully thought out.

I think talking to an intelligent customer service person is hard to beat. In my experience, as you start learning more information in an experience, you have questions, and the quicker those questions can be answered, the happier I am, and the more I am feeling I am designing the best possible experience with a service, like a hotel or a restaurant. I might discover, "Oh, you don't have a table at 6:30, but you have one at 6:20? Great!" But would a UI [user interface] give me that? They might say, "Could you come at 6:43?" I don't know if ML [machine learning] or AI [artificial intelligence] can do that, but I think humans are an important part of that creative problem solving process.

Another problem we have to worry about is: if our computers are doing all of this work for us, what are humans going to do? I think there's lots of things humans can do; there are many more fruitful and fulfilling things in life than taking people's reservations over the phone. However, until that outlet has been established, people could end up idling or unemployed. We took away jobs in manufacturing and the coal industry. Not that we shouldn't have, but we didn't think about what we can do with all those [unemployed] people. In this country, the idea of freedom also comes with this idea of autonomy, that everyone is responsible for themselves. That can lead to problems, and I think we need to think about that as we design people out of our systems. This also connects to the idea of "reshoring"—bringing manufacturing back to this country but having automated machines do the work.

I think one of the confounding factors in our society in America, and probably elsewhere, is the disparity of wealth that is taking place. We have tremendous wealth [concentrated] in a very small percentage [of people], we have a very large percentage of lower-middle class, and we have another percentage that's in poverty. This is a very dangerous place to be, both economically and socially. If there is no middle class with disposable income to buy products, volumes are going to go way down—and everyone knows that volume is the key to a company's success. We can't all sell Bugattis, Gucci shoes, and Armani suits; you are not going to have a vibrant economy [in that situation].

On top of that, there is this disparate social perspective, where you have people that are alienated from the mainstream America in terms of wealth and opportunity. It may not be the case, but it's their perception; they feel dejected and cast off, so they form their own kind of togetherness. If their values are disconnected from the values that have made this country, what they are to date, we see very dangerous things happening. So, we need to bring those people back into our economic system. We need to make them feel loved. And the rich people need to make that happen. It can't be the other way around.

The more we have machines doing this work, the more we cast people off. To me, this is a very dangerous thing that we're doing. And to what end? Someone with a lot of money buys some automated equipment to the tune of $100,000,000 in order to make things that a factory full of people could have made, that would have cost $30,000 to ramp up production. It takes a rich person to do this—and they do it. They cut out all of those people they would pay and all of the profit goes to a very small number of people (after that huge investment is paid off). Before, that money was distributed across all kinds of economic strata, and now we're not are doing that. As a result, if you think of the fabric of our society as soil, we are stripping all the nutrients out of it.

SF: *What are the most important traits future designers must possess? Why?*

MK: I think a mastery of HCD is important—not only for designers to practice it themselves, but also to run teams that will use it. Some might think that if a director of engineering or marketing takes a course in design thinking, or a workshop about HCD, they can then return to their company and run a team practicing HCD. Maybe some of them can, but it's unlikely. I really think that people running those teams should be designers, and they should learn that in design schools. Then, as an integrated team consisting of designers, engineers, and businesspeople, they can connect with their audience to solve problems or design products.

Designers also need to better understand the system that they're part of: the system of the world. Design schools have to start teaching these systems and the *languages* of these systems to designers. Otherwise, designers are going to continue to have very little credibility in the real world, and are going to be marginalized, seen as just stylists. HCD has tremendous value to everything we do and yet it continues to be an afterthought.

It's important for designers to learn how to work on interdisciplinary teams; how to speak the language of design, business, and engineering. The design language they know, but they can't use the language of design to tell an engineer the value of that compound curve that's frustrating that engineer. Neither the engineer nor the businessperson cares if a curve looks beautiful, but they do care if it drives sales and if it's more ergonomic. So, the designer needs to learn to think like they do and communicate in their language the value of the designs that they come up with.

SF: *What obstacles or challenges do you foresee for the futures of either design industry or design education?*

MK: Getting design schools to equip designers to speak those languages I mentioned above. That's challenging. I tried for a long, long time. I tried to get one particular design school to adopt business and engineering curriculum, to own this whole integrated approach to designing products and solving problems. The problem was that the deans and department heads didn't understand how that could work, so they resisted. I was able to do this at MIT because the institution has business and engineering programs, and fortunately they weren't too scared of design.

SF: *On a personal level, what is your hope for tomorrow's designers? For the design industries?*

MK: I want people who are running the world to be designers because I know the world will be beautiful. I know that it will be done thoughtfully, and with sensitivity to all the factors in life: sensitivity to the environment, to the earth, and to how we experience our day. I don't think lawyers and politicians think about that one bit. They figure that's all up to designers. Meanwhile, they design policies, methods, and processes that clog our lives with junk.

Future designers, on the other hand, will be sensitive to our world, our systems, and our policies. They inherently have an ethos that is sensitive to all of these things, from race relations to the environment. HCD is at the heart of that and very similar to the system of democracy. We have people who have needs, the citizens, and we have our representatives—let's call them designers—that spend time with their local constituents to understand their needs. Then, these representative-designers travel to Washington D.C. where they design policy, products, and services for the citizens. When designers do this, they understand that integrity is a critical part of that process. I think people who are currently [developing governmental products and services] don't understand how important integrity is; they don't advocate for their stakeholders or constituents. Rather, they advocate for something between their constituents' needs and their own personal gains that includes protecting their political careers. I think designers are a lot more selfless.

HCD and politics share very similar processes: you understand what stakeholders need, then you advocate for them, and then you build something. Hopefully, when you're done, the solution you created maps directly to stakeholders' needs. The same thing should happen with government and policy.

SF: *What advice would you give design educators as they prepare students for the future design industries?*

MK: First, give our designers confidence and enable them to go out into the world to make an impact. In order to have that impact, our design students and graduates need to understand the languages of engineering and business. If you're a design educator who doesn't understand or teach business and engineering along with your design, you can collaborate with faculty and schools that do.

All my courses have collaborated with a business or engineering faculty member from another school. They and their students loved the integration! We had business or engineering students working with design students, or all three working together. They had two different faculty members with different perspectives, modeling different ways of being and seeing, along with the possible roles that they can have in life. Engineers might think, "Maybe I want to be a designer," and designers could say, "Maybe I want to be an engineer," or "I want to be in marketing." This kind of cross-pollination is not only critical to the objective of empowering designers and design, it's also a fabulous way to invigorate everyone involved, including the faculty.

There are design faculty and designers that do understand business and engineering, and I think design institutions need to hire them. Design schools are not doing that right now because they tend to hire people in their own image—and they need to understand that their image is not perfect. Design schools need to understand their limitations and expand by designing a set of criteria that are comprehensive. Then, find those people who check all the boxes, who meet the rubrics of the "ultimate" design educator.

In undergraduate design curricula, there are many ways to incorporate business and engineering. At a bare minimum, take some of the design projects and involve students from other disciplines. For example, in apparel design, this doesn't mean working with illustrators or textile designers. It's about working on a project or two with students and/or faculty from business studies or material science. The design students and business students might collaborate on a project together, but the actual lectures or curriculum that's delivered to those two cohorts will be unique to their programs or disciplines. That's one relatively non-invasive way [to promote interdisciplinary learning opportunities].

The IDM [Integrated Design & Management] program at MIT is incredibly integrated. It's on the other end of the spectrum and it has a whole host of problems. For example, our cohort is made up of one-third designers, one-third engineers, and one-third business professionals. So, what curriculum do we teach? Students enter the program with five or six years of experience in their disciplines. Are we going to teach people how to render? Are we going to teach people how to do a cash-flow projection? Are we going to teach people how to do a CAD model? One-third of our students are experts on those things at any given moment, and so they'll be bored. Yet, the other two-thirds of them will be overwhelmed. It can be very challenging in that way, too.

We are not trying to create better designers, or engineers, or businesspeople; we're trying to create leaders. This is about having sensitivity for all the disciplines, so that we can better conduct that "orchestra." If you don't know how to play the oboe, it's hard for you to figure out how to use an oboe as a conductor.

# Section II
# Design Education

# 5 Introduction to Design Education
## The Historical and Contemporary Contexts of US Higher Education

### Introduction

Higher education has become an American cultural phenomenon. Beginning with just nine students who attended the nation's first college in 1636 and growing to an estimated twenty million students in approximately 4,000 degree-granting postsecondary institutions nationwide to date, the US has established an unparalleled system of tertiary-level education (National Center for Education Statistics [NCES], 2020b). This is no surprise given the great esteem Americans afford education. Derek Bok (2013), former President of Harvard University (1971–1991; 2006/2007, interim), notes "Americans have long displayed a high regard for education. Already in the 19th century, the United States was a leader in requiring young people to attend primary school and, later, high school" (p. 80). By the middle of the 20th century, US higher education was well on its way to becoming the colossus it is presently: between 1940 and 2018, the number of higher education institutions in the nation grew by 153% (NCES, 1993, 2020b). The expansion of tertiary education across the US has led to its significant contribution to the nation's economy; in 2018/2019 alone, the nation's degree-granting postsecondary institutions spent $632 billion US (in current dollars), leading some critics to opine about the "the creeping corporatism of the American university" (deBoer, 2015, n.p.; NCES, 2021b).

Amid this success are deeply rooted challenges that burden the US higher education system and its students—namely its affordability and, resultantly, the accessibility of a college degree. The unprecedented 247% increase in tuition costs (in constant 2019/2020 dollars) during the past forty years (1979/1980–2019/2020) for full-time students in degree-granting postsecondary institutions has become a barrier to higher education for a large portion of Americans (NCES, 2019c). This can be attributed to several factors. First, the total cost of attending college has grown significantly due to institutions' fierce competition to draw and maintain students, which leads to an increase in schools' expenditures for things such as marketing, student services, campus resources, and new programs. Second, "salary

DOI: 10.4324/9781003049166-7

stagnation"—the low increase of salaries that has not kept pace with inflation rates—has affected most Americans since the mid-1970s. While college costs have skyrocketed, US wages have increased only marginally. Third, resources for grants and scholarship funds have decreased, forcing students to take on exorbitant loans to pay for their educations, which easily can cost them $120,000 US for an undergraduate-level degree. When combined with several other key factors, the ever-rising cost of college is causing alarming numbers of undergraduates to face undue hardships throughout college, which often lead to experiences of strained emotional health and a high number who drop out of college.

The barrier of rising costs faced by college students is prompting academicians and policy makers to devise proposals aimed toward alleviating the financial burden. These include developing three-year bachelor's programs (as opposed to the traditional four-year track), reducing or cutting ancillary services, and expanding online education. While the feasibility and implications of such proposals remain to be seen, it is essential for design educators to understand the full context of the US higher education system, which strongly influences both how students develop as young adults and how they experience learning in the classroom. The scope of this chapter addresses the key areas of the growth and success of US higher education, the affordability of a college degree, and the consequential student experience. In conclusion, this chapter lists proposals that aim to improve the affordability and accessibility of college.

## The Success of American Higher Education

American higher education has achieved worldwide recognition for its influence, quality, and scale. Recent international rankings show ten of the top twenty universities globally are in the US (Quacquarelli Symonds [QS], 2021). Among the top ten globally ranked tertiary-level programs, the US contains the top eight for arts and humanities, the top six for natural sciences, the top seven for finance, the top six for social sciences, and the top eight for psychology (QS, 2021). In fact, "[m]ore than half of all Nobel laureates in science and economics since World War II did their most important work while serving on faculties in [colleges and universities in the US]" (Bok, 2013, pp. 1–2). US schools have long been the choice of international students, while other nations—including China, South Korea, and Saudi Arabia—have sought to build in-country "world-class" universities and degree structures that closely resemble those of the US (Bok, 2013). To meet international demand, many leading US universities, including Cornell, Georgetown, and New York University, have opened outposts in other countries with notable success.

America's design schools are equally esteemed internationally. Six of the top ten globally ranked design schools are in the US; among globally ranked design programs, the US contains the top three for architecture, the top four for interior design, and the top five for graphic design, to name a few (Ancheta, 2020; Arch2o, 2021; QS, 2021). America's world-renowned design schools are also situated within comprehensive universities, such as Stanford University's Hasso Plattner Institute of Design, The New School's Parsons School of Design, and Massachusetts Institute of Technology's School of Architecture and Planning. Worldwide esteem for US design education is so strong that international students often represent high portions of total student enrollment at many US design schools, including HGSD (54%), CCA (40%), Parsons (45%), and RISD (36%) (California College of the Arts [CCA], 2022; Harvard University Graduate School of Design [HGSD], 2019; Rhode Island School of Design [RISD], 2021; The New School, 2021).

## *The Growth of Institutions, Degrees, and Student Enrollment*

The rapid growth in the number of institutions for American higher education began in the mid-19th century. In just seventy-four years, from 1860 to 1934, 632 new institutions of higher education were founded, for a total of 932 schools nationwide by 1934 (Goldin & Katz, 1999). By 2017, 4,313 accredited postsecondary institutions offered degrees in the US (NCES, 2020b). Mirroring this growth is the spike in degrees annually conferred to students. For the ten-year period of academic years between 2006/2007 and 2016/2017, the number of associate's degrees conferred increased 38% (728,000–1,006,000) and bachelor's degrees increased 28% (1,525,000–1,956,000) (NCES, 2019c). In fact, among the thirty-seven mainly western countries that make up the Organisation for Economic Co-operation and Development (OECD), the US surpassed the organization's average (49% US and 44% OECD) for the quantity of twenty-five to thirty-four-year-olds that had attained tertiary education in 2018 (Organisation for Economic Co-operation and Development [OECD], 2019).

The surge in undergraduate enrollment has propelled this growth (Figure 5.1). Between 1960 and 2017, there was a 212% increase of high school graduates who made up the total fall enrollments of first-time degree/certificate-seeking students in degree-granting postsecondary institutions (NCES, 2021a). Today, about 80% of all US high school graduates will enter college at some point in their lives—a stark difference from 1940 when just 14% went on to college (Bok, 2013; NCES, 2019a, 2021a). In fact, in the thirty-year time span from 1987/1988 to 2017/2018, the conferral of bachelor's degrees alone has doubled (NCES, 1993, 2019b). Additionally, there has been a marked increase of international students choosing to study in the US: in just eighteen years (2000–2018), the number of foreign tertiary-level students in the US doubled to a total of 1,094,792 students (NCES, 2019d). Students from Asia represent the highest percentage (69%) of the international population in US institutions, with China (33%), India (18%), and South Korea

## 58  Design Education

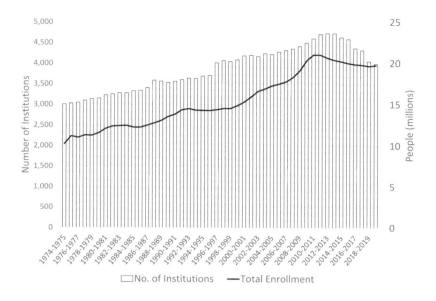

*Figure 5.1* Number of US degree-granting postsecondary institutions and their total fall enrollment, 1974–2020.

Source: NCES, 2020b, 2021a.

(5%) ranking among the top three nations represented globally (NCES, 2019d; OECD, 2019). No longer a homogenous campus environment populated with an elite, US-centric majority, contemporary campuses contain both domestic and international students who represent highly diverse backgrounds, experiences, and beliefs that greatly enrich the academic and social communities of their institutions.

### Growth in US Design Education

Many US design schools are experiencing similar spikes as young adults increasingly pursue design-related careers. For instance, enrollment rose 219% between 2000 and 2021 at Savannah College of Art and Design (SCAD) and 50% at Harvard University Graduate School of Design (HGSD) between 2007 and 2018 (HGSD, 2019; Lebryk, 2016; Savannah College of Art and Design [SCAD], 2022). At Parsons School of Design, enrollment increased 54% between 2007 and 2021 (The New School, 2021; Towers, 2018).

Furthering this growth are emergent design programs that have been developed in response to both the evolving needs of the design industries and students' interests. For example, in the twenty-two years between 2000 and 2022, SCAD added forty-nine degree programs, twenty-four majors, and fifty-five minors (SCAD, 2022). Parsons added sixteen new graduate-level design and design-related programs, including Industrial Design, Transdisciplinary Design, and Design and Management, within the first two decades of this century. Over the span of just twelve years (2006–2018), Massachusetts College of Art and Design pivoted the offerings of its fine arts and design programs from an even split of 50% and 50% to approximately 30% and 70%, respectively (Seltzer, 2019). The growing number of design graduates and design programs underscore the increasing roles design—and design schools—play in developing our future world.

## The Costs of Higher Education

The annual cost of attending college in the US, including tuition, fees, room, and board, varies widely, from approximately $25,000 to over $80,000 depending on the institution's size, location, reputation, and more. US design schools align with these averages, with many currently surpassing $70,000 per year in total annual cost to attend. The increase in the average cost has been particularly steep over the past four decades (Figure 5.2), rising 187.6% at four-year private nonprofit institutions and

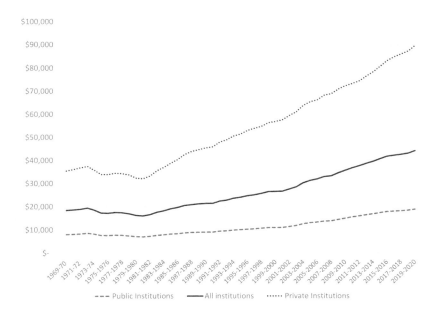

*Figure 5.2* Average undergraduate tuition and fees and room and board rates charged for full-time students in degree-granting postsecondary institutions, 1969–2020 (in constant 2019/2020 USD).

Source: NCES, 2020a.

177.5% at four-year public institutions (from $17,340 to $49,870 and from $7,910 to $21,950, respectively, in constant 2019 dollars) (Bustamante, 2019). By 2036, the cost of tuition and fees to earn a four-year degree is expected to average $303,503 and $162,818 at private and public colleges, respectively (Jacimovic, 2020).

Why has college become so expensive? There are three main reasons. The first is the growing competition between institutions to draw and retain students. This often requires extensive budgets allocated to things such as greater marketing and outreach; campus-based services and resources; exorbitant salaries for "star" faculty, coaches, and leadership; advanced instruction and program development; and new campus construction. The cost of operating a design school can be even more expensive due to its comparatively low endowments, studio-based learning that requires large physical spaces and small class sizes, and the continuous cycle of implementation and replacement of the advanced technologies used in design.

The second reason is the decades-long "salary stagnation" experienced by most Americans since the mid-1970s. Researchers note that since 1973, the real median family income (the value paid to employees after being adjusted for inflation) has risen just 0.6% per year (in 2019 constant dollars) (Furman, 2021). Meanwhile, since 1975, the annual cost of tuition and fees for full-time students in degree-granting postsecondary institutions rose approximately 3% year-over-year (in 2019/2020 constant dollars) (NCES, 2020a). Thus, the ability to afford college today—despite financial aid—remains burdensome for most students and their families. Whereas former generations commonly paid for college by working a summer job, those earnings today will barely cover the cost of textbooks or art/design supplies. As a result, nearly half of full-time students and 80% of part-time students work during college (NCES, 2020c). In fact, one in ten full-time undergraduates works thirty-five or more hours per week (NCES, 2020c).

The third reason is the inadequate growth of financial aid. Between 2010/2011 and 2018/2019, there was a 12.7% decrease in total aid given to full-time equivalent (FTE) undergraduates (from $214 billion US to $187 billion US, in 2018 dollars), while the average tuition cost increased 17.4% at four-year private nonprofit colleges during the same period (Baum et al., 2019; NCES, 2020d). The decrease of federal grants during this period contributed to the growing cost of college: expenditures for Federal Pell Grants, given to low- and moderate-income students, dropped by 32%, while funding for Federal Work Study and the Federal Supplemental Educational Opportunity Grant dropped by approximately 10% and 13%, respectively (Baum et al., 2019). The grants that have increased are not keeping pace with the spiking cost of college; the total grant aid for undergraduate students rose just 7.4% ($108.9 billion US to $116.9 billion US, in 2018 dollars) between 2010/2011 and 2018/2019 (Baum et al., 2019). While some advances in financial aid have occurred, it simply is not enough: the financial barrier to college is becoming increasingly unscalable for far too many students (Baum et al., 2019).

These and other factors lead approximately 60% of students to take out loans, all of which contribute to the current national student loan debt of $1.6 trillion US shared by forty-five million Americans (Federal Reserve Board, 2020; Friedman, 2020). Among public and nonprofit college graduates, 65% leave with an average outstanding loan balance of approximately $30,000 US that takes an average of twenty years to pay off (Cengage, 2019; The Institute for College Access and Success, 2019). Thus, the combination of reduced federal aid and steep increase in college costs has caused the average debt per degree recipient to rise by nearly 20% and 31% among graduates of private and public nonprofit four-year colleges, respectively, between 2002/2003 and 2018/2019 (Baum et al., 2019). Moreover, subsidized federal direct loans (for which interest is paid by the government while students are in school) have been cut steeply from 60% to 29% between 1998/1999 and 2018/2019 (Baum et al., 2019). This further increases students' debt as student borrowers are forced to resort to nonfederal education loans that typically do not offer subsidies and have interest rates significantly above prime interest rates (Baum et al., 2019). The magnitude of the nation's student debt crisis is illustrated by the 18% of federal loan borrowers who were in default on their student loans in 2019 (Baum et al., 2019).

*Negative Effects on the Student Experience*

The growth of what some have dubbed "the cost disease" of US higher education has produced significant negative effects across US campuses. For instance, a survey of 86,000 participating students across 123 US colleges revealed 45% of respondents were food insecure (e.g. had limited or uncertain availability of nutritionally adequate and safe food or the ability to acquire such food in a socially acceptable manner) in the past thirty days (Goldrick-Rab et al., 2019). During the previous year, 56% of respondents were housing insecure (e.g. the inability to pay rent or utilities, or the need to move frequently) and 17% were homeless (Goldrick-Rab et al., 2019). These factors decrease students' physical and emotional well-being and, consequently, their capacity to learn. The percentage of undergraduates that cited finances as negatively impacting their academic performance nearly tripled (6.4%–16.2%) between 2009 and 2019 (American College Health Association, 2009, 2019).

The sudden, dramatic decline in undergraduates' emotional health—with financial insecurities being a contributing factor for many students—has been pronounced. According to the American College Health Association (2009, 2019), in just ten years (2009–2019), the number of undergraduates reporting they had been diagnosed or treated by a professional in the past twelve months for depression doubled (10%–20%); the number of students being treated for anxiety more than doubled during the same period (11%–24%). The consequences of depression and anxiety can be dire: of the 40% of students in the US who drop out of college each year, approximately 65% report doing so due to mental health-related reasons (Gruttadaro & Crudo, 2012; Kirp, 2019). (See Chapter 11 for a full discussion about the growing mental health crisis among undergraduates in the US.)

These and other challenges students experience can affect how—and if—they complete their degrees. Nationwide, approximately 60% of first-time, full-time undergraduate students earn a diploma in six years, while only 41% receive them within the traditional four-year period (NCES, 2019e). Among the Association of Independent Colleges of Art and Design (AICAD) schools, the average graduation rate is 63% (Association of Independent Colleges of Art and Design [AICAD], 2021). For others, including Parsons, RISD, and The Cooper Union, graduation rates typically exceed 80% (Parsons School of Design, 2021; RISD, 2021; The Cooper Union, 2022). The inability to complete an undergraduate degree within four years greatly increases students' debt, while dropouts face diminished life and career trajectories. And, as noted by David Kirp, emeritus professor of public policy at the University of California, Berkeley, the graduation crisis impacts the general public since "[as taxpayers] we are contributing a ton to these students and really not getting anything back on our investment. If you look at it as an ethical question, it's a big deal. If you look at it as an economic question, it's a big deal" (as quoted in Gordon, 2019).

## Potential Solutions

As the cost of college grows increasingly more expensive, it is incumbent upon academic and federal organizations to develop strategies that improve the affordability and accessibility of higher education. In doing so, institutions can better support their communities' diversity, which is an important factor in ensuring students receive the greatest swath of input from the widest possible audience. This is important as fostering an educational environment that is truly diverse is a critical component to providing students with the greatest opportunities to learn and grow. To address this challenge, wide-ranging proposals from researchers and policy makers are gaining increased attention and support. These include:

- **Offering three-year bachelor's degrees**. Historically, these have been unfavored by most undergraduates. However, the cost savings over a traditional four-year program may shift their views. Diverse scenarios—such as running the school year according to trimesters, condensed coursework, and/or granting substantial course release

during the first year for exceptional design students—will enable undergraduates to reduce their educational costs and enter the workforce one year earlier.
- **Scale-back and/or cut ancillary services.** Attracting and sustaining students has led colleges to spend exorbitant sums on resources and services that were previously unthinkable on campuses (e.g. waterparks, valet service). While some amenities are beneficial, others are absolutely unnecessary and inflate students' costs. If colleges want to enroll socioeconomically diverse students, students who want to access higher education without incurring crippling debt, dropping out, or forgoing college altogether, they must make challenging decisions around which amenities to forfeit.
- **Enlist federal oversight.** The college tuition system is akin to an oligopoly; institutions annually raise tuition and fees largely because their peers do. A centralized federal agency, working collaboratively across all private and public US institutions, would oversee tuition increases as necessary. For this oversight team, a key goal would be to prevent arbitrary spikes in the costs of tuition and fees. It also would provide counsel on budget development for truly necessary campus expenses. Oversight would include reassessing the crisis around federal financial support that has decreased and/or not kept pace with tuition inflation.
- **Increase faculty development.** Faculty development ensures educators are provided with the most advanced pedagogical training they need to be effective when working with students. By strengthening teachers' abilities to work with students through pedagogical development, more teachers will foster environments in which students will become more engaged and feel better supported. As a result, students will be less likely to leave the institution, thus helping improve retention and graduation rates. Students' matriculation supports institutional budgets, which will retain a solid stream of operating income from this tuition, which, when managed effectively, can mitigate the need for tuition inflation. This is particularly relevant for design schools, which are often heavily tuition-dependent (as opposed to having a large endowment from which they can draw additional resources when needed).
- **Expand online education**. While online education has existed for decades, it was not until the outbreak of COVID-19 in 2020 that online education became ubiquitous across institutions of higher education—even at studio-based design schools. The sudden, widespread adoption of online education showed teachers and students alike that many courses are viable online. For the institution, online education reduces the need for operating costs associated with utilities, maintenance, and occupying physical space, while enabling higher enrollment in the unlimited classroom "space." The financial savings can enable the reduction of both institutional expenses and tuition costs.

While there are implications, drawbacks, and impediments to these and the other proposals gaining attention in the field, they offer viable paths to decreasing students' costs.

## Conclusion

US higher education makes significant contributions to the nation's economy, serves nearly twenty million national and international students annually, and awards over two million degrees each academic year. American design schools contribute to this through their advanced programs and curricula, along with their exponential growth during recent decades. However, the tertiary educational system is encumbered with the ongoing, escalating challenges that impact the affordability of and subsequent accessibility to a college degree. As the cost of attending college rises steeply, greater numbers of students are forced to incur previously unimagined levels of debt. These costs force them to work part-time or full-time jobs while enrolled, or leave school without completing their degrees. To alleviate students' financial burden, researchers are devising solutions that include accelerated three-year bachelor's degrees, reduced spending on ancillary college institutional resources and services, and expanded online coursework that can lead to significant cost savings. Design schools in particular need to examine these options, as they are usually highly tuition-dependent due to their comparatively low endowments.

## Section II: Design Education

This section discusses the key factors that have helped shape and continue to impact design higher education in the US. The chapters that follow examine:

- the historical influences and subsequent development of contemporary design education in the US;
- speculations on the future design school experience, namely through advanced technologies that include artificial intelligence (AI), virtual reality (VR), and non-fungible tokens (NFTs);
- key industry, financial, and technological dynamics that can significantly evolve design education; and
- the unique design educational systems and industrial marketplaces located in four culturally diverse nations (Argentina, China, Italy, and the UK) that have the potential to inform US design educators and subsequently assist them in advancing their own academic practices.

Awareness of these and other factors that help propel design education forward is vital to ensuring design educators' pedagogical practices and curricula evolve successfully and, in doing so, optimally support students' learning and opportunities for success.

# References

American College Health Association. (2009, Spring). *American College Health Association-national college health assessment II: Reference group executive summary*. https://www.acha.org/documents/ncha/ACHA-NCHA_Reference_Group_ExecutiveSummary_Spring2009.pdf

American College Health Association. (2019, Spring). *American College Health Association-national college health assessment II: Undergraduate student executive summary*. https://www.acha.org/documents/ncha/NCHA-III_Fall_2019_Undergraduate_Reference_Group_Executive_Summary.pdf

Ancheta, M. (2020). The 10 best graphic design schools in the world. *CareerAddict*. https://www.careeraddict.com/best-graphic-design-schools

Arch2o. (2021). *Top 10 interior design schools around the world*. https://www.arch2o.com/10-best-interior-design-schools/

Association of Independent Colleges of Art and Design (AICAD). (2021). *Parents*. https://www.aicad.org/parents/

Baum, S., Ma, J., Pender, M., & Libassi, C. J. (2019). Trends in student aid 2019. *College Board*. https://research.collegeboard.org/pdf/trends-student-aid-2019-full-report.pdf

Bok, D. (2013). *Higher education in America*. Princeton University Press.

Bustamante, J. (2019, June 7). Average cost of college & tuition. *Educationdata.org*. https://educationdata.org/average-cost-of-college/

California College of the Arts (CCA). (2022). *Fast facts and figures*. https://www.cca.edu/admissions/facts/#section-facts-figures

Cengage. (2019). *2019 Cengage student opportunity index*. https://embed.widencdn.net/pdf/plus/cengage/qwntsqxbxh/todays-learner-student-opportunity-index-infographic-1015733-final.pdf

deBoer, F. (2015, September 9). Why we should fear University, Inc. *The New York Times*. https://www.nytimes.com/2015/09/13/magazine/why-we-should-fear-university-inc.html

Federal Reserve Board. (2020, May). *Report on the economic well-being of U.S. households in 2019, featuring supplemental data from April 2020*. https://www.federalreserve.gov/publications/files/2019-report-economic-well-being-us-households-202005.pdf

Friedman, Z. (2020). Student loan debt statistics in 2020: A record $1.6 trillion. *Forbes*. https://www.forbes.com/sites/zackfriedman/2020/02/03/student-loan-debt-statistics/#76f4bfe7281f

Furman, J. (2021, August 5). Income growth for the typical American family has slowed since the early 1970s. *The Peterson Institute for International Economics*. https://www.piie.com/research/piie-charts/income-growth-typical-american-family-has-slowed-early-1970s

Goldin, C., & Katz, L. (1999). The shaping of higher education: The formative years in the United States, 1890 to 1940. *Journal of Economic Perspectives*, 13(1), 37–62.

Goldrick-Rab, S., Baker-Smith, C., Coca, V., Looker, E., & Williams, T. (2019, April). College and university basic needs: A national #realcollege survey report. *The Hope Center for College, Community and Justice*. https://hope4college.com/wp-content/uploads/2019/04/HOPE_realcollege_National_report_digital.pdf

Gordon, L. (2019, August 15). National college dropout rates are a scandal, UC author says. *EdSource*. https://edsource.org/2019/national-college-dropout-rates-are-a-scandal-uc-author-says/616248

Gruttadaro, D., & Crudo, D. (2012). College students speak: A survey report on mental health. *National Alliance on Mental Illness.* https://www.nami.org/getattachment/About-NAMI/Publications-Reports/Survey-Reports/College-Students-Speak_A-Survey-Report-on-Mental-Health-NAMI-2012.pdf

Harvard University Graduate School of Design (HGSD). (2019). *GSD annual report 2017–2018.* https://l87r32c95dp1hz05tig4px11-wpengine.netdna-ssl.com/wp-content/uploads/2019/04/GSD128_2018_Annual-Report-_04_23_2019_reduced-size.pdf

Jacimovic, D. (2020). *Average college tuition in America* [Infographic]. https://whattobecome.com/blog/average-college-tuition/

Kirp, D. (2019). *The college dropout scandal.* Oxford University.

Lebryk, T. (2016). Graduate School of Design's enrollment soars skyward. *The Harvard Crimson.* https://www.thecrimson.com/article/2016/10/20/GSD-growth-brings-change/

National Center for Education Statistics (NCES). (1993). *120 years of American education: A statistical portrait.* https://nces.ed.gov/pubs93/93442.pdf

National Center for Education Statistics (NCES). (2019a). *High school graduates, by sex and control of school; public high school averaged freshman graduation rate (AFGR); and total graduates as a ratio of 17-year-old population: Selected years, 1869–70 through 2029–30.* https://nces.ed.gov/programs/digest/d19/tables/dt19_219.10.asp

National Center for Education Statistics (NCES) (2019b). *Bachelor's, master's, and doctor's degrees conferred by postsecondary institutions, by sex of student and discipline division: 2017–18.* https://nces.ed.gov/programs/digest/d19/tables/dt19_318.30.asp?current=yes

National Center for Education Statistics (NCES). (2019c). *Digest of education statistics 2018.* https://nces.ed.gov/programs/digest/d18/

National Center for Education Statistics (NCES). (2019d). *Foreign students enrolled in institutions of higher education in the United States, by continent, region, and selected countries of origin: Selected years, 1980–81 through 2017–18.* https://nces.ed.gov/programs/digest/d18/tables/dt18_310.20.asp?current=yes

National Center for Education Statistics (NCES). (2019e). *Indicator 23: Postsecondary graduation rates.* https://nces.ed.gov/programs/raceindicators/indicator_red.asp

National Center for Education Statistics (NCES). (2020a). *Average undergraduate tuition and fees and room and board rates charged for full-time students in degree-granting postsecondary institutions, by level and control of institution: Selected years, 1963–64 through 2019–20.* https://nces.ed.gov/programs/digest/d20/tables/dt20_330.10.asp

National Center for Education Statistics (NCES). (2020b). *Degree-granting postsecondary institutions, by control and level of institution: Selected years, 1949–50 through 2019–20.* https://nces.ed.gov/programs/digest/d20/tables/dt20_317.10.asp

National Center for Education Statistics (NCES). (2020c). *The condition of education: College student employment.* https://nces.ed.gov/programs/coe/pdf/coe_ssa.pdf

National Center for Education Statistics (NCES). (2020d). *The condition of education: Price of attending an undergraduate institution.* https://nces.ed.gov/programs/coe/indicator_cua.asp#:~:text=At%20public%204%2Dyear%20institutions%2C%20average%20tuition%20and%20fees%20were,2010%E2%80%9311%20(%2430%2C500)

National Center for Education Statistics (NCES). (2021a). *Total fall enrollment of first-time degree/certificate-seeking students in degree-granting postsecondary institutions, by attendance status, sex of student, and level and control of institution: 1960 through 2029.* https://nces.ed.gov/programs/digest/d20/tables/dt20_305.10.asp

National Center for Education Statistics (NCES). (2021b). *The condition of education 2021: Postsecondary institution expenses.* https://nces.ed.gov/programs/coe/indicator/cue

Organisation for Economic Co-operation and Development (OECD). (2019). *Education at a glance 2019: OECD indicators.* https://www.oecd.org/education/education-at-a-glance/EAG2019_CN_USA.pdf

Parsons School of Design. (2021). *Admission FAQ.* https://www.newschool.edu/parsons/admission-faq/

Quacquarelli Symonds (QS). (2021). *World university rankings.* https://www.topuniversities.com/university-rankings/world-university-rankings/2021

Rhode Island School of Design (RISD). (2021). *About.* https://www.risd.edu/about/

Savannah College of Art and Design (SCAD). (2022). *SCAD president: Defining accomplishments.* https://www.scad.edu/about/scad-president/defining-accomplishments

Seltzer, R. (2019, February 7). Art school shakeout. *Inside Higher Ed.* https://www.insidehighered.com/news/2019/02/07/art-schools-show-signs-stress-what-can-liberal-arts-colleges-learn

The Cooper Union. (2022). *Retention and graduation rates.* https://cooper.edu/admissions/facts/retention-graduation-rates

The Institute for College Access and Success. (2019, September). *Student debt and the Class of 2018.* https://ticas.org/wp-content/uploads/2019/09/classof2018.pdf

The New School. (2021, November 11). *Institutional research: Almanac & trends.* https://www.newschool.edu/provost/institutional-research/

Towers, J. (2018). *Faculty and staff town hall.* Data presented at the Bi-Annual Parsons Faculty and Staff Town Hall, New York, NY, February 2018.

# 6 The Design School Experience

The foundation of US design education was established through centuries of evolving formal and informal academic models led by the public and private sectors. Although these models varied in scale, accessibility, and purpose, they all responded to their respective contemporary zeitgeists. For some, such as the medieval European craft guilds, students entered into a highly structured apprenticeship-based education before gaining admission into the guilds' bureaucratic marketplaces. Others, such as the Staatliches Bauhaus, encouraged students to create a future utopian society in which highly industrialized design could improve daily life for the masses.

Today, the diversity of educational models vary, yet they are unified under two premises, namely that students learn by making and that curricula prepare students for professional practice. The present global environment continues to evolve design education: erupting in the 21st century, the nation's design educators continue to debate the pedagogical balance between theory and practice—particularly in undergraduate education. This, along with other explorations of online education, artificial intelligence, and the evolving nature of design practice all combine to fuel speculations about the future of the design school experience.

There are seemingly endless forms of design education that span centuries and cultures. For the scope of this chapter, select key moments in the Western Academy that made a deep impact on US design education are described to provide a general overview while also providing contexts for the other chapters.

## Apprenticeships and the Craft Guilds

The European craft guilds that blossomed during the medieval period and flourished well into the 18th century represented both a formal association of artisans and an approach to design education through apprenticeships. While design-oriented community groups and education systems previously existed, these new groups were more formal assemblies, emblematic of the significant rise of urbanization during medieval Europe. The

DOI: 10.4324/9781003049166-8

confluence of growing city populations, expanding marketplaces, and increasing wealth attracted highly skilled craftspeople who were able to satisfy the urban elite's growing demands for luxury goods. As these communities of specialized craftsmen grew in scale, so too did their desire to exert control in the attendant marketplaces through unification, thus leading to the establishment of formal craft organizations called "guilds."

A key function of guilds was to establish standards and maintain a high quality of craftsmanship among their members. To support these standards, an educational system was imposed whereby aspiring guild members were required to complete distinct stages of learning in order to be recognized as master craftsmen. As student-apprentices, aspirants learned basic techniques and practical knowledge from a master craftsman for several years. Upon the completion of a qualifying piece of work that met their guilds' standards, the students became journeymen and could work for other masters and earn wages. With these journeyman roles, the craftsmen received certificates from their masters (or the guilds themselves) that enabled them to "journey" inside and/or outside their respective countries to advance their studies from other masters. After three years, each journeyman returned to his home to produce a masterpiece that showcased his best abilities. If this masterpiece was approved by all guild members, the student then became a master craftsman. Along with gaining market entry, status, and political influence, he went on to become a teacher of new student-apprentices.

Contemporary design education draws from aspects of the guild system in many ways, including the teacher-as-master practitioner role. This person is one who imparts general industry standards and practices within the studio classroom. The guild framework also provided a platform for the development of formalized academic institutions in Europe. For instance, three of the world's oldest institutions of higher education—the universities of Bologna, Oxford, and Paris—originated as guilds of students (as at Bologna) or of masters (as at Paris) (Rashdall, 1895). As Ogilvie (2004) explains, guilds supported their members by creating shared norms, exchanging information, and undertaking collective political action. These early design communities advanced themselves while sustaining the quality of their craft through structured apprentice-based education. However, critics have cited multiple issues arising from the formation of guilds. Through their rigid control over members and territorial struggles, guilds hindered free market economies for art and design. They also closely guarded knowledge and this protected knowledge, combined with the issues mentioned above, resulted in stifled innovation (Ogilvie, 2004).

The French Revolution's wave of egalitarianism established laws that promoted free trade and, consequently, most European guilds disbanded or were forbidden outright. Strict legislation affected the guild system, but it was the 19th century's rise of industrialization and the growing middle class' desire for affordable mass-produced design that irrevocably altered the system. Products that were once labor-intensive and time-consuming to make—and thus out of reach for all but the wealthy—were finally made accessible to the masses through the industrialization and free market creation of the 19th century. Additionally, as demands for equality and equity in society and education gained traction through the radical cultural and political shifts of this period, increased criticism of social hierarchies and oppressor/oppressed dynamics further undermined the guilds' educational and organizational models.

## The École des Beaux-Arts

The late 18th century discourse that promoted egalitarianism and classicism—and subsequently influenced European design education—is exemplified through France's École des Beaux-Arts that was formed from the consolidation of the individual academies devoted to architecture and the fine arts in 1819 (Davis, 2017). The École's conservative ethos and instructional methods drew heavily from the tenets of classical Greek and Roman arts; its coursework prioritized the theories of ancient precedents across subjects that included drawing, painting, sculpture, engraving, and architecture. Unlike the craft-oriented guilds, the École aimed to elevate design education "from craft to philosophy and discourse, with a focus on beauty in the logic of classical buildings of ancient Rome and the Italian Renaissance" (Chafee, 1977, as cited in Davis, 2017, p. 10). To achieve this, the curriculum employed lectures and drawing exercises that involved such activities as detailed analyses of exemplary classical buildings.

Prospective applicants to the École were first required to learn foundational and practical skills from an outside master or independent workshop for approximately two years. Students who passed an examination and matriculated undertook formalized studies that consisted of lectures and competitions (*concours d'emulation*) that were judged by academy members. Throughout their studies at the École, students progressed at their own rate and, upon successful completion of all *concours*, advanced to the final level that required more advanced, finished work. The École's pedagogy emphasized active learning, practical content, art and design history, practitioner-led teaching, and design theory—emphases that continue in the curricula of today's US design schools.

The École remained the steadfast model for European art and design education up to WWI. After the war, new post-war attitudes sparked radically different lifestyles and desires for "modernism" that looked *forward*—a stark contrast to the École's reverence for the *past*. Fierce cravings for modernism were particularly acute in the devastated economy of post-war Germany. German artists and designers devised ways to modernize their society and resume positive international status.

However, to create this new society, founders of this new world of design required a new form of design education.

## The Bauhaus

Arguably the single most important modernist art school of the 20th century, the Staatliches Bauhaus (1919–1933) strongly influenced the primary structure for American art and design higher education (Figure 6.1). Through its core objective of unifying art, craft, and technology, the Bauhaus aimed to eradicate the distinction between form (aesthetics) and function (usefulness) in design, thus harmonizing artistry with industrial mass production. This approach had a strong influence that rippled throughout the 20th century across numerous art and design disciplines—including architecture, typography, interiors, textiles, furniture, graphics, and industrial design. However, the school's ideologies went well beyond merely the execution of design practice; they strove "to address the problems of how society could and should be changed by harnessing mechanical production to spread the power of art throughout all levels of society" (Heskett, 2002, p. 20).

In the aftermath of WWI, Germany entered a deep economic recession and was forced to rebuild its economy and international standing.

*Figure 6.1* The Bauhaus at Dessau.
Source: Claudio Divizia/Shutterstock.com.

Concurrently, widespread national liberalism fostered radical experimentation across the arts in Germany. Creative movements, including the Expressionist *Die Brücke* ("The Bridge," 1905–1913) movement and post-Expressionist *Neue Sachlichkeit* ("New Objectivity," 1920–1933) movement, promoted forward-thinking modernism. This was propelled by the belief that humans have the power to create, improve, and reshape their world (Vink, 2019). It was amidst these post-war economic, social, and cultural shifts that Germany embraced technology, machine production, and modern styles to rebuild its industrial prowess and global status. At the same time, this yearning to look forward among the vanguard also carried the preceding Arts and Crafts Movement's beliefs that art should serve the needs of society and that form follows function. The result—particularly under the shadows of the *Neue Sachlichkeit* movement that favored rational, functional, and sometimes standardized design stripped of superfluous detail and excess—was a reimagining of design education and industries.

Following Hermann Muthesius' government-funded study *Das Englische Haus* ("The English House," 1904–1905) that advocated for the implementation of art-oriented workshops in Germany's handicraft schools, the Weimar School of Arts and Crafts and the Weimar Academy of Fine Arts merged in 1919 to form the Staatliches Bauhaus. The school's primary aim was radical for its time: to unify all the arts and, as proclaimed by its architect-director Walter Gropius, to "create a new guild of craftsmen without the class distinctions that raise an arrogant barrier between craftsman and artist" (Gropius, 1919, n.p.). This new design education sought to "turn out artisans and designers capable of creating useful and beautiful objects appropriate to this new system of living" (Griffith Winton, 2016, n.p.). The school's coursework and teaching reflected this directive by prioritizing the development of modern, rational, and functional design that could fulfill the needs of a larger, mass society—and thus rebuild the German economy. Further reflected in this egalitarian, communal spirit were students who came from a range of social and educational backgrounds. These principles remained resolute throughout the tenure of the School's three directors and three different geographic locations in Weimar (1919–1925), Dessau (1925–1932), and Berlin (1932–1933).

In Weimar, Gropius appointed the avant-garde painter, writer, and theorist Johannes Itten to the position of deputy director. Itten greatly influenced the school's initial pedagogical emphases on romantic medievalism and its attendant reverence for practical skills, crafts, and techniques—a clear vestige from the earlier Arts and Crafts Movement. Students were first introduced to Bauhaus ideals through the *Vorkurs* (preparatory course), which integrated theory and application before they progressed to specialized workshops that included metalworking, weaving, pottery, and wall painting (Figure 6.2). However, Itten's curricular emphasis on

*The Design School Experience* 73

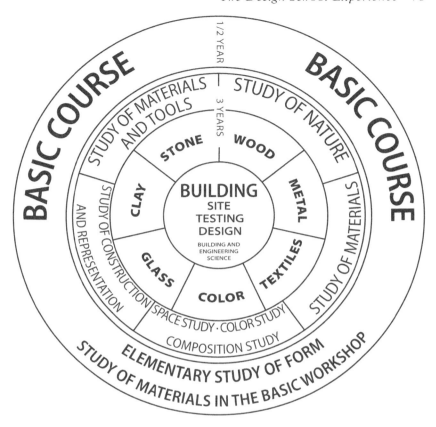

*Figure 6.2* Gropius' curriculum schema displaying students' sequence of learning, from the outer ring (the *Vorkurs*) to the centralized areas of disciplinary study.

nurturing students' spiritual and personality development soon contrasted with Gropius' increasingly scientific and modernist approach that "want[ed] an architecture adapted to our world of machines, radios, and fast cars" (Gropius as quoted in Curtis, 1996, pp. 193–194). In 1923, Itten resigned, and László Moholy-Nagy refashioned the *Vorkurs* as a program that embraced technology and the social function of art, yet retained the original core teaching of art and design fundamentals.

Due to mounting political pressure and decreased funding from the increasingly conservative Weimar government, the Bauhaus moved to the industrial town of Dessau in 1925. Considered by many scholars to be the school's heyday and most fruitful period of activity, the Dessau years gave rise to new academic departments, such as architecture and advertising, and discipline-specific workshops that included metalworking, textiles, cabinetmaking, typography, painting, and photography.

Pedagogy continued to stress practical, commercial applications of design, and, in some cases, this procured commissions from external professional partners. These opportunities gave the school additional financial support and offered students "real world" design experience—a practice that continues across many US design schools today. Essential components of this ethos were its emphases on design creativity and modernism, namely through experimentation, problem-solving, and a reimagining of the artistic process that was more akin to scientific research than to the humanities (Borteh, 2010).

These educational practices were strengthened when Hannes Meyer replaced Gropius as director in 1928. Unlike Gropius's educational foci on universal form and the study of nature, Meyer's educational model adopted scientific and social criteria that received an equal level of curricular attention as those that focused on other aspects of the design process (Davis, 2017). Across courses and levels, students were taught to produce practical and "purely rational" design. Under Meyer, student presentations now included technical drawing, charts, graphs, and, in some instances, communal work that developed externally commissioned products such as lamps, wallpaper, and advertising. Despite the projects' financial and creative achievements, Meyer was dismissed after just two years by Dessau's Mayor under the accusation of leftist political activity. His successor, Ludwig Mies van der Rohe, reworked the curriculum to further emphasize architecture and created a new interior design department. He also halted the Bauhaus' manufacture of goods so that the school could focus on teaching.

Following the Nazi Party's victory in the municipal elections of 1931, the Bauhaus at Dessau was dissolved in 1932. In absence of government support, Mies established the Berlin iteration of the Bauhaus as a privately run school of architecture with smaller workshops in other areas. At this time, Mies again reworked the curriculum so that studies were reduced to six semesters, the *Vorkurs* was only required for students lacking previous sufficient training, and teaching was emphasized. In order to acquire practical experience, students were expected to work on any and all construction during their own time. While the new curricular model reduced students' potential for making money through external projects, they were able to sell their designs to the Bauhaus for later commercialization. Ultimately, when the Nazi regime gained national control in 1933, the school—long considered "un-German" and a front for radical communists—was forced to close.

Subsequently, many Bauhaus luminaries fled Europe and continued their teaching with considerable success in the US. Gropius and Marcel Breuer taught at the Harvard Graduate School of Design, where Gropius chaired the Architecture Department (1937–1952) and implemented a Bauhaus pedagogy focused on modernism. In Chicago, Mies directed the College of Architecture, Planning, and Design at the Illinois Institute of Technology, and Moholy-Nagy founded the New Bauhaus (now the Institute of Design at Illinois Institute of Technology). Josef Albers headed the painting program at the legendary Black Mountain College in North Carolina before moving to Yale University, where he chaired their new Department of Design. These and other Bauhaus leaders promoted their educational philosophies that soon spread across US art and design schools and ultimately affected the course of design curricula and pedagogy from that point on.

## Contemporary Design Education in the US

Currently, the leading design programs in the US are now closely aligned with the Bauhaus' principle of connecting theoretical and intellectual pursuits with practical skills and techniques to produce designers who can solve problems for a modern industrial society. Curricula continue to link fine arts ("pure art") with crafts ("applied art") so that graduates are able to produce useable designs that give the human experience aesthetic and spiritual weight (Savel, 2019). It is through this practice that institutional mission statements and design pedagogy underscore the capacity design has for changing society; students are taught today, as they were at the Bauhaus, that design can radically transform daily life and contribute to the greater good of society.

The assortment of design disciplines offered today represents an extensive choice for area of study. Undergraduate- and graduate-level programs include the design of products (e.g. graphic design, packaging design, industrial design, fashion design), environments (e.g. architecture, interior design, urban design), and services and experiences (e.g. user experience design, information design, universal design). While program offerings and academic structures vary widely across design schools, undergraduates typically complete a "Foundation Year" where they learn the fundamental skills and principles of general art and design before entering three years of a specialized program major. Upon entering the major, emphasis is placed on building the skillsets associated with the practice. The advanced semesters challenge students to refine their design processes and aesthetics through theory- and skill-based design assignments. In most instances, curricula offer a comprehensive academic experience: studio-based core and complementary elective courses address active learning ("doing and making"), while liberal arts courses provide students with contextual and critical thinking skills. Some programs (like the Bauhaus') invite brands or guest critics to work with students on select projects, thereby reinforcing the students' learning with industry application. While these experiences support the courses' defined learning outcomes, they also offer students important insights into the professional experience. The typical undergraduate capstone experience is the development of a thesis and portfolio that showcase the student's abilities and launch them into the professional world.

While many of these practices continue, the beginning of the 21st century witnessed the start of a marked shift in US design education that continues today. Increasingly, vocational emphases and previously "siloed" disciplines are giving way to new, advanced educational models that encourage cross-discipline collaboration and prioritize a greater understanding of the interconnectivity of design and daily life. Lydia Matthews, Professor at Parsons School of Design, describes this new direction by stating, "[designers] recognize that they need to have an understanding of world systems, whether they're economic, social, ethnographic, or cultural. At the same time, social scientists … are beginning to understand that the systems they work with are, in fact, designed, and that there's a fundamental need to communicate visually and materially across cultures and in a globalized condition" (quoted in Agid, 2008, p. 13). To achieve this, US design education is rebalancing the necessity of imparting technical skills to students while simultaneously fostering conceptual thinking that aims to solve the complex problems of the world. As described by Don Norman, noted author and professor at the University of California, San Diego, "[d]esign is … about interacting with the world. To deal with today's large, complex problems, design education needs to change to include multiple disciplines, technology, art, the social sciences, politics, and business" (quoted in Akkawi, 2017, n.p.). In the professional sector, designers are being sought for both their abilities to make useful things that look good *and* their abilities to think and work across design disciplines.

The need for designers to have this breadth of skills has prompted a spike in interdisciplinary studies and degrees throughout the US. Design school curricula are now promoting and encouraging students' openness to integrating new insights into the design process itself so they may gain "design dexterity" and become nimble in working across different design spaces—both literally and figuratively. The porous nature between formerly siloed design disciplines and the increasing overlap with alternative academic fields (e.g. the social sciences and engineering) enables students to acquire the most desired design skills of the future, which, according to a recent survey of over 9,000 design professionals, include: adaptability (to technological and social change); cross-functional and multi-disciplinary skills; strong communication and listening skills; empathy; and storytelling (American Institute of Graphic Arts & Google, 2019). Concurrently, designers are encountering technologies that will have a profound impact on the future of design, namely artificial intelligence and machine learning, augmented reality and virtual reality, and online buyer behavior tracking and modeling. Through the incorporation of these measures and its continual evolution, design education will remain relevant to both future job markets and design practices overall.

# References

Agid, S. (2008). Re: Imagining Parsons—How Parsons' new academic structure is shaping design education in the 21st century. *Re:D, 26*(2), 10–15.

Akkawi, Y. (2017, August 22). The future of design education is ... no design education. *Inc.* https://www.inc.com/yazin-akkawi/the-future-of-design-education-is-no-design-educat.html

American Institute of Graphic Arts & Google. (2019). *AIGA 2019 design census.* https://designcensus.org/

Borteh, L. (2010). Bauhaus movement overview and analysis. *The Art Story.* https://www.theartstory.org/movement/bauhaus/

Chafee, R. (1977). The teaching of architecture at the École des Beaux-Arts. In A. Drexler (Ed.), *The architecture of the Ecole des Beaux-Arts* (pp. 61–109). Museum of Modern Art and MIT Press.

Curtis, W. (1996). *Modern architecture since 1900* (3rd ed.). Phaidon Press.

Davis, M. (2017). *Teaching design: A guide to curriculum and pedagogy for college design faculty and teachers who use design in their classrooms.* Allworth.

Griffith Winton, A. (2016). The Bauhaus, 1919–1933. In *Heilbrunn timeline of art history.* The Metropolitan Museum of Art. http://www.metmuseum.org/toah/hd/bauh/hd_bauh.htm

Gropius, W. (1919). *Program of the state Bauhaus in Weimar* (H. Weaver, Trans.). http://ghdi.ghi-dc.org/sub_document.cfm?document_id=4133

Heskett, J. (2002). *Design: A very short introduction.* Oxford University Press.

Ogilvie, S. (2004, May). Guilds, efficiency, and social capital: Evidence from German proto-industry. *Economic History Review, 57*(2), 286–333.

Rashdall, H. (1895). *The universities of Europe in the Middle Ages.* Clarendon Press.

Savel, N. (2019, February 4). How Bauhaus redefined what design could do for society. *The New York Times.* https://www.nytimes.com/2019/02/04/t-magazine/bauhaus-school-architecture-history.html

Vink, A. (2019). *Postmodern artists: Creators of a cultural movement.* Lucent Press.

# 7 Speculations on the Future Design School Structure

*Benjamin Stopher and Tobias Revell*

## Introduction

As Bill Gates famously said, "We always overestimate the change that will occur in the next two years and underestimate the change that will occur in the next ten." This perspective is useful when trying to consider any future design school experience on a ten-year horizon. Within the context of the design school, it is likely that post COVID-19, the changes that will happen in national, regional, political, economic, and socio-technical contexts will directly impact the institution. It is important to acknowledge that all of these factors move slower than technological innovation. This chapter will explore four near-future Speculations looking at different ways in which these factors might shape design education's future. These Speculations, of course, are partial and bound by the authors' experience in the context of UK higher education. We do not think each—if any one—will happen, but they are archetypes and imaginings already discussed and referenced in the design education community and thus deserve closer examination.

Our Speculations can also be thought of within the context of Joseph Voros' (2003) "Futures Cone," which visualizes possible futures, plausible futures, and probable futures over time. This method—well understood in speculative design—enables us to use specific examples as ways to map out coordinates in the general futures space and allow the reader to imagine the spaces in between and around them. Below, we present our Speculations of the future of design schools in the UK. However, the reader should be aware that the trends in the UK system likely will be paralleled in design educational systems in other countries around the globe.

## Speculation One: Status Quo, Like Now, but More

In the future, the Big Design School dominates, with increased amounts of centralization, metricization, and bureaucratization. Now, with a cap on fees and a reduction in the threshold at which students pay back their loans looming, it is likely that the focus of the universities in the UK is on

DOI: 10.4324/9781003049166-9

frugality, and the need to maximize income will only increase (Weale, 2021). With funding also tied to key performance indicators like the Research and Teaching Excellence Frameworks and rankings, there is an imperative for universities to maximize their performance across these metrics to attract students and income, gain government favorability, and plug funding gaps. However, as scholars have noted, rankings and metrics tend to manufacture competition, confirming "what everyone already 'knew' about which institutions were the 'best'" and create conditions where "every university is *expected* always to strive to improve" (Brankovic, 2021, p. 11).

In this future, the master/student art school dynamic is still strong in many design schools that inherit their "banking pedagogy" (whereby teachers "deposit" knowledge into the minds of receptive students) from the art academies of the 19th century (Freire, 2000). The idea of a student learning from an "eminent" practitioner through the production of material forms has come under significant pressure as arts schools have become affiliated with or absorbed by modern universities. But the promise of this is powerful for potential students who, attracted to the celebrity of big-name design educators and graduates, are considering their choices for design education. This culture is increasingly in conflict with both the academicization of the design school and the waning of the inclination to accept orthodoxy by information-rich students, who now have more control, choice, and consumer rights than ever. Many students are also much savvier to, and less accepting of, the hierarchies through which eminent practitioners have been elevated to their positions.

Finally, in terms of subject, Big Design Education will likely see a homogenization of approaches. In the drive to appeal to the business-minded interests of government and student applicants who are considering their employability, courses focusing on productivity-oriented disciplines like user experience, service design, design thinking, and so on will likely see a boost in enrollment, while critical or radical specializations will likely see a decline. This divide would be further cemented following industry calls to produce more employable graduates (Marshall, 2020) and by an increased influence of corporations and other businesses in shaping curricula that would "entail partnerships between the largest tech companies in the world and elite universities" (Walsh, 2020). This would leave smaller, regional universities in weaker positions in the market.

## Speculation Two: AI Studios and the Metaverse

In the future, the design school is "meta." The creative technology/Internet nexus creates a techno-determinist view of the design school experience that is at the mercy of machine learning technology, the coming so-called Metaverse, students as content creators, and the monetization of creativity through non-fungible tokens (NFTs). Here, universities follow Silicon Valley as it moves to rebrand the Internet as the "Metaverse"—a fully immersive, brand-driven landscape that integrates social networks, gaming, e-commerce, and streaming with technologies like artificial intelligence (AI), augmented reality (AR), virtual reality (VR), and cryptocurrencies. Huge amounts of financial and social capital have been invested to make this deregulated "ultimate company town, a megascale Amazon that rolls up raw materials, supply chains, manufacturing, distribution, and use and all its related discourse into one single service. It is the black hole of consumption" (Bogost, 2021, n.p.).

This scenario is the design school COVID-19 pandemic online experience at giga-scale. Enrollments increase by orders of magnitude at the elite design schools, from thousands to hundreds of thousands, as advanced AI-augmented analytics allow for the simulation of the student feeling of a unique, responsive, autonomous learner's journey through the university's mostly online campus. This is all supported by an apparatus of near-constant surveillance that utilizes AI and other machine learning tools to measure student engagement and achievement. Automated processes and machine learning are also used for the creation of learning materials. Generative briefs, projects, and learning outcomes are created automatically to respond to the specific needs and competencies of individual students.

In terms of the subject, the massive expansion of creative AI tools in industry and education, such as Google's Teachable Machine (Teachable Machine, n.d.) and Runway machine learning (Runway, n.d.), makes designers, at best, more akin to collaborative partners with automated tools and, at worst, AI-trainers (Saboo, 2021). AI, machine learning, and other automated processes are fully embedded in creative software. Resultantly, there is a clear need for designers to become technology savvy, for without this skill, they will be left behind. However, further expansion of the monopolies of big software companies has increased their jurisdiction over the futures and careers of students and thus has the potential to impact the scope of their practice by tying them to proprietary digital tools (Carter, 2021).

The recent emergence of NFTs, where digital artworks/files are tokenized via blockchain implementations and then traded for crypto currencies, has some interesting potential consequences for the future design school experience. Once NFTs become more widely adopted, design students' visual experiments can go viral and appreciate in value quickly. In this design school environment, students come to be *influencers* in the *design space,* instant superstars, and the parts of design education that cannot be digitized or monetized wilt through lack of both perceived and monetary value.

## Speculation Three: The Networked Studio and Other Dreams

In the future, the school is a network. As opposed to the centralized, surveilled, and highly commercialized school of our previous Speculation, this one bases its foundation more on its community, using the digital network to build new relationships, provide care and support, and challenge centralized hierarchies. It features current staples of the design school experience, such as streamed-in guests and collaborators, remote participation in events, cross-cohort reading groups, and the formalization of these network practices as the organizing principle of the design school. The global COVID-19 pandemic shuttered the physical resources of design schools across the world and created the opportunity for design schools to be organized around a network rather than a place. However, that approach has yet to be intentionally pursued at scale.

To suggest that design schools will exist entirely without physicality would be unrealistic, although the on-site, in-person nature of learning is being questioned (White, 2020). Instead, it is useful to think of this physicality as another network attribute—one that has as important a place in the school/network as the digitally mediated components. The idea of a rhizomatic or connected-knowledge environment is not new. But the acceleration of scholars opening their closed networks more widely as they transition to online delivery due to the pandemic has been noticeable, as the marginal difference in presenting to forty of your own institutions' students in-person or adding another cohort online has proved opportune and possible for some (Ansari, 2021).

Part of this unbundling of the institutional edifice (Craig, 2015) presents a newfound opportunity to challenge the hegemony of power built up within these institutions. Projects like "Designing the Pluriversity" (Center for Philosophical Technologies, n.d.) draw on Arturo Escobar's (2018) concept of pluriversality to decolonize the institution through collaborative and place-based means. While still being spatially placed, the Shared Institute (n.d.), which is based in Portugal but has a fully global presence, aims to "decentralise design discourse and practice … serving literally as a shared space for design research" (n.p.). Other examples include the UK-based Feral Art School (n.d.), a co-op of art educators who teach adults in venues across the city of Hull, England, and the New School of the Anthropocene (n.d.), an alternative school for the humanities launched as part of a cadre of co-op universities.

These new organizations gain legitimacy not from being in a particular place with a particular legacy or history but from the strength of the networks that support them and that they support. The imperative, then, is to work with existing communities' needs and drivers rather than mass appeal to students either physically or digitally.

## Speculation Four: The Post-Crisis "No-School"

In the future, there is no design school. The traditional institutional boundaries and silos have collapsed under political, financial, and technological pressure. Rather, design education lives in fully or quasi-autonomous new groupings, co-ops, and movements. Instead of enormous capital investments topped up by fees, these "no-schools" are small, mobile, and eclectic, traveling to points of crisis or need and functioning on barter and donation (Woolard, n.d.).

Extracurricular, non-credentialed, and responsive learning groups that have positioned themselves against the status quo survive and become the norm. These no-schools focus on responding to specific design briefs in specific places, embedding in and working with local communities to develop curricula that respond to their needs. These groupings generously give training, expertise, and support to learners. The small resource base, open-source assets, and the technologically mediated approach of these collectives enable them to thrive, while big, heavy, debt-laden institutions flounder. Additionally, their independent nature allows them to focus on critical technical skills and approaches deemed unfavorable to employability-focused corporate certificates and universities.

We can see the beginnings of these groupings in organizations like Hackers & Designers (n.d.), Nø School Nevers (n.d.), School SOS (n.d.), and in online equivalents like Trust.Support (n.d.). These autonomous communities bear greater resemblance to the guild-like nomadic structure of medieval European universities. However, they are founded on post-digital principles and operate as "decentralised institutions that are financed, owned, and governed by their own members" (GVN908 & ARB, 2021, n.p.).

As a result of this co-ownership and participatory governance structure, the subject, focus, and form of these new no-schools are highly organic and flexible, taking on and shedding expertise, tools, and platforms as necessary to respond to particular emergent briefs or phenomena. This makes them ably suited to respond to projects that emerge quickly and carefully, as their agile form can change easily and adapt to a rapidly evolving world. Where "design education in all its forms, has [focused] upon creative innovation without due regard for what was destroyed in the process, be it material, values, ideas, cultures, knowledge or practices" (Fry, 2017, p. 3), these schools are uniquely positioned to integrate nimbly with and respect existing practices and knowledges instead of stiffly responding to the klaxon of "disruption."

In this world, the professionalization of design means that it is embedded across all subjects in the STEM-dominated university world. Lawyers, physicists, marketers, and bankers all receive elements of design thinking and practice as a part of their education. The last bastions of radical, critical practice live in the itinerant but flourishing underground movement of the no-schools.

## Conclusion

The four potential futures for design education we have presented here are, of course, speculations. They each individually instantiate a set of specific concepts that are all emerging in tandem and in tension with the post-pandemic design school environment. These concepts include: the pressures of tougher institutional financing against the drive to make design education more accessible; demands for greater response to climate and social justice; the necessity for employable skills; and the diffusion of design across other disciplines as a method for problem-solving against the perception of "expertise" required to become an accomplished practitioner.

It is most likely that in different places and at different times, we will see variations on these unique visions come to the fore, celebrated as harbingers of the future only for them to fall prey to the next set of geopolitical and global financial shifts that expose them as outdated. The design school is always playing catch up, always becoming the next thing, always seeking to reinvent and justify itself in the world—and that is likely to be the only constant for the next few decades, whatever happens.

## References

Ansari, A. (2021). *Modernity + Coloniality*. https://modernitycoloniality.com/
Bogost, I. (2021, October 21). The metaverse is bad. *The Atlantic*. https://www.theatlantic.com/technology/archive/2021/10/facebook-metaverse-name-change/620449/
Brankovic, J. (2021). Academia's Stockholm Syndrome: The ambivalent status of rankings in higher education (research). *International Higher Education, 107*, 11–12.
Carter, E. (2021, November 11). The rise and fall of Adobe Inc. *Substack: Design Harder*. https://designharder.substack.com/p/adobe
Center for Philosophical Technologies. (n.d.). *Designing for the pluriversity*. https://www.c-p-t.org/projects/designing-the-pluriversity
Craig, R. (2015). *College disrupted: The great unbundling of higher education*. St. Martin's Press.
Escobar, A. (2018). *Designs for the pluriverse: Radical interdependence, autonomy, and the making of worlds*. Duke University Press.
Feral Art School. (n.d.). *Feral Art School: Courses*. https://www.feralartschool.org/courses/
Freire, P. (2000). *Pedagogy of the oppressed*. Continuum.
Fry, T. (2017). Design education in a broken world. *The Studio at the Edge of the World*. http://www.thestudioattheedgeoftheworld.com/uploads/4/7/4/0/47403357/fry-designeducation.pdf

GVN908 & ARB. (2021, August 2). Moving castles: Modular and portable multiplayer miniverses. *Trust.* https://trust.support/feed/moving-castles

Hackers & Designers. (n.d.). *About.* http://hackersanddesigners.nl

Marshall, C. (2020, September 5). Google introduces 6-month career certificates, threatening to disrupt higher education with "the equivalent of a four-year degree." *Open Culture.* https://www.openculture.com/2020/09/google-introduces-6-month-career-certificates-threatens-to-disrupt-higher-education.html

New School of the Anthropocene. (n.d.). *New School of the Anthropocene.* https://newschoolanthropocene.wordpress.com/

Nø School Nevers. (n.d.). *Nø School Nevers 2022.* https://www.noschoolnevers.com/

Runway. (n.d.). *Create impossible video.* https://www.runwayml.com

Saboo, S. (2021, May 10). Prompt engineering: The career of future. *Medium.* https://medium.com/nerd-for-tech/prompt-engineering-the-career-of-future-2fb93f90f117

School SOS. (n.d.). *About us.* https://www.schoolsos.xyz/

Shared Institute. (n.d.). *About.* https://shared.institute/

Teachable Machine. (n.d.). *About.* https://teachablemachine.withgoogle.com/

Trust.support. (n.d.). *Trust.support.* http://trust.support

Voros, J. (2003). A generic foresight process framework. *Foresight, 5*(3), 10–21.

Walsh, J. D. (2020, May 11). The coming disruption: Scott Galloway predicts a handful of elite cyborg universities will soon monopolize higher education. *New York Magazine.* https://nymag.com/intelligencer/2020/05/scott-galloway-future-of-college.html

Weale, S. (2021, September 27). Outcry over proposal for lower student loan repayment threshold. *The Guardian.* https://www.theguardian.com/money/2021/sep/27/students-in-england-irate-over-reports-of-early-loans-repayment

White, D. (2020, September 17). Desituated art school (a provocation). *David White.* http://daveowhite.com/desituated/

Woolard, C. (n.d.). *TradeSchool.coop.* https://carolinewoolard.com/system/tradeschoolcoop/

# 8 The Future of Design Education

Interview with Tim Marshall, Deputy Vice-Chancellor, College of Design and Social Context and Vice-President, Royal Melbourne Institute of Technology University, Melbourne, Australia

## Introduction

US design education is facing an uncertain and tenuous future. The COVID-19 pandemic that left unprecedented and indelible impacts on people's lives, the global design industries, and the broader sector of US higher education necessitates a reimaging of design education if the nation's design schools and programs are to remain relevant, successful, and sustainable. This chapter presents an interview with Tim Marshall, Deputy Vice-Chancellor, Design and Social Context and Vice-President at the Royal Melbourne Institute of Technology University. Prior, Marshall served as Dean of Parsons School of Design (2006–2009) and Provost and Executive Vice President of Academic Affairs at The New School (2009–2020) where he led a major restructuring of design education. Within the discussion, Marshall examines the key factors impacting design education and provides recommendations for how US design schools and programs can advance strategically for success in this highly changeable future.

## Interview

STEVEN FAERM: *What attributes or characteristics make the US design education so distinct from other global design education leaders? Will these characteristics evolve in the near future?*

TIM MARSHALL: If I looked across the history of US design higher education, there was a long period in the past where I would have said that the design profession, in certain respects, was ahead of education, and that education was playing catch up—though I don't think this is still true. We had new approaches to design and design thinking emerging sometimes in the Academy and some business schools, and more often in companies like IBM and IDEO, while [US design schools] were, for the most part, still pursuing guild-like approaches to design craft. In other places, like the UK and Australia, I'd say the opposite was true. Design schools are a little ahead of the more

DOI: 10.4324/9781003049166-10

conservative design industries. But, in the US, I think that has begun to change over the last five to ten years, and nowhere more prominently than at Parsons [School of Design]. Parsons has had an impact in the US in that regard, as well as elsewhere.

The approach taken at Parsons was basically channeling certain things happening in the industry and tech and what was happening in Europe[ean design education]. A couple of other places in North America were starting to do that, but not too many. In Canada you had the Rotman School of Management setting up a design lab, while in the US you had Stanford University setting up their "d.school" with IDEO—places without a design school in the traditional sense of it. So, you had universities acquiring and pushing a notion of design, and it's a bit like the classic scenario where precisely because you *don't* have a design school you can actually move more quickly into that space; you don't have the legacy problem.

US design schools were really hanging on to a traditional notion of "design-at-all-costs" for a long time—some still are for some degrees—and not adapting those approaches to contemporary design, which is pushed by what is happening in the world and the fact that we, in design schools, had that very scary thing happen: we got what we wished for in that people started to take design as a very serious player in larger societal issues. It's something designers had always desired, to move up in the "food chain" and be part of the decision-making process in order to bring their skills to more complex questions and issues like sustainability and social equity.

So, we got what we wished for. Then there was some resentment about that because when you get what you wish for, you have to give some things up. Nothing comes for free. So, some of those traditions— the guild-like logic where we kept design and some practices of design to ourselves—had to be given up progressively in order for us to have the impact in the world that we actually aspire to. Therefore, there's an inherent tension between those two ambitions that were confronted. You can't have that kind of impact and behave like a guild, as a closed community not willing to allow others to come in and fully take advantage of what design has to offer.

Then, there are some very basic structural questions that have nothing to do with anything but bureaucracy that impact US design education. For instance, Scandinavia, Northern Europe, the UK, and Australia all have creative, practice-based PhDs. The US has not really had these, and still doesn't, which is purely due to its [bureaucratic] structure of higher education. It's not because those other countries were somehow ahead of the curve but because design schools in many of those countries were, like they often are in the US, *independent*. And then, purely for administrative and financial reasons, those countries' governments decided to have [design schools] absorbed into universities. When they absorbed them into universities, they were absorbed into a different type of university than the one in the US because to become a university is very hard, and the use of the term "university" is very extended. But once you have that status, the whole university has access to a PhD. In other words, you don't have to go to the State Education Board to get an approval for every PhD you want to run. Also, their government funding incentivizes schools to have PhDs, whereas in the US, it's pure expense. Most [US] design schools are not wealthy—they don't have large endowments and they don't receive large grants—so they don't have the same mechanisms to fund doctoral students.

SF: *As US design education evolves, what emergent design programs or new academic models are needed? What lies ahead?*

TM: There's been so much talk of disruption, of breaking this or breaking that, which I detect in a multitude of ways. In the US, I learned of a design and business incubator making pitches. The people running it were all about disrupting [the system]. However, if you listened closely, most of the pitches weren't about disruption. They were actually about a new form of reconciliation between the layers in our lives in the virtual and physical, biological and spatial, and temporal realities that we live in at the same time. They were about how to be more mindful of the way we live, how to reconcile the digital back into our fuller lives rather than see everything as purely disruptive.

There's that aspect of how we deliver design education as COVID-19 has pushed design schools into the virtual space of learning because the faculty had been resistant [to online teaching], and actually there's been a bit of a backlash amongst the undergrads because [online learning is] robbing them of their college experience in some respects. In the fashion world, and other material worlds, it's also robbing students of that highly material-based, body-based experience.

By the same token, it would be mad not to learn from this period and take forward an approach in which designers can be educated in ways that prepare them for the reality of the world they're entering, where they're going to be expected to operate "multimodal" all the time, across time, distance, and cultures in different ways. That's going to be the norm, and it's going to be expected. So I think we have to educate students not just on craft but also to understand the craft in the context of shifting political issues, in the context of technology, and transformations like that. If students are able to philosophically and intellectually grasp the implications of this world as it's emerging—be able to be a great designer in *that* context—then I think we'll have fantastic students. I think there will be people absolutely hungry for designers with that capacity. That's why we made the changes at Parsons: it's recognizing that simply going out and saying, "I'm really great at 'X', but I know nothing about this other stuff" isn't going to cut it anymore. This isn't doing design students or the design industry justice. It's not allowing graduates to show what design is capable of doing in the fullest sense of the work.

SF: *What obstacles or challenges do you foresee for design education?*
TM: The economic model of US higher education, particularly the tuition-driven model, needs a massive shakeup. It's simply too expensive, and because it's so expensive, it no longer opens opportunity for social and economic mobility. It actually reinforces underlying class structures. Though with exceptions, that would be the general rule because the [financial] sacrifices it's asking people to make are just too great.

On the other side, as always happens, there are unaccredited providers who are moving into that space. And we may find there are more and more students who forsake or at least minimize their engagement with the traditional design school model—the four-year bachelor's degree in a $40,000-plus per year system—by finding other ways and pathways by either not going to school at all or by enrolling for just one or two years. Traditional four-year design schools have to be prepared to give a lot up if they are to meaningfully address this economic issue. Simply scratching around for a few more scholarship dollars might help, but I don't think it's going to get us there. So I think the financial aspect of the educational system is a massive challenge, not just to students but also to the whole premise of education and the opportunities we seek to keep alive.

When it comes to the obstacles stopping us from addressing the challenges in front of us, some of it is the classic cliché of thinking the old brands would be the ones that would do best in the online environment. But how come Sears and Roebuck didn't succeed while Amazon does just fine? It's a question of how you take legacy institutions that are undergoing tremendous stress and strain by the impact of changes that are happening beyond themselves and transform them.

In that sense, the brand value of higher education probably has more persistence than in some of those other business areas, but I would not take it for granted. One reason why we can't take it for granted, especially in the US, is the massive financial impact. If all we want to do is graduate rich children, then fine. But if you're really true to your mission and if you want to survive [as a design school], you have to do the thing that is so extraordinarily difficult, which is you have to become the very thing that you fear most, namely that you're about to get taken out of business by a nimble, smart operator who reads the landscape of, say, fashion, and realizes, "Wow! There are a lot of students studying it, it's the second biggest industry in the world, and we want a piece of that action." They can then disrupt the traditional [educational] providers largely by doing two things, which is doing it at scale and then using that to hire the very best faculty, all while making design education more affordable for students. The reason why it hasn't happened yet is because the scale part is very hard to figure out for design education in general.

We did see a test of this, but it went "south" because the first wave of "for-profits" did a version, or were on their way to doing a version, before the government stepped in due to their gouging and exploitative things. But as has happened in other parts of virtual industries, there's a new wave of them saying, "Told you so," and come in later, such as Coursera and Udacity. So the early adopters lost a lot of money and everyone thought this online model wouldn't work. Then, after five to ten years, the second wave comes in, learning the lessons of the early adopters and figuring that out, and eventually takes the world by storm.

We're also learning what "online" really means, because what you learn from online education is the real value of face-to-face. Given you can find all the knowledge, skills, and techniques you want virtually, what is the value of coming together to learn? Minerva has a version of that which basically says [the value of face-to-face learning] is *social*, which is not surprising. They bring students together in dorms as a community who then learn together online. They flip the model so that the *faculty* can be distributed and can bring tremendous talent to bear because the faculty are distributed and students don't all have to live in [costly cities]. They can actually have a different lifestyle which, post-COVID-19, is an even bigger deal. People's lifestyles mean a whole different thing than what they did before. So how can design educators work with that rather than resist it? Obviously, in design education, access to studio spaces is important. But you could bring together thirty [design] students from ten different design schools, set up a studio, get faculty from around the world, employ technicians, and operate in a cheaper location with cheaper faculty and professionals paid hourly.

Educationally, I think it's going to be a reconfiguration of skills and knowledge in social, collaborative, virtual, and in-person contexts. They're just getting shaken around and reconfigured in terms of where you go to pick up your skills and other kinds of cultural, social, and economic sophistication to operate in the modern world, and where you pick up approaches to sustainability, cross-cultural work, and experiential opportunities. This is Minerva's model. They rebuilt the model and turned it inside out so that students receive cross-cultural opportunities, get the social experience, and learn from high-level faculty from around the world. This isn't the version I'd apply to a design school—but I don't think design schools should be sitting around, thinking there isn't a Minerva-like approach that's going to impact design education. It's not going to be exactly the same model, but there will be something. There are just too many students who want to study design, and there are too many students from wealthy backgrounds who want to study design to think that there aren't going to be players out there who will do "Minerva-like moves."

This way of rethinking the educational and social patterns is probably going to be *one* strand of what happens next, and [think of] what that now frees you to do when you consider those other opportunities. Because on the economic side, if you can relocate to a little farm somewhere, it's a hell of a lot cheaper than Manhattan. That's not trivial!

SF: *How has the virtual learning experience (necessitated by COVID-19) reshaped the ways design schools will approach the future?*

TM: Because of COVID-19, the idea of being in dense cities now has a whole darker complexion to it, so people are re-evaluating their lives in different ways. Whether that lasts or not, it's impossible to say. But you don't have something like COVID-19 rip through a society and not have something change in the long-term. Education, at minimum, has to figure out how to be much more dynamic with learning and lifestyle patterns, as well as the live realities of our students, understanding that the regimented structure—spring and fall, year one, two, three, four, and course after course—is not the only way that people are going to get a viable education. I'd be amazed if we're still talking about that conventional educational structure in five to ten years.

Going back to the previous question, one of the biggest hindrances and roadblocks for change is the conservatism of these legacy institutions and their faculty. COVID-19 pushed faculty into becoming familiar with online learning at a rate that was ten-times faster than anyone anticipated. That was a massive breakthrough for institutions. It didn't happen in quite the same way for students, because there was almost an opposite effect—particularly for undergraduate students who felt the experience wasn't the "real deal." I think students felt they were robbed of the social experience as much as anything else.

So the real post-COVID-19 breakthrough is with faculty, if it allows institutions to build and rethink in the ways we've been talking about: a more complex delivery model that is much more responsive to the live realities of our individual students and their capacity to progress and move through design programs in different ways, be it be it virtually or in-person. I think this answers the economic and the access question as well. We now have the means to be dynamic, flexible, and responsive to the students, so it's really up to us. It's not a technological barrier and it's not a pedagogical barrier. So now the task is beholden on us to think acutely about face-to-face or virtual education, about distribution, about being in different geographies, and how we can redesign our programs to provide greater access to students who simply cannot afford the education.

SF: *What advice would you give design educators as they prepare students for the future world?*
TM: I'll underline something I said earlier: the ways we traditionally taught studio-based education gets given up in the transformation, but then something else gets taken up. Universities have been largely built through faculty teaching students who want to specialize in their [disciplinary] area. But this new world will require us to teach far more students who want to learn *something* about our areas but don't necessarily want to *specialize* in it. And there's resistance during that transition because there is a perceived hierarchy in which people won't take you seriously if you're taking an elective or doing a minor, thinking it's not the "real deal." I think that's a huge mistake for several reasons. One is that we want more people in this society to understand design and what it has to offer. You won't achieve that if all you ever do is teach in a guild-like way to specialist students. At The New School, for example, philosophy professors taught fashion students who never wanted to become philosophers and it changed the faculty's whole conception [of fashion design]. And many of those fashion students now enter the world with a deep appreciation and love of philosophy while being designers. That's what we need to do. We need philosophers who "get" design, we need businesspeople who "get" design, we need urban planners who "get" design. They will only "get it" if there are opportunities for diverse students to work together in different ways. To achieve that, educators need to take the non-design students seriously and offer them as good of an education [as the design students].

Students are coming to us from more diverse and mixed backgrounds. The logic of "The kid that's not good with the books but is good in the art room goes to art school" is broken. So, students are coming in with this rich mix of skills and capacities and abilities and then, after graduation, they're entering a world which is much more complex and offers opportunities for people and designers in vastly greater ways than twenty years ago. If design programs remain structured like a funnel, students will enter school with this diversity and then exit it with a diversity of opportunities—and programs will just put them through a "cattle race" in between. This makes no sense. That system neither reflects where the students are at when they come to us, nor the world of opportunity they're going into as graduates. So, I think schools have to better reflect these two realities: the world of the students coming to them and the world the students are graduating into.

I advise design faculty to not hold on to their students too tightly. [Teachers should] encourage them to move broadly, to pursue other interests. I think these [experiences] will be deeply enriching for students and help them successfully operate in the post-studio world. Generally speaking, simply learning how to design clothes in a classroom, ninety hours a week for four years, is not going to cut it anymore. It's starting to show in successful designers who come from more complex backgrounds and educations. Educate the design students broadly. Let them be broad and be part of a completely different ecosystem in the modes of learning, who you're teaching, how you're teaching, and what kinds of experiences you're facilitating for your students.

That's what I think is going to be a dramatic change from the traditional studio-based four-year education.

# 9 Global Directions
## Unique Approaches to Design Education

*Verónica Fiorini, Susan Orr, Benjamin Stopher, Arturo Tedeschi, and Christine Tsui*

### Introduction

Around the world, design education has become a powerful force in shaping global and national cultures, economies, and societies. In some regions of the world, design education possesses deeply embedded roots that continue to intertwine, expand, and evolve. In other regions, however, the very concept of "design" and the establishment of formal design education are simultaneously burgeoning and rapidly advancing.

This chapter examines the unique approaches to design education and industry of four culturally diverse nations: Argentina, China, Italy, and the UK. In each nation's respective section, contributing authors discuss the histories, current practices, and future prospects of their countries' design industries and educational systems. By learning about these and other diverse approaches to global design education, design teachers, administrators, and programs can better reflect upon and strategically plan for the future of their contribution to these changes.

### Argentina

*Verónica Fiorini*

Guy Julier (2010) defines the ethos of design as one that combines discourses, beliefs, structures, and relations: "the culture of design as a process implies the existence of collective norms of practice, shared within certain contexts or through them" (p. 20). Therefore, in order to shed light on some local distinctions and peculiarities that are unique to the Argentine market, it is important to begin by defining select topics regarding the panorama of design development in Argentina.

To understand the relationship between Argentine design and its industry, we first need to examine the nation's changing economic models during the second-half of the 20th century. Throughout this period—particularly during the presidencies of Juan Perón (1946–1952; 1952–1955; 1973–1974)—Argentina was transformed by different

DOI: 10.4324/9781003049166-11

stages of economic and industrial development. The Peronist governments initiated two successive five-year plans (1947–1951; 1951–1955) that sought to significantly deepen and broaden Argentina's industries and markets by:

- establishing a single governmental body that oversaw all measures of exportation/importation;
- administering import quotas;
- financing industrial activities through the Banco de Crédito Industrial and the Central Bank;
- regulating the classification, packaging, and quality certification of exportable products;
- promoting and forming specific and new product areas; and
- managing the transference of resources between different sectors of the nation's economy (Kosacoff, 2003).

The government's initiatives yielded strong results: Argentina's gross domestic product (GDP)—the final value of the goods and services produced within a country during a specified time period—rose 77% between 1961 and 1969 (World Bank, n.d.).

However, despite this promising growth, the national economy soon plummeted. Argentina's simmering political discord erupted in the late 1960s and sparked a series of unstable leaderships and governments. These and various unsuccessful fiscal policies contributed to the nation's economic volatility throughout the ensuing decades. Most importantly, both the domestic and export demands for Argentine-produced industrial goods decreased; the "domestic demand for these goods had been hit by the influx of competitive imported products, and export demand for them had been reduced by the exchange rate policy which had caused the [Argentine] peso to become greatly overvalued" (Kosacoff, 2003, p. 152). In the twenty years between 1969 and 1989, Argentina's GDP dropped 175%; in fifteen years between 1975 and 1990, real per capita income fell by over 20% (Veigel, 2005; World Bank, n.d.). As Kosacoff (2003) notes, Argentina's degree of industrialization during the early 1990s was analogous to its level in the 1940s.

Between 1982 and 1990, economic stabilization became a constant goal of Argentine economic policy-makers; the country aimed to increase its exportations of locally made goods and drastically decrease importations (Kosacoff, 2003). This goal of increasing local industry contributed to the formalization of design education in Argentina: by the 1980s, university degrees were offered in graphic, industrial, fashion, and textile design at the University of Buenos Aires, and in later years at private institutions, such as the University of Palermo, among others. The schools' curricula reflected the nation's aforementioned goals along with the growing desire to form a stronger cultural identity via design. Devalle (2009) posits "[design] does not settle in an empty imaginary of social meaning, nor does it enable the problem of form outside of the characteristics of the production, circulation, and consumption of objects" (p. 398). In this respect, Devalle highlights the synthesis between the modern mode of conceiving the practices of architecture and design (seen as cultural customs), emerging industrial design, and the socially minded Peronist ideals for national industrialization. A more locally sustained design industry, led by a growing population of locally educated designers, has since emerged.

It is noteworthy that at the end of the 1990s, the lack of large-scale businesses in which designers of the different disciplines could work generated a great number of small businesses ("signature designers") that were managed by their own project creators. They were characteristic in the city of Buenos Aires following the severe economic and political crisis of 2001, and in underdeveloped neighborhoods such as Palermo, which offered these emergent designers affordable retail space. Thus, graduates across different areas of design were able to develop successful small-scale businesses with high profit margins, substantial levels of innovation, and low- to medium-scale production outputs despite having significant technological limitations. As a result, small signature designers/manufacturers emerged and promoted dialogue between local craftsmanship and industry. For example, two representative trademarks that developed from this period are the brand Juana de Arco (launched in 1998 and featuring hand-printed fabrics) in fashion design and the retail store Calma Chicha (founded in 1996 to showcase locally produced goods) in the areas of industrial and interior design.

We may summarize some distinctive aspects of Argentine design industry and design education since 2001 thusly:

- **Relation to design industry.** In Argentina, the prevailing business model is small industries and design businesses led by independent designers. Design goes hand-in-hand with project management; there is no sharp division between the different stages of the product's supply chain. The designers tend to create and sustain their own business dealings, being their own producers and consultants in a broad practice of sales, marketing, and other forms of self-promotion.
- **Profile of the design graduates.** The constant, fluctuating changes that are characteristic of the Argentine industrial economic models generate highly flexible and versatile designer profiles and attributes. The uncertainty of Argentina's economic stability strengthens certain business skills of the designers, who may work equally in a job at a large business, create their own design brand, and develop products for independent shops. These unique, distinct opportunities expose designers to the broader marketplace and thus provide them with an awareness of diverse markets, consumer behaviors, and business models.

- **Perspectives for teaching design.** Argentine schools employ a design pedagogy that is focused on concept and discourse: investigation and critical analysis are key phases of all design projects. Aspects related to the search for inclusive, social, and sustainable outlooks are key factors in contemporary and future approaches for the local Argentine design practices. To complement students' design studies, business courses are provided, thus preparing graduates to better understand attendant practices and launch their own "signature" small-scale design businesses.
- **Approaches to technology and production.** Dialogue between the industrial and craftwork aspects, as well as medium- and small-production scales, are central issues of "design + technology" in Argentina. Because of the difficult access we have to the latest technologies and industrial processes, Argentine designers generate innovative solutions with limited resources. It is precisely this strategy that has become one of Argentine design's strengths on the regional level.
- **Identity and tradition.** In several areas of design, the search for references in Argentine traditions also becomes the material for certain project discourses that hold dialogues with other latitudes. In the fashion design field, a notable example can be seen in the work of Pablo Ramirez—a designer who, throughout his career, has referenced Argentine cinema, certain aspects of Argentine religious culture, and local small-town customs in his work. These types of references and intercultural notes are quite distinctive in the broader sense of Argentine design.

In summary, Argentine design education is focused (in the academic perspective) on a general, versatile, and highly flexible training for changing contexts and constructive challenges with limited resources of materials and/or advanced technologies. The development of design among Argentine designers is centered on the symbolic and the cultural discourses of design, as well as the ability to innovate in conceptual terms. A unique mixture of the European design inheritance (Bauhaus—Ulm, through the central figure of Tomás Maldonado) with Latin America's relatively "young" design industry in search of its local identity guides the nature of design education in the broader region. In this sense, Argentine design education leverages the intertwining of these two lines of discourse: the linking of the European heritage with local Latin American views in the context of great socio-economic uncertainty.

These linked discourses embrace not only, as Margolin (2005) proposes, design as an activity, a product, and a cultural practice, but also as a "meta-discourse" in terms of design education models. The ideas conceived in the "heat" of modernity have constructed key guidelines to think about design projects and wider academic models in Argentina not as crystallized monoliths but as malleable hybrids, in the sense of a fragmented identity that is mixed and in dialogue with Latin American discourses.

It is possible to think that these approaches to design may become more visible in global scenarios to the extent that it not only shows *what we are*, but also *what we want to be* through Argentina's own point of view. In this sense, local design remains a strategy that selects, relates, and maintains a dialogue with other subjects and sights from different latitudes. After all, an approach that limits the question of identity to certain forms, materials, or techniques becomes a reductionist point of view (Fiorini, 2015). In the future, it will be essential for us to continue accentuating our roots in our ways of thinking and processing influences inherent to our culture, and the connections we have with other diverse sociocultural scenarios and contexts.

# China

*Dr. Christine Tsui*

## Introduction to Design Education in China

For centuries, Chinese artisans—including ceramicists, glassware makers, metalsmiths, and textile workers—received training through a deeply rooted master and student-apprentice workshop model. In 1903, the government inaugurated the nation's first educational system that included arts and crafts courses from the primary to university levels (Pan & Pan, 2018). These courses taught students artistic and technical drawing skillsets for producing crafts and objects, which kept the phases of design creativity and production distinctly separated (Yuan, 2003). Soon after, in 1906, the Liangjiang Normal School initiated the first formal higher education program for drawing and crafts; pupils were trained in the arts of paper cutting, wood carving, textile weaving, embroidery, metal work, technical drawing, and more (Pan & Pan, 2018; Yuan, 2003).

Arts and design education gained additional advancements during this period. One notable example occurred under the Minister of Education Cai Yuanpei (1898–1940), who changed the Qing Dynasty's (1644–1912) educational principle of "Five Honors" (Honor the Emperor, Honor Confucius, Honor Collaboration, Honor the Military, and Honor Practicality) to a new model of "Five Educations," which were Military Education, Practical Education, Moral Education, Worldview Education, and Art Education (Pan & Pan, 2018). Cai felt that art education should replace religion because the study of aesthetics could replace the function of religion in fulfilling the spiritual needs of the public (Pan & Pan, 2018). Cai soon established art departments within comprehensive universities and thus fortified the nascent foundation of design higher education in China.

### Chairman Mao's Era (1949–1979)

Founded in 1949, The People's Republic of China adopted a highly centralized political system and, accordingly, a highly centralized and unified national higher education system. All Chinese industries were controlled by ministries located in Beijing; academia, manufacturing, and trade were each contained in a vertical system under their respective bureaus. The system regulated all areas of academia, including job placements for university graduates. Today, however, most Chinese universities are administrated by provincial or municipal government; only a limited number continue to be centrally and directly supervised by the Ministry of Education.

China's high-quality handicrafts (e.g. cloisonné enamelware, embroidery, and similar design-related products) became a significant profit engine for China during the 1950s. This was largely due to their high demand, smaller investment capital requirement (compared to the mass technological industries), and an abundance of Chinese craft workers. To further expand China's handicraft industries, the first public school dedicated to design, the Central Academy of Arts and Crafts (CAAC), was formed in Beijing in 1953. The Academy's primary objectives were to cultivate creative design talent for traditional arts and crafts and to serve the proletariat (Pan & Pan, 2018). At CAAC, three programs were launched simultaneously: Textile Design, Ceramic Design, and Visual Communication.

Despite these burgeoning, hopeful beginnings, the Cultural Revolution (1966–1976) shuttered all Chinese universities, thus stalling the advancement of design higher education.

### Modern Design Education (1980–Present)

Formal design education reemerged in the 1980s by prioritizing traditional arts and crafts traditions and increasing the nation's manufacturing commerce. Design studies—placed under "arts and crafts" departments—focused on industrial growth, and coursework was limited to ceramic design, fabric design, environmental design, interior design, furniture design, and industrial design (Pan & Pan, 2018). However, as Chinese students began to study abroad in the US and Europe, they bought back new ideas for strengthening China's design industries and schools. Subsequently, a new modern concept of "design" began to proliferate across both sectors.

Since the 1990s, there have been three particularly notable changes in design education. First, in 1993, The National Catalogue of Higher Education officially split the study of design across the two discrete fields of Arts and Engineering. The fashion design program is the only subject that was split between these two fields: fashion design (artistic) focuses on creativity, drawing, and artistic representation of clothing, whereas fashion design (engineering) focuses on pattern cutting, business management, and marketing coursework. Second, in 1998, the Ministry of Education revised the name of "arts and crafts education" to "design education." The third notable change pertains to the terminology used for art and design education. In the Chinese system, people use the terms of "grandson," "son," and "father" to differentiate academic prestige/hierarchies. In 2012, The National Catalog upgraded the Arts and Design Programs from "son" and "grandson" to the positions of "father" and "son," thus elevating the status of design education in China.

Collectively, these changes illustrate the growing value and importance placed on design education in China and its consequential expansion. Today, there are over 2,000 tertiary-level schools that offer design programs in China (Beijing Industrial Design Center [BIDC], 2020).

### *The Modern Design Industries in China (1980s–Present)*

Similar to how China's design education system evolved, so too has the development of China's design industries been both expansive and systematized. Its progress has occurred in four distinct phases (Zhongzhuang, 2018) (Table 9.1).

As a result of this extensive planning and advancement, contemporary Chinese designers are fully equipped to perform every phase of the design process—from conceptual ideation to industrial production to global marketing and retailing—within the nation's increasingly influential space in the global marketplace.

### *Design in China Today*

Today, China's design industries are primarily located in the "design capitals" of Shanghai, Beijing, and Shenzhen. Each city has its own design industry focus and attendant attributes. Beijing, the nation's capital,

*Table 9.1* The four phases of growth in the Chinese design industries

| Phase | Years | Change |
|---|---|---|
| "Learning" | 1978–1988 | China learned design from the West. |
| "Exploring" | 1989–1998 | China explored the meanings of design and practiced design. During this phase, companies attempted to integrate Chinese culture with the Western design philosophies. |
| "Maturing" | 1999–2009 | China endeavored to elevate its self-confidence in design, rather than believing the Chinese can only follow Western design. |
| "Impacting" | 2010–present | Chinese design yields more influence in a wider spectrum of design fields globally. |

contains many state-owned companies that specialize in large-scale projects. As a result, it attracts designers in the environmental design fields (e.g. infrastructure, landscape, architecture). Beijing also develops design for the technology industries (e.g. artificial intelligence [AI], new energy vehicles, and new materials), thus attracting professionals from that sector also (BIDC, 2020). Conversely, Shanghai attracts more global design firms because of its openness and long history of contact with the West. Shanghai excels in both traditional design industries, such as clothing and advertising, and emergent areas such as AI, the Internet of Things (IoT), virtual reality (VR), and augmented reality (AR) (BIDC, 2020). Meanwhile, the newer city of Shenzhen attracts more recent design graduates; the city is situated in the Guangdong-Hong Kong-Macao Greater Bay Area and, thus, is a bourgeoning center for the international design industry (BIDC, 2020).

Design graduates typically standardize their careers through one of four business models:

1 state-owned companies that mainly perform large-scale infrastructural work, such as transport systems, architecture, and urban planning;
2 large, privately owned companies that offer comprehensive design services;
3 small-scale studios that offer services in a specific design discipline; and
4 self-employed/freelance-oriented work whereby designers work for design firms as independent contractors.

Within these models, designers usually operate in one of three distinct service formats:

1 "pure" design services (such as the comprehensive service of fashion design sketching, technical packages, and garment prototyping);
2 a combination of design and production services (such as for clothing/shoe businesses, and licensed product development, including games and animations); and
3 "total solution provider" services that offer a total design solution for clients.

One example of a "total solution provider" is the privately owned Rocco Design Group (RDG). The Group maintains offices in seven cities and aims to provide "one-stop innovative services" for their clients (Rocco Design Group [RDG], n.d.). RDG offers wide-ranging services that include industrial design, brand design, licensed products, space and service design, research and supply chain management, digital design solutions, and more for an array of markets that include IoT, AI, the medical and health sectors, education, transportation, and the air, space, and military industries.

*Future Prospects: Design Education and Industry*

Numerous changes are foreseen in China's design education system and industries. Top among these are the following items:

- There will be an increasing need to formalize intellectual property protection for design.
- There is high demand for designers in the high-technology fields such as AI, user interface, and VR. Design education will respond by adding coursework and possible programs in these areas.
- Digital transformation across the design industries is inevitable. Consequently, design students and current professionals will be increasingly required to learn new technologies, such as 3D design software.
- There will be a greater synthesis between science and design. This will result in the relevant changes across design school curricula required to keep up with this rapidly evolving trend.
- The growing industrial power of China and increasing tensions between China and the US are helping to increase the sentiment of nationalism in China, thus affecting the design industries. For example, more local consumers in China will favor elements with traditional Chinese features. This could affect design curricula and teachers' pedagogy. Coursework might increasingly address "the indigenous design quality and cultural values of Chinese products" rather than strictly adhering to Western ideals and/or inclinations as done previously (Yu & Jerrard, 2018, n.p.).
- By 2026, it is expected that "a total of 500 million people [in China] will be classed as the middle class—creating a rapid growth in demand for consumer goods" (Barboza, 2010, as cited in Yu & Jerrard, 2018, n.p.). China's market growth is the fastest in the world, yet comparatively, design education has not kept pace. The rapidly growing middle class, design industries, and desire for seamless applications of design across all business sectors (e.g. AI, VR, and digital networking) will result in the creation of additional design schools to train highly in-demand designers.

In the decades ahead, the design industries will play a greater role in advancing China, both economically and culturally. It is therefore imperative for the teaching of design (via the design schooling systems, curricula, and teachers' pedagogical training) to be re-examined and strengthened. In doing so, China will be primed to produce designers who are equipped to innovate and advance the nation—and the world—throughout the 21st Century.

# Italy

*Arturo Tedeschi*

## The Origin of Italian Design

Italy has a long-established design tradition rooted in the material culture of craft and industry of the early 1900s and cultivated with originality and prestige starting in the 1950s. The end of WWII led Italy to a prosperous period of socioeconomic transformation characterized by the passage from a purely rural economy to a new industrial one that focused on mechanical industry. The most dynamic sector was automotive and led by Fiat, which had succeeded in setting up a solid and competitive company renowned for its iconic and affordable vehicles. The symbol of this age is represented by the Fiat 500 (1957), the precursor of city cars (Figure 9.1). Designed by Dante Giacosa, 500 was a revolutionary project that defined a new urban mobility and, consequently, triggered a transformation in the habits and lifestyles among Italians.

This project aligns with an ideal trend already begun by the Vespa scooter (1946) and seems to mark a first trajectory for Italian design research that is characterized by the combination of technical excellence

*Figure 9.1* The Fiat 500 (1957).
Source: Keystone/Getty Images.

with a unique style to promote a friendly and easy design aesthetic, or "language." This approach to design is also found in the archetypal and vaguely anthropomorphic moka pot by Bialetti (1933): the coffee maker embodies the Italian attitude to create objects imbued with semantic value and the ability to generate an emotional response. Similar, exemplary contemporary products are by the Italian brands Alessi, Seletti, and Kartell.

*The Link between Industry and Design*

The period usually referred to as the "Italian economic miracle" (1958–1963) is well connected to the "motorization" and transformation of Italian consumer society. Albeit short, this period set up the modern industrial culture in Italy. A symbolic case is represented by the success of Olivetti in the design and development of typewriters and computers. President Adriano Olivetti, an influential manager and man endowed with cultural awareness, combined the attention to technology with an extreme care for design. He transformed a family business into a modern industrial group that achieved the vision to develop innovative, globally appreciated products and to distribute them through a worldwide network. The Olivetti direction aimed to create excellence and innovation in industrial design through an unprecedented vision of workers' conditions: Olivetti opened the factory to intellectuals, writers, and artists who offered their creative contributions to design. Among the most famous projects were the Valentine typewriter (by Ettore Sottsass) and the first personal computer in history, Programma 101 (by Mario Bellini).

In parallel with industrial innovation, a gradual disappearance of traditional small businesses (carpenters, blacksmiths, cobblers, etc.) occurred due to their transformation into small manufacturers. Such scaling up is particularly evident in the north-central area of Italy where small businesses gathered together to form the base clusters of the current "industrial districts." This new model did not affect the quality of products and the artisanal approach, despite the production process moving from traditional manufacture hosted within small shops to well-organized, structured factories. This unique ability to successfully merge craft and industrial production established the foundation of the so-called"Made in Italy"— a production with low technological content but characterized by unparalleled attention to details and finishing.

*The Made in Italy*

The 1950s and 1960s represent the moment when companies benefited from economic expansion and increased spending due to the increase of Italy's per-capita income. If the first symbol of this economic shift is seen in the aforementioned Fiat 500, a second one is seen in home living—a new business territory ruled by small sectors (furniture, furnishings, textiles, and ceramics). In general, Italians started to "live" better, to dress and eat better, and to ultimately develop what can be called an "art of living" that was proudly shown off to the rest of the world. Above all, cinema and advertising helped to shape in consumers a well-defined idea of Made in Italy as an expression of refinement and quality (e.g. Ferrari cars and brands like Gucci, Armani, and Natuzzi) that was shown mainly through the so-called "triple Fs" of Made in Italy: Food, Fashion, and Furniture.

## Design Education in Italy

While industrial design emerged as a relevant and autonomous discipline in the 1950s, the formal education of the Italian designer essentially passed through the faculties of architecture and engineering for decades in the 20th century. The establishment of the first design school (Scuola Politecnica di Design di Milano, 1954) was based on the principles of experimentation and innovation. It was in 1993 that the first degree course was established by Politecnico di Milano (School of Design), which has conferred academic autonomy to the design disciplines. The current program offerings are divided between public and private schools (Table 9.2).

Design education is structured around a pragmatic approach aimed at equipping students with creative problem-solving skills, the abilities to fully control the creative process, and the skillsets of visual communication and storytelling. The Italian design tradition, which is deeply connected with the concept of Made in Italy, emphasizes the semantic and emotional values of objects to engage all the senses. Qualities of functionality, user-friendliness, sustainability, and safety are complemented by a vision where products are capable of triggering an emotional response and inspiring the user. In a society based on data and digital technologies, where functionality is somehow a given value, the design student is often invited to meet immaterial and unmeasurable needs, such as those belonging to the dimension of rituals, imagination, and myth. Accordingly, both educational and creative processes embrace a top-down approach where students formulate a general framework with general goals, followed by a refined and detailed project development. For example, a possible design brief for a living room lamp will ask students to consider the item as an episode of the user's daily story, rather than just a functional object. *How can a lamp make someone living alone in a city feel better when they come back home?* The answer is not obvious and it is probably beyond the technical features, materials, assembly, or smartphone control. Maybe a resin monkey holding a bulb is a valid answer (see the "Monkey Lamp" by Seletti)?

*Table 9.2* Public and private design schools in Italy

| Main public schools | Main private schools |
| --- | --- |
| *Scuola Politecnica di Design (Milan)*<br>Product Design, Interior Design, Web and Digital Design, Transportation and Car Design, Food Design.<br>*School of Design—Politecnico di Milano (Milan)*<br>Industrial Product Design, Communication Design, Fashion Design, Interior Design, Digital Design and Interaction, Industrial Product Design and Engineering, Design for the Fashion System, Digital Design and Interaction, Naval and Nautical Design.<br>*Architecture and Design Department—Politecnico di Torino (Turin)*<br>Design and Visual Communication, Systemic Design, Interior Design, Exhibit and Retail Design.<br>*Design and Arts—Università IUAV di Venezia (Venice)*<br>Fashion Design and Multimedia Arts, Industrial Design and Multimedia, Product Design and Visual Communication.<br>*Faculty of Design and Art—Libera Università di Bolzano (Bolzano)*<br>Design and Arts, Eco-Social Design, Interaction and Transmedia Space.<br>*Design—Politecnico di Bari (Bari)*<br>Industrial Design. | *Domus Academy (Milan)*<br>Design, Experience, Fashion, Business.<br>*Istituto Marangoni (Milan)*<br>Fashion, Arts and Design.<br>*Istituto Europeo di Design(IED)(located in several Italian cities)*<br>Design, Fashion, Visual Arts, Communication.<br>*Nuova Accademia di Belle Art (NABA)(Milan)*<br>Design, Media Design, Fashion, Scenography, Graphic Design, Communication.<br>*Istituto Superiore per le Industrie Artistiche (ISIA) (located in several Italian cities)*<br>Product Design, Product Chart, Ceramics.<br>*Istituto d'Arte Applicata e Design (IAAD)(Torino & Bologna)*<br>Transportation Design, Interior Design, Textile and Fashion Design, Social Innovation Design. |

The distinction between public and private design schools reflects the significant difference in the educational/pedagogical approach. The public universities are more focused on the technological aspects and cultural roots of the project. As an example, polytechnic schools continue the traditional and technical expertise in automotive and transportation design. In contrast, private schools structure their courses by focusing on interdisciplinary workshops and collaborations with external partners, thereby providing connections with professional design practices and companies. Schools like Domus Academy and Marangoni offer students the experience of working aside the most famous brands of Made in Italy, from fashion to industrial design (e.g. Armani, Versace, Bulgari, Flos, Natuzzi, and Technogym). A central role is given to teachers and mentors who are chosen from the most important designers and opinion leaders; these teachers transfer their knowledge to the classroom by sharing information about the latest practices and trends. The flexibility of private schools is also reflected in the offer of short-courses and open conferences. Future trends for both public and private design schools will certainly involve the introduction of new didactic tools oriented to develop students' skills in digital research, the IoT, and data interpretation and visualization—as well as a deep understanding of the interaction between the physical and digital worlds, offline and online, with the purpose of connecting and exchanging data with devices and systems over the Internet.

If such an interaction usually leads to pure and neutral aesthetics, recent approaches in this direction show the technology integration in Italian products does not lead to a minimalistic language, but, rather, to an original, expressive, and colorful result—as seen in Scavolini's Dandy Plus kitchen (2020) by Fabio Novembre. Thanks to the integration of Amazon Alexa, Dandy Plus is a "speaking" and digitally connected kitchen, but with a pop concept and a strong and playful aesthetic approach: it reveals itself as a clear homage to the most expressive Italian design, characterized by soft curves, decorative textures, and bright colors.

## The United Kingdom

*Dr. Susan Orr and Dr. Benjamin Stopher*

In this short case study, we report on the particular context of design education at University of the Arts London (UAL) as a means to reflect on the position of contemporary design education in the UK.

### Design Industries and Contexts

This first section explores the relationship between design education and design industries.

The design industries in the UK have become a major source of economic growth in recent decades. Consequentially, the role of the arts university has grown in both providing the conditions for innovation and growth (Maioli et al., 2021) in this sector, and—not unproblematically—for providing labor to emerging new industries (Bakhshi & Windsor, 2015). Given this, it is worth briefly exploring the history shaping the political economy of design education within the UK arts university context and considering its relationship to the design industries.

Contemporary approaches to design education in the UK are heavily influenced by two distinct traditions: those of the trade and craft schools of the 19th century and those of the arts schools of the 20th century (Frayling, 1987). These art schools incorporated the countercultural revolution of the 1960s and, specifically, embraced the emergence of critical theory (Newall, 2018). When this was combined with contemporary art that rejected representation, a new market was created, one where ideas held primacy (Lippard, 1997). It is important to note that while UK art schools were proudly part of a progressive cultural revolution, they continued to be spaces where primarily white and male supremacy dominated. Consequently, women's and Black voices (Bailey et al., 2005) struggled to be heard, and power relations and hierarchies were left unchallenged (Llewellyn, 2015).

As the 20th century drew to a close, the arrival of the Internet started the universal digitization of the design sector, and new forms of design materiality and design consumption developed at an increasingly fast pace (Leung, 2008). This forced the design sector—including design education—to grow rapidly as it expanded its place in the every-day lives of citizens through their interaction with digital products, services, and culture (Kimbell, 2019).

UAL's emergence as an *arts university* has many roots, but most important amongst these were the broad recognition of the cultural value embedded within London's storied arts schools and the political desire across the 20th century to bring this cultural capital both into the knowledge economy and the Academy. UAL's status as an arts university was conferred in 2004, following its life as a federation of colleges that can trace themselves back to the aforementioned trade and craft schools of the 19th century.

Within UAL, this history and context is foundational as it shapes many of the ways we think about the design industries and the pedagogy of our design courses. For example, we revere ideas—particularly of the conceptual kind—and have a deep commitment to making and craft as a knowledge-producing activity. These instincts can be traced directly through our history (Rughani et al., 2016).

Within the 21st century, we would argue that the process of becoming an arts university has seen UAL turn outwards, embrace its epistemic and societal responsibilities, and broaden its conception of design education; UAL's "Design Against Crime" initiative is an example of this. These changes were accompanied by the wider educational turn and the academization of the art school. This development in design education shifts the focus from being exclusively an individual creative practice to ensuring that the practice is connected to a broader set of understandings of the challenges facing society, both locally and globally. Within UAL, there is an increasing recognition of the ways a creative university makes a contribution to the UK design industries.

## *Design Pedagogies*

This second section examines signature pedagogies in design education and introduces key concepts that underpin design education at UAL.

At UAL, much work has been done to articulate the signature pedagogy of creative education. Drawing on the work of one of the authors (Orr, 2018) and others (e.g. Deakin & Webb, 2016), the pedagogical focus has been on developing a "voice" for studio-based education that unpacks what can be tacit educational practice. The concept of inquiry is central to our understanding of creative learning at UAL. As a specialist arts university, we have been able to design all aspects of our pedagogy and assessment practices to support the pursuit of creativity.

All our design students are assessed against five criteria: inquiry, knowledge, process, product, and communication. This clearly conveys to students that we value the journey of creative development—the process—as much as we value the product of that journey (Orr & Shreeve, 2017). We also ground students in active learning; it is their inquiry that is the compass that directs their creative development. The five assessment criteria shape all aspects of curriculum, pedagogy, and assessment approaches and are a reflection of both an institutional-level concept of signature pedagogies for creative education and our history of creative inquiry through making.

In addition to our common assessment criteria, we have developed the Creative Attributes Framework (CAF) (UAL, 2020a). Drawn from our experience of creative education at scale, this establishes the attributes that enable students to thrive in the design industries. The nine attributes are grouped in three sections:

- *Making things happen:* Proactivity, Enterprise, and Agility;
- *Showcasing your talents to others:* Communication, Connectivity, and Storytelling; and
- *Life-wide learning:* Curiosity, Self-efficacy, and Resilience.

Developing these attributes helps our graduates achieve sustainable and ethical careers. As a result, the CAF has brought maturity to our approaches to employability and enterprise. The relevance and application of the CAF can be seen through design students who graduate and successfully begin careers during periods of global crisis (e.g. COVID-19), as students with these attributes are equipped to cope with the uncertainty of the moment. Additionally, we believe these attributes are "future proofed" and avoid the trap of listing skills that become obsolete with the arrival of new technologies and new roles in the design industries.

*Speculations*

Given the above, it is worth speculating about things that we feel will shape design education for UAL in the coming years. These can be summarized in three categories: **political and social relations, technology,** and **knowledge production and interdisciplinarity.**

**Political and social relations** inform all aspects of cultural discourse at present. Design education is no exception (Resnick, 2019).

Structural inequality also surfaces in relation to the university's teaching, learning, and curriculum—as can be seen in projects co-produced with students investigating the "decolonizing" of design education (Abdulla et al., 2018). Our students also demand critical reflection in this domain by pursuing campaigns such as the "UAL so white," by drawing attention to a design curriculum that was seen by our Students' Union at the time as "pale, male, and stale." Student and staff activism, and the University's response to this, has led to a partnership between students and staff who are working together to develop a decolonialized arts practice. One recent output includes two decolonizing-the-arts curriculum "zines" that have been created through a collaborative student and staff partnership. The university's Teaching, Learning, and Employability Exchange supported this work and brought a renewed focus on addressing educational inequality into its teacher development activity, such as its MA Academic Practice in Art, Design, and Communication.

At UAL, responses to this social and political context can be seen within and beyond design education at all levels. At the institutional level, UAL has establish both the Decolonizing Art Institute which "seeks to challenge colonial and imperial legacies and drive social, cultural and institutional change" (UAL, 2021, n.p.) and the Social Design Institute which "uses research to change how designers and organizations design [for social good]" (UAL, 2020b, n.p.)—both of which represent significant institutional efforts to engage with the wicked problems of design education. Given this context, the speculation that political and social relations will play a large part of design education in the coming years should not be surprising. However, the urgency with which this work is being undertaken is significant, and we would hope to see design programs at UAL having a far more explicit engagement with these urgent agendas in the coming years.

**Technology** has radically reshaped both the teaching and practice of design in all disciplines over the last twenty years (Figure 9.2). Design education has become increasingly concerned with things that cannot be done readily by machines (Bakhshi et al., 2015), such as understanding human need in an increasingly complex design ecology and conceptual design schemes that cohere complex organizational needs with tangible action (Irwin et al., 2015).

At UAL, this has resulted in significant growth in the interaction, user experience (UX), and service design disciplines in the last fifteen years, along with associated research interest of UAL academics (Stopher et al., 2021). This technology context is also evident at UAL in the development of the Creative Computing Institute, which works "at the intersection of creativity and computational technologies" and delivers courses across creative disciplines to UAL students (UAL, 2020c, n.p.). This Institute was formed, in part, in recognition of the fact that some designers need advanced technical fluency in order to define and shape the tools that, in turn, shape their practice. For example, this means that undergraduate students can add an additional year of study to their other undergraduate degree and graduate with a BA (Hons) Design (with Creative

*Figure 9.2* Prototype for a solar balloon that floats above a city by day and lights its streets by night.

Source: Tim Ireland/PA Images via Getty Images.

Computing). As engagement with technology becomes more demanding, we expect to see more opportunities for undergraduates to augment their design studies with this kind of technical learning.

**Knowledge production and interdisciplinarity** are key forces shaping design education in the UK. This can be traced back to when UK art schools transitioned into full universities, a transition that stems from the political choice to bring arts education into the Academy (Wilkinson, 2020). In this process, design education has had to build a narrative about its contribution to the academic knowledge (Darbellay et al., 2017). This has resulted at UAL in, for example, the development of a substantial program of practice-based PhD work.

This trend will intensify due to key instrumental forces such as research assessment, challenged-based framework for innovation funding, national industrial strategy priorities, and associated and emerging knowledge exchange framework (Kaner, 2020). All of this demands that design education develops better ways of integrating knowledge and methods from other academic disciplines and continues to develop its understanding of the unique value of the design disciplines.

## Chapter Summary

The four nations featured in this chapter demonstrate the ways in which a region's history, socio-political systems, communities, and inherent cultures directly shape and drive its approaches to design industry and education. While these countries exhibit distinct circumstances and aims, they also share common themes that can, in turn, prompt us for reflective discourse for guiding and shaping our own unique trajectories in design education. These themes include:

- **Design as a knowledge-producing activity.** The orientation of the design industries has evolved from local crafts to centralized industrialization to innovative knowledge economies. Accordingly, contemporary design has surpassed its basic roles (function and aesthetics) to become something that offers radically new ideas, particularly in conceptual terms. Design education is thus responding by pivoting from its longstanding vocational focus to a focus on the development of conceptually oriented inquiry for innovation. Students' success will be contingent upon the continuation of interdisciplinary coursework that promotes diverse ways of seeing, understanding, conceptualizing, ideating, making, and presenting design ideas. The crossovers between design and science and technology will be particularly advantageous in advancing design industry and education.
- **Design as national identity.** While some nations have cultivated a mature design identity for decades (Italy and the UK), others are in the formative stages of development (China and Argentina). Regardless of their level of maturation, each nation demonstrates a growing desire to celebrate and hone its unique cultural identity via design, rather than blindly following globally homogenous (e.g. "Western") ideals. Designers (and design schools) are looking inwardly to identify, define, and accentuate acutely the symbolic and cultural discourse of design—their nation's aesthetic "brand"—that is unique to their region. This shift can be attributed to numerous reasons, including recent hyper-globalization, the desire to increase local businesses for sustainability and build local economy, and rising consumer interests for showcasing more diverse and inclusive design.
- **Design as social responsibility.** Around the world, consumers and corporations are increasingly attuned to the impact design makes on our lives and our planet. The power of design is being leveraged to address the challenges facing society, both locally and globally; design industries and educators are shifting their focus from teaching individual, myopic design practices toward those that engender connections to and the syntheses of a broader understanding of the world's challenges. In this way, design practice becomes issues-driven for greater social responsibility (see Chapter 3 for full discussion).
- **Design as an immaterial agent.** Digital transformation across the global design industries is accelerating rapidly, particularly following the emergence of COVID-19. Today's market requires designers

to use digital tools for day-to-day operations. The widespread adoption of virtual prototyping, AI, VR, and IoT are just some areas that will radicalize all sectors of design industry, education, and consumption. At the same time, a dichotomy exists in designers' and students' growing appreciation for craft and other practices in design that *cannot* be digitized or automated—such as the development of creative processes that strategically target and subsequently fulfill consumers' emotional needs (e.g. self-actualization and well-being). These two immaterial agents of design—the digital and the psychological—will determine the direction of future design industries and schools' curricula.

When we incorporate these themes into our work as design educators, we improve our pedagogy, curricula, and institutions and subsequently have a positive impact on our students—both today and in the future.

# References

Abdulla, D., Prado de O Martins, L., & Schultz, T. (2018). *Decolonising design education: Ontologies, strategies, urgencies*. Platform Editions.

Bailey, D. A., Boyce, S., & Baucom, I. (2005). *Shades of Black: Assembling Black arts in 1980s Britain*. Duke University.

Bakhshi, H., Frey, C. B., & Osborne, M. (2015, April 17). Creativity vs. robots. *Nesta*. https://www.nesta.org.uk/report/creativity-vs-robots/

Bakhshi, H., & Windsor, G. (2015, April 21). The creative economy and the future of employment. *Nesta*. https://www.nesta.org.uk/report/the-creative-economy-and-the-future-of-employment/

Barboza, D. (2010, August 15). China passes Japan as second-largest economy. *The New York Times*. https://www.nytimes.com/2010/08/16/business/global/16yuan.html

Beijing Industrial Design Center (BIDC). (2020). *The blue book of design industry: Annual report on the development of design industry in China (2019–2020)*. Social Sciences Academic Press.

Darbellay, F., Moody, Z., & Lubart, T. (Eds.). (2017). *Creativity, design thinking and interdisciplinarity*. Springer.

Deakin, F., & Webb, C. (2016). *Discovering the post-digital art school*. UAL, Fred and Company.

Devalle, V. (2009). *The journey of form: Emergence and consolidation of graphic design (1948–1984)*. Paidós.

Fiorini, V. (2015). Consumer trends, innovation and identity in fashion: Transformations in the teaching of Latin American design. *Cuaderno, 53*, 79–89.

Frayling, C. (1987). *The Royal College of Art: One hundred & fifty years of art & design*. Vintage.

Irwin, T., Kossoff, G., & Tonkinwise, C. (2015). Transition design provocation. *Design Philosophy Papers, 13*(1), 3–11.

Julier, G. (2010). *Design culture*. Gustavo Gili.

Kaner, J. (2020). KEF, TEF, REF and all that: The current state of art & design higher education in the UK. *Design and Technology Education: An International Journal*, 25(1), 9–12.

Kimbell, L. (2019). What if there were more policy futures studios? *Journal of Futures Studies*, 23(4), 129–136.

Kosacoff, B. (2003). The Argentine industry: A thwarted restructuring process. In *Production and work in Argentina: Photographic memory 1860–1960* (pp. 149–158). National University of Quilmes.

Leung, L. (2008). *Digital experience design: Ideas, industries, interaction*. Intellect Books.

Lippard, L. R. (1997). *Six years: The dematerialization of the art object from 1966 to 1972*. University of California.

Llewellyn, N. (2015). *The London art schools: Reforming the art world, 1960 to now*. Tate.

Maioli, S., Di Novo, S., Fazio, G., Sapsed, J., & Vermeulen, W. (2021). *The UK's international creative trade: A review of the official data sources*. Newcastle University.

Margolin, V. (2005). *The routes of design*. Nobuko.

Newall, M. (2018). *A philosophy of the art school*. Routledge.

Orr, S. (2018). 21st Century art school curriculum: Highways, by-ways and leaving a trail. *Bauhaus Now*, 3(3). https://www.bauhauskooperation.com/kooperation/project-archive/magazine/experience-the-bauhaus/highways-byways-and-leaving-a-trail/

Orr, S., & Shreeve, A. (2017). *Art and design pedagogy in higher education: Knowledge, values and ambiguity in the creative curriculum*. Routledge.

Pan, G., & Pan, Q. (2018). *History of Chinese design education*. John Wiley & Sons. https://onlinelibrary.wiley.com/doi/full/10.1002/9781118978061.ead042

Resnick, E. (2019). *The social design reader*. Bloomsbury.

Rocco Design Group (RDG). (n.d.). *Company profile*. www.lkkdesign.com

Rughani, P., Raban, W., & Al-Maria, S. (2016). *The creative stance*. Cornerhouse.

Stopher, B., Fass, J., Revell, T., & Verhoeven, E. (2021). *Design and digital interfaces: Designing with aesthetic and ethical awareness*. Bloomsbury.

University of the Arts London (UAL). (2020a). *Creative Attributes Framework*. https://www.arts.ac.uk/about-ual/teaching-and-learning-exchange/careers-and-employability/creative-attributes-framework

University of the Arts London (UAL). (2020b). *UAL Social Design Institute*. https://www.arts.ac.uk/ual-social-design-institute

University of the Arts London (UAL). (2020c). *UAL Creative Computing Institute*. https://www.arts.ac.uk/creative-computing-institute

University of the Arts London (UAL). (2021). *UAL Decolonising Arts Institute*. https://www.arts.ac.uk/ual-decolonising-arts-institute

Veigel, K. F. (2005). *Governed by emergency: Economic policy-making in Argentina, 1973–1991*. Princeton University.

Wilkinson, R. G. (2020). Creative arts personal pedagogy vs marketised higher education: A battle between values. *International Journal of Art & Design Education*, 39(3), 536–549.

World Bank. (n.d.). *GDP growth (annual %): Argentina*. https://data.worldbank.org/indicator/NY.GDP.MKTP.KD.ZG?locations=AR

Yu, P., & Jerrard, B. (2018). The challenges and transformation of design education in contemporary China. *MATEC Web of Conferences*, *176*. https://www.researchgate.net/publication/326118134_The_Challenges_and_Transformation_of_Design_Education_in_Contemporary_China

Yuan, X. (2003). *The vicissitudes of Chinese artistic design education*. Beijing Ligong Daxue Chubanshe.

Zhongzhuang, X. (2018). The historical development of Chinese design since the Open-Door Policy. *Sohu*. https://www.sohu.com/a/257738366_160238

# Section III
# Design Pedagogy

# 10 Introduction to Design Pedagogy

## What Is Pedagogy?

Pedagogy is commonly understood as the method of teaching. As both an art and a science, it is a process of educating students that considers all the interactions and acts that take place during learning (Davis, 2017). Pedagogical processes are diverse and include how teachers and students learn together, develop language associated with the discipline and the curriculum, connect course content with students' lives, and engage with complex thinking. Pedagogy, at its best, responds to and strengthens students' cognitive, social, political, and emotional development. Thus, pedagogy can foster many positive outcomes in students, including: enhanced social development and well-being; the ability to have thoughts, ideas, beliefs, and practices challenged through critical thinking for higher learning; a deeper understanding of and sensitivities to cultural differences; the aptitude to engage meaningfully with others; and the capacity to challenge assumptions and biases, seek alternatives, and persevere when learning. Pedagogy is fundamental to the preparation of students to live more dynamically, both in their professional lives and in society.

Pedagogy plays a vital role in shaping the learning environment; it defines the relationships among students, teachers, and the subject of study (Pendoley, 2019). The teacher's chosen pedagogical methods are influenced by the specific learning environment, cognitive theory, students' backgrounds and interests, and the students' unique needs. These, collectively, influence the teacher's actions, judgments, and teaching strategies. And, while well-developed curricula, learning outcomes, and standards are critical components of design education, "they aren't at the forefront of great learning and teaching. Pedagogy is" (Pendoley, 2019, n.p.). A curriculum either succeeds or fails due to teachers' abilities to *teach* students (i.e. pedagogy). The development of advanced pedagogy is particularly important in design education. This is because college-level design faculty, hired for their subject knowledge and professional experience, rarely receive direct preparation to teach (Davis, 2017). This means colleges are taking design professionals and placing them in the classroom with little to

DOI: 10.4324/9781003049166-13

no training in education or pedagogy. These new teachers are then left to "sink or swim" in their new jobs, depending on how adaptable they are to the academic environment and the practice of teaching.

This section draws attention to the importance and complexity of design pedagogy—and its impact on students, schools, and faculty—with an eye to encouraging design schools to increase their institutions' measures that support and strengthen their faculty's teaching practice.

## Key Approaches to Pedagogy

There are extensive theories and categories of pedagogy. The following four approaches are particularly relevant to design higher education:

1 **Behaviorist pedagogy** stems from the theory of Behaviorism researched by Edward Thorndike (1874–1949), Ivan Pavlov (1849–1936), and B.F. Skinner (1904–1990). This pedagogical approach is teacher-centered: teachers repeat positive reinforcement (or other stimuli) for good behaviors until they become conditioned in the student while correcting less desired behaviors through consequences—a system of rewards and punishments termed "operant conditioning." In behaviorist design pedagogy, the teacher leads activities as the perceived authority. These activities are visible and structured and commonly include lectures, direct instruction, demonstrations, and rote learning. While behaviorist pedagogy may offer some benefits (it often produces results quickly), it can undermine students' opportunities for agency, autonomy, deep learning, and long-term motivation.
2 **Constructivist pedagogy**, based on the pedagogical research of Jean Piaget (1896–1980), posits people learn through experiences and reflection. Sometimes described as a "progressive teaching style," this method places the student at the center of the learning. Rather than passively acquiring knowledge from teacher-authorities, students actively construct knowledge that is based, in part, on their *own* previous experiences and knowledge. When using this approach, the teacher's role is to develop and facilitate activities—such as project- and inquiry-based learning—that build students' knowledge constructions. Constructivist pedagogy is "a dynamic process comprising successive stages of adaption to reality during which learners actively construct knowledge by creating and testing their own theories of the world" (Wray, 2006, p. 51). Resultantly, working through a constructivist pedagogy, design students acquire heightened agency, autonomy, and ownership of their education that, in turn, engender deeper learning and intrinsic motivation.
3 **Social constructivism pedagogy** builds upon Piaget's theories through the work of Lev Vygotsky (1896–1934). Whereas constructivism focuses on the development of knowledge within the *individual* mind,

social constructivism posits knowledge is shaped by the individual's *society*. Vygotsky contended it is impossible to separate learning from its social context. This is due, in part, to the role language and culture play in how we come to understand our world: together, they provide a framework for how we experience, communicate, and understand reality (Vygotsky, 1934/1987). As such, Vygotsky believed learning should be a *collaborative* process since "all cognitive functions originate in (and must therefore be explained as products of) social interactions" (Berkeley Graduate Division, n.d., n.p.; Vygotsky, 1978). Social constructivism pedagogy combines student-centered and teacher-guided approaches to learning while simultaneously integrating students into the wider learning community through social activities (e.g. group discussions, collaborative design work).

4 **Liberationism pedagogy** is rooted in the work of Paulo Freire (1921–1997). Freire's ideologies emphasize the relationship between politics and education and, in particular, the ways dominant, privileged groups impede the advancement of disadvantaged groups within unjust societies. In his seminal text, *Pedagogy of the Oppressed* (1970), Freire notes, "[a]n act of violence is any situation in which some men prevent others from the process of inquiry," and that "[a]ny school which does not foster students' capacity for critical inquiry is guilty of violent oppression" (p. 74). Liberationism pedagogy aims to eliminate oppression and emancipate students by democratizing the learning environment—*students'* voices (not teachers') are centralized in the classroom. In practice, this approach provides students greater freedom through their education. They are given more choice in: what they learn and how they learn it; how to showcase their knowledge throughout the iterative/final stages of design assignments; and the best ways to lead discussions, decide lesson topics, and/or plan weekly schedules. To further this student-centered pedagogy, teachers offer opportunities that target different learning styles and situate themselves "side-by-side" with students so that everyone learns and discovers the subject *together*.

A preliminary understanding of these critical pedagogies is essential due to their impact on students' cognitive and emotional development, sense of community, and professional preparation. Although presented above as discrete pedagogical approaches, often teachers work with a combination of tools from across these four theories in order to ensure they best meet the needs both of their students and of their own teaching styles. Each pedagogical approach plays an important role in design education, but the balance used between them will be dependent upon the situation's context, students' needs, and the teaching goals. While these four approaches are ubiquitous across most higher education settings, "signature pedagogies" are especially important in design education.

## The Signature Pedagogies of Design

Signature pedagogies are "the types of teaching that organize the fundamental ways in which future practitioners are educated for their new professions" (Shulman, 2005, p. 52). For instance, medical students accompany doctor-professors during clinical rounds and many business schools employ the "case method" to study business. The critical role played by signature pedagogies (aside from imparting disciplinary content) is to promote ways of thinking or "habits of mind" that help students "act, behave, and think like practitioners, albeit with the structures, constraints and affordances of a pedagogic university environment" (Orr & Shreeve, 2018, p. 88). Signature pedagogies are important not only due to their pervasiveness across professionally oriented academic institutions (including design schools), but also because they ultimately shape the character of the future practice and symbolize the values and hopes of the profession (Shulman, 2005). Moreover, the signature pedagogy of design implicitly defines what counts as knowledge and how this knowledge is analyzed, criticized, accepted, or rejected (Shulman, 2005).

Lee Shulman (2005) notes every signature pedagogy contains three structures that build students' *knowledge* ("habits of the mind"), *values/ethics* ("habits of the heart"), and *skills* ("habits of the hand") of the profession. These structures are:

1 The *surface structure* consists of what are considered the "typical" operational aspects of teaching and learning. Activities include design briefs, lectures, critiques, technical demonstrations, questioning and answering, and other teacher-student interactions that create knowledge ("habits of the mind").
2 The *deep structure* contains a set of assumptions about how disciplinary knowledge should be imparted to students. In design education, students are immersed directly into active design thinking, practice, and creation, while simultaneously learning key theories of design that will shape how they act and think as designers. This simultaneous immersion begins at the entry level, unlike in other academic disciplines where students first master ideas (theory) before application (practice). To engage these combined processes, design students conduct design research, sketch, create prototypes, prepare diagrams, and perform other activities that synthesize theory with practice. Thus, students learn to think creatively and analytically like professionals while simultaneously mastering core skillsets ("habits of the hand").
3 The *implicit structure* is the moral dimension that imparts values ("habits of the heart"). It embodies the "beliefs about professional attitudes, values, and dispositions" that are passed from teacher to students (p. 55). In design education, this structure manifests

through teachers' design briefs, examples shown to students, comments made during critiques, and the selection of students for special opportunities (e.g. awards and public profiling) (Davis, 2017). In some respects, this structure acculturates students in the taste culture of design (Anthony, 1991).

Across design programs, teachers leverage aspects of the four signature pedagogies discussed above, each of which activates these three types of structures.

### *The Powerful Tool of the "Crit"*

The critique (or, "crit") is a pedagogical practice whereby design students present their work for instructor- and peer-review in the studio classroom (Figure 10.1). It is perhaps the most frequently used tool of the signature pedagogies. "Crits" enable students to gain a critical, analytical approach to design while simultaneously teaching students to articulate their thoughts verbally and to defend their work. This equips students with skillsets that are invaluable in the professional world.

The studio classroom also plays a key role in design signature pedagogy because it "helps structure what can and does take place when students learn" (Orr & Shreeve, 2018, p. 90). For instance, typical studio classrooms show no obvious front of the room whereby students face the

*Figure 10.1* The studio critique.

Source: BalanceFormCreative/Shutterstock.com.

teacher or lecturer. Rather, students assemble around work areas so they can experiment and collaborate together, observe and comment on others' works, and maintain primary focus on their work, not the teacher. Students work autonomously while the teacher "circulates among the work areas and comments, critiques, challenges, or just observes" (Shulman, 2005, p. 54). Consequently, the teacher is perceived less as the sole authority for knowledge and more as a supportive, "side-by-side" collaborator with students. Other tools of design signature pedagogies include: design briefs that launch project-based learning; projects set by industry partners that give students "real world" experience; learning through materiality and making (including in digital realms); discipline-specific terminology; design research methodologies; and visual development of work.

These and other design signature pedagogy tools are tremendously powerful in design education: they impact how we teach, how students are socialized and acculturated into design practices, and how professional behaviors and attitudes are shaped. As today's design students will be tomorrow's design professionals, these tools directly impact the future direction of design industries. They also make aspects of pedagogy routine so that teachers and students can spend less time planning and establishing fundamental classroom practices and more time teaching and learning complex subject matter (Shulman, 2005). Their habitual nature simplifies daunting, intricate challenges, thus enabling teachers and students to advance from merely thinking *about* knowledge to thinking *with* knowledge (Shulman, 2005). At the same time, design educators must be aware that such routine can cause rigidity, perpetuate repetitive actions or responses (namely "perseveration," or the act of persisting with an approach in spite of its failure to produce success), and force all types of learning to fit a limited scope of teaching (Shulman, 2005). Therefore, it is imperative that design educators leverage the tools of signature pedagogies to ensure an optimal teaching environment for the design studio. Additionally, design educators must constantly examine their own performance within the signature pedagogies frameworks to ensure they are not falling into the rigidity and limitations that Shulman warns us about above.

## Section III: Design Pedagogy

This section introduces select, key topics that can inform, advance, and strengthen design teachers' pedagogy and students' learning. They include:

- undergraduates' holistic development;
- design students' cognitive and emotional transitions from high school to design school;
- advanced pedagogical methods for design educators;

- preparation and support structures for design educators; and
- leading traits of highly effective educators.

The power of design pedagogy must not be underestimated. As this section will show, the ways we impart knowledge, cultivate teacher-student relationships, form classroom communities, design and facilitate learning, and evolve our pedagogical approaches all leave indelible impressions on students who, as graduates, will shape our design industries. After all, to see the future of design industries, one only needs to observe a classroom as design educators, our teaching—our pedagogies—contribute directly to the creation of our future world.

## References

Anthony, K. (1991). *Design juries on trial: The renaissance of the design studio*. Van Nostrand Reinhold.

Berkeley Graduate Division. (n.d.) Social constructivism. *University of California, Berkeley*. https://gsi.berkeley.edu/gsi-guide-contents/learning-theory-research/social-constructivism/#:~:text=He%20argued%20that%20all%20cognitive, integrated%20into%20a%20knowledge%20community.

Davis, M. (2017). *Teaching design: A guide to curriculum and pedagogy for college design faculty and teachers who use design in their classrooms*. Allworth.

Freire, P. (1970). *Pedagogy of the oppressed*. Herder and Herder.

Orr, S., & Shreeve, A. (2018). *Art and design pedagogy in higher education: Knowledge, values and ambiguity in the creative curriculum*. Routledge.

Pendoley, R. (2019, March 23). If we don't work on pedagogy, nothing else matters. *Age of Awareness*. https://medium.com/age-of-awareness/if-we-dont-work-on-pedagogy-nothing-else-matters-c1a61207ff92

Shulman, L. (2005). Signature pedagogies in the professions. *Daedalus, 134*(3), 52–59.

Vygotsky, L. (1978). *Mind in society: The development of higher psychological processes* (Cole, M., Ed.). Harvard University Press.

Vygotsky, L. (1987). Thinking and speech. In R. Rieber, & A. Carton (Eds.), *The collected works of L.S. Vygotsky* (Vol. 1, pp. 37–285) (N. Minick, Trans.). Plenum. (Original work published 1934).

Wray, D. (2006). Looking at learning. In J. Arthur, T. Grainger, & D. Wray (Eds.), *Learning to teach in the primary school* (pp. 46–56). Routledge.

# 11 Young Adult Development

## Introduction

Despite the fact that undergraduates commonly experience complex cognitive and emotional development during their college years, there has been relatively scant research investigating development in the eighteen to twenty-five-year-old age-group—the time when "emerging adulthood" is commonly marked (Arnett, 2004). The first scholarly conference discussing this age demographic was held in 2003 (Arnett, 2004). However, during the past decade, this distinct period of young adulthood has been studied increasingly by researchers whose advanced scientific findings are enabling educators in higher education to better understand and subsequently support their students.

For young adults, this period consists of biological, social, and cultural development, as well as cognitive and emotional. Research shows the top three measures of achieving adulthood are assessing one's abilities to make independent decisions, become financially independent, and accept responsibilities for one's self (Arnett, 2004). These formative years can be especially unstable and emotionally turbulent for those who are transitioning out of the family home and into the college lifestyle. Undergraduates, particularly those who move away from home to attend college, often are not accustomed to several factors that can greatly impact their development, namely the long periods of time away from family and friends, the extended hours of instruction, the greater academic demands, and the heightened peer competition. Successfully navigating this adjustment and its accompanying developmental processes typically requires greater autonomy, self-reliance, and the setting aside of childhood fantasies by adopting a more realistic lifestyle that comports with the changing life requirements on the part of the student (Marcia, 1980). (See Chapter 12 for a comprehensive overview about design students' experiences during college.)

Young adulthood also affords diverse opportunities to explore issues of selfhood (Chickering, 1981). This period is commonly used as a temporary delay in the maturation of individuals, one in which they learn to meet obligations and make adult commitments before becoming full

DOI: 10.4324/9781003049166-14

adults (Erikson, 1968). It can be during this phase that individuals undergo radical identity change through exploration, engagement with life offerings, and "free-role experimentation" so that they may establish enduring decisions (Erikson, 1968). For most young people, this period preceding the full commitment to adulthood is an exciting opportunity for them to discover and transform themselves. Among design students, for example, it is not uncommon for them to explore and change their creative and artistic preferences, professional and personal goals, and styles of personal appearance. Thus, identity is never static and it is always evolving for young adults in this stage of development (Marcia, 1980).

The attendant developmental shifts in selfhood can, however, prove challenging for many young adults. Feelings of instability commonly arise during this period as identity formation requires changing the way one functions in the world, questions their values, and alters their habits (e.g. Erikson, 1968). Concurrently, these young adults must engage regularly in activities that are increasingly complex so they gain greater competence in preparation for full adulthood (Hamilton & Hamilton, 2004). These feelings intensify due to the psychosocial transition from the dependent world of adolescence into the more self-directed lifestyle of adulthood (e.g. Arnett, 2004). Marcia (1980) notes a positive self-construction of this identity is critical: if one's identity is underdeveloped or weak, "the more confused the individual is and likely to rely on external sources for self-evaluation" (p. 159).

## The Emergent Generation of Design Students

While the aforementioned developmental processes and attendant characteristics can be found across recent generations of young adults, current undergraduates possess distinct and unique attributes due to living in a remarkably different world than the one inhabited by earlier generations. Today's students "grew up in an era of school shootings, the Great Recession, the Occupy Wall Street movement, protests over police brutality, and the legalization of gay marriage—all streamed on their devices and followed through hashtags on social media—making today's students worried about money, anxious about the future, and more inclusive of differences in identity" (Selgino, 2018, p. 8).

The section below presents select key attributes commonly found in the emergent generation of young adults. It is important to note that while these attributes have been observed in large populations participating in diverse research studies, they are presented as generalizations and not absolutes. After all, not every person experiences the same situations or environments in the same way. However, it is by acquiring a general understanding of and sensitivity toward these common attributes that design educators will be better prepared for working with this unique student generation.

## A Greater Focus on Diversity, Inclusion, and Social Justice

College students today are part of "the most diverse generation in modern American history, and its members are attentive to inclusion across race, ethnicity, sexual orientation and gender identity" (Selgino, 2018, p. 4). The pluralistic racial and ethnic makeup of the US has been, and will continue to be, ever-shifting; for example, between 2016 and 2050, predictions show a decreasing percentage of the population who are White (down 22%) and increasing percentages among those who are Hispanic/Latinx (up 44%), Black or African American (up 7%), Asian (up 50%), and "other" race or mixed races (up 67%) (United States Census Bureau, 2018, as cited in Poston, 2020).

These and other societal changes—including the #MeToo and Black Lives Matter movements, national policy debates on immigration, the US electing its first African American president, emerging awareness of transgender rights, and gay marriage legislation—are leading young adults to be more attentive to inclusion, diversity, social equality, and human rights. The high level of support for social justice among this generation is suggested by the over 90% of young adults who "strongly agree" or "somewhat agree" that gays and lesbians should have the legal right to adopt a child, the nearly 60% who believe forms and online profiles should include additional gender options beyond the binary "male" and "female," and the 77% who say a company's diversity would be a deciding factor on accepting a job offer (McGregor-Kerr, 2019; Parker & Igielnik, 2020; Stolzenberg et al., 2020). Additionally, the amount of first-year college students who support the abolition of the death penalty has risen by approximately 50% over the past two decades (Sax et al., 1998; Stolzenberg et al., 2019a). This generation's ethos is "we"-centered and one in which the majority of young peoples' concerns center around the well-being of others rather than just themselves (Seemiller & Grace, 2017).

## Perceptions of Career and College

The Great Recession (2008) and the emergence of COVID-19 (2020) reshaped the nation's social, political, and economic landscapes. US industries contracted, students' parents lost jobs and siblings moved back home, and the housing market collapsed. Instead of growing up in a strong economy abundant in financial and professional opportunities, young people were jarred into confronting a highly uncertain and unstable future. As a direct result of these and other cataclysmic events, young adults increasingly prioritize their future financial security: over 85% of teens worry about finding a job and 82% of first-year college students believe "being well off financially" is important, which is an all-time high in a survey going back to 1967 (Twenge, 2017).

Young people's prioritization of their financial futures directly impacts their shifting perceptions of college. Rather than seeing it as a place simply to learn about things of interest and obtain a general education, college is seen by the emergent student generation as a place to obtain the training and education required to be employed fully in stable, in-demand careers (Selgino, 2018). Consequently, since the 2008 Recession, enrollment in the humanities majors has declined, while matriculation into more career-oriented majors has risen: for instance, between 2008 and 2018, the bachelor's degrees conferred in philosophy and English language and literature have dropped by 22% and over 27%, respectively, while there have been marked increases in engineering (up 78%), biological science (up 49%), health professions (up 120%), and computer science (up 107%) during the same period (National Center for Education Statistics [NCES], 2019). This generation's pragmatism is directly influencing their perceptions of a college degree's value and its ability to provide future job security and professional success. A recent survey found 67% of young adults (10% higher than the previous generation) believe college is an important stepping-stone to future success and only 25% (38% less than the previous generation) believe they can have a rewarding career without going to college (Pearson, 2018). It is of no surprise, then, that nearly 70% of young people in the US enroll in college immediately following high school graduation—40% more than just two generations prior, in 1980 (NCES, 2020).

While college-bound students may deem their college education as "essential," these students are also more averse to debt than past generations. This cohort wants to avoid the exorbitant student loans assumed by previous undergraduates and widely publicized by the media. In fact, "[l]ess than a fifth of teens expect loans to be the main way they pay for college" and "less than half of freshmen who started college in 2016 took out loans, compared with 61 percent in 2001" (Selgino, 2018, p. 19). The Great Recession and COVID-19 decimated many families' college savings, making paying for college even more challenging for students and more pressing that they get the most out of the experience—an experience that can deliver a significant return on investment in the form of jobs with living wages and career stability.

To mitigate costs and debt, prospective students are comparing the "deals" and optimal scholarship packages that colleges and universities are now offering them, at a level unseen by any other generation. High school students' worries about college costs are so high that nearly 60% of them now save for college and approximately 20% feel the cost of higher education is the top societal concern, above unemployment, healthcare costs, and other endemic worries felt across the US (Romney, 2018; Selgino, 2018). Young people today confront a radically different predicament of affording college compared to previous generations, such as Baby Boomers, who could pay their college tuition, room, and board simply by working summer jobs. Among those who forgo college altogether, a staggering 75% cite financial concerns as the leading reason (Selgino, 2018).

### The Rise of Digital Technology and Attendant Stressors

For the emergent generation, technology is not merely a tool: it is a way of life (Kalkhurst, 2018). Today's young adults represent the first generation to be born after the popularization of the World Wide Web. Subsequently, the widespread use of the Internet and the adoption of smartphones (95% of young adults own or have access to one) are hallmarks of this generation (Anderson & Jiang, 2018). Unlike previous generations, which have had to find ways to integrate these technological tools and have had to reshape their everyday lives around them, today's students are "digital natives"; they were born into and have grown up with personal technology ubiquitous in their lives (Nicholas, 2020). Technological advancements impact users both positively and negatively. The easy accessibility to information and communication channels afforded by the Internet and smartphones enables students to broaden their knowledge base, quickly develop friendships from around the world, be more proactive about their learning, and connect with friends and family more frequently than any previous generation.

At the same time, while these technologies can be beneficial, studies indicate excessive engagement with them can negatively affect the user's well-being. Today, the average person uses their smartphone 20% more often than they did in 2015; each day they spend 195 minutes (3:15 hours) on their device, for a total of over forty-nine days per year (Brandon, 2019; MacKay, 2019). Additionally, 85% of smartphone users check their devices while speaking with friends and family, 80% check them within the first ten minutes of waking up, 40% look at their devices while driving, and 25% wake up to use them at night (Brandon, 2019; Wheelwright, 2021). Among teens in particular, approximately 33% bring their phones to bed at night, 45% say they are online on a near-constant basis (a figure that nearly doubled in the four years between 2014 and 2018), and average over seven hours of waking time of screen media per day (Anderson & Jiang, 2018; Brandon, 2019; Rideout & Robb, 2019).

The extreme usage of smartphones, particularly the frequency of electronic messaging sent and received, prevents people from feeling "unplugged" and can make them seem less present during any given situation in real life; the constant influx of messages on these phones engenders in people a state of anxiety and urgency to respond, no matter the recipient's present situation and activity. As one doctor asserted, "In the past, you may go out and meet with your friends and talk about something, but when you got home you'd go to sleep. The difficulty now is you can't really turn things off. We don't necessarily have downtimes to recharge and get our bearings straight again" (Thompson, 2017, n.p.). Remaining forever "on" via smartphones has become a normative behavior for many people, subsequently elevating stress levels that weaken cognitive, physical, and emotional health (Levitin, 2015). Teens are especially vulnerable: 33% of those who spend two hours or more per day on electronic devices are likely to have at least one suicide-related incident, and for those using devices five or more hours per day (versus one hour), they are 66% more likely to have at least one suicide-related incident (Twenge et al., 2018).

Social media platforms—which are often used to showcase subscribers' seemingly "perfect" lives and enable them to give and receive validation and reassurance through streams of "likes" and positive comments—contribute further to excessive screen time, deteriorating mental health, and changing social and interpersonal dynamics. Since 2007, 189% more first-year undergraduates spend six or more hours per week engaging with their digital social networks, with approximately one-third of them spending eleven or more hours per week using social media (Pryor et al., 2007; Stolzenberg et al., 2019b). The correlation between time spent on these platforms and users' well-being is evident: data reveals incoming undergraduates who spent two hours or fewer on social media during their senior year of high school were 11.7 percentage points less likely to feel anxious than those who spent eleven hours or more (Stolzenberg et al., 2019b) (Figure 11.1).

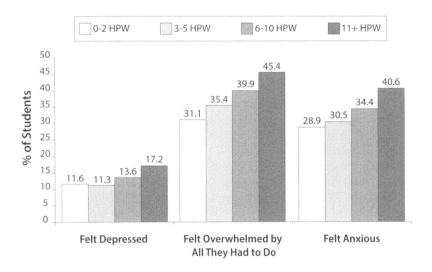

*Figure 11.1* Emotional well-being, by hours per week using social media (% indicating "frequently").

Source: Adapted from Stolzenberg et al. (2019b).

For some users, the abundance of "perfect" online personas that are viewed over extended periods of time becomes "normalized" by the viewer, who then compares themselves to these personas and inevitably feels as if they are "less than" the people behind these personas. As a result, this causes harm to their sense of self and level of confidence. For example, in one survey, responses from the women participants showed that an increased use of social media is linked to decreased self-assessed intellectual self-confidence (49.7% for zero to two hours and 45.5% for eleven or more hours rating their intellectual self-confidence as at least above average) (Stolzenberg et al., 2019b). In another study, the number of teens "who agreed with the statement, 'I feel like I can't do anything right' reached all-time highs in recent years, zooming upwards after 2011"—precisely when smartphones became ubiquitous and screen time surged among teens (Twenge, 2017, p. 100). Within the classroom, design educators frequently describe the emergent student generation as being increasingly reluctant to speak in class, take risks on assignments, and commit to decisions in their work because they might be "wrong," make a "mistake," or be "bad" at the associated task. This shift in behavior is likely attributable to their worries that they will not be "perfect" like everyone else—who they see only positive depictions of online. In fact, when over 600 college professors were surveyed by McGraw-Hill Education in 2017, 70% stated students were less willing to ask questions and participate in class than they were five years earlier (Stolzenberg et al., 2020).

The stark increasing use of (and sometimes addiction to) screen time is contributing to students' decreasing in-person socialization skills. These are interactions that allow individuals to build social skills, develop empathy, learn and understand body language, navigate emotions, and create relationships. In 2020, compared to those in 1998, 81% more young people socialized with friends for five or less hours per week, 47% fewer students spent sixteen or more hours per week socializing, and 74% fewer students spent six hours or more per week partying (Sax et al., 1998; Stolzenberg et al., 2020). One outcome of these shifting behavioral patterns has been the 40% decline in the markers for empathy among college students, which has occurred during the past fifteen years, a trend that researchers link to the omnipresence of digital communications (Turkle, 2015). As McGregor-Kerr (2019) asserts, "All in all, [today's young adults] are increasingly disconnected from human relationships" (n.p.).

Face-to-face social interaction is about more than simply cultivating benefits cited above. For decades, medical research has shown that positive social interaction promotes and strengthens physical and emotional health. In one particular study, a strong social connection was found to lead to a 50% increased chance of longevity, an increase in the strength of the body's immune system, faster recovery from disease, elevated levels of self-confidence and empathy, improved emotional regulation skills, and lowered susceptibility to depression and anxiety (e.g. Seppälä, 2020). In a study of undergraduates from 2010 to 2019, it is evident that the decreasing socialization among undergraduates is contributing to a 21% increase of survey respondents reporting they "felt very lonely within the past year" (54.4% and 65.6% in 2010 and 2019, respectively) (American College Health Association [ACHA], 2010a, 2019a). It is no coincidence that undergraduates who self-reported their general health as either "very good" or "excellent" decreased by 25%, while those who self-reported it as "fair" or "poor" jumped by 143% during the same nine-year period (ACHA, 2010b, 2019b). Whichever came first—the generation's increasing feelings of depression, anxiety, and loneliness or the extreme amounts of time spent on smartphones and social media—there is a clear link between well-being and screen time.

## The Multitasking Lifestyle and Its Subsequent Impact on Cognition

Researchers speculate one reason why people aren't "unplugging" from screen time and thus contribute to these rising statistics is because multitasking has become an expected, normative behavior in US society. Americans widely believe engagement in multiple activities simultaneously will increase productivity. However, studies reveal multitasking can actually *reduce* productivity by as much as 40% (Cherry, 2020; Rubinstein et al., 2001). This is partly due to the brain's neurological functions; specifically, when a person learns anything new while multitasking, the new knowledge is transmitted to the wrong part of their brain required to store the information for use in the future. So, if a student studies while watching television, the information from the coursework enters the striatum (a region of the brain for storing new procedures and skills, but not facts and ideas) rather than the hippocampus (where new information is stored and organized in ways that make it easier to retrieve facts and ideas). The impairment of cognition during multitasking was shown in another study that revealed heavy multitaskers were worse at sorting out relevant information from irrelevant details (Ophir et al., 2009). Moreover, the time wasted by multitasking can be considerable. Studies show it takes a person approximately twenty-three minutes to resume tasks at the depth where they left off following an interruption (Mark et al., 2008). The seemingly harmless activities of replying to texts, reading an email, or clicking between smartphone screens while performing schoolwork can waste enormous amounts of time while simultaneously exacerbating mental fatigue and stress among students.

Thus, when a design student's attention is spread across multiple tasks rather than "unitasking," they are unable to focus on their design work itself, and a sequence of negative consequences occurs. For example, assignments take longer to complete, subsequently decreasing the amount of time available for socialization and rest. The student can experience mental and creative exhaustion due to dropping in and out of the material and having to recall what was just recently reviewed or created. Memory and creativity are impaired due to the divided attention and, consequently, academic performance declines. Conversely, studies reveal people who practice mindfulness, which employs the process of unitasking, remember their work better, are more efficient with their time and accomplish more in the same amount of time, experience fewer negative emotions when undertaking the work, and produce work that is usually more creative and of higher quality (Konnikova, 2012; Levitin, 2015). There is mounting evidence that suggests simply *having* the opportunity to multitask is harmful to cognitive performance. As one study found, the distraction caused by a student's knowledge of an unread email in their inbox while trying to study can reduce that student's intelligence quotient (IQ) by ten points (Levitin, 2015).

## *An Unprecedented National Mental Health Crisis*

Such factors as these (e.g. a tenuous financial climate, extreme screen time, and decreasing socialization) are causing undergraduates to experience emotional challenges like never before. Incoming college students' self-reported emotional health has continued to decline over the past three decades. In 2016, for the first time ever, the majority of undergraduates described their mental health as "below average" (Twenge, 2017). The ACHA's annual surveys (2010a, 2019a) of approximately 48,000 undergraduates at ninety-three US institutions display particularly dramatic changes in students' well-being. In just nine years, there were increases in those "feeling things were hopeless" (up by 27%), who "felt overwhelming anxiety" (up by 42%), who "felt so depressed that it was difficult to function" (up by approximately 60%), who cited anxiety and depression as academic impacts (up by 70% and 102%, respectively), and who "seriously considered suicide" (up by 122%). The swift increase of suicide is especially alarming; the national suicide rate among persons aged ten to twenty-four years old was statistically stable from 2000 to 2007 but increased by 57.4% between 2007 and 2018 (Curtin, 2020). Suicide is the second-leading cause of death among college-aged students, with an estimated 1,100 undergraduates in the US taking their own lives annually (David, 2019; Seelye, 2018).

The emotional health crisis among young people is further evidenced by the increasing number of students seeking help. A recent survey of approximately ninety US colleges showed that in just six academic years (Fall 2009 to Spring 2015), counseling center utilization increased by an average of 30%–40%, while enrollment increased by only 5% (Center for Collegiate Mental Health [CCMH], 2021). It can be difficult for students to gain access to counseling. In a survey of 476 colleges, students must typically wait six business days for their first appointment with a counselor (though at some colleges the wait for a first appointment can take nearly two months) and approximately half (46%) provide students an average limit of twelve psychological sessions per academic year—a grossly inadequate amount to significantly reduce the mental health crisis that is escalating across US campuses (LeViness et al., 2020).

It behooves institutions to increase mental health services, as they can make a profound impact on the student population, particularly with regard to student retention rates. A recent survey at over 200 campuses showed nearly "two-thirds of center clients report that counseling services helped them remain in school and helped them improve their academic performance. This is evidence that counseling services are functioning as a 'high impact practice' that directly and positively impacts student retention and engagement" (LeViness et al., 2020, p. 23). Faculty must learn as much as they can about this critical stage of life by taking classes that examine young adult development and mental health. This will equip faculty better to identify and assist students in need. Once this goal is met, they can help guide students to the appropriate campus services.

## *Prolonging Adolescence*

In the US, young adults are growing up in a world filled with turmoil that has rarely been seen in the past. They were born into a post-9/11 nation. They grew up witnessing escalating public shootings and terrorism. They use smartphones that facilitate near-constant communication. They are confronting an increasingly arduous and financially volatile job market while observing unprecedented levels of political and social discord. These, and a myriad of other factors, are instilling pronounced worry and fear in the emergent generation. This is leading them to focus on and prioritize more acutely their physical and emotional safety and security (e.g. Twenge & Park, 2019).

This greater focus is suggested by the rising numbers of young people choosing to delay certain lifetime milestones in US culture that commonly signify one's passage from adolescence into early adulthood. Rather than taking risks and challenges, they are making choices that require relatively low risk and can provide greater physical and emotional safety and comfort. For example, between 1989 and 2020, fewer twelfth graders obtained a driver's license (down by 29%), tried alcohol (down by 34%), or had a paid job (down by 33%) (Miech et al., 2021) (Figure 11.2). Additional data shows between 1990 and 2016, fewer twelfth graders went out without their parents (down by almost 7%)

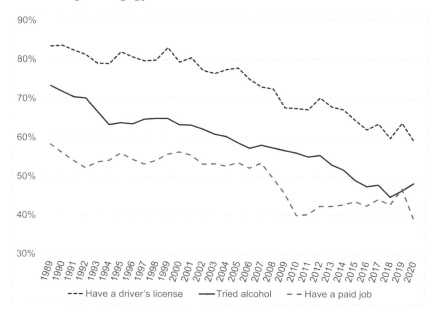

*Figure 11.2* Percentage of twelfth-grade students who have a driver's license, who have ever tried alcohol, and who have a paid job, 1989–2020

Source: Miech et al. (2021).

or on dates (down by approximately 25%), and fewer had sexual intercourse (down by nearly 24% across all high school levels) (Twenge & Park, 2019). These statistics are important in that they demonstrated the significant decline in engagement by the emergent generation in the "adult-like" activities that inherently challenge and prepare young people for adulthood by providing opportunities for greater responsibility, independence, and stronger interpersonal skills.

In keeping with this theme of reduced risk, current students are notably less likely to want to engage in dissenting viewpoints. Over the past few years, there has been a spike in disinviting (or attempting to disinvite) speakers across US campuses. The main driver for this is the fact that the students find the speakers' topics or backgrounds unsettling, challenging, or controversial. In the four-year periods of 2000–2004 and 2016–2019, there were 47 and 145 attempted and completed disinvitations, respectively, an increase of 209% (Foundation for Individual Rights in Education, 2021). The reasons for these incidents vary but, as Twenge (2017) asserts, "[m]any disinvitations are framed in terms of preserving the 'health' or 'safety' of students—usually not physical health or safety but emotional health or safety" (pp. 155–156).

Rather than engaging in formative opportunities that typically bolster one's self-confidence, independence, maturity, coping mechanisms, and preparation for full adulthood, the emergent generation is spending more time isolating, more time virtually "socializing" via screen time, more time hanging out with their parents, and more time avoiding and preventing "uncomfortable" conversations. Unlike previous generations of young people, who at an earlier age enthusiastically pursued adulthood so they could feel "grown up," the emergent generation is less eager to do so; one study (Smith et al., 2017, as cited in Twenge, 2017, p. 45), found that today's "college students (vs. students in the 1980s and 1990s) scored markedly higher on a measure of 'maturity fears.' [They] were more likely to agree 'I wish that I could return to the security of childhood' and 'The happiest time in life is when you are a child.' They were less likely to agree 'I would rather be an adult than a child' and 'I feel happy that I am not a child anymore'" (p. 45). For this population, the entire developmental trajectory, from childhood to adolescence to adulthood, is now delayed.

## Conclusion

The relatively short period of young adult development is complex and arduous, yet is vitally formative in students' lives. At its best, the process enables them to "lead healthy, satisfying, and productive [lives], as youth and later as adults, because they gain the competence to earn a living, to engage in civic activities, to nurture others, and to participate in social relations and cultural activities" (Hamilton & Hamilton, 2004, p. 3).

Yet for a growing number of undergraduates, this developmental process is increasingly fraught with challenges, worries, and concerns due in part to their engagement in a radically different world and lifestyle than the previous generations. Consequently, they possess significantly different characteristics, priorities, viewpoints, ideologies, and life goals—along with a need for greater academic and emotional support than their predecessors. To promote students' successful learning and holistic development better, design educators must understand more deeply the characteristics of young adult development, how and why the emergent student generation is different from preceding ones, and then utilize advanced pedagogical methods that can help them strategically address these critical issues in students' lives. Examples of these select pedagogical methods are provided in Chapter 15.

## References

American College Health Association (ACHA). (2010a). *National college health assessment: Fall* 2010 *reference group executive summary*. https://www.acha.org/documents/ncha/ACHA-NCHA-II_ReferenceGroup_ExecutiveSummary_Fall2010.pdf

American College Health Association (ACHA). (2010b). *National college health assessment: Fall* 2010 *reference group data report*. https://www.acha.org/documents/ncha/ACHA-NCHA-II_ReferenceGroup_DataReport_Fall2010.pdf

American College Health Association (ACHA). (2019a). *National college health assessment: Spring* 2019 *reference group executive summary*. https://www.acha.org/documents/ncha/NCHA-II_SPRING_2019_US_REFERENCE_GROUP_EXECUTIVE_SUMMARY.pdf

American College Health Association (ACHA). (2019b). *National college health assessment: Spring* 2019 *reference group data report*. https://www.acha.org/documents/ncha/NCHA-II_SPRING_2019_US_REFERENCE_GROUP_DATA_REPORT.pdf

Anderson, M., & Jiang, J. (2018). Teens, social media & technology 2018. *Pew Research Center*. http://www.pewinternet.org/2018/05/31/teens-social-media-technology-2018/

Arnett, J. J. (2004). *Emerging adulthood: The winding road from the late teens through the twenties*. Oxford University.

Brandon, J. (2019, November 19). These updated stats about how often you use your phone will humble you. *Inc*. https://www.inc.com/john-brandon/these-updated-stats-about-how-often-we-use-our-phones-will-humble-you.html

Center for Collegiate Mental Health (CCMH). (2021, January). *2021 Annual report*. https://ccmh.psu.edu/assets/docs/2020%20CCMH%20Annual%20Report.pdf

Cherry, K. (2020, March 26). How multitasking affects productivity and brain health. *Dotdash Verywell*. https://www.verywellmind.com/multitasking-2795003

Chickering, A. W. (1981). *The modern American college: Responding to new realities of diverse students and a changing society*. Jossey-Bass.

Curtin, S. C. (2020, September 11). State suicide rates among adolescents and young adults aged 10–24: United States, 2000–2018. *National Vital Statistics Reports*, 69(11), 1–10.

David, E. (2019, October 9). Rising suicide rates at college campuses prompt concerns over mental health care. *ABC News*. https://abcnews.go.com/Health/rising-suicide-rates-college-campuses-prompt-concerns-mental/story?id=66126446

Erikson, E. H. (1968). *Identity: Youth and crisis*. Norton.

Foundation for Individual Rights in Education. (2021). *Disinvitation attempts*. https://www.thefire.org/research/disinvitation-database/#home/?view_2_per_page=1000&view_2_page=1

Hamilton, S. F., & Hamilton, M. A. (Eds.). (2004). *The youth development handbook: Coming of age in American communities*. Sage Publication.

Kalkhurst, D. (2018, March). Engaging Gen Z students and learners. *Pearson Higher Education*. https://www.pearsoned.com/engaging-gen-z-students/

Konnikova, M. (2012, December 15). The power of concentration. *The New York Times*. https://www.nytimes.com/2012/12/16/opinion/sunday/the-power-of-concentration.html

LeViness, P., Gorman, K., Braun, L., Koenig, L., & Bershad, C. (2020). AUCCCD annual survey: 2019. *The Association for University and College Counseling Center Directors*. https://www.aucccd.org/assets/documents/Survey/2019%20AUCCCD%20Survey-2020-05-31-PUBLIC.pdf

Levitin, D. (2015). *The organized mind: Thinking straight in the age of information overload*. Viking.

MacKay, J. (2019, March 21). Screen time stats 2019: Here's how much you use your phone during the workday. *RescueTime*. https://blog.rescuetime.com/screen-time-stats-2018/

Marcia, J. (1980). *Handbook of adolescent psychology*. Wiley and Sons.

Mark, G., Gudith, D., & Klocke, U. (2008). The cost of interrupted work: More speed and stress. In *Proceedings of the SIGCHI Conference on Human Factors in Computing Systems*, 107–110.

McGregor-Kerr, P. (2019, September 3). Gen Z: What to expect from the next workforce. *Harvard*. https://www.harvard.co.uk/gen-z-workforce/

Miech, R. A., Johnston, L. D., Bachman, J. G., O'Malley, P. M., Schulenberg, J. E., & Patrick, M. E. (2021, October 26) *Monitoring the future: A continuing study of American youth (12th-grade survey), 2020*. Inter-university Consortium for Political and Social Research.

National Center for Education Statistics (NCES). (2019). *Bachelor's degrees conferred by postsecondary institutions, by field of study: Selected years, 1970–71 through 2017–18*. https://nces.ed.gov/programs/digest/d19/tables/dt19_322.10.asp

National Center for Education Statistics (NCES). (2020). *Recent high school completers and their enrollment in college, by sex and level of institution: 1960 through 2019*. https://nces.ed.gov/programs/digest/d20/tables/dt20_302.10.asp

Nicholas, A. (2020). Preferred learning methods of Generation Z. *Salve Regina University*. https://digitalcommons.salve.edu/cgi/viewcontent.cgi?article=1075&context=fac_staff_pub

Ophir, E., Nass, C., & Wagner, A. D. (2009). Cognitive control in media multitaskers. *Proceedings of The National Academy of Sciences for the United States of America*, 106(37), 15583–15587. https://www.pnas.org/content/pnas/106/37/15583.full.pdf

Parker, K., & Igielnik, R. (2020, May 14). On the cusp of adulthood and facing an uncertain future: What we know about Gen Z so far. *Pew Research Center*. https://www.pewresearch.org/social-trends/2020/05/14/on-the-cusp-of-adulthood-and-facing-an-uncertain-future-what-we-know-about-gen-z-so-far-2/#:~:text=Members%20of%20Gen%20Z%20are,as%20it%20existed%20before%20smartphones

Pearson. (2018, August). *Beyond millennials: The next generation of learners*. https://www.pearson.com/content/dam/one-dot-com/one-dot-com/global/Files/news/news-annoucements/2018/The-Next-Generation-of-Learners_final.pdf

Poston, D. L. (2020). 3 ways the US population will change over the next decade. *PBS*. https://www.pbs.org/newshour/nation/3-ways-that-the-u-s-population-will-change-over-the-next-decade

Pryor, J., Hurtado, S., Sharkness, J., & Korn, W. (2007). The American freshman: National forms Fall 2007. *Higher Education Research Institute, UCLA*. https://www.heri.ucla.edu/PDFs/pubs/TFS/Norms/Monographs/TheAmericanFreshman2007.pdf

Rideout, V., & Robb, M. B. (2019). The Common Sense census: Media use by tweens and teens, 2019. *Common Sense Media*. https://www.commonsensemedia.org/sites/default/files/uploads/research/2019-census-8-to-18-full-report-updated.pdf

Romney, L. (2018). How youth plan to fund college. *College Savings Foundation*. https://www.collegesavingsfoundation.org/press-releases/how-youth-plan-to-fund-college/

Rubinstein, J. S., Meyer, D. E., & Evans, J. E. (2001). Executive control of cognitive processes in task switching. *Journal of Experimental Psychology: Human Perception and Performance*, 27(4), 763–797.

Sax, L., Astin, A., Korn, W., & Mahoney, K. (1998). The American freshman: National norms for Fall 1998. *Higher Education Research Institute, UCLA*. https://www.heri.ucla.edu/PDFs/pubs/TFS/Norms/Monographs/TheAmericanFreshman1998.pdf

Seelye, K. Q. (2018, May 7). M.I.T. is not responsible for student's suicide, court rules. *The New York Times*. https://www.nytimes.com/2018/05/07/us/mit-student-suicide-lawsuit.html

Seemiller, C., & Grace, M. (2017). Generation Z: Educating and engaging the next generation of students. *About Campus*, 22(3), 21–26.

Selgino, J. (2018, September). The new generation of students: How colleges can recruit, teach, and serve Gen Z. *The Chronicle of Higher Education*. https://highland.edu/wp-content/uploads/2018/12/NewGenerationStudent_i.pdf

Seppälä, E. (2020, March 23). *Social connection boosts health. Even when you're isolated*. https://emmaseppala.com/connect-to-thrive-social-connection-improves-health-well-being-longevity/

Smith, A., Bodell, L. P., Holm-Denoma, J., Joiner, T., Gordon, K., Perez, M., & Keel, P. (2017). I don't want to grow up, I'm a [Gen X, Y, Me] kid: Increasing maturity fears across the decades. *International Journal of Behavioral Development*, 41(6), 655–662.

Stolzenberg, E. B., Eagan, M. K., Aragon, M. C., Cesar-Davis, N. M., Jacobo, S., Couch, V., & Rios-Aguilar, C. (2019a). The American freshman: National norms Fall 2017. *Higher Education Research Institute, UCLA*. https://www.heri.ucla.edu/monographs/TheAmericanFreshman2017-Expanded.pdf

Stolzenberg, E. B., Eagan, M. K., Romo, E., Tamargo, E. J., Aragon, M. C., Luedke, M., & Kang, N. (2019b). The American freshman: National norms Fall 2018. *Higher Education Research Institute, UCLA*. https://www.heri.ucla.edu/monographs/TheAmericanFreshman2018.pdf

Stolzenberg, E. B., Aragon, M. C., Romo, E., Couch, V., McLennan, D., Eagan, M. K., & Kang, N. (2020). The American freshman: National norms Fall 2019. *Higher Education Research Institute, UCLA*. https://www.heri.ucla.edu/monographs/TheAmericanFreshman2019.pdf

Thompson, D. (2017, April 17). More Americans suffering from stress, anxiety and depression, study finds. *CBS News*. https://www.cbsnews.com/news/stress-anxiety-depression-mental-illness-increases-study-finds/

Turkle, S. (2015). *Reclaiming conversation: The power of talk in a digital age*. Penguin.

Twenge, J. (2017). *iGen: Why today's super-connected kids are growing up less rebellious, more tolerant, less happy—and completely unprepared for adulthood*. Atria.

Twenge, J., Joiner, T., Rogers, M., & Martin, G. (2018). Increases in depressive symptoms, suicide-related outcomes, and suicide rates among U.S. adolescents after 2010 and links to increased new media screen time. *Clinical Psychological Science*, 6(1), 3–17.

Twenge, J., & Park, H. (2019). The decline in adult activities among U.S. adolescents, 1976–2016. *Child Development*, *90*(2), 638–654.

United States Census Bureau. (2018). *2017 national population projections tables: Main series.* https://www.census.gov/data/tables/2017/demo/popproj/2017-summary-tables.html

Wheelwright, T. (2021, April 21). Cell phone behavior in 2021: How obsessed are we? *Reviews.org.* https://www.reviews.org/mobile/cell-phone-addiction/#:~:text=re%20not%20alone.-,On%20average%2C%20Americans%20check%20their%20phones%20262%20times%20per%20day,ve%20fallen%20into%20our%20screens

# 12 Students' Transition from High School to Design School

### Introduction: Two Discordant Worlds

Design students often feel disconnected upon reaching their design programs. This is a direct result of the discordant academic emphases between their high school and undergraduate design experiences.

Across the US, design higher education is responding to the design industries' need for professionals who are able to create innovative products, rethink business systems, and understand the broader business and environmental contexts of their industries. The technological advances and expanding access to the global marketplace that spiked during the first decade of the 21st century afforded designers increased opportunities globally to outsource the production of their goods at greatly accelerated rates and reduced costs. Globalization eliminated certain kinds of work in the US altogether and led to the consequential "knowledge-based economy" of today, in which design innovation is critical for sustaining successful operations, both within the traditional design industries and across many other industries as well (see Chapter 3 for a full discussion).

In response to the knowledge-based economy and design industries' attendant demands, many US design schools are augmenting their undergraduate curricula rooted in Bauhaus principles (which emphasize the practical skills of learning by making) with the conceptual skills that prioritize design thinking and interdisciplinary practice. Across all years of undergraduate study, fundamental design skills (e.g. drawing and prototyping) are co-taught with skills and subject areas that promote design thinking; these include advanced research methodologies, conceptualization, ethics, philosophy, sustainability, sociology, and global issues. This increased application of interdisciplinary practice encourages students to "understand the socio-cultural, political, and commercial implications that design can have in society" and to become innovators and social entrepreneurs in the new design industries (Muratovski, 2010, p. 385).

DOI: 10.4324/9781003049166-15

Despite this evolution occurring across US design education, the majority of the nation's high school art/design education (particularly those in public systems) has remained unchanged for decades. Curricula across the nation's high schools remain focused on honing students' technical and vocational skills (such as perspective drawing, digital aptitudes, and craftsmanship) rather than on incorporating the aforementioned skillsets prioritized by design schools and sought by design industries. Course syllabi commonly feature highly prescribed assignments that emphasize observational drawing, realistic representation, and uniform project outcomes so that students fulfill the requirements of rigid learning agendas. Because high schools have remained unresponsive to the advances occurring in design higher education and industry, the accompanying art/design curricula poorly prepare students for their transition into the "conceptual deep-end" of design school.

These discordant academic foci cause many design students to experience pronounced difficulties during their transition from high school to design school because they must leap across the ever-widening chasm between the two contrasting educational environments with little guidance. Furthermore,

> the deeply rooted beliefs and attitudes towards design education and practice these students developed and nurtured throughout their formative years of pre-college studies must now yield to new—and at times, radically different—beliefs, methodologies, and emphases. The associated cognitive and emotional demands can be destabilizing because students' ways of existing within and understanding the world around them are upset by the foisting of new mindsets, creative processes, and assessment criteria for what constitutes "successful" design work. As a result, most first-year design students undergo multiple crises during which they question their personal identities, academic competencies, career choices, and life goals.
>
> (Faerm, 2020, pp. 61–62)

Thus, many first-year design students' academic and personal experiences are compromised—which is particularly damaging as the transitional period occurs during a period in their lives when they are also undergoing extensive personal development. Rather than experiencing a smooth cognitive and emotional transition from high school to design school, these students must overcome unnecessary and preventable challenges.

This chapter examines design students' transition between high school and design school by illuminating the common challenges and experiences unique to first-year design undergraduates, including: students' academic preparation; the curricular and pedagogical contrasts between the US secondary- and tertiary-level art and design education; the features and impacts of support systems; and students' cognitive and emotional development during their first year of design school. In conclusion, recommendations are provided for pre-college and undergraduate educators, directors, and programs on how to adopt key strategic initiatives to improve their students' transition to design school.

## The Emotional and Cognitive Development of First-Year Design Students

> I never knew it would be so different, so difficult, and so memorable.
> (Design school senior, in Faerm, 2020)

### Research Background

Most available data about undergraduates' first-year experiences are typically acquired by surveying students across all institutional types. However, a study by this author (Faerm, 2020) examines the experiences and challenges unique to students at design schools specifically. Engaging nearly 150 design school undergraduates and alumni through surveys, focus groups, and case studies, the data collected in this study was analyzed using Perry's (1970) Theory of Intellectual and Ethical Development, a sequential continuum that illustrates the process of learning that is common among undergraduates (Figure 12.1).

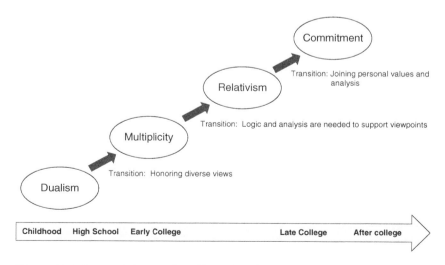

*Figure 12.1* Perry's Scheme of Intellectual and Ethical Development.

The scheme consists of the four states (or "positions") of students' experience, namely dualism, multiplicity, relativism, and commitment in relativism. They include:

1 **Dualism.** Students view knowledge in concrete and dichotomous terms such as good/bad and right/wrong. Learning is an information exchange: knowledge is seen as facts given by authorities (teachers) who possess the "correct" answers. Students view their role as one that requires them to memorize correct answers and deliver them back accurately. They view every problem as solvable yet often defer to authorities for the solution or answer.

2 **Multiplicity.** Students move into this second stage when cognitive dissonance occurs (e.g. when experts disagree, or the teacher does not have all the answers). Students honor diverse views when the right answer is not yet known. All opinions are valid, there are conflicting answers, and peers become more legitimate sources of knowledge. Students learn how to find the right answer on their own, think more independently, and begin to construct analytical thought processes. Although students still seek the "correct" answers, they put more trust in their "inner voice" rather than automatically deferring to authority for the solution.

3 **Relativism.** The move into this third stage occurs when the student recognizes the need to support opinions through reasoning methods and logical analysis. All opinions no longer appear equally valid, and the use of evidence and argument allows the student to evaluate the validity of different viewpoints. Knowledge and solutions are defined more contextually and qualitatively. In this stage, students question their own viewpoints as well as their teachers', who still are valued experts, but whose opinions now are open to scrutiny.

4 **Commitment in Relativism.** The final stage involves the integration of knowledge learned from others with personal experiences and reflection to arrive at conclusions. These conclusions (and subsequent commitments) in areas such as politics, careers, and relationships are made by recognizing intrapersonal diversity of goals, interests, and needs. As such, this stage can be viewed as initiating ethical development made from the vantage point of relativism rather than increasing cognitive complexity (Evans et al., 2010). Additionally, there is an acceptance of uncertainty and the tentative nature of life. Students place value on their ongoing development and an openness to new experiences.

Undergraduates typically move through some or all of these positions during the college years, though some may "stall" or "retreat" during the progression if they experience a lack of confidence or feel overwhelmed. In these scenarios, challenging the student's current thinking

144  Design Pedagogy

while offering support that encourages risk-taking and lessens the likelihood of retreating can promote successful advancement from one position to another (King, 1978).

Although Perry's stages of development are commonly found in most undergraduates across diverse academic institutions, certain characteristics and experiences are unique to first-year design students. For them, the college experience involves distinct challenges that consequently affect their cognitive and emotional development before, during, and after their transition from high school to design school.

*Pre-College Experiences*

In the study mentioned above, prior to design school, nearly all (95%) of the study's participants stated they studied art/design, and a full 75% indicated they took art/design courses offered by their high schools. Despite this widespread preparatory experience, nearly one in five (19%) stated their high school-level art/design courses—described as "rudimentary," "superficial," and "lacking depth"—left them ill-prepared for the demands of design school. In fact, just 17% of participants stated their high schools taught conceptual thinking, which is a key component of design school coursework. In contrast, a vast majority of students reported that their high school art/design assignments were "textbook-ish" projects that prioritized representational work, drawing from observation, and students' standardized project outcomes that adhered to mandated learning goals. To access diverse creative approaches—a principal element sought by design schools in applicants' portfolios—a significant quantity of participants (48%) enrolled in supplementary external pre-college programs (e.g. summer courses). The shortcomings of high school-level art/design education were so pronounced among participants that it led some to believe acceptance to design school is unlikely *unless* one enrolls in such extra-curricular coursework.

While participants noted that these and other hurdles had varying degrees of impact on their development, one widespread challenge stood out above all others: the dearth of practical and emotional support for students when they applied to design schools. High school advisors, frequently described by participants as uninformed about design schools, instead encouraged students to pursue more conventional professions at traditional colleges—*particularly* if the student achieved high academic performance. This lack of support left students feeling alone and as if they had to "fend for themselves." As one student expressed, "I informed [my advisor] of my interest in design, and the only thing she did for me was pull out a book of universities I should consider. All of the pre-college preparation was the result of the efforts of myself." Another noted, "[During high school] I was told by a guidance counselor…women choose to major in art to get their 'Mrs. Degree.' [He] though because

I had good S.A.T. scores, I should choose a 'normal' university and a different career/major path." The advisors' lack of knowledge and, at times, negative stereotypes about design careers echoed the concerns of the participants' parents, who questioned both the financial investment of a design school education and the feasibility of professional opportunities after graduation.

Consequently, more than one-third of respondents (38%) and one in five (20%) cited their advisors and parents, respectively, as the *least* helpful for their transition into design school. For some students, this lack of support—particularly parental support—left them feeling they needed to overachieve in design school, thereby justifying the validity of their academic and professional goals. As one participants described, "[M]y parents were on the fence about spending so much money on design school, so I felt like it was a decision I had to *truly* want and fight for. This maybe helped me because I knew it was a big choice that I was making for myself, and I had to perform." Others felt the challenges ultimately strengthened their holistic development because, as one stated, "it taught me that I had to be independent if I was going to pursue a career in design. And, in design school, you have to be self-motivated [to succeed]!" For some students, this need for increased independence boosted their confidence and subsequently their self-directedness.

### *The Curricular Gap Between Academic Levels*

Upon entering design school, the stark contrasts between high school- and college-level design education—pedagogy, course assignments, learning goals, assessment criteria, and critique methods—were immediately felt by students. Their high school's "straightforward assignments" that "did not allow for out-of-the-box thinking" and required them to "translate what you CAN see before you" within highly prescribed parameters (e.g. media and format that prioritized technical proficiency through realistic representation rather than creativity or personal expression) were suddenly replaced by abstract, conceptual project briefs in design school; these assignments required first-year undergraduates to formulate and defend highly personal and innovative project deliverables that were assessed through radically different rubrics than those used in high school.

This commonly experienced pedagogical dissonance was widely criticized by study participants, with one asserting, "It really felt like starting this life from scratch. In high school, [art/design] class was all about learning techniques, but [design school] is where I learned what a concept is and how to develop it." The severity of the pedagogical gap is suggested by the nearly 50% of survey participants who selected "learning new art/design coursework/subjects" as one of the *most* challenging aspects of the transitional experience. The students' inexperience with conceptualization resulted in an accelerated "crunch period" during which they needed to grasp these new ways of thinking quickly during a condensed amount of time in the first year—thus intensifying their emotional, physical, and mental stress. One student, reflecting on his very first assignment in design school, stated:

> [W]e had a class where we had to do a *lot* of conceptual thinking. Really intense theory-thinking and that's when I felt everything was so overwhelming. [The first assignment] was: "How do you measure time?" I was stumped with that! That was one of the first times I was *really* overwhelmed…and freaked out just because each week I'd go to class and continue hitting a wall, and my teacher would see it and bring it up. They're just like, "Oh, I see you're really struggling with this." But…you get to that point where you're like, "I have *no* idea where to go with this."

For many of these design students, their inexperience with conceptualization often generates substantial amounts of stress. Unlike typical undergraduates, the design students' inexperience with conceptual design thinking—and the consequential need to master the skillset rapidly during a condensed amount of time in the first year—means they had to devote additional hours to their already high academic workloads in order to compensate for this inexperience. This accelerated crunch period intensified stress in all areas of the students' lives. Additionally, the narrow focus of design studies—unlike high school coursework that spanned multiple subjects—creates a difficult phase of adjustment for students and increases any existing psychological or emotional challenges they are already facing. Participants shed light on the experience by noting, "I realized that creative thinking…could actually be more stressful than working on essays or studying for math tests," and, "It was exhausting being creative 24/7 for five different classes all focused on creating art/design. It *really* took a toll on me emotionally."

Moreover, the shifted understanding for what constitutes successful work required students to replace previous values, mindsets, and practices instilled during their formative years of high school with new ones promoted by design school. The radical pivot in mindset—and related sense of personal identity—exacerbated the typical first-year challenges they experienced as undergraduates (e.g. homesickness and increased workloads). For example, unlike high school critiques that "lacked depth and meaningful feedback," design school critiques were described by some participants as "intense," "terrifying," "harsh," and "spiteful," and came as culture shock. Students were suddenly expected to present masterfully and defend conceptually driven choices after having spent the entirety of their previous art/design education presenting prescribed responses to tactical assignments. The shift in pedagogical orientation from high school to design school curricula is so great that it led many participants to cite in-class critiques as one of the *biggest* challenges during the first year of design school. As one participant expressed, "it's not just about making. You also have to be able to talk about [your work] conceptually. That's what I had the hardest time with." Many participants, when asked how high school art/design courses could improve, stated secondary-level programs should require students to present their work in similarly structured critique formats, thus enabling them to become comfortable with public speaking well before entering college-level studios.

*Design Students' Personal Development During the First Year*

Although most students entering design school received adequate support primarily targeting practical topics (e.g. "tips for time management"), there was a marked absence of support addressing emotional challenges (e.g. "how to ease homesickness"). For example, despite widespread beliefs that college is the best four years in one's life, participants emphasized feeling "overwhelmed" and "paralyzed" during their first year because, as one described it, "You have no idea what you got yourself into and every day is [an emotional] struggle." Similarly, imposter syndrome—which is pervasive among design students who went from being "star artists" in their high schools to feeling like "small fish in big ponds"—destabilized many students' identities. This caused them to reassess their talent, college choice, and career goals. These feelings were so widespread among research participants that it led many to state their first year, of all their years, contained the greatest level of self-doubt. Yet, for others, the new extreme competition *positively* impacted them; it intensified their desire to prove themselves and to succeed, often resulting in an elevation of their academic performance and self-directed goals.

Students widely cited one especially positive experience during their first year of design school, that of entering a newly supportive community that finally "understood" them. No longer feeling like marginalized "outcasts" in homogeneous hometowns, many participants relished the design school's heterogeneous communities, "meeting other artistically-minded people," and "finally not being a weirdo! Design school helped me find my tribe I still align with today"—thus nurturing each other's personal growth. Students' emotional and cognitive support was better met by the campus community and peer-to-peer support that cultivated trust and long-term friendships. These associations prompted them to advance from dualism (in which the teacher is the sole provider of knowledge) into multiplicity (in which peers become more legitimate sources of knowledge).

Accordingly, there was a marked shift in how first-year design students perceived their roles as learners. Initially, many respondents displayed

148  *Design Pedagogy*

clear dualistic traits, including focusing on pleasing teachers, rather than themselves, and avoiding "incorrect" answers. However, by the end of or immediately following their first year, numerous participants had advanced from the stage of duality to the stage of multiplicity. One student illustrates this shifting mindset when noting:

> [At first,] I worked so hard to please my teachers but not myself. [C]oming from [high school], it's still all about grades. I was still in that zone, even though I said I didn't care about grades. But I feel I was on the verge of figuring it out, like, this is really for *me*. After freshman year, I was finally in the mindset of "I should do what *I* want to do whether or not it pleases someone else."

Another student, echoing this move between stages, believed it occurred as a direct result of being told by others to make her *own* decisions, rather than simply to accept answers given to her. While she felt the progression was uncomfortable and that missteps occurred, her advancement to multiplicity bolstered her confidence, identity, and purpose as a learner. As she expressed, "Toward the end of [first] year, I finally realized that it is my work, it is my time put into it, and my thoughts, ideas, and dreams. I need to worry about making myself happy and trying new things." This pivot from achieving for others to achieving for one's self led students to feel more invested in their self-constructed goals, to experiment and explore more, and ultimately to develop projects they felt were optimal representations of themselves.

In conclusion, when participants were asked if their overall transition into design school was easy and fluid, 40% either "agreed" or "strongly agreed," 41% "somewhat agreed," and almost 20% "disagreed" or "strongly disagreed." Given the majority of design students (approximately 60%) experienced varying levels of challenges during their transition into design school, it is incumbent upon secondary- and tertiary-level design educational institutions and educators to implement actions that better support students' cognitive and emotional development during their transitional experience. The need is particularly salient when contextualized by the growing undergraduate population that is simultaneously preparing for adulthood while prolonging its complete arrival (see Chapter 11 for full discussion).

## Supporting the Student's Transition into Design School

To better support design students during their transition into design school, a series of initiatives—each based on data findings that target the key challenges faced by participants—are recommended below for both secondary- and tertiary-level design educators (Table 12.1).

Table 12.1 Initiatives to support design students' transition into design school

| Education level | Recommendations |
| --- | --- |
| Secondary design education: Junior and senior levels | **Art and design career panels.** Artists and designers present autobiographical "from student-to-practitioner" stories to students, parents, teachers, and guidance counselors. These aim to counter negative stereotypes, demystify professional opportunities, and alleviate anxieties around design studies and future career options. Panelists provide teachers with valuable insights into the future of design practices and education, which can help them develop relevant curricula in secondary-level art/design education. Subsequently, students receive more meaningful guidance on portfolio development and design school applications.<br><br>**Introducing conceptual thinking.** Conceptually focused assignments are incorporated into advanced pre-college coursework to introduce students to diverse research methods, conceptual and speculative thinking, and unorthodox design processes. Advanced coursework may also include interdisciplinary assignments that enable students to cross-over and synthesize disciplines, address global issues, explore systems-thinking, and generate projects that focus exclusively on innovative design process rather than traditional "polished" portfolio pieces. Emphasis is placed on developing a personal, authentic, and unique approach to the coursework rather than meeting strict assignment guidelines for homogenous results from all students.<br><br>**Build a solid critique culture.** Secondary-level art/design teachers should observe critiques at local art and design colleges so they can better understand the new emphases in design education and strengthen their own critique methods and skills. Observing critiques will provide them with meaningful professional development and pedagogical support. A critically-based presentation and critique cultural environment is designed and implemented throughout the advanced levels of art/design coursework. Students' cognitive and emotional development will be strengthened and their future transition into design school will be more fluid and less stressful.<br><br>**Course credit for external art/design coursework.** High schools grant course credit for external art/design courses that meet pre-approved requirements (e.g. learning outcomes, contact hours, etc.). Credit may be given for individual courses (such as intensive summer studies offered by colleges) or for a cluster of courses that, collectively, fulfill academic requirements. The practice will offer great benefit to those students who attend high schools at which, for whatever reason, suggested changes cannot be implemented. The external coursework is necessary for students to develop the required skillsets and competitive portfolios for successful design school applications. |

(Continued)

Students' Transition from High School to Design School   149

150  Design Pedagogy

Table 12.1 Initiatives to support design students' transition into design school (Continued)

| Education level | Recommendations |
| --- | --- |
| Secondary and tertiary design education | **Faculty development workshops about young adult development.** At both levels, institutions provide faculty development workshops that examine the leading theories of young adult development, contemporary research that exists surrounding the generation of incoming students, and the general aspects of emotional and cognitive development that occurs during the transition from adolescence into full adulthood.<br><br>These workshops will provide practical and actionable research-based best teaching practices that respond to the specific attributes, learning styles, and other features of the current student generation.<br><br>**Student development workshops about emotional and cognitive development.** Similar in scope and breadth as those for faculty, these workshops aim to decrease students' sense of feeling imposter syndrome, to increase their confidence around independence and autonomy, and to let them know they are sharing common challenges. By understanding their own developmental trajectories, students will be better able to contextualize their identities, goals, and benchmarks of young adulthood.<br><br>Moreover, design school-level workshops will address those issues not commonly discussed by student services, such as overcoming homesickness and other commonly experienced emotional challenges that occur during the transitional period. |
| Tertiary design education: First year | **Redefining personal success.** Information is provided for students to redefine "success" in the design school context. Focus is on the tools students may adopt to overcome imposter syndrome, talent doubt, and feelings of inadequacy. Students are encouraged to self-define personal success so they can move out of dualism and into higher stages of intellectual and emotional development.<br><br>The materials will promote greater independence and preparation for self-authorship, a key trait of full adulthood. Encouragement of the increase of personal agency will provide students with greater ownership of their academic learning experiences. This will increase feelings of motivation and desire for achievement (see Chapter 18).<br><br>**Peer-to-peer mentorship system.** Upper-level students are paired with first-year students so they may meet regularly and offer support by listening to their challenges, give advice, propose solutions, and provide general guidance. While students may also meet with professional advisors, faculty, and counselors, the peer-to-peer dynamic affords first-year students insights from the more tangible, "lived" experience of the upper-level students. This dynamic fosters privacy, trust, and a sense of candidness; students may feel reluctant to share certain challenges with school administration but will share those challenges with a peer mentor.<br><br>Moreover, given the surge of students seeking support services, particularly for emotional challenges, this initiative offers more immediate support to students *before* seeking student support services (see Chapter 11). |

Source: Faerm (2020).

## Conclusion

It is essential that US secondary education and design higher education closely examine the substantial disconnect between their two pedagogic and curricular emphases. The existing gap creates a disjointed academic experience for students and subsequently imposes undue challenges for many undergraduates during their first year of design school. The implementation of research-led initiatives—such as the adoption of conceptually-driven assignments during the more advanced secondary-levels of art/design studies—will narrow the curricular and pedagogic gaps, thus reducing a significant portion of students' challenges during this period. By adopting the above initiatives, design students' cognitive and emotional development will be better supported during their transition into design school, which will lead to sustained holistic success for young adults.

*A version of this chapter was first published in The International Journal of Design Education, Vol. 14, No. 4.*

## References

Evans, N., Forney, D., & Guido-DiBrito, F. (2010). *Student development in college: Theory, research, and practice.* Jossey-Bass.

Faerm, S. (2020). Students' cognitive and emotional development during the transition from high school to design school. *The International Journal of Design Education*, 14(4), 61–78.

King, P. M. (1978). William Perry's Theory of Intellectual and Ethical Development. *New Directions for Student Services*, 1978(4), 35–51.

Muratovski, G. (2010). Design and design research: The conflict between the principles in design education and practices in industry. *Design Principles and Practices*, 4(2), 377–386.

Perry, W. Jr. (1970). *Forms of intellectual and ethical development in the college years.* Holt, Rinehart, & Winston.

# 13 Developing Competent Pedagogy
## A Web of Practices

### Introduction

Similar to how we hold our students accountable for high-quality performance, we, as design educators, must hold ourselves to the same level of accountability for high-quality teaching. Whether we are first-semester teaching novices, well-seasoned educators, or somewhere in between, our pedagogy requires continuous attention and development. In particular, what constitutes "teaching"—and how these ideas and practices can best address our ever-shifting contexts—must remain the primary question we address. In order to do so, we must seek new input so we can learn how we can improve every interaction we have with students. This chapter, presented in four parts, describes how design educators may strengthen their pedagogy through a triangulation of theory, research, and practice.

"Part 1: What is a 'Teacher'?" outlines the teacher's role beyond that of the perfunctory "knowledge provider" in traditional, teacher-centered learning environments. Today, a new, more advanced role is required to accommodate several key macro factors that actively influence the teaching profession, including the significant changes occurring in US higher education, the evolving attributes of undergraduate design students, and the shift in design industries that require increasingly diversified skillsets from designers. To address these and other increasingly pressing challenges faced by US design education, a more expansive, multifaceted role—the "teacher-mentor"—is presented and discussed.

Next, "Part 2: The Model Three: What We Can Learn from Singapore, South Korea, and Finland" uncovers three nations' internationally extolled educational systems that prepare teachers for this advanced role of "teacher-mentor." Each nation's rigorous tertiary-level teacher preparation programs, emphasis on maintaining strong organizational support systems for entry-level teachers, and ongoing faculty development initiatives are examined. Select strategies are then provided for how US design educators and institutions may successfully leverage these nations' select best practices in teacher preparation, development, and support.

DOI: 10.4324/9781003049166-16

Building on Parts 1 and 2, "Part 3: Critically Reflective Teaching" discusses how design educators can self-develop and hone their pedagogy through the effective, sustainable methods of reflective practice. This part begins with the essential question we must *continuously* ask ourselves as design educators: "How do I know when my teaching is effective and my students are learning?" Critically reflective teaching is examined through its fundamental tenets, the ways it can be promoted, and its subsequent benefits for teachers' pedagogy, students' development, and design schools' success.

To conclude, "Part 4: What Makes an Effective Educator?" contextualizes the previous three parts by situating their key ideas within active teaching practice. Doctor Katherine Boles, former program director at Harvard University's Graduate School of Education, discusses the shared key attributes of the highly effective educators she has known in her fifty-year teaching career. Through examination of these attributes in diverse contexts, core pedagogical attributes can be identified and used by design educators and schools to improve their pedagogy.

## Part 1: What Is a "Teacher"?

What is a "Teacher"? What key roles do they play? How can these roles evolve to better suit the emergent generation of design students? Traditionally, teachers are often perceived as disseminators of information who then assess learning based on students' abilities to accurately reiterate said information. This "banking system" of pedagogy, a term coined by education theorist Paulo Freire, involves the "depositing [of] information into the student brain eventually to be cashed like bank notes at exam and grading time" (Graff, 2003, p. 234). This established system was based on the concept of information scarcity; teachers (particularly pre-Internet) dispersed knowledge to students who had few other ways to access that knowledge (Lanier, 1997). However, the overabundance of free information today from seemingly endless sources has transformed both how students learn and the role of the design educator. The role of the educator has additionally been impacted by the growth of online education, the escalating costs of college tuition, and an increasingly complex and nuanced generation of undergraduates who possess diverse learning styles and needs from teachers. Consequently, the future of design higher education necessitates all design schools and educators to offer compelling reasons for *why* students should choose to enroll in *their* schools and remain in *their* classrooms.

Students' choices of which colleges to attend and programs to enter increasingly center on the quality of design teachers' pedagogy. This, in turn, compels the improvement and recontextualization of the educator's role. The outdated approach of "teaching as telling"—a generalized distribution of facts/skills for subsequent assessment of students' learning

154  *Design Pedagogy*

*Figure 13.1* The studio classroom.
Source: Monkey Business Images/Shutterstock.com.

(a simple transaction)—must give way to uniquely customized pedagogy that is student-centered (a meaningful relationship) (Figure 13.1). This means design educators must remain experts in disciplinary content while fusing their design expertise with artful, targeted, and diverse pedagogy. This synthesis advances the role of the educator. It transitions that role from a siloed "teacher" to that of a holistic "teacher-mentor" who deftly intertwines their disciplinary knowledge with a deep awareness of pertinent aspects of students' emotional and cognitive development. As William Arthur Ward (1921–1994) famously espoused, "The mediocre teacher tells. The good teacher explains. The superior teacher demonstrates. The great teacher inspires."

To develop this advanced teacher-student mentorship model, the following pedagogical methods can be employed:

1  **Educate and develop the whole person**
   Research studies (e.g. Bain, 2004) reveal the best teaching and learning occur when focused attention is given to the intellectual, creative, social, and emotional development of each student—in addition to their professional development. These areas interconnect and complement one another for students' holistic learning and growth. The philosopher Jean-Jacques Rousseau, in his esteemed treatise on education, *Emile* (1762/2002), cites the consequential value of this pedagogical approach when the tutor-narrator states, "Life is the trade

I would teach [my student]. When he leaves me, I grant you he will be neither a magistrate, a soldier, nor a priest; he will be a man" (n.p.). In this model, the teacher's role "is to counsel students as they grow and mature—helping them integrate their social, emotional, and intellectual growth—so the union of these occasionally separate dimensions yields the abilities to seek, understand, and use knowledge; to make better decisions in their personal lives; and to value contributing to society" (Lanier, 1997, n.p.). By incorporating an understanding of the full scope of student development into their pedagogy, design educators better prepare them to flourish as professional, creative, and resourceful individuals—in both the design fields and wider society.

2 **Cultivate relationships with students**
In one study, when asked about the most influential learning experience of their lives, people commonly cited the positive relationships they had with teachers as most important (Bain, 2004). It is critical that educators expose students to new perspectives, inspire reflective moments, provide support during challenging situations, and influence their future goals. To cultivate such rewarding relationships and outcomes as these, design educators must acutely understand each student's unique background, learning style(s), goals, interests, needs, and current level of skills and knowledge.

The focus of these relationships spotlights the need for every student to be identified as a unique individual who aspires to reach their own level of achievement rather than expecting a prescribed and standardized level of achievement across all students. A more targeted and personalized pedagogy can be created by the teacher, one that begins from where the student is and then primes them for digging down to a creative and intellectual depth that is challenging to the student where they currently are, yet is achievable for them. As Dr. Christina Villarreal of Harvard's Graduate School of Education states, "[t]he syllabus is merely a skeleton shaped by [teachers'] lived experiences and expertise, and the muscles, tissues, tendons, and heart come from [their] students" (Hough, 2019).

3 **Create classroom community**
A design student's sense of classroom community can make a significant impact on their academic performance. After all, learning does not happen in the student's mind alone; it also occurs through social interactions with peers, teachers, the school community, and the world at large (Speicher, 2009). For instance, in one study, 87% of student-participants believed the creation of a caring and committed learning community contributed significantly to their successful completion of their programs (Harris, 2001). Similarly, "the largest contributors to student satisfaction and success [are] the caring attitude of the instructor and the supportive environment

156  *Design Pedagogy*

created by fellow students" (Tebben, 1995, as cited in McKinney et al., 2006, p. 281).

What can design teachers do to promote a sense of community among students? Researchers McKinney et al. (2006) assert that the following six elements are required to produce a positive sense of community:

- **Connection.** Throughout the course, teachers create opportunities for students to learn about one another on a personal level beyond rote/perfunctory peer-to-peer classroom engagement (e.g. design critiques, reading discussions).
- **Participation.** Regular class discussions, as pairs or small groups of students, promote a deeper sense of community by allowing participants to share personal insights, ask questions, offer advice, and obtain different perspectives.
- **Safety.** Optimal learning can only happen when students feel the classroom is a supportive "safe space" in which they can take risks, fail without negative judgment, and engage openly.
- **Support.** When students are strategically paired up for short collaborative peer-tutoring opportunities, students' sense of community increases. For example, a student who struggles with drawing could be paired with a highly skilled partner who performs guided demonstrations and shares advice for improvement.
- **Belonging.** A sense of belonging is a prerequisite for a successful community. Asking individual students about their weekends, learning about their other courses, and openly expressing to them the value they each bring to the classroom are examples of ways to bolster their sense of belonging.
- **Empowerment.** Inviting students to codesign select course content, vote on certain course-related issues, plan personalized weekly deliverables that meet due dates, and engage in other areas that provide agency promote feelings of unification, value, and empowerment among students.

### 4  Design learning opportunities

The power of teaching greatly lies in how educators design learning experiences. Strategic, targeted learning experiences need to respond to every unique student cohort and adjust to each individual student. They should provide a diverse array of thoughtfully crafted opportunities for students to develop the skills, creativity, and knowledge required to solve design problems. Contrasted with the aforementioned "banking system," this approach sees teaching as a responsive and carefully engineered environment that employs strategies, tools, and techniques that will support and encourage students' learning.

The more varied and dynamic these learning opportunities are, the greater the probability of students' satisfaction, engagement, motivation, and academic success. Examples of these types of opportunities include group- and individually performed design exercises during class; lectures and presentations; design-related demonstrations; discussion or critique groups containing varied numbers of students; readings; and reflective writing. Activities like these address and support the diverse spectrum of learning styles—including auditory, visual, verbal, logical, kinesthetic, and inter/intrapersonal—throughout the course.

5 Facilitate learning

While design teachers should be authorities, they should not be authoritarians. Whereas the former role enables students to benefit from teachers' advanced knowledge, the latter can undermine students' learning and autonomy, as well as teacher-student dynamics. To ensure a more positive environment, the teacher's role needs to pivot—from that of a "sage-on-the-stage" who broadcasts content for students' passive consumption to that of a "teacher-mentor" who designs and facilitates learning experiences—and thus complement the teacher-student mentorship model. In this model, teachers are facilitators of learning: they observe and occasionally guide students and resist prematurely interjecting their ideas, opinions, and/or solutions during students' quests for knowledge. This enables students to construct their own meanings, relationships, and understandings of the design processes. Consequently, students are able to self-author their educational experiences and become stronger, more resilient, and more flexible designers.

This is not to say design teachers may not teach, only that they may not teach in certain ways—and that teaching involves more than simply feeding information to passive student-consumers. When we, as teachers, choose to stand on the literal and figurative periphery of the class to facilitate and guide students' self-directed learning, a partnership—that of a shared intellectual and creative responsibility—emerges, one which enables both teacher and student to be participatory co-learners who create new knowledge together (Lanier, 1997). Thus, simply by "stepping back," teachers empower students to self-discover and consequently develop greater agency, intrinsic motivation, and subsequent learning. As Brookfield (1995) notes, "[d]iscussions in which teachers are mostly silent are often regarded as the best discussions of all. We walk away from animated conversations dominated by students' voices with a sense that our time has been well spent" (p. 12).

Facilitated leaning can occur in many ways. For example, students may be asked to write their own design briefs to solve; devise in-class design exercises that address predetermined learning objectives; lead peer discussions and debates; and formulate other creative ways to "design their design education" and fulfill course requirements.

Socratic questioning (asking open-ended questions) also facilitates learning and repositions students from passive consumer to active learner. By using this pedagogical method, teachers prompt students to probe beneath their surface-level thinking. Categorically, these Socratic-style questions aim to:

- Clarify thinking and rationale ("Could you put it another way?" or "Can you give an example?");
- Challenge assumptions ("Is that always the case?" or "How did you reach that assumption?");
- Encourage analysis or reasoning through a concept ("How do these approaches compare/contrast?");
- Investigate other viewpoints or perspectives ("What is an alternative?" or "How would ... respond?");
- Probe implications/consequences ("How does ... affect ...?" or "What does this mean for ...?");
- Question the question ("Why do you think I asked ...?").

Engaging in this form of facilitated learning leads students to discover the structure behind their own thoughts, establish and clarify well-reasoned decisions and solutions, and experience metacognition ("thinking about thinking"). Consequently, students experience deeper, more self-directed learning. The result is an elevation in students' autonomy, creativity, and intrinsic motivation.

6  **Instill the love of learning**
The principle, "If we succeed in giving the love of learning, the learning itself is sure to follow," famously expressed by John Lubbock, is fundamental to the teacher-student mentorship model. When teachers promote this feeling in students, the love of learning for the sake of learning marked benefits for the student emerge. These include students' heightened intrinsic motivation; more positive associations with the course and the design discipline itself; higher levels of engagement, effort, and perseverance; and improved academic performance (see Chapter 18). This instilled love of learning extends well beyond design school and remains a lifelong attribute of the professional designer—a significant advantage in the ever-changing design industries that requires designers to possess the most current knowledge.

7  **Constantly question, evolve, and improve pedagogical methods**
As teachers, the pedagogical methods we use to foster meaningful relationships and dynamic learning opportunities must be examined and advanced in an iterative way that results in an ongoing improvement of the methods. This involves undertaking a sustained inquiry into how and why we, as teachers, employ specific pedagogical methods. It requires that we question the efficacy of different techniques we employ and refine our practice accordingly. It entails checking our

own progress, adapting to the ever-shifting student needs and environmental contexts, and making appropriate changes in our teaching when needed.

To excel during this ongoing process, our own stance must be that of the perpetual learner who is "constantly trying to improve their own efforts to foster students' development, and never completely satisfied with what they already achieved" (Bain, 2004, p. 20). Our teaching must not become a mechanistic, prescribed script to follow. Rather, it requires consistent examination and improvement if we are to elevate our design pedagogy from a mere profession to a dynamic and innovative art that advances students and, consequently, future design industries.

## *Summary*

Optimal teaching and learning require design educators to adopt a more multifaceted, expansive, and iterative pedagogical approach. The teacher's traditional and necessary roles—disciplinary expert and knowledge provider—must synthesize with the concept of the "teacher-mentor," one who strategically assesses and addresses the cognitive and emotional development of every unique student. This advanced role involves developing more meaningful relationships with students; finding creative ways to nurture classroom community; designing strategic and targeted learning opportunities; adopting facilitated teaching methods; gaining increased awareness of the connections between cognition and emotion throughout the learning process; and viewing the teaching practice as an ongoing journey of continuous improvement. A more artful, holistic educational experience results, thus priming design students for success throughout their academic, professional, and personal lives.

## Part 2: The Model Three: What We Can Learn from Singapore, South Korea, and Finland

US design education would greatly benefit from studying best educational practices from around the world. While doing so, educators and program directors may personalize these proven best practices in order to strengthen their own, distinct Academies.

The internationally extolled educational systems of Singapore, South Korea, and Finland share remarkable similarities. The educational capabilities of these nations, in just a few decades, have risen from inauspicious beginnings to become preeminent globally in both economic and educational successfulness. Massive educational reforms, deep cultural respect for teachers, fiercely competitive and rigorous teacher educational programs, and extensive professional development for educators have led students from these three countries consistently to outperform other nations on global assessments (such as The Program for International Student Assessment, or "PISA"). Consequently, this has led to a high level of global admiration for these countries' systems.

What can US design education glean from these nations' pre-college educational practices that are more successful than our own? How can we, as college-level design educators, appropriately select best practices for our own teaching and institutional contexts? The following section briefly surveys each of the three leading nations' educational systems, approaches to teaching and learning, and teachers' professional training and ongoing development. Finally, an outline of applicable best practices with suggestions for how each may be implemented by US design higher education is provided.

## *Singapore*

Singapore is an extraordinary success story. Beginning in the 1970s and attaining notable achievement in 1997 through the transformative "Thinking Schools, Learning Nation" initiative, Singapore has "evolved into a global economic powerhouse through an educational system centered on developing strong, highly qualified teachers" (Faerm, 2015, p. 205). The nation's rapid ascent from a resource-poor island to a leading nation came about because of its inaugural Prime Minister Lee Kuan Yew (1959–1990). Mr. Lee's strategy, he famously proclaimed, was "to develop Singapore's only available natural resource: its people." The investments made by Mr. Lee and his successor Goh Chok Tong (1990–2004) have been highly successful: Singaporean students are among the world's highest achievers (placing within the top three nations on PISA tests since 2009 when it was first administered in Singapore), and the nation was ranked as the number one most competitive economy (out of 141) in 2019 (Geiger & Crotti, 2019; Organisation for Economic Cooperation and Development [OECD], 2019e).

Singapore operates a highly centralized educational system. The Ministry of Education (MoE) oversees virtually all aspects of the system, including funding allocation for schools; curriculum guidelines and assessment; and teacher credentialing, recruitment, professional development, and promotions. This centralization allows Singapore to acquire both the very best parts (teachers, schools, and policies) and a broader, holistic understanding of these parts (La Londe & Liew, 2019).

For many reasons, teaching is a highly respected profession in Singapore. These reasons include the high value placed on teachers in Confucian culture, the great success and international esteem for Singapore's students and educational system, and the widely known rigorousness of the nation's teacher education program (National Center on Education and the Economy [NCEE], 2020). The respect and prestige for the teaching profession are reflected by a recent survey of teachers in forty-eight countries that participated in the OECD's Teaching and Learning International Survey (TALIS): in Singapore, 72% of teachers surveyed "agree" or "strongly agree" that their profession is valued in society—greatly surpassing the average among the participating nations, which was 26% (OECD, 2019a).

Singapore's commitment to education is exemplified by its heavy investments in teacher recruitment, training, and mentorship. Every year, the top third of students are recruited by the MoE for entrance into the nation's only teacher preparation program. This program is run by the National Institute of Education (NIE), an autonomous school situated within one of the most esteemed institutions in Singapore, Nanyang Technological University (ranked second in Asia and twelfth in the world) (Quacquarelli Symonds, 2022). The application process is widely considered grueling and includes a written essay that probes at applicants' sense of professional ethics; panel interviews that consider the candidates' personal qualities that make a good teacher; intensive reviews of applicants' academic records; assessments of their contributions to their school and community; and a live lesson demonstration that is a gauge of the applicant's disposition and "presence" as a teacher (NCEE, 2020). Just one out of eight applicants is accepted, and upon entering the NIE, students receive a full tuition package along with a full beginning teacher's salary that increases after they have completed training and receive their teaching certification (NCEE, 2020). Teachers are also offered generous scholarships by the MoE and NIE when they pursue graduate and doctoral degrees in either Singapore or abroad (NCEE, 2020).

Depending upon their level of education when entering the NIE, students enroll in programs that range from two to four years; these include the Diploma in Education, the Postgraduate Diploma in Education, and the Bachelor of Arts/Science (Education) (NCEE, 2020). The ethos of these programs "reflect the features of a knowledge-based, skills-oriented, and practice-based curriculum" (La Londe & Liew, 2019, p. 135) and "are focused on pedagogy and connections between educational subjects, rather than on advanced academic training within a specific subject" (NCEE, 2020, n.p.). Both one's mastery of subject content and the craft of teaching, then, are essential to becoming a successful teacher in Singapore.

Mentorship is widely embedded into the nation's academic culture: in Singapore, more novice teachers (54.5%) had an assigned mentor than many other nations participating in a recent OECD TALIS study, ranking Singapore fourth out of fifty other nations for this practice (OECD, 2019a). During their first year, beginning teachers continue to attend courses in classroom management, counseling, reflective practices, and assessment offered by the NIE and MoE. This ongoing teacher education is sometimes supplemented with teacher-led workshops hosted by each school; these peer-to-peer activities encourage the sharing of ideas, support career development, advance faculty's research and pedagogy, and create a highly collegial work environment (Faerm, 2015).

Teachers enter one of three distinct career tracks: Teaching, Leadership, or Specialist (research and policy) (NCEE, 2020). As noted by La Londe and Liew (2019), teachers' election into and advancement through these tracks is based on the Enhanced Performance Management System, a centralized performance appraisal system that "allows for quantitative, standardized comparisons of teachers' observable competencies and measurable contributions" (p. 135). So, while all teachers receive annual raises during their first three years of teaching, subsequent raises are based on exhaustive evaluations across sixteen areas (including the contributions teachers make to school and community); these raises are available as part of promotions along the career tracks—promotions that include not only salary increases but also additional training and mentorship opportunities (NCEE, 2020). Schools also offer a generous system of bonuses whereby teachers can receive retention bonuses (approximately $1,500 to $3,600 US per year, paid every three to five years) and performance bonuses (totaling up to 30% of their base salary) based on annual evaluations (NCEE, 2020; Singapore Teachers Union, 2020). Furthermore, the MoE monitors teachers' salaries in relation to other professional salaries to ensure pay rates are competitive and adjusts them accordingly (NCEE, 2020).

Thus, Singaporean teachers feel highly incentivized to strengthen their teaching practice, participate and contribute to the school and community, and advance professionally. It is no wonder that teachers feel highly valued by Singaporean society and that the nation's educational system is so strong.

### South Korea

The South Korean proverb "Don't even step on the shadow of a teacher" reflects the nation's deep respect for education. South Koreans commonly attribute their nation's transformation—from one of the poorest in the world to the twelfth-largest economy—to their strong commitment to and investment in education (Paik, 2020); South Korea spends more funding on education (approximately 5.4% of its GDP) than the OECD average (5.0%) (OECD, 2019b). The financial investment and other supportive measures have yielded considerable success: South Korea's literacy rate has risen from just 22% in 1945 to 99% today (Paik, 2020). South Korean students are perennial top performers on international assessment tests, and (as of 2015) 98% of men and women aged twenty-five to thirty-four completed upper secondary education—the highest percentage in the OECD (NCEE, 2020). Tertiary education rates of South Koreans are also among the highest in the world; approximately 70% of those between the ages of twenty-five and thirty-four had earned a tertiary qualification in 2018 and roughly 94% of undergraduates who enter a bachelor's program will finish—the highest among OECD counties in both areas (OECD, 2019b; NCEE, 2020).

South Korean's reverence for education is reflected in the prestige and popularity of the teaching profession. Teaching is the most popular career choice among young South Koreans, and 80% of teachers cited teaching as their first-choice career (versus the 67% average in OECD countries and participating economies) (NCEE, 2020; OECD, 2019a). South Korean teachers earn relatively high wages and have job stability, high job satisfaction, and elevated social status. The most successful teachers "command packed stadium attendance and are treated like rock stars," and the teacher attrition rate is slightly over 1% per year (Edghill, 2015, n.p.; NCEE, 2020). In fact, the social status of teachers is ranked the sixth highest out of thirty-five countries polled, and on a recent survey of fifty countries, South Korea ranked fourth for the percentage of teachers (67%) who "agree" or "strongly agree" with the statement that their profession is valued in society—versus the OECD average of 26% (OECD, 2019a; Varkey, 2019).

The application and hiring processes for teaching positions are rigorous and competitive. Applicants must first take a national employment test that ranks them based on quantitative scores (NCEE, 2020). Once hired, teachers enter a school-run three-stage program that ensures they become highly skilled educators. In the first stage, these new teachers undergo two weeks of pre-employment training concentrating on the more practical aspects of teaching (e.g. classroom management). Next, they receive six months of post-employment training, managed by senior administration and teacher mentors, who provide the new teacher with "instructional guidance and evaluation, classroom supervision and instruction on clerical work and student guidance" (NCEE, 2020, n.p.). Finally, the process concludes with two weeks of follow-up training that engages teachers in reflective practice; through the use of presentations, reports, and discussions with peers, new teachers share with each other what they have learned during the program (NCEE, 2020).

Teachers' ongoing professional development is prioritized in South Korea. Teachers with three or more years of service are required to participate in a 180-hour professional development program to qualify for a Grade I certificate that, in turn, allows them to apply for advanced positions such as Master Teacher. The role of Master Teacher is a leadership position that may be granted following fifteen years of experience and requires positive school recommendations, extensive committee screening, teaching observation reports, and required training (NCEE, 2020). Master Teachers lead peer mentorship, professional development, and curriculum design while continuing their teaching. As in the Singaporean system, this peer-to-peer work fosters closer, collegial environments where ideas and challenges may be more easily shared with experienced colleagues. In fact, a comparatively high percentage of South Korean teachers (68%) typically participated in a network of teachers formed specifically for peer-development support, ranking South Korea fourth out of fifty nations in this area (OECD, 2019a). Aside from offering practical teaching support, this peer mentorship also provides invaluable emotional support, which can be particularly helpful for new, inexperienced teachers who commonly face challenges during the early stages of their careers.

Teachers' professional development is further supported by the Teacher Competence Development Assessment, which includes evaluative feedback from peer faculty, school leaders, students, and students' parents. The final report from this assessment determines a teacher's individualized development plans based on their professional level along with assessing their eligibility for a research sabbatical (NCEE, 2020). Teachers are highly incentivized to participate in professional development since promotion depends on a system that awards points for professional development as well as noteworthy performance assessments and other criteria. Moreover, "[b]ecause training is worth points for teacher promotion, there is a direct connection between teachers' participation in professional development and advancement on the career ladder" (NCEE, 2020, n.p.). The system's success in incentivizing faculty to pursue professional development is shown by the high percentage of South Korean teachers (98%) that had participated in at least one professional development activity in the twelve months prior to a survey in 2018, along with the average number of different professional development activities in which they participated (5.7 activities versus the OECD average of 4.0 activities) (OECD, 2019a).

*Finland*

Like Singapore and South Korea, Finland has become a model of rapidly achieved academic and economic success through educational reform. Beginning in the early 1970s, Finland adopted a new centrally administrated educational system that prioritized widespread equity and high quality. Leveraging this system enabled Finland to transform itself from a poorly educated, agrarian-based society into one of the most literate, modern, and economically successful societies and knowledge-based economies of today. Finland has been consistently ranked among the most globally competitive nations by the World Economic Forum since the early 2000s—an achievement that is particularly remarkable given the nation's recovery from a banking crisis and near economic collapse in the early 1990s. The Finnish people are among the most educated in the world: approximately 48% of young people obtain a bachelor's degree (or equivalent) during their lifetime while approximately 24% obtain a master's degree (or equivalent) during their lifetime (ranking sixth and fourth, respectively, among thirty-seven other OECD nations) (OECD, 2019c).

Vital to Finland's educational and economic successes is the fact that Finnish culture considers education a "necessary and a potential investment—not just expenditure—in helping to develop innovation and adopting more innovation throughout the economy" (Sahlberg, 2010, p. 107). For example, Finland's public expenditure on tertiary educational institutions as a percentage of GDP is comparatively high (5.4%), ranking second highest among thirty-nine other OECD nations (OECD, 2019c). This ardent cultural and economic support for education has contributed to the consistently high placements of Finnish students on international assessment tests. Finnish students' ongoing success on such tests (e.g. PISA) has contributed to the ongoing surge of interest from other nations who wish to better understand Finland's model approach to education. International interest is so high that Finland's MoE has had to create a unit exclusively dedicated to helping foreigners learn about their system (NCEE, 2020).

What makes Finland's educational system one of the most successful and highly esteemed in the world? Many of its hallmarks are shared by Singapore and South Korea, while others remain unique to Finland. Teaching is a highly revered and popular profession; it typically ranks among the most popular career paths for students and is a highly admired profession amongst Finns (NCEE, 2020; Pollari et al., 2018). Consequently, acceptance into teacher education programs is extremely competitive and highly selective, "admitting only one out of every ten students who apply. The result is that Finland recruits from the top quartile of the college-bound cohort" (NCEE, 2020, n.p.). Schleicher (2019) notes those who aren't accepted often turn to medical or law school instead, thus indicating the high level of prestige of the teaching profession.

Applicants to education programs must first take an entrance exam and, following this preliminary screening that includes an extensive review of their academic achievements and extracurricular activities, advance to the next stage. It is during this stage that applicants are evaluated for suitability for the teaching profession. The assessment methods used during this second stage depend upon the institution; however, they commonly include individual and/or group interviews, questionnaires, group tasks, and observed teacher-like activities (NCEE, 2020; Pollari et al., 2018). Only those candidates with a clear aptitude for teaching—along with excellent academic performance and strong motivation to become teachers—are admitted.

The track to becoming a teacher offers no shortcuts. On average, it takes prospective teachers five to six years of university studies in both subject content and teacher education to receive the required master's degree and qualifications (NCEE, 2020). Finnish teacher education is heavily research-based; coursework includes experimental pedagogy and education-oriented scientific research that aim to cultivate prospective teachers' innovative and analytical attitudes toward teaching (NCEE, 2020; Pollari et al., 2018). Degree candidates are also taught how to teach—with a strong emphasis on applying research-based state-of-the-art practices. Thus, the aim of this research- and practice-based teacher education is "to educate students to be able to make educational decisions based on rational argumentation, in addition to their intuitive insight" (Pollari et al., 2018, p. 12). The resulting synthesis between theory and practice deepens teachers' holistic understanding of teaching and, consequently, strengthens their problem-solving capacity through research-based initiatives and decision-making.

Finland's rigorous teacher education programs produce exceptionally qualified educators who are highly trusted and respected in Finnish society. This high level of trust affords teachers and schools tremendous autonomy in their work. For example, school inspections were abolished in the 1980s, and while municipal authorities offer supervision and Finland's National Core Curricula framework and learning objectives must be followed, Finnish schools and teachers have great flexibility and autonomy in curriculum design, materials selection, pedagogical methods, and student assessment formats (Pollari et al., 2018). Furthermore, the elimination of school inspections—which commonly caused disruption and pressure among faculty—gives teachers more time to advance and hone their pedagogy, curriculum, and research. Most Finnish teachers perform these tasks outside the classroom throughout their professional careers (Pollari et al., 2018).

Teachers' ongoing professional development is advanced through formal and informal peer- and school-led initiatives. Although the government mandates teachers participate in at least three days of professional development each school year, the average Finnish teacher spends seven days per school year on professional development, with some municipalities arranging large, multi-school training events (NCEE, 2020). Faculty development is further supported by lower-than-average net teaching time: per year, Finnish teachers spent around 100 hours less in the classroom teaching than the respective OECD averages (OECD, 2019d). This allows teachers to spend their remaining professional hours on other activities that support their professional growth, including mentoring and collaborating with peers, designing innovative and personalized lessons, conducting research, and attending training sessions (NCEE, 2020). As Saavedra et al. (2018) note, these activities "provide the support needed to make sure that the best pedagogical practices are implemented in every classroom" for equity in high-quality education (n.p.).

The Finnish approach to students' development is equally comprehensive. Rather than assessing the quality of education merely by students' test scores and acquired skillsets, the guiding ethos of *"bildung"* underpins Finnish education. *Bildung*, originally a German concept, emphasizes education that focuses on student cultivation by unifying philosophy and education in order to develop both personal and cultural advancement. Across academic levels, *bildung* aims to strengthen students' intellectual, moral, emotional, and civic sensibilities so they may "see the relations between things—between self and society, between a community of relationships in a family and a town" and thus develop more complex inner selves (Brooks, 2020, p. 27). This student-centered approach to cognitive and emotional development is particularly notable during students' final two years of high school. During these years, students in the academic track work with faculty to self-design an education plan they complete at their own pace; students may even enroll in subject-focused schools (e.g. the arts, sciences, music, or sports) to suit their interests and goals best (NCEE, 2020). Students determine their own weekly targets, choose tasks to perform, collaborate with peers in small groups, and attend workshops that, in turn, guide inquiry-focused learning and cultivate the student's independence and sense of agency. This self-directed, tailored learning experience heightens students' sense of responsibility, confidence, engagement, motivation, and ultimately their personal and academic success.

## US Need for Utilizing Global Best Practices for Design Higher Education

Utilizing the common best practices shared by these three nations will collectively strengthen the future of US design higher education, its educators, and its students. These practices include the following:

1 **Assessing candidate's aptitude for teaching**
   When hiring design educators, schools must increasingly consider and screen candidates' design education/professional experience *and* their aptitude for teaching via select methods that include observed teacher-like activities during the interview process. These mock teaching activities enable school leadership to evaluate the candidates' interpersonal skills, communication style, and capacity to lead and facilitate learning through design briefs, approach to studio classroom management, subject knowledge, and overall potential as a design educator.

2 **Incorporate subject knowledge with teacher education**
   Teachers' training strongly correlates with students' success, which subsequently builds and sustains institutional reputation. Therefore, it behooves US design schools to invest in teachers' preparation both during recruitment and throughout their careers. Design schools must provide teacher training opportunities—such as workshops, certificate programs, and graduate degrees in design education— for their faculty across all levels of teaching expertise. As noted by

Hu and Huang (2019), "teachers' sense of preparedness has a significant impact on their sense of self-efficacy, which directly influences teaching effectiveness" (p. 45). Design teachers' mastery of subject content *and* the craft of teaching, then, are imperative for effective design education.

3 **Adopt a holistic view of teaching and learning through practice, theory, and research**
Optimal teaching requires the triangulation of practice, theory, and research. When leveraged together, these three approaches provide teachers with an arsenal of knowledge from which they may strategically select and apply methods to meet students' individual, unique needs best. Ongoing practice hones teachers' intuitive insights and diverse approaches. Theory and research offer deeper understandings of cognition, student development, and pedagogy so that teachers' decisions and problem-solving skills are both well-grounded and strengthened. Theory and research also provide teachers with a better understanding of the shifting design student generation, and this, in turn, informs how pedagogy may be strategically evolved to ensure student success. Thus, design educators must become lifelong learners of design (subject content) and teaching (practice and theory).

4 **Build an institutional culture that prioritizes teachers' professional development (TPD)**
Teachers' professional development (TPD) offers innumerable benefits. TPD enables design educators to strengthen their teaching skills, gain more sensitive insights into design student development, discover effective studio classroom management techniques, and continually improve curriculum. TPD also strengthens community and collegiality: TPD enables teachers to emerge from their classrooms—where they are typically isolated from other teachers—and participate in critical activities with their peers. These activities allow them more easily to discuss challenges, glean insights, share research, engage in mentorship, and receive practical and emotional support—all of which positively affect teachers' morale, job satisfaction, and teaching effectiveness. These, in turn, impact students' success and design school enrollment retention. Additionally, through TDP, teachers experience greater self-efficacy, care and respect from their institution, and an enhanced sense of status.

Research demonstrates teachers' level of engagement with TPD is an indicator of teacher quality and results in teachers feeling more prepared to employ student-centered pedagogy—an increasingly necessary pedagogical approach for the emergent generation of undergraduates (Faerm, 2015; Hu & Huang, 2019). Furthermore, teachers with stronger preparation "typically stay in teaching significantly longer, as do those who receive high-quality mentoring in their first year on the job. This preparation and subsequent retention develop a closer and more supportive community, greater institutional memory, and faculty who are more deeply invested in their school's success" (Faerm, 2015, p. 204).

5  **Create a robust system for evaluating and rewarding effective teaching**
Design schools must mirror the teacher cultivation activities of high-achieving educational systems by employing their best practices for assessing and rewarding effective teaching. These practices include:

- exhaustive teacher performance evaluations that contain detailed TPD plans;
- point-based systems for teachers' ongoing development (e.g. participation in TPD) that then contribute toward annual evaluations;
- added promotional levels that teachers feel motivated to climb;
- bonuses given for outstanding teacher performance and years of service; and
- teaching performance-based salary increases, sabbaticals, and research grants.

Currently, US design schools (and US higher education more broadly) commonly offer little support in these areas. For instance, full-time faculty typically climb just three promotional levels over the course of their teaching tenure, namely Assistant, Associate, and "full" Professor. These roles are based on an amalgam of teaching, institutional service, and research/creative practice that are reviewed annually and determine promotions in professorial rank. Part-time faculty are typically performance reviewed through classroom observations and students' course evaluations. If US design education is to strengthen and prepare better for the future, it must adopt a markedly more robust system for spotlighting, supporting, and rewarding effective teaching.

## Part 3: Critically Reflective Teaching

"How do you know when your teaching is effective and your students are learning?"
"How can your teaching be more responsive?"

Questions such as these are increasingly vital for design higher education. Educators are experiencing a shifting design student generation, evolving curricula, greater demands for accountability, and volatile design industries. The complexities around these variables require design educators to question their pedagogical practices more deeply for their own professional development and to enable them to increase their students' learning. Reflective practice is a powerful tool to improve one's quality of teaching and learning outcomes.

## What Is Critically Reflective Teaching?

"Reflection," in simplest terms, means "contemplation." Educational reformer and philosopher John Dewey (1933) defined "reflective thought" as "active, persistent, and careful consideration of any belief or supposed form of knowledge in the light of the grounds that support it and the further conclusions to which it tends" (p. 118). In teaching, reflective practice is a well-defined and crafted action that aims to make the implied explicit for evaluation and positive action (Loughran, 2002). Reflective practice draws attention to areas of our teaching that may be problematic so that our practices may be improved. It requires "[a] disposition to inquiry incorporating the process through which students, early career and experienced teachers structure or restructure actions, beliefs, knowledge and theories that inform teaching for the purpose of professional development" (Zwodiak-Myer, 2012, p. 5).

A critical aspect of reflective teaching is that it extends well beyond the scope of mere instruction and course content. It prioritizes introspection around *what* is being done, *why* it's being done, and *how well* it impacts students' knowledge acquisition (Mathew et al., 2017). Brookfield (1995) notes critical reflective practice has two distinct purposes: "to understand how considerations of power undergird, frame, and distort educational processes and interactions" and "to question assumptions and practices that seem to make our teaching lives easier but actually work against our own best long-term interests" (p. 8). Reflective practice is necessary because we are "[t]o some extent ... prisoners trapped within the perceptual frameworks that determine how we view our experiences" (Brookfield, 1995, p. 28). The conscious and unconscious assumptions and biases we hold may distort, blur, or constrain our teaching and how we view situations. Moreover, if our biases are left unchecked or we remain unresponsive to the evolving design school environment, these biases may undermine our professional development, students' learning, and the value the educational institution provides.

## The Fundamental Tenets of Reflective Practice

While many scholars (e.g. Dewey, 1933; Schön, 1984) offer varying perspectives of reflective practice, all perspectives share several fundamental principles. First, reflective teaching is an ongoing, career-long learning process. In reflective teaching, the teacher seeks to understand better the effects of their teaching and connect more meaningfully with students. Teachers do this with the goal of promoting ideal teaching and learning experiences. Second, reflective teaching requires teachers to question their practices and identify any problems, perplexing or curious situations, or similar concerns that should be addressed. As Loughran (2002) asserts, "[w]hat that problem is, the way it is framed and (hopefully) reframed, is an important aspect of understanding the nature of reflection and the value of reflective practice" (p. 33). Third, the reflective process relies heavily on the individual's professional experiences in developing analyses for and evaluating their teaching. At the same time, incorporating theory and peer mentorship into the reflective process enables teachers to identify more clearly and examine more effectively past actions and events. Over time, the new learning is incorporated into the teacher's existing knowledge, enabling the teacher to reach a higher level of understanding (Schön, 1984). Overall, the reflective process requires seeing things from different viewpoints to "probe beneath the veneer of a [one-dimensional] commonsense reading of experience. [Reflective teachers] investigate the hidden dimensions of their practice and become aware of the omnipresence of power" (Brookfield, 1995, p. 7).

*Promoting Critically Reflective Teaching*

The core of critical reflection lies in hunting down the assumptions and biases we possess that prevent us from viewing our "true" selves. To gain this perspective, we must move "from the dance floor to the balcony" so that we can better assess and comprehend the full extent of a situation, its participants (e.g. students), and ourselves (Heifetz & Linsky, 2002). Brookfield (1995) offers four methods that we can use to gain a more salient picture of who we are and what we do as design educators. They include the following:

1 **Autobiographical reflection.** Self-reflection, the foundation of critical reflection, involves the introspection of our autobiographies as learners and teachers so that we become aware of the internal assumptions and instinctive reasonings that guide how we teach (Miller, 2010). We explore our formative experiences as students (the positive and the negative), which have shaped our teaching practices. For instance, past positive experiences may guide what we seek to emulate, while negative ones are those we want to avoid exhibiting. This reflective method includes reviewing teaching journals, student/peer feedback, personal goals/outcomes, and/or role model profiles.
2 **Our students' perspectives.** Placing ourselves in our students' roles offers the greatest long-term effect in evolving our pedagogy (Brookfield, 1995). The process is especially beneficial to those who have been teaching and/or in professional practice for so long that over time they forget their own experiences as students. This method seeks to understand better students' cognitive and emotional challenges during the learning process by considering their experiences, anxieties, difficulties, blockages, and views of our teaching. These perspectives serve as a starting point for developing an effective curriculum, teaching more responsively, fostering empathy, and

grounding our educational processes (Brookfield, 1995). After all, "[w]ithout this knowledge all the pedagogic skill in the world means very little, since that skill may unwittingly be exercised in ways that confuse or intimidate learners" (Brookfield, 1995, p. 94).

3 **Peer mentorship**. Inviting colleagues to view our practice through their unique perspectives is the key to revealing our habits and discovering possible solutions to problems and concerns in our teaching. Peers' feedback allows us to reexamine our teaching methods more consciously so they may be reframed, expanded, and strengthened. Moreover, mentorship provides emotional support, a sense of connectedness, and the feeling that we are not alone in our challenges. This assurance fosters greater confidence, autonomy, and motivation within teachers and subsequently bolsters their teaching quality, students' learning, the academic community, and the value of the design school. The process can involve informal conversations, teaching observations, reviews of materials (e.g. syllabi or teaching philosophies), workshops, and similar opportunities that encourage teachers to share their experiences in order to remove "the shroud of silence in which our [teaching] practice is wrapped" (Brookfield, 1995, p. 35). (See Chapter 22 for a full discussion.)

4 **Scholarly literature**. Research on higher education can provide us with multiple, diverse perspectives on a specific issue. The materials help us "name" our experiences and practice, gain alternative interpretations and suggestions for familiar situations, further challenge our assumptions and biases, and clarify situational contexts (Brookfield, 1995). Like peer mentorship, these external perspectives may reveal that issues we might perceive as personal failings or challenges could actually be issues related to external factors, such as a school's structural or cultural conditions. This newfound awareness, in turn, prevents self-blame, conserves emotional energy, and subsequently improves our confidence in teaching (Brookfield, 1995).

To promote these reflective practices, a variety of methods may be employed, including video recordings, peer observations, and professional support groups. Video recordings (easily made with smartphones) provide us with factual depictions of ourselves in the classroom. They show us the balance of teacher-to-student discussion, the quality of design critiques and instruction, and the time we allow students to reflect and respond. Recordings also reveal our classroom "performance," namely our use of effective gestures, body language, space, vocal modulations, facial expressions, and other characteristics that affect learning and teacher-student dynamics (see Chapter 16).

Peer observations provide further insights into our teaching. Inviting a colleague to watch, analyze, and critique our teaching may feel uncomfortable, particularly due to the connection between classroom observations and high-stakes assessments such as reappointments, promotions, and tenure reviews. Additional discomfort may be felt by those who experience "imposter syndrome," fearing their "true inadequate selves" will be revealed to their colleagues. Therefore, it is important to pre-evaluate peer candidates. These candidates should possess substantial experience and be people with whom you feel trust and are comfortable. It is also common for observations to be reciprocal to ensure mutual benefit. A preliminary discussion whereby each colleague shares specific areas they'd like observed will ensure observations are focused and offer useful feedback. Observations should evenly contain positive and constructive feedback, offer detailed suggestions for improvement, and may even describe the observer's own challenges and how they were addressed. Good feedback is *specific* feedback.

Professional support groups provide a third method to promote critically reflective teaching. In these groups, teachers gain new perceptions of their practices through their colleagues' stories, feedback, suggestions, and assessments. While the meeting formats can vary, their overarching purpose is to allow group members to share their personal experiences as educators. Colleagues listen to one another and respond with their perspectives and critical analysis. We do so to gain objective perspectives on those areas of our teaching that may be taken for granted or otherwise need closer attention. Throughout the process, group members must remain vigilant in detecting "groupthink," a phenomenon whereby members mutually reinforce negative assumptions or dispositions (Brookfield, 1995). Participants may also help experienced teachers detect long-standing, self-fulfilling routinized teaching frameworks that close them off from alternative, more effective perspectives (Brookfield, 1995). These support groups elevate our teaching practice by recognizing its complexities and by promoting a more publicly active culture of pedagogical discourse in design higher education.

## *The Benefits of Reflective Teaching Practice*

Reflective teaching practice offers extensive benefits. It allows us to see our teaching as continuous development and improvement. For example, the pressure to be the "perfect" design teacher often thwarts self-assuredness. However, there is no "perfect" in the reflective teaching practice; rather, it reminds us that professional development is a never-ending process. When we openly question ourselves, we create a professional environment in which we value in each other the ability to accept change and risk failure (Brookfield, 1995). Students also benefit since teachers who make their own thinking public (and thus open to discussion) typically have classes that are more interesting, stimulating, and challenging for students (Osterman, 1990). As a result of reflective teaching practice, teachers are able to communicate and deliver course content better and promote more meaningful teacher-student relationships (Leitch & Day, 2000).

Reflective teaching produces feelings of groundedness and intention in our practice as teachers. Rather than fate, serendipity, or even luck shaping our educational processes, reflection reveals and affirms the personal agency—and the responsibilities—we have as teachers (Bartlett, 1990). By acting with intention, having purpose in our actions, and discovering deeper meaning in our work, we can achieve greater fulfillment as more self-directed and empowered professionals (Brookfield, 1995). Moreover, our abilities to communicate clearly our educational agendas and rationalized pedagogical methods establish our credibility with students and this, in turn, engenders greater trust within the learning environment (Brookfield, 1995).

Reflective practice also illuminates hegemonic assumptions, namely "those that we think are in our own best interests but that have actually been designed by more powerful others to work against us in the long term," and ultimately best serves those in power (Brookfield, 1995, pp. 14–15). These assumptions are commonly embedded in schools' culture to the point of remaining unnoticed and accepted as "The Way." Reflective practice aims to destabilize these assumptions so that we may discover alternate, improved methods that better address the goals, needs, and ambitions of our evolving design students, ourselves, and our academic communities. It is through reflective practice that we model the behaviors we hope to instill in our students and see them promoted by our design school's leadership. Reflective practice leads us through sustained critical inquiry to yield new ideas that will lead to significant leaps in learning, innovation, and positive change, affecting all parties, from individual students to the design school as a whole.

Yet, such critical inquiry that aims to disrupt the status quo (and possibly fail) is risky and thus potentially avoided; "[b]elief in the stable state serves primarily to protect us from apprehension of the threats inherent in change. Belief in stability is a means of maintaining stability, or at any rate the illusion of stability" (Schön, 1970, n.p.). After all, reflective teaching practice fundamentally asks us to deconstruct our ways of knowing and being in the world. The resultant personal change that comes from engagement in reflective practice commonly produces turbulent feelings of loss, bewilderment, and a general uncertainty of the worth and value of our teaching and of ourselves (Loughran, 2002). However, by adopting the outlined methods and support systems, these challenges are outweighed by the promise of remarkable benefits, including the development of a deeper body of knowledge into the epistemology of teaching practice—potentially through academic textbooks, scientific papers, and academic journals—that will serve to strengthen future design educators, institutions, and industries.

# Part 4: What Makes an Effective Educator?

*Katherine C. Boles, Ed.D.*

*Former Program Director and Senior Lecturer,
Harvard Graduate School of Education*

Teaching is both a performing art and an intellectual endeavor, a beautiful duality fueled by creativity, rigor, and passion. Teaching is a dance, an empathic, disciplined dance. It moves through time and space, integrating the knowledge, interests and goals of students, the teacher's knowledge of subject matter, the techniques and craft of teaching, and the personalities—the unique strengths and the particular needs—of individual students.

An educator can only be considered effective if, as a result of the work that the educator and the learner have done, the learner can do something new or better or differently. The teacher can know that she has been effective if the learner behaves differently and/or thinks and acts more deliberately and critically. This essay will tease out the ingredients of highly effective teaching—content, pedagogy, and relationships—to show how these ingredients can be combined within effective instruction, to consider and appreciate the complexity and nuance of what makes an educator effective.

My thinking about this topic is built on the impressions, insights, and analyses gathered and experienced during my fifty-year teaching career in a wide range of educational settings. I taught at the pre-college level for over twenty years, and then following my completion of doctoral studies in education, I became a faculty member at the Harvard Graduate School of Education. My thinking has also been shaped by the highly effective educators I consulted before writing this essay; their teaching practice spans diverse academic levels and disciplines—from public elementary and high schools to Harvard University.

No matter their academic settings, highly effective educators all share two common attributes. First, they love teaching. One colleague remarked, "I get a 'high' from walking into the classroom. It's like being on a zipline on a mountain. There's always that energy, the energy of solving problems and empowering [students] so that they can make their own decisions."

Second, while effective educators develop and hone their expertise over many years, each one can identify particular people and/or events that set them on this path to highly effective teaching. Many cite their own experiences as students with extraordinary teachers who inspired them. For instance, one teacher recounted the instructional strategies of a college music teacher: "a charismatic lecturer who had mastery over his demonstrations, his prose, his questions, his flow, that I observed and carried over into my own teaching." Others remembered teachers who had mentored them in their own work as professionals. Another praised the quality of her teacher education program where student teachers were taught how to become a "reflective team of teachers, giving and receiving feedback." She remarked that through this experience she had learned to be "both a designer [of course content] and a teacher." My own experience was that I was inspired to embark on a teaching career while I regularly observed a unique first-grade teacher who demonstrated with her every move that teaching can be a beautiful work of art.

Teachers vary significantly. There are those whose strongest connection is with the *content* of their subject and others for whom a particular *pedagogical method* defines their practice. There are teachers who make deep, powerful *connections* with each student. Some effective teachers bring profound cultural knowledge of their students' backgrounds and aspirations to every lesson. Others have important professional relationships that enrich them intellectually and emotionally, while some are brilliant loners.

In the end, however, fine teaching is built on a very personal combination of three essential ingredients.

### The Three Ingredients of Effective Teaching

No matter what it was that inspired individuals to become teachers, or where they honed their craft, the result—fine teaching—always consists of three elements:

- Deep understanding of **content**;
- Strong and continuously evolving **pedagogy**;
- Expansive, respectful **relationships** with students and colleagues both inside and outside of the classroom/educational organization.

The proportion of each ingredient is very personal to the teacher and the setting; the combination may vary at different times in a teacher's career, but all three elements must exist and they must be "live"—that is, always active and evolving.

Effective instruction is typically orchestrated by the individual teacher and determined by the students she teaches. But teaching is not merely personal: it must respond to the organization and the culture in which the teacher works. What/where the teacher teaches, the students' ages and their cultural backgrounds, the priorities of the school/university—all of these factors exert powerful influences on the teacher's pedagogy. However, when all is said and done, it is the teacher's own values, vision, specific methods, and personal style that determine what goes on in a classroom.

Trust is the cement that binds together these three ingredients—and it takes many forms. The teacher must have trust in herself, confidence in her subject and her ability to teach it; trust in her colleagues, the administration, and the students; and trust in the institution within which she works. Trust permits risk-taking. If a teacher is not able to take risks, the teacher's repertoire is severely limited, and she is less likely to discover better teaching methods. Through trust, the content, pedagogy, and personal relationships are woven together. Let's examine each:

1 **Content**
The effective teacher must have a good understanding of the subject matter and ongoing curiosity, as well as the motivation to look for new ways of approaching the content, and access to engaging materials that engender more learning and deeper understanding.

I have taught everything from primary-level counting skills to secondary-level literary analysis in French to graduate-level organizational theory. These widely different academic subjects and settings may appear to have little in common. But they made similar demands with respect to my content knowledge of each subject. Knowledge of the subject matter, combined with *determination* to teach it well, propels the teacher toward effective teaching. One teacher explained, "I think my rigorous teaching comes from understanding the content well enough so that I can build multiple pathways to it. The content is much more far-reaching than the boundaries of the given curriculum."

2 **Pedagogy**
Pedagogy (the "how" of teaching) is inextricably linked to content, to the learners' ages and prior knowledge, and to the teacher's own level of experience. The pedagogical moves of a novice differ greatly from the elegant methods of a veteran who has had numerous opportunities to teach a certain lesson, notice the results, adjust strategies for the whole class or for individual students, experiment with alternate methods, make mistakes and then fine-tune her responses, and expand continuously her own pedagogical repertoire. The effective teacher, over time, learns to match her actions more closely to students' needs and characteristics. The teacher organizes and paces content so that it becomes progressively more challenging and interesting. She learns to vary strategies, to have a broad repertoire of activities that develop or recapture students' engagement, and move them closer to mastery of the particular subject.

The effective educator also choreographs how a lesson will unfold or evolve, how different parts of the content and process will ultimately fit together—while ensuring the lessons have momentum. An effective teacher senses what a student may need in the moment and moves quickly to provide support or challenge to that student. She is fluent with a wide repertoire of "just-right" moves that encourage the students, lead them to reflect more analytically about their own work, and stimulate the learners to move toward and then experience mastery and accomplishment.

When I was a novice teacher in the pre-college levels, my repertoire of instructional moves was limited. For example, I struggled with how to organize my classroom. Yet, what I lacked in organizational skills I made up for with my enthusiasm, my passion for the subject, and my determination to create a stimulating learning environment. By observing veteran colleagues whose pedagogies I respected, I learned to vary my approaches: mini-lectures, small group activities, hands-on projects, dramatic presentations to illustrate ideas, and more. The rich diversity of my instructional repertoire enhanced students' learning, motivation, and success. I also worked on a teaching team to learn how to expand and strengthen my pedagogy. My own joy and confidence grew enormously.

Years later, when I began teaching at Harvard, I was struck by how these same pedagogical strategies were transferable to my university teaching. I varied my teaching strategies within graduate-level three-hour courses by including in every class mini-lectures, whole- and small-group discussions, and projects that students self-identified to meet their individual needs. I discovered that my university colleagues were teaching their classes in ways that were similar to mine. Though the professors' methods were unique, their teaching contained many of the same elements of effective teaching that I had crafted in my pre-college classrooms.

There are particular professors who stand out. A veteran professor at Harvard, whose large, popular statistics classes were renowned for both rigor and effectiveness, is among them. Following every class session—which he videotaped—he'd screen the recording to notice which of his teaching moves or materials could have been clearer or could have enhanced students' learning. He noted which students he might have shortchanged and then sent detailed e-mails to every one of those students to rectify his mistakes.

Another professor, who currently teaches the History of Music at Harvard, varies the elements of every class session, orchestrating his lectures, presentations, demonstrations, and videos. He ensures that each of his 100 undergraduates has the opportunity to think and write about a provocative question during each class session. He gives regular short written quizzes to check that he is teaching the content effectively and that his students understand what he was trying to teach them.

Effective educators evaluate their teaching methods and student learning *constantly*. They self-evaluate in myriad ways: students' oral responses to unexpected questions; students' written responses to challenging questions about dilemmas in the field; and diverse performances, projects, and demonstrations that highlight the students' learning. All of these formal and informal student evaluations enable effective educators to assess the quality and effectiveness of their own pedagogy.

3  **Relationships**
Communication in an educational setting is a dance with many partners—students, administrators, staff, and colleagues. **Relationships with students** are built on both cultural awareness and knowledge of the individual: the teacher's caring, rigor, and compassion must make sense to the learner. The effective educator recognizes the value of these relationships with students and makes sure that her teaching is responsive to their culture, their interests, and their individuality!

One of the professors I interviewed makes a point of having a personal, individual meeting sometime during the semester with each of her approximately 150 students in the course. She also makes it a point to address students individually by name in the large lecture hall. She knows them all well enough to support and warmly encourage those who are reluctant to speak. Another colleague who teaches both pre-college and college-level courses commented on the importance of relationships in both settings. She explained, "Every student, it doesn't matter if they're 5 years old or 50, wants to be seen and heard and recognized and believed in. The effective educator believes in her students, always believing that they can *construct* as well as *receive* knowledge."

The effective educator must know and understand the students in her class, whether they live in marginalized communities or come from privilege. She must develop close ties with every learner and act with empathy. Deep understanding and empathy enable the educator to recognize each student's strengths and areas that need growth. The result is an increase in student trust, and increased student trust enables the teacher to assess more accurately her own effectiveness as an educator.

**Relationships with colleagues** that are built on networking and collaboration enrich the teacher's repertoire. The range of actions that come naturally to a teacher is expanded by encountering "I'd never have thought to do that" methods. Successful teachers see the benefits of working together for mutual self-interest.

I began working with my colleague Vivian Troen in the early 1980s, and shortly after, for the first time in my career, I was co-planning with another educator, teaching lessons collaboratively, and then honestly assessing the results. We built strong relationships with students and went on to build new relationships with other teachers who had been intrigued by our partnership. We worked with our administrators to create more teacher teams; we co-authored books and articles on teaching, teacher teams, and teacher rounds; and for over twenty years, we shared what we had learned about teams and teaching with teachers and schools around the world. Our relationship was the key to all we accomplished.

*Conclusion*

An effective educator introduces learners to concepts or ideas they have never considered or reacquaints learners with ideas they had previously dismissed or never fully understood. An effective educator engages learners with ideas they can accept, reject, modify, or expand: ideas that can enhance their thinking. An effective educator opens new worlds to learners and then systematically leads them through the process of incorporating new learning into their lives, their work, and (often) their identities.

I knew I was an effective educator when I was introducing ideas that I knew to be important and that the students had never before considered. I could see the students processing and adapting the ideas—and making them their own. I knew students were learning when I could see them grappling with ideas that were not new to them but which they had never critiqued or seriously considered, when I could see them critiquing their own beliefs and assumptions, or when they realized that they knew more at the end of a semester than they had assumed they would ever know. Then, and only then, I felt effective.

Teaching is indeed a complex and multifaceted profession. The context in which the teacher teaches matters—enormously. The organizational culture, interpersonal relationships with colleagues, and the levels of financial and technical support either make teachers' work easier—or much harder—to do. Educators, no matter their settings, who experience inadequate support in these vital areas often leave teaching early in their careers. I was among the lucky ones: I worked in well-resourced institutions with fascinating colleagues, supportive administrators, and eager students. These factors allowed me to take risks with the content of my teaching and my pedagogy. Indeed, I was encouraged to take risks in the academic settings in which I taught. The risk-taking and the support (both are essential) enabled me to try out new ideas, make mistakes, and then improve my practice.

However, teaching, at its core, is all about learning for students and teachers alike. As one university colleague remarked:

> I teach because I learn. Every time I teach, if I'm "on" and paying attention—when it's really working—I'm learning a new perspective, a new point of view, both about my content and about my relationships. Maybe the essence is the hunger and willingness to learn from others. What am I learning about? I'm learning about content and relationships. What's going to work with one student isn't

going to work with another student. Learning is the big umbrella. That student said something I'd never thought about before, and I'm intrigued. My teaching is about my learning.

Teaching is a dance, an exciting set of moves and skills that bring knowledge and joy to the learner and to the teacher herself. There is deep satisfaction in fine teaching, some of which I hope I have managed to convey in this essay.

## References

Bain, K. (2004). *What the best college teachers do*. Harvard University Press.
Bartlett, L. (1990). Teacher development through reflective teaching. In J. C. Richards, & D. Nunan (Eds.), *Second language teacher education* (pp. 2002–2014). Cambridge University Press.
Brookfield, S. (1995). *Becoming a critically reflective teacher*. Jossey-Bass.
Brooks, D. (2020, February 14). This is how Scandinavia got great. *New York Times*, section A, p. 27.
Dewey, J. (1933). *How we think*. D.C. Heath.
Edghill, L. (2015, October 12). Why do South Korean teachers get the rock star treatment? *World News Group*. https://world.wng.org/2015/10/why_do_south_korean_teachers_get_the_rock_star_treatment
Faerm, S. (2015). Building best practices for fashion design pedagogy: Meaning, preparation, and impact. *Cuaderno, 53*, 189–213.
Geiger, T., & Crotti, R. (2019). Top 10 most competitive economies in the world. *World Economic Forum*. https://www.weforum.org/agenda/2019/10/competitive-economies-world/
Graff, G. (2003). *Clueless in academe*. Yale University Press.
Harris, B. (2001). The power of creating a spiritual learning community. *Adult Learning, 12*(3), 22–23.
Heifetz, R., & Linsky, M. (2002). *Leadership on the line: Staying alive through the dangers of leadership*. Harvard Business Review Press.
Hough, L. (2019, Fall). The making of a lecturer: Christina Villarreal. *Harvard Graduate School of Education Ed. Magazine*. https://www.gse.harvard.edu/news/ed/19/08/making-lecturer-christina-villarreal
Hu, A., & Huang, L. (2019). Teachers' professional development and an open classroom climate: A comparative study of Norway, Sweden, South Korea, and Taiwan. *Nordic Journal of Comparative and International Education, 3*(1), 33–50.
La Londe, P., & Liew, W. (2019). Teacher preparation in Singapore. In C. A. Lubienski, & T. J. Brewer (Eds.), *Learning to teach in an era of privatization: Global trends in teacher preparation* (pp. 127–147). Teachers College Press.
Lanier, J. (1997, July 1). Redefining the role of the teacher: It's a multifaceted profession. *Edutopia*. https://www.edutopia.org/redefining-role-teacher
Leitch, R., & Day, C. (2000). Action research and reflective practice: Towards a holistic view. *Educational Action Research, 8*(1), 179–193.
Loughran, J. J. (2002). Effective reflective practice: In search of meaning in learning about teaching. *Journal of Teacher Education, 53*(1), 33–43.

Mathew, P., Mathew, P., & Peechattu, P. (2017). Reflective practices: A means to teacher development. *Asia Pacific Journal of Contemporary Education and Communication Technology*, 3(1), 126–131.

McKinney, J., McKinney, K., Franiuk, R., & Schweitzer, J. (2006). The college classroom as community. *College Teaching*, 54(3), 281–284.

Miller, B. (2010). Brookfield's four lenses: Becoming a critically reflective teacher. *Faculty of Arts Teaching and Learning Committee, The University of Sydney*. https://valenciacollege.edu/faculty/development/courses-resources/documents/Brookfield_summary.pdf

National Center on Education and the Economy (NCEE). (2020). Top performing countries. *Center on International Education Benchmarking*. https://ncee.org/what-we-do/center-on-international-education-benchmarking/top-performing-countries/

Organisation for Economic Cooperation and Development (OECD). (2019a). *TALIS 2018 results: Teachers and school leaders as lifelong learners*. https://www.oecd-ilibrary.org/education/talis-2018-results-volume-i_1d0bc92a-en

Organisation for Economic Cooperation and Development (OECD). (2019b). *Korea: Education at a glance*. https://www.oecd.org/education/education-at-a-glance/EAG2019_CN_KOR.pdf

Organisation for Economic Cooperation and Development (OECD). (2019c). *Finland: Overview of education system*. https://gpseducation.oecd.org/CountryProfile?primaryCountry=FIN&treshold=10&topic=EO

Organisation for Economic Cooperation and Development (OECD). (2019d). *Finland: Education at a glance*. http://www.oecd.org/education/education-at-a-glance/EAG2019_CN_FIN.pdf

Organisation for Economic Cooperation and Development (OECD). (2019e). *OECD ilibrary: PISA*. https://www.oecd-ilibrary.org/education/pisa_19963777

Osterman, K. F. (1990). Reflective practice in education. *Education and Urban Society*, 22(2), 133–152.

Paik, W. (2020, April 9). What the U.S. can learn about education during crisis from South Korea's wartime example. *The Hechinger Report*. https://hechingerreport.org/opinion-what-the-u-s-can-learn-about-education-during-crisis-from-south-koreas-wartime-example/

Pollari, P., Salo, O.-P., & Koski, K. (2018). In teachers we trust—The Finnish way to teach and learn. *i.e.: Inquiry in Education*, 10(1), 1–17. https://digitalcommons.nl.edu/ie/vol10/iss1/4

Quacquarelli Symonds. (2022). *World university rankings*. https://www.topuniversities.com/university-rankings/world-university-rankings/2022

Rousseau, J.-J. (2002). *Emile*. (B. Foxley, Trans.). Gutenberg. (Original work published 1762). http://www.gutenberg.org/cache/epub/5427/pg5427.txt

Saavedra, J., Alasuutari, H., & Guitierrez, M. (2018, December 28). Teachers and trust: Cornerstones of the Finnish education system. *World Bank*. https://blogs.worldbank.org/education/teachers-and-trust-cornerstones-finnish-education-system

Sahlberg, P. (2010). *Finnish lessons: What can the world learn from educational change in Finland?* Teachers College Press.

Schleicher, A. (2019, January). The secret to Finnish education: Trust. *OECD Observer*. https://oecdobserver.org/news/fullstory.php/aid/6126/The_secret_to_Finnish_education:_Trust.html

Schön, D. (1970, November 15). The loss of the stable state (Lecture 1). In *The Reith Lectures*. BBC Radio 4. https://www.bbc.co.uk/programmes/p00h65rn

Schön, D. (1984). *The reflective practitioner: How professionals think in action*. Basic Books.

Singapore Teachers Union. (2020). *FAQ tenure*. https://stu.org.sg/index.php/faq-tenure/

Speicher, S. (2009, February). IDEO's ten tips for creating a 21st century classroom experience. *Metropolis, 27*(8), 80.

Tebben, S. (1995). Community and caring in a college classroom. *Journal for a Just and Caring Education, 1*(3), 335–344.

Varkey, S. (2019). Give teachers the respect they deserve. *The Korea Times*. http://www.koreatimes.co.kr/www/opinion/2020/02/197_280249.html

Zwodiak-Myer, P. (2012). *The teacher's reflective practice handbook: Becoming an extended professional through capturing evidence-informed practice*. Routledge.

# Section IV
# Design Classrooms

# 14 Introduction to Design Classrooms

## A Workbook of Effective and Strategic Teaching Methods for Design Educators

As design educators, we assume enormous responsibilities for our students. We introduce them to new worlds and guide them through the process of adopting new knowledge into their lives, their careers, and, often, their identities (Brookfield, 2013). We influence students' lifetime goals, perspectives on the consequences of their work, and their roles in the world (Davis, 2017). We choreograph environments in which students feel able to take risks, explore options, develop alternate solutions, challenge staid design thinking, and, perhaps most importantly, innovate. We directly influence how our students experience the world, both now and in the future.

In our professional roles, we prepare future designers to be able to shift nimbly and be flexible throughout their careers in the constantly evolving design industries. We also model "soft skills," such as socialization, teamwork, organization, stress management, resilience, empathy, active listening, diplomacy, and integrity to students. We impart values that travel well beyond our campuses and ultimately affect entire communities. In every teacher-student engagement, no matter how long or short—or how formal or informal—it may be, we intellectually, creatively, and emotionally develop students for success in the wider society. Thus, we help shape society itself. As Davis (2017) surmises, "colleges and universities prepare productive citizens who shape the world we live in through the type of inquiry a design education instills. This is not a responsibility faculty can leave to chance or view only as student preparation for employment" (p. 2).

We must keep pace with the accelerated rate at which knowledge is emerging across the design practices. Accordingly, our teaching skillsets need to be both extensive and malleable; they must meet the rapidly evolving needs of students and administrators and must be honed over time. These skillsets include the abilities of:

- working effectively with others from diverse cultures and backgrounds;
- mentoring learners with different abilities and interests;
- promoting inclusivity, equity, and social justice;

DOI: 10.4324/9781003049166-18

- engendering community and social cohesion;
- employing new technologies and academic supports into our pedagogy; and
- remaining abreast of complex, nuanced school policies (Zwozdiak-Myers, 2012).

Concurrently, the cultivation of "emotional intelligence"—which is one's capability to be consciously aware of, actively manage, and thoughtfully articulate one's emotions, particularly in relation to others in situations of both harmony and discord—is an essential complement to this collection of teaching skillsets. For example, when we engage with students, we balance structure and freedom, navigate difficult conversations and conflicts, cultivate trust and respect, inspire and motivate, gauge levels of competency and understanding, and appropriately customize pedagogical methods to support many individual students optimally. Indeed, our design pedagogy is an extensive and ever-evolving process that requires proactive continuous learning on the teacher's part.

The impact made by our teaching is both very significant and highly consequential. Effective teaching, regardless of its disciplinary context or grade level, can produce a sea change across our nation's higher education systems and, subsequently, in global economies. Scholars have long maintained that teacher effectiveness is the single most dominant factor affecting both student academic gain and student retention. Research reveals (Sanders & Rivers, 1996; Wright et al., 1997) the following:

- Students who receive three ineffective teachers consecutively may achieve at levels that are as much as 50 percentile points lower than students who receive three highly effective teachers consecutively.
- Following ineffective teachers, students in classrooms with effective teachers will make academic advances, but not enough to make up for lost time spent with an ineffective teacher.
- As a teacher's pedagogy strengthens, lower achieving students are the first to benefit; this can have a markedly consequential effect on student retention and attendant institutional revenue.

From this research, a "pedagogical ecosystem" emerges, one where a student's level of learning corresponds to a teacher's level of pedagogy, which, in turn, correlates with the level of teacher training and support an institution provides its faculty (Figure 14.1).

Still, many design teachers underestimate their impact on students, assuming they are but one brief, minor contributor to their students' four-year undergraduate education. However, in one survey of over 1,600 undergraduates (Light, 2001), graduating seniors were asked "Can you think of any particular faculty member who has had a particularly important impact on you? In shaping the way you think about yourself,

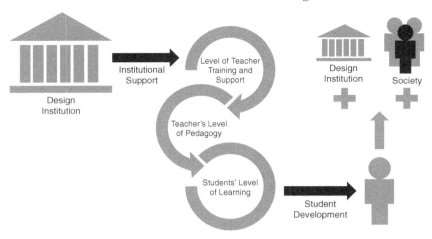

*Figure 14.1* The Pedagogical Ecosystem.

or life, or the world around you, or your future?" (p. 104). Among the respondents, 89% identified and described in great detail a specific professor who had a major impact on them, and two-thirds of these students named *several* faculty members who had been critical in their college lives. As Pendoley (2019) further opines:

> Ask anyone about the most important learning experiences of their lives, and they will tell you about someone who gave them insight into themselves and the world. They won't tell you about curriculum. They won't tell you about standards. And they won't tell you about funding models. We spend a lot of time talking about those things because they matter. But, they aren't at the forefront of great learning and teaching. Pedagogy is.
>
> (n.p.)

This data clearly demonstrates that we, as design educators, hold significant influence over the development of our students. We must therefore increasingly acknowledge the inherent power design educators—and their *teaching skillsets*—hold.

Yet, a paradox arises. Despite the vital role pedagogy plays in students' and alumni's successes—and subsequently the institution's success—tertiary-level design educators rarely receive pedagogical training or support. They are typically hired based on their success and recognition as professionally active designers and/or researchers (work that often takes precedence over teaching). They are subsequently placed in a classroom where they must teach themselves how to teach through self-instruction and trial and error. While some of these faculty enter the teaching profession with strong skills for interacting with students and are able to construct meaningful educational experiences that impart advanced knowledge and design expertise, many other faculty members may take years to develop as educators, years during which "the consequences of their early struggles [negatively] affect generations of students who enroll in their classes" (Davis, 2017, p. 1). There are those, too, who "sink" rather than "swim" because they lack any access to pedagogical training or support because neither are provided by their institutions. As a result, they exit the teaching profession prematurely, thus preventing design schools from cultivating a stable, well-prepared faculty that is committed to their roles as educators for the long term.

Conversely, when academic institutions provide effective and strategic teaching methods for design educators, this training can largely preempt these undue struggles and negative outcomes—particularly when introduced at the beginning of the teacher's career. Over time, the sustained support of continuing education enables design educators to strengthen their pedagogical aptitudes that are fundamental to increasing their sense of agency, self-efficacy, motivation, personal agility, confidence, job satisfaction, initiative, and performance. These gains not only benefit the students and the institution: they also enable the design educator to become a "teacher-mentor"—a new, advanced role that is becoming increasingly vital to the future of US design education (see Chapter 13 for full discussion).

## Section IV: Design Classrooms

Building upon the previous three sections' research, theories, and assessments, this section provides design educators with extensive, practical approaches to developing effective and strategic pedagogy. Throughout the following chapters, emphasis is placed on situating these techniques within the contexts of the emerging design student generation and the teacher-mentor role. These practices include:

- teaching methods to target the attributes of the emergent design student population;
- interpersonal practices that work to build trust and help manage conflict effectively;
- procedures for crafting well-designed syllabi;
- strategies that foster dynamic pedagogy and class sessions;
- techniques to bolster students' motivation and subsequent success; and
- ways of successfully cultivating an inclusive learning environment.

The synthesis of these with the other diverse practices presented in this section provides the reader with ideas for creating optimal learning experiences for design students.

As design educators, one of our fundamental roles is to provide our students with the knowledge they need to become successful professional designers. Directly connected to this is our duty to cultivate a learning environment in which students can develop into creative, resourceful, and responsible citizens. When we commit to strengthening our teaching skillsets—such as those discussed in this section—we make a promise to ourselves that we will transform our students positively and, subsequently, help shape the future of the world. As Linda Darling-Hammond, professor emerita at Stanford University's Graduate School of Education, astutely notes, "We have all kinds of educational reforms underway in the United States—curriculum reforms, governance reforms and so on—but at the end of the day, if you don't have a strong supply of well-prepared teachers, nothing else in education can work" (in Spector, 2019, n.p.).

## References

Brookfield, S. (2013). *Powerful techniques for teaching adults*. Jossey-Bass.

Davis, M. (2017). *Teaching design: A guide to curriculum and pedagogy for college design faculty and teachers who use design in their classrooms*. Allworth.

Light, R. (2001). *Making the most of college: Students speak their minds*. Harvard University.

Pendoley, R. (2019, March 23). If we don't work on pedagogy, nothing else matters. *Medium*. https://medium.com/age-of-awareness/if-we-dont-work-on-pedagogy-nothing-else-matters-c1a61207ff92

Sanders, W., & Rivers, J. C. (1996). *Cumulative and residual effects of teachers on future student academic achievement*. University of Tennessee Value-Added Research and Assessment Center.

Spector, C. (2019, July 29). If you don't have a strong supply of well-prepared teachers, nothing else in education can work. *Stanford University Graduate School of Education*. https://ed.stanford.edu/news/if-you-don-t-have-strong-supply-well-prepared-teachers-nothing-else-education-can-work

Wright, S. P., Horn, S. P., & Sanders, W. L. (1997). Teacher and classroom context effects on student achievement: Implications for teacher evaluation. *Journal of Personnel Evaluation in Education*, 11(1), 57–67.

Zwozdiak-Myers, P. (2012). *The teacher's reflective practice handbook: Becoming an extended professional through capturing evidence-informed practice*. Routledge.

# 15 A Practical Guide to Teaching the New Design Undergraduates

This chapter builds on the research and theories of young adult development along with the emergent generation's attributes and mindsets that are presented in Chapter 11. These generational characteristics include:

- students' growing need for personal choice, agency, and personalization in learning;
- new perceptions and expectations of the college experience and future careers;
- extreme periods of screen time and addiction to smartphones;
- rising fears of being "imperfect" and of making cataclysmic mistakes;
- declining in-person socialization; decreased expressions of empathy;
- multitasking behavior, reduced attention span, and not feeling fully "present" in situations; and
- the prolonging of adolescence due, in part, to a heightened focus on personal safety and security.

As explicated in Chapter 11, while these attributes have been evidenced in numerous research studies containing large, diverse populations of young adults in the US, they are not absolutes; rather, these characteristics are generalizations that may aid design educators in better understanding and subsequently engaging with their students.

Presented below are the key attributes detailed in Chapter 11, followed by practical pedagogical techniques that strategically target each attribute for design students' holistic success (Table 15.1).

At its best, design education supports the cognitive, emotional, and personal development of all students—students who will graduate and go on to help construct our future society. At its worst, the Academy marginalizes and disenfranchises these students, thus potentially becoming irrelevant and inconsequential in both the educational and professional contexts. It is therefore necessary for us, as design educators, to understand better how and why our students' attributes are evolving.

DOI: 10.4324/9781003049166-19

Table 15.1 Practical teaching strategies for the new generation of design school undergraduates

| Attributes and mindsets | Implications for teaching |
| --- | --- |
| **Personal choice, agency, and personalization** | Our design students were raised in a world filled with choice, where seemingly everything could be personalized to meet their own unique, personal needs. Accordingly, the principle "no one way suits all" guides their thinking and expectations toward learning, along with their need to feel unique and to expect tolerance of their diversity. How can students "design" their design education in your course? To answer this question, you must provide students with choice and agency in their learning experiences by offering customizable ways to meet learning outcomes, approach assignments, and engage in class. Agency elevates students' dedication and investment in the work and results in deeper learning.<br>Sample approaches you can use include the following:<br><br>• Ask students how they would like to structure particular class sessions. From a learning perspective, which formats do they feel will be most engaging? Class-wide activities, one-on-one meetings, and/or small-group reviews? Which content areas will need more or less attention, based on students' current knowledge and skillsets? List several options, ask students to suggest additional formats, and then collaboratively determine the session's agenda.<br>• Allow students to choose a reading from a short, curated list of texts that equally meet the session's learning aims.<br>• When scheduling guest speakers or field trips, offer three choices and facilitate a discussion about each option before students decide which one will best target their educational and professional goals.<br>• Determine how many weeks should be allocated to each project. Based on students' learning goals, which projects deserve more time? Which ones require less? During the first class session, review the syllabus and, through class-wide discussion, ask students to determine the projects' schedules. For example, if there are fifteen sessions and three projects, the weekly breakdown could be 5:5:5, 4:5:6, 3:6:6, or 2:4:9. Immediately following the conclusion of the first project (when students have a clearer sense of the course), review the plan with students, solicit feedback, and adjust the plan if needed. |

(*Continued*)

194  *Design Classrooms*

*Table 15.1* Practical teaching strategies for the new generation of design school undergraduates (*Continued*)

| Attributes and mindsets | Implications for teaching |
|---|---|
| **Perceptions of career and college** | The Great Recession (2008), COVID-19 (2020), increasing inflation of college fees, and other factors have piqued students' concerns over the economy, personal finances, and their careers. Thus, while students appreciate and enjoy learning design theory, they also want to know how these abstract ideas relate to their practical professional preparation. They want to know that the concepts learned in their courses will have broader implications on their ability to succeed in design careers in the future.<br>To allay students' concerns:<br>• Begin by asking students, "Why do you want to be an 'X'?" to promote deeper reflections on their chosen careers. Then, based on their answers, ask subsequent questions such as, "What drives you about 'X'?" and "What scares you about 'X'?" This guided reflection can strengthen and clarify students' academic and professional goals.<br>• Frequently relate design theory to "real world" applications by providing tangible examples.<br>• Ask students to reflect on how the course material applies to their chosen careers. Journaling, small-group discussions, and class-wide conversations are methods that can promote students' abilities to link the material to their professional development.<br>• Invite guest speakers from the design industries to enhance students' learning and answer questions about their careers and the profession.<br>• Support students' internship pursuits so they actively connect course material with field application in "real time" and not in the distant future, after graduation. Internships can also lead to ongoing professional mentorship both during and after the intern experience.<br>• The emergent group of undergraduates values direct and honest conversations. Facilitate frank in-class discussions about the design industries, skillsets sought by employers, the current and future job markets, and the challenges of building a design-oriented career. |

(*Continued*)

Table 15.1 Practical teaching strategies for the new generation of design school undergraduates (Continued)

| Attributes and mindsets | Implications for teaching |
|---|---|
| **Smartphone addiction** | While it is clear smartphones are here to stay, we—and our students—need to develop more self-aware relationships with our devices. Students should be taught about the importance and benefits of moderating smartphone usage. These benefits include dramatically improved emotional and physical health, cognition, and general well-being. Conversely, extensive studies show extreme smartphone usage fuels anxiety, increases depression and loneliness, diminishes one's ability to concentrate and think creatively, encourages self-absorption, disturbs sleep, negatively affects academic and work performance, and more. It is incumbent on us teachers to present living models of moderated cellphone usage and best practices; after all, students pattern their behavior on what they observe from those in leadership-level positions.<br><br>• At the start of every class, ask students to power off their phones or to leave them on a side table. Note: it is imperative that *you* do so, also.<br>• Although students may initially balk at this request, most students will quickly understand the benefits of "unplugging" during class. Students typically express they feel more present, are more engaged in discussions, achieve stronger cognitive focus, and have more positive and productive learning experiences when their phones are set aside.<br>• As with all your requests, explain the facts and logic behind this policy. For instance, aside from the aforementioned cognitive and emotional impacts caused by excessive usage, studies suggest a student's use of their devices during class degrades not only their own performance but also the performance of those around them due to the inherent distraction their presence presents in the classroom. Additionally, strong social skills are essential for job interviews, networking opportunities, personal relationships, and more. Students must be made aware that expertise with these skills are far more important to their futures than multitasking and distracting technology.<br>• You can also access extensive resources about this topic online and provide this information to students to subsequently gain "buy-in" to the practice from the class. |

(*Continued*)

Table 15.1 Practical teaching strategies for the new generation of design school undergraduates (*Continued*)

| Attributes and mindsets | Implications for teaching |
|---|---|
| | Students can also be given tools for moderating their smartphone usage outside of class. Examples include:<br><br>• Keep your phone silenced and in another room when doing schoolwork. Research suggests it takes a person approximately twenty-three minutes to resume a task at the depth where they left off following an interruption (e.g. a text).<br>• When working, wait until you feel distracted or fatigued (e.g. forty-five minutes), and then allow yourself a five-minute break to check your phone. Adhering to the five-minute rule is essential: set a timer to ensure you do not exceed the timeframe.<br>• At bedtime, silence your phone and keep it in another room or in a closed drawer where it is out of sight (and temptation).<br>• If necessary, use a phone app that automatically limits your screen time.<br>• Power off phones and place them out of sight whenever you are with friends, in meetings, or participating in other social activities. Be fully present, engaged, and respectful of others by giving them your undivided attention. They will appreciate your focus, and this will subsequently strengthen the positive aspects of your relationships.<br>• As an experiment, cut your screen time in half for one week. Over the course of that week, track how you feel. (In doing so, you may find that overall you feel happier, less anxious, and better connected to others and activities.)<br>• Schedule routine periods to "unplug" from your devices so that you can recharge your emotional, cognitive, and physical selves. Reiterate to students the significant benefits of doing so and the risks of not doing so. |

(*Continued*)

Table 15.1 Practical teaching strategies for the new generation of design school undergraduates (Continued)

| Attributes and mindsets | Implications for teaching |
|---|---|
| Fear of being "imperfect" and making mistakes | The extremely competitive design school environment, social media, and other stress-inducing factors lead many design students to believe everyone but them is more talented, a bigger success, and "perfect." Additionally, extreme social and academic pressures, coupled with hyper-involved parents, contribute to students having few opportunities to take significant risks and make mistakes. Thus, many scholars believe young people are consequently afforded too few chances to practice and develop resilience. Accordingly, avoiding mistakes at all costs—and enabling the perpetuation of a crippling fear of failure—can have a profoundly negative influence on some students' approach to learning in the design studio. To mitigate students' possible fears of failure, promote resilience and consequently optimize their learning: <br><br> Confront and destabilize fear. <br><br> • Facilitate a class-wide discussion about fear. What is it? Why do we have it? What are we afraid of *specifically*? Ask students to define explicitly their fears by writing them down so they can visualize and externalize them. This process can greatly decrease their fear, stress, and anxiety. <br> • Alternatively, ask students to anonymously list on a notecard two to five fears concerning their work, academic performance, career trajectory, or other topics. Then, either: <br>   i   Collect and review the cards and transcribe dominant fears and themes on the board. As a group, brainstorm suggestions for how someone could alleviate each fear; or <br>   ii  Collect and shuffle the cards, form pairs or small groups of students, and randomly distribute several cards to each grouping. Ask each team to list possible solutions and present their ideas to the class. <br><br> Normalize "failure" as a critical part of learning. <br><br> • Facilitate no- and low-stakes (non-graded) in-class activities throughout the semester that allow students to "play" and make mistakes in a supportive, relaxed environment. Allowing students to fail often and routinely builds their coping mechanisms around failure, encourages exploration, and engenders deeper learning. For example, one activity could be a "speed sketching" exercise: in fifteen-second intervals, students move to different sketching "stations" that are placed around the room to iterate quickly from the previous design idea drawn by a classmate. Another activity is the "30-minute design challenge" wherein student teams collaboratively solve a specific design brief. |

(*Continued*)

Table 15.1 Practical teaching strategies for the new generation of design school undergraduates (*Continued*)

| Attributes and mindsets | Implications for teaching |
|---|---|
| | • Shortly before each class ends, allow students to begin the upcoming week's homework. This can enable you to preempt students' questions, misunderstandings, and any other potential impediments before they complete it independently.<br>• Omit a "final" project deliverable. Instead, offer an assignment that focuses on the design process as the ultimate goal. For example, this might be a sketchbook filled with extensive research and "raw" design iterations that typically precede "polished" presentations.<br>• If your course contains several design projects, allow students to drop their lowest grade before determining their final course grades.<br><br>Deliver detailed feedback.<br><br>• Living in a world of continuous "likes" and streams of feedback means the emergent generation is accustomed to and values ongoing feedback and guidance in shorter "bursts" rather than in the form of a singular exhaustive final project assessment. This includes frequently offering students assurance they are learning and progressing forward.<br>• The emergent generation appreciates a gentler approach during design critiques. At the same time, its members prioritize logic and facts, along with sincerity and authenticity—particularly in academic assessments. During critiques, provide students equal amounts of constructive and positive feedback that are reinforced by clearly articulated rationales. |

(*Continued*)

Table 15.1 Practical teaching strategies for the new generation of design school undergraduates (*Continued*)

| Attributes and mindsets | Implications for teaching |
|---|---|
| | Analyze success and promote personal agency. |
| | • What is "success?" It can take many forms. Ask students to reflect on the diverse definitions of "success" so they may discover areas where they are succeeding through their own agency.<br>• Provide biographical information about design leaders who overcame setbacks through grit and determination. This will help students better understand that hardships are an inherent part of personal and professional development, and that they can be overcome. It can also help them realize that their failures, no matter how big or small, are not always a determining factor for their success. In fact, initially perceived "failures" can become remarkable successes—like the "failed" adhesive that led to the development of Post-It Notes.<br>• Provide a learning experience (e.g. a short essay or design project) that prompts students' reflections on a period when their grit, determination, and perseverance led to successful outcomes in adversarial situations.<br>• Emphasize a growth mindset. This will encourage students to embrace challenges, rather than feel overwhelmed by them and avoid them. To promote a growth mindset:<br>   i  Assure students they will eventually master the skillset(s) over time (use the key word "yet" during discussions to remind students that skills are developed over time);<br>   ii  Praise effort, perseverance, and determination;<br>   iii  Normalize the fact that some students struggle and do not "get it" right away;<br>   iv  Commend students' strategies and quality of thought in the work, not just the final project outcome;<br>   v  Remind students that learning is a personal experience. As such, everyone progresses at different, alternating speeds before reaching the final class session *together*.<br><br>Additional pedagogical techniques that promote a growth mindset are provided in Chapter 18. |

(*Continued*)

200  *Design Classrooms*

*Table 15.1* Practical teaching strategies for the new generation of design school undergraduates (*Continued*)

| Attributes and mindsets | Implications for teaching |
| --- | --- |
| **Decreased in-person socialization** | The emergent generation is spending significantly less time socializing face-to-face than prior generations. Studies show undergraduates are exhibiting increasing levels of loneliness, anxiety, stress, and depression, along with decreasing levels of empathy.<br><br>In-person socialization offers exponential benefits. It allows people to "read" their counterpart's body language, facial expressions, and vocal intonations to help them refine their communication skills and develop their empathy. It enables them to build and better navigate inter- and intrapersonal relations, and thus form stronger emotional bonds with others. These interactions reduce stress and anxiety, bolster the body's immune system, promote longevity, and enhance physical and emotional well-being—as well as offering numerous other cognitive and emotional advantages and gains. To promote in-person socialization during class, and thus support students' holistic development, the following pedagogical techniques can be employed:<br><br>• Explain to students the mental and physical benefits of in-person socialization. For example, these engagements decrease stress and anxiety that, in turn, engender better neural functioning and focus. Consequently, learning, academic performance, and professional preparation are strengthened.<br>• Offer diverse ways for students to participate so that everyone feels included and can engage at their own comfort level. Select strategies include:<br>    i   Large class-wide discussions;<br>    ii  Small-group conversations;<br>    iii Peer-to-peer sharing;<br>    iv  Development of word clouds and other "real time" responses that are projected or documented on the board during class discussions;<br>    v   Brainstorming and mapping exercises via Post-Its or a similar format.<br>• Offer text- and visually based activities so that students' differentiated learning and communication styles are supported. |

(*Continued*)

Table 15.1 Practical teaching strategies for the new generation of design school undergraduates (Continued)

| Attributes and mindsets | Implications for teaching |
|---|---|
| | Students' empathy can be developed and strengthened in many ways. For example: <br><br>• Prompt more discussions, written reflections, and projects that explore *others'* experiences, emotions, and situations. Explicitly ask students to put themselves in another person's situation and identify what emotions that person may be feeling. <br>• At the conclusion of group design projects, ask students to write two reflections: <br>   i  a reflection about themselves during the project; and <br>   ii a reflection about how they think their group members experienced the project. <br>• Facilitate role-play exercises, debates, and similar opportunities wherein students must assume perspectives that are different from their own. <br>• When appropriate, make socio- and ethnographic research part of a project. In-person interviews, community observations, and similar methodologies that place students vis-à-vis the individual and community help students acquire active listening skills and a more authentic understanding of people, both of which lead to an increased capacity for empathy. <br>• Assign an "opposite designer" project. Sometime after the course's first project (when students have a sense of each other's aesthetic sensibilities), facilitate a class-wide discussion whereby classmates determine one another's "opposite designer." Students then research their assigned designer's biography, design processes, and professional work. Using this material as a guide, students develop their *own* design project in the assigned opposite design style. The pedagogic goal is for students to experience a different, "foreign" mindset and approach to design while simultaneously honing their critical thinking. <br><br>The "Mid-Project Swap" is another version of this project. Its methodology is as follows: <br><br>1  Students begin an assigned project; <br>2  At midpoint, students swap projects (through lottery or class vote) with one another; <br>3  Each student interviews their counterpart to discuss the work at its midpoint, their peer's initial vision and goals for the project, and other vital design criteria; <br>4  The new student then completes their counterpart's assigned work by adhering to their partner's original intents (e.g. aesthetics, design deliverable(s), and target audience); <br>5  During class-wide final critiques, each student assesses their counterpart's completed work. <br><br>In this version, students can engage face-to-face, develop deeper empathic understandings, and subsequently cultivate a more robust classroom community. |

(Continued)

202  *Design Classrooms*

*Table 15.1* Practical teaching strategies for the new generation of design school undergraduates (*Continued*)

| Attributes and mindsets | Implications for teaching |
|---|---|
| **Multitasking and not feeling "present"** | For many people, multitasking has become a normative practice. Yet this behavior commonly escalates the individual's anxiety, stress, and inabilities to feel fully "present" in situations. Among undergraduates, research shows the average student manages five digital screens at once and has an eight-second attention span. Attributes like these make it necessary for design educators to adopt new pedagogical methods for the emergent generation. These practices include:<br><br>• At the start of every class:<br>   i  Write the session's agenda on the board so that students can reference it throughout the class.<br>   ii  Review the session's goals and discuss how they relate to the previous class, the current project, and the course's broader learning outcomes. As always, explain the session's rationale (the "why" behind these goals) and not just its content (the "what" in the agenda).<br>   iii  Instruct students to power off their phones and stow them away out of sight.<br><br>• As an example, a well-structured three-hour session could then run as follows:<br>   i  Beginning ten minutes: review the last session as a foundation for today's new material.<br>   ii  Middle 160 minutes: introduce new material and occasionally reference prior learning to effectively construct more advanced knowledge for students.<br>   iii  Final ten minutes: briefly describe how today's session primes students for the upcoming homework assignment and the next session.<br><br>• Begin every assignment by showing the full scope, path, and aims of the work. Proceed by offering students step-by-step, "bite-sized" amounts of information along the way—as opposed to big progressions that could overwhelm their attention spans.<br>• Every session should offer several discrete experiences that keep the class moving. Design demonstrations, class-wide discussions, team activities, videos, structured critiques, and periods of reflective writing are some ways to target different learning styles (e.g. visual, auditory, and kinesthetic) so that all students remain engaged and focused.<br>• Promote "unitasking" and its subsequent benefits (e.g. explain the twenty-three minutes it takes someone to resume a task at the depth where they left off following an interruption/diversion). |

(*Continued*)

Table 15.1 Practical teaching strategies for the new generation of design school undergraduates (*Continued*)

| Attributes and mindsets | Implications for teaching |
|---|---|
| **Prolonging adolescence: the need for safety and protection** | Spikes in national terrorism, marked political discord, two recent economic collapses, and over-involved parenting are just some of the factors that have impacted our current college students' childhoods, mindsets, and attendant perspectives on life. Thus, compared to previous populations, data reveal increasing numbers of current undergraduates are choosing to grow up more slowly, are more concerned about their safety and security, are proceeding more cautiously in life both outside and inside the school environment, and overall are significantly more risk averse than previous generations.<br>Attributes such as these can be supported through the following pedagogical techniques:<br><br>• When appropriate, allow students to set their own comfortable pace. For example, although a project's due date should be held, how that deadline is met can be unique to each student's preference and learning style.<br>• Provide students with time to make meaning of their learning before they share that meaning with others. A common practice is "Think—Pair—Share," whereby students first reflect on information before discussing it with a classmate and then sharing it with the whole class.<br>• Provide ongoing reassurance to students by emphasizing you are "on their side" and that you provide them with feedback because you want to help ensure they succeed. Explicitly stating to a student, "I want you to succeed" can engender trust, heighten motivation, and subsequently catapult them to success.<br>• Frame criticisms as the best path toward better academic performance and professional preparation.<br>• Be a "life coach": offer appropriate advice if/when a student asks for guidance about topics beyond the project at hand—such as career pathways, other academic courses, time management, stress reduction, and similar areas that are essential to their holistic development. This is a core attribute of the teacher-mentor described in Chapter 13—a new role that is becoming increasingly vital to the future of design education.<br>• It is worth remembering that some students may, at times, feel scared or exhibit more cautious behaviors than their peers. Take more time to build mutual trust with them consciously, connect them with the wider community, and promote a safe learning environment in which students are unafraid to take risks, experiment, and fail. (See Chapters 17 and 19 regarding building trust and community.) |

(*Continued*)

Table 15.1 Practical teaching strategies for the new generation of design school undergraduates (Continued)

| Attributes and mindsets | Implications for teaching |
| --- | --- |
| | At the same time, it is critical to teach students:<br><br>• To be comfortable with discomfort and, in doing so, build vital coping mechanisms and life-skills.<br>• The values and benefits of differing voices, even when we disagree with them.<br>• How to debate—and not silence or censor—differing viewpoints, no matter how upsetting or uncomfortable they may be. (As US President Barrack Obama famously asserted, "Feel free to disagree with somebody, but don't try to just shut them up …").<br><br>Accordingly, a pedagogical balance should be employed: one that simultaneously involves being compassionate toward students' needs *and* instilling in students the values and tools that will prepare them for the professional world and full adulthood. |

In doing so, we are better prepared to craft dynamic learning environments through our teaching methods. The pedagogical techniques presented in this chapter serve as a starting point for design educators in their continual exploration of innovative educational practices. These practices that support students also strengthen design curricula, programs, and institutions for our students—and our world.

# 16 Teaching as Performance

## Introduction

Teaching, at its best, is a performative practice. The moment we enter the design classroom, we set the tone and course of study for every student. By incorporating dynamic uses of our voices, bodies, and classroom spaces, we are able to engage, inspire, and motivate students. These performative practices, in turn, enhance students' learning, their relationship with the design discipline, and their academic success. This strongly pertains to the student-centered, studio-based learning environments of design higher education; as highly perceptive young adults, design students possess sophisticated abilities to "read" and process the autonomic and idiosyncratic nonverbal communication we emit. It is therefore imperative to remind ourselves that, as design educators, we are capable of transforming indifference into piqued enthusiasm through well-crafted performative teaching for our student-audience. Through our performances, we represent the discipline we teach and act as role models for the aspiring designers we educate.

Despite the significance of performance in teaching, it is given scant attention in design education. Many teachers assume course content—and its delivery through verbalization and subject-related visuals—is the primary way to impart knowledge and communicate with students. However, researchers (e.g. Mehrabian, 1971) posit approximately 93% of all face-to-face communication is nonverbal. The small percentage of verbal communication primarily stimulates cognition (learning) in the student, whereas the greater percentage and pervasiveness of nonverbal communication (e.g. body language and vocal tone)—which sometimes *replaces* verbalizations—stimulate affective meanings in students (e.g. their feelings and attitudes toward the course, learning material, and the teacher) (McCroskey et al., 2006). Emotions are powerful motivators and frequently drive students' actions—including their levels of engagement, learning, and intrinsic motivation (see Chapter 18).

Our teaching performance plays a pivotal role in establishing rapport with students. Research reveals negotiations conducted by phone are

DOI: 10.4324/9781003049166-20

typically won by the person with the strongest argument, "but this is not so true when negotiating face-to-face, because overall we make our final decisions more on what we see than what we hear" (Pease & Pease, 2004, p. 10). Body language is critical in these scenarios since it accounts for 60%–80% of the impact made in negotiations (Pease & Pease, 2004). As teachers, we regularly "negotiate" with our students by asking them to adopt new beliefs, gain knowledge, take risks and experiment, and trust us during periods of uncertainty. This sense of trust sometimes can be forged immediately; people typically form an impression of someone within ten seconds in one-on-one settings and sixty seconds in group settings, like classrooms (Cooper, 2019). It is therefore essential that design educators develop and hone effective and positive body language. As a result, students are more apt to trust us, understand we value their points of view, see us as capable and competent, sense our support, and ultimately feel cared for and understood (Pease & Pease, 2004).

## Key Components of Effective Teaching Performance

While there are extensive methods for developing effective nonverbal communication, several techniques for design educators are provided below. These include the effective uses of presence, voice, body language, and spatial relationships. As with all forms of communication, consideration should be given to cultural differences that may influence how certain behaviors are perceived by students.

### *Presence*

The aphorism, "If you fail to prepare, you are preparing to fail," underscores the importance of preparation in producing effective teaching performance. Preparation for each class includes priming ourselves to exude *presence*, "a state of alert awareness, receptivity, and connectedness to the working of both the individuals and the group in the context of the learning environment" (Henik, 2018, n.p.). Like a maestro mounting a podium, a teacher with presence generates excitement and respect among students simply by entering the room. Presence is crucial to gaining and holding students' attention, classroom management, and creating the excitement that makes students eager to learn from us. Conversely, a poor sense of presence—as shown through such actions as mumbling, slouching, avoiding eye contact, crossing arms, and arriving late—undermines our credibility and our students' trust in us. Rather than being captivated by us, students will check their emails, text, doodle, or find other ways to disengage from our lackluster teaching performance. In this case, teachers are less likely to be respected or trusted by students.

Presence is a skill, a tool we can acquire. We can develop it by focusing on our relationships with students, remembering *why* we teach, and honing our inner confidence. One technique to improve your presence is to mentally rehearse how you envision yourself teaching and want the class to proceed shortly before each class. Imagine how articulate you will be; envision your fluid and deliberate body movements, your effective use of the classroom, and the positive, cheerful energy you will give—and receive. In addition to this technique, another ability we can access is that of positive memory recall. By remembering a positive memory, you put yourself into a positive and confident state of mind. Doing so before each class can help bolster your confidence and subsequently improve the quality of your presence in the classroom.

Simple exercises such as these can help release mood-elevating endorphins and dopamine and boost your confidence, which help improve your presence. After all, a teacher's presence and confidence (not to be confused with arrogance) are *vital* to teaching effectively as they promote respect in the classroom and provide a foundation for trust, which allows for more student positive risk-taking. This, in turn, increases learning opportunities, fosters authentic teacher-student relationships, enables teachers to address the unknown resourcefully, and reassures students we are qualified educators (Henik, 2018).

*Voice*

Students excel when their emotions are engaged during the learning process. One way to stimulate students' emotional engagement is to convey our inherent passion for what we are sharing with them through expressive vocal inflection, diction, volume, and choice of words. As educators, it is critical that we master effective vocal communication for teaching performance. By learning and practicing variations of these features in our presentation, educators can master them to the point where they can be used to instill a sense of presence in students and attain the attention they and their students deserve (Henik, 2018). The incorporation of variations in tone of voice, well-timed pauses, and tempo changes can emphasize key learning points, enthusiastically bring students into the discourse, draw their attention to critical learning areas, and prevent vocal monotony and subsequent student disengagement that often accompanies it.

Our use of vocal patterning should take into account specific goals, audiences, surroundings, and related contexts (Cooper, 2019). Vocal styles of inflection, volume, and tone can dramatically affect our intentions, teacher-student relationships, action outcomes, and even our reputations. For example, asking "Why are you late?" can evoke starkly different meanings depending upon the manner of delivery, such as whether it is being shouted, warmly expressed, or whispered. The physical context can also impart significant meaning and emotional impact. There are tremendous differences in how to handle a conversation based on whether that conversation needs to take place across a large, crowded design studio as class begins, or said during office hours when the teacher and student are in private, closer proximity.

Synchronizing our intonation, inflection, and pace of speaking with those of our students is another effective way to establish rapport and subsequently improve learning. When we adjust our vocal patterns to reflect those of our counterpart, the counterpart is more likely to feel comfortable, enjoy our conversation, develop a sense of trust, and become better connected with us (Pease & Pease, 2004). When that counterpart is a student, it draws the student further into our teaching. Furthermore, because the rate of speed of a person's speech gives us an idea of the rate at which their brain can absorb and analyze information, it is important not to speak at a rate that is faster than the student's (Pease & Pease, 2004). Doing so may cause the student to feel pressured and potentially form negative views of the teacher, the message, and the course. To prevent such undue pressure, it is essential not to rush students, but rather to observe pauses in students' speech and appear relaxed and ready to listen during learning activities.

*Body Language*

Without a single word, our body language can welcome or reject students, affirm or contradict our words, reinforce or undermine our spoken message, or convey our emotional state. Body language is the first thing our students perceive about us when we enter the classroom. When we teach, our body's stance, positions, gestures, and movements enhance and amplify the spoken messages we deliver. The interrelationship between our body and our emotions must be thoroughly considered: the body "works in conjunction with the brain to send and expel certain messages that define emotions, often leading to subconscious visual cues that may give away the true thoughts and feelings of a given individual without their even realizing what they are doing" (Cooper, 2019, p. 55).

Given the impact our body language can have on students' perceptions, emotions, and subsequent learning experiences, attention must be given to the following techniques of teaching performance:

1 Stance
   Our physical stance outwardly communicates our emotions. When our shoulders, neck, and back are relaxed and in alignment, we appear alert, confident, and eager to engage with students. Conversely, body language conveyed through things such as a hunched back, inwardly rotated shoulders, and protruding stomach can communicate insecurity, disinterest, lethargy, anxiety, sadness, or fear (Cooper, 2019). A negative, unapproachable demeanor is also conveyed when folding one's arms across one's chest, standing

behind a desk, and using other physical barriers that block access to the front of the body.

To promote a positive and welcoming stance, avoid such barriers. Ensure you are literally and figuratively close to students whenever possible. Make sure that the physical space of your classroom allows you to move freely about so you can situate yourself near students. One critical expression of openness includes facing the student with whom you are communicating and directing your heart toward the student's without any barrier in between. This particular posture communicates that you are interested, engaged, receptive, and respectful toward the student.

Ultimately, your aim is to establish a positive stance that conveys confidence without appearing arrogant and concurrently works to cultivate a positive rapport with students. One way to quickly establish rapport with a student is to mirror their positive body language. This is a common phenomenon that subconsciously occurs between people who are fond of each other, such as friends, and it leads our counterparts to feel accepted and well-liked due to the "in-synch" attitudes that arise as a direct result of perceiving the in-synch body language. These attitudes, in turn, foster the feeling you are easy to be with, help forge an unspoken bond and unified front, promote mutual understanding and agreement, and often produce a sense of security in the student (Pease & Pease, 2004).

2 The face

Because it is the typical focal point of in-person communication, the face is the most critical tool for displaying body language (Cooper, 2019). Our facial expressions easily convey our emotions and attitudes, and their abilities to lower or elevate others' emotions can either close the proverbial "gap" and draw you together *or* lay the foundations for distrust, frustration, confusion, and other negative emotions in our observer(s). The best way to establish a positive first impression and sustain engagement is simply to smile. For students, a teacher's smile encourages, draws them in, and conveys the teacher's pleasure in working with them. A smile's effect can be positively contagious: the more we smile, the more positive other people's attitudes and responses will be to us (Pease & Pease, 2004). Research reveals "most encounters will run more smoothly, last longer, have more positive outcomes, and dramatically improve relationships when you make a point of regularly smiling …" (Pease & Pease, 2004, p. 89).

Appropriate eye contact also establishes positive, trusting relationships with students. It promotes rapport, shows we are self-confident and comfortable with students, and conveys our interest in listening to students. However, like body language, context matters: in certain instances, too much eye contact can be perceived as a dominating behavior and/or feel intimidating to the receiver. Researchers (e.g. Cooper, 2019) note several select important patterns and interpretations of eye movements. These include the following:

- Looking away mid-conversation can suggest discomfort with the conversation or environment, a subconscious desire to disengage and leave, or low confidence.
- Downward glances may express submission or shame.
- Upward glances can suggest boredom, uncertainty, or haughtiness.
- Sideway glances often suggest repulsion, irritation, or disagreement.
- Rapid blinking can appear arrogant or reveal distress.

Understanding the possible meanings behind eye movements enables us to interpret our students' nonverbal cues and strengthen our teaching performance for optimal learning and teacher-student relationships.

3 <u>Arms and hands</u>
The positioning of arms and hands also communicates emotions. While relaxed arms at one's side suggest receptiveness, openness, and willingness to engage, an arms-folded across the chest posture frequently denotes nervousness, defensiveness, unacceptance, or "an attempt to put a barrier between the person and someone or something they don't like" (Pease & Pease, 2004, p. 93). A barrier also arises when an object is held with both hands in front of the body in a protective or defensive way; this may suggest the person is protecting themselves or disinterested in engagement. Although we may assume such positions because they feel comfortable, because we are physically feeling cold, or for any other innocuous purpose, it is important to consider how arm and hand positions may convey negative nonverbal communication to students and thus understand how to avoid them whenever possible.

Hand gestures offer especially complex emotional "vocabulary." As Pease and Pease (2004) note, their range of nonverbal communication is expansive. Some common hand gestures in the context of teaching include the following:

- *Open palms* during conversation suggest openness, sincerity, honesty, and acceptance. They can also convey a genuine interest in questions and answers in a nonthreatening way. However, the same verbal response with concealed palms suggests the person is lying. Palms-up is nonthreatening, while palms-down shows authority.
- *Hands clasped together behind the back* display superiority, power, and confidence since the person is exposing the vulnerable areas (heart, stomach, etc.) of the front of their body.

- *Holding hands at crotch level* (for men) subconsciously protects vulnerable areas and may indicate insecurity or submission.
- *Clenched hands* commonly express a frustrated, anxious, restrained, or negative attitude.
- *One hand gripping the other's wrist* shows frustration and an attempt at self-control.
- *"The Steeple"*—a gesture given when the fingers of one hand are placed over the fingers of the other hand and form a "church steeple"—can be perceived as haughty, smug, or arrogant, and resultantly undermine a teacher's intentions to appear welcoming, trustful, and persuasive.
- *Free hands,* removed from pockets and displayed openly, show receptiveness and having nothing to hide.

In addition to using these techniques to communicate better with your students, they can also affect your internal experience. Simply taking a particular pose can alter our emotions through cause and effect. For instance, uncrossing your arms and extending open palms in a welcoming stance will resultantly produce feelings of confidence within ourselves. As our minds influence our bodies, so too do our bodies influence our states of mind.

4 <u>Legs and feet</u>

While many people are acutely aware of their faces, arms, and hands—and thus more conscious of faking these gestures—they are less aware of how they communicate with their legs and feet (Pease & Pease, 2004). Therefore, legs and feet offer significant clues about someone's authentic attitudes. For instance, while the upper body posture may indicate one thing (e.g. the person is politely facing us during a conversation, meaning they are engaged), the lower body may indicate another altogether (e.g. the feet pointed toward a door or away from us, meaning they wish to exit the engagement) (Cooper, 2019). Numerous studies (e.g. Pease & Pease, 2004) reveal these leg and feet gestures can communicate the following signals:

- *Crossed legs* (when sitting or standing) can suggest reticence, defensiveness, uncertainty, and/or disapproval (whereas legs in an open stance convey openness and acceptance).
- *Crossed ankles* may signify nervousness, anxiety, or fear.
- *Restless legs* commonly indicate boredom, nervousness, disinterest, and a desire to leave.
- *Toes point* to where the person wants to go or their direction of interest.
- *Placing one leg forward with one leg back* when standing may indicate discomfort with the conversation and/or situation, and a desire for distance.

As with all nonverbal communication, awareness of how these bodily gestures may be perceived by students should encourage us to adopt positive nonverbal teaching performance strategies. Understanding these gestures also provides possible clues into our students' attitudes that, in turn, allow us to guide situations appropriately.

*Spatial Relationships*

Design demonstrations, project critiques, and attendant studio-based teaching and learning activities involve teachers and students regularly negotiating one another's personal space, which is "the area individual humans actively maintain around themselves into which others cannot intrude without arousing discomfort" (Hayduk, 1978, p. 118). The amount of personal space required by the student—which expands and contracts due to varying factors (e.g. national/cultural norms and interpersonal relationships)—can affect their feelings of comfort and safety (Little, 1965; Welsch et al., 2019). Intruding upon a student's personal space can undermine their learning. For example, impinging on a student's personal space may evoke a "fight-or-flight" response in the student. This response results in negative physiological changes that occur within the body when someone uninvited enters their personal space. It is therefore imperative that design educators gain awareness of the commonly demarcated "zone distances" of personal space that influence students' emotions.

While personal space varies from culture to culture, researchers (e.g. Hall, 1966) have divided the radius circling the body into multiple subregions commonly observed among North Americans (Figure 16.1). These include the following:

- Intimate space. In this area, estimated to be between 6 and 18 inches away from the body of the individual, the person only allows those who are most emotionally close to them. Examples include parents, lovers, and close friends.
- Personal space. Extending from 1.5 to 4 feet, this distance is considered comfortable when working with individual students, conversing at functions and parties, and standing with those we know relatively well.
- Social space. This space, between 4 and 12 feet, is typically used for more formal social and business activities with acquaintances or strangers like new colleagues, storekeepers, and delivery people.
- Public space. Covering 12–25 feet (or more), this is a comfortable distance for public speaking and addressing sizeable student cohorts in large classrooms.

The effective use of space for teaching performance includes seating positions. During project reviews, collaborative discussions, and similar

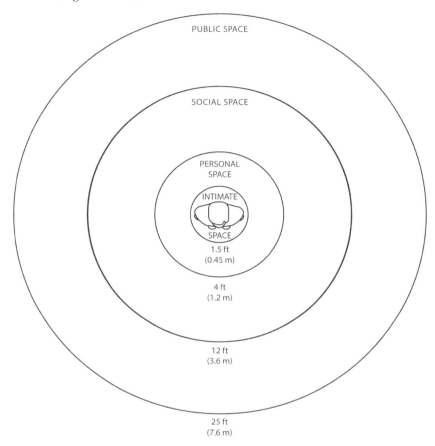

*Figure 16.1* Interpersonal distances.
Source: Adapted from Hall (1966).

engagements, the positioning between teacher and student fosters certain moods. For instance, Pease and Pease (2004) note the following seating arrangements commonly generate the accompanying dynamics (Figure 16.2):

1  The L-shaped position is used to foster friendly, nonthreatening conversation where each person can offer good eye contact, observe and use positive gestures, and avoid territorial division. It is an ideal position when teaching or advising students.
2  The side-by-side position is chosen when two people are working on a task together or think alike. It is intuitively taken when conducting a demonstration (e.g. illustration rendering) or similar action that

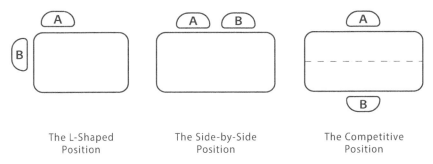

Figure 16.2 Seating positions.

suggests collaboration. However, it is important that neither party feel as if they have encroached on the other's intimate space.

3 The competitive position "can create a defensive, competitive atmosphere and can lead to each party taking a firm stand on [their] point of view because the table becomes a solid barrier between both parties" (p. 334). Outside of domestic contexts, this position is often used during negotiations or when playing chess. Yet in social settings, such as dining, it is seen as conversational rather than confrontational. Research reveals when people assume this position they speak in shorter sentences, recall less of what was said, and are more likely to argue.

While particular situations may not offer seating choices, an understanding of how these positions may affect design teacher-student dynamics will enable teachers to enter each engagement better equipped to promote positive teacher-student relationships.

## Conclusion

Teaching performance plays a significant role in cultivating and advancing students' learning and success as emergent designers. As such, concerted attention must be given to teachers' effective uses of their presence, vocal intonation and patterning, word choice, body language, and spatial relationships vis-à-vis students that can support and enhance students' academic experiences. When executed correctly, these performative practices elevate students' levels of motivation and engagement, positive perceptions of their coursework and the design disciplines, and subsequently the quality of their learning. It is through a well-crafted, positive teaching performance that optimal teacher-student relationships may emerge and thus support our design alumni's personal and professional successes—and subsequently, the design industries' advancements.

## References

Cooper, B. (2019). *Body language mastery: The ultimate psychology guide to analyzing, reading and influencing people using body language, emotional intelligence, psychological persuasion and manipulation*. Brandon Cooper.

Hall, E. (1966). *The hidden dimension*. Doubleday.

Hayduk, L. (1978). Personal space: An evaluative and orienting overview. *Psychological Bulletin*, *85*(1), 117–134.

Henik, S. (2018, June 19). Developing your classroom presence. *Edutopia*. https://www.edutopia.org/article/developing-your-classroom-presence

Little, K. (1965). Personal space. *Journal of Experimental Social Psychology*, *1*(3), 237–247.

McCroskey, J., Richmond, V., & McCroskey, L. (2006). *An introduction to communication in the classroom: The role of communication in teaching and training*. Allyn & Bacon.

Mehrabian, A. (1971). *Silent messages*. Wadsworth.

Pease, A., & Pease, B. (2004). *The definitive book of body language*. Bantam Dell.

Welsch, R., von Castell, C., & Hecht, H. (2019). The anisotropy of personal space. *PLoS ONE*, *14*(6), 1–13.

# 17 Classroom Dynamics
## Trust and Conflict

## Introduction

Classroom dynamics—commonly defined as the interactions between teachers and students—are, inevitably, the most emotionally loaded aspects of the learning environment. As teachers, we are responsible for helping guide and shape these dynamics so they may positively affect our students' experiences. The subsequent impact of classroom dynamics on students' learning and well-being can be expansive and long-lasting: a Gallup-Purdue University report (2014) reveals "if graduates had a professor who cared about them as a person, made them excited about learning, and encouraged them to pursue their dreams, their odds of being engaged at work more than doubled, as did their odds of thriving in their well-being" (p. 4). Conversely, if students complete a course hating the experience "they [are] less likely to continue learning, or even to retain what they had supposedly gained from the class" (Bain, 2004, p. 7). Such outcomes as these make it incumbent upon design teachers to maintain concerted awareness of the complex relationships between teachers and students and students and students, and to continuously foster a positive learning environment.

Classroom dynamics are formed by a broad, extensive array of factors. This chapter focuses on two that are particularly determinant in shaping classroom interactions: **trust** and **conflict**. Meaningful relationships—and attendant learning opportunities—cannot flourish without trust. Positive classroom dynamics require emergent conflicts between participants to be managed and resolved successfully. The necessity of trust and conflict resolution are key to students' and faculty's well-being: in some cases, frequent encounters with unruly or disengaged students (due to high conflict and/or low trust) can cause educators to dread teaching and, at times, depart prematurely from the profession (Boice, 2000).

DOI: 10.4324/9781003049166-21

## Trust in the Design Classroom

"Coming to trust another person is the most fragile of human projects. It requires knowing someone over a period of time and seeing their honesty modeled in their actions. College classrooms provide the conditions in which people can learn to trust or mistrust each other" (Brookfield, 1995, p. 26). This fragile, complex nature of trust-building is pronounced in academic environments due in part to their culture: demarcated roles, rules, guidelines, teacher-student hierarchies, and assessments of students' personal creative expression are just some factors that impact the development of trust in design classrooms.

Trust is vital to the design classroom because it engenders feelings of security and support in both students and the community as a whole. These feelings, in turn, enable students to feel unafraid of being judged, remain vulnerable, take risks, and ultimately perform at their best. It is through such personal experiences and in trusting environments that design innovation can occur.

Analyzing data from 360 assessments of 87,000 leaders, researchers Zenger and Folkman (2019) identified three key attributes that typically instill trust in people:

1 <u>Positive relationships.</u> Building positive relationships requires educators to view undergraduates as adults as well as actively promoting cooperation between others, being generous with our time and attention as educators, emphasizing peer learning, and remaining connected to the concerns of others.
2 <u>High expertise and good judgment.</u> Students' formation of trust is closely linked to how they perceive their teacher's level of knowledge, depth of experience, and use of good judgment. This includes the teacher's aptitude for anticipating and responding quickly to problems and concerns.
3 <u>Consistency.</u> Reliability, matching words with actions, honoring commitments and promises, and setting good examples are essential to building trust. As teachers, it is necessary for us to model in ourselves the behaviors we want to see in our students. Some key questions for introspection in this area include: "Are you genuinely open to new ideas?", "Do you take risks in your *own* scholarship/creative practice?", "Have you explored new teaching methods?" One of the most powerful ways we can positively impact the tone of our design classrooms and our students' holistic development is to live the values we espouse (Brookfield, 1995).

Trust builds slowly and incrementally, over the course of many diverse moments. Whether through classroom design demonstrations, office hours, hallway interactions, or occasional emails, there is always an opportunity to develop trust with and between students. This requires adopting an "anthropological lens" to understand better each student's unique values, needs, concerns, and interests. In doing so, we can build meaningful relationships, make good judgments, and show consistency in our actions.

Additional strategies that develop trust in the classroom include:

- <u>Facilitating group interactions frequently.</u> Throughout the semester, cultivate group cohesion to reduce the "psychological distance" between participants. This can be accomplished by facilitating interactions between students, such as "peer-to-peer design tutorials," so they can casually interact and bond. As teachers, we can share with students our favorite movies, vacation spots, and other personal information to show our "human" side. Additionally, these frequent interactions do more than simply build trust: they prevent feelings of alienation among students, which, in turn, reduces the potential for disruptive behaviors in classrooms (Kearney & Plax, 1992).
- <u>Discuss your pedagogy.</u> Explaining our pedagogical methods and rationales with students engenders trust in several ways. For example, these discussions help reduce the impact of teacher-student hierarchies on students (and thus promote opportunities for critiques and evaluations of our teaching methods), prevent students from assuming hidden agendas or motives on our parts, support class-wide fairness and inclusion, and heighten students' overall engagement in and connection to the learning experience (Brookfield, 1995). When we discuss our teaching methods with students, it conveys that our pedagogy comes from a "well-thought-out rationale grounded in experience" and is something we take very seriously. Furthermore, if discussions are accompanied by brainstorming select ideas with students, they are apt to trust the teacher more quickly (Brookfield, 1995, p. 109).
- <u>Foster a democratic design classroom.</u> Sharing decision making in our learning environment is essential for trust. Brookfield (2013) states three core principles that substantiate a democratic system:
    - Widely different groups and perspectives are engaged in facilitating communal affairs;
    - Participants are granted equal, full access to all available resources and knowledge so they can be fully aware of the possible routes to take, make the most well-informed decisions, and understand potential consequences of their decisions and actions;
    - Members, by incorporating new and/or unfamiliar perspectives, identify and challenge dominant ideologies and associated practices that historically have gone largely unquestioned.

In design classrooms, these principles promote shared intellectual responsibilities as students "design" their design education. For example, select areas in our syllabi can be revised if students feel one project needs reframing or more time than another assignment (see Chapter 20). Additionally, we can begin some classes by asking students "What do you need *most* from today's class?" or "How should we structure today's session?" to target their needs better at that particular stage of the project and course. Co-designing curriculum and classes with students makes them co-creators of their learning (rather than passive receivers of an education). Students come to understand they *own* their education, because they co-created it, and thus take greater responsibility for their personal success. As a direct result, a more collaborative teacher-student relationship built on trust emerges.

This is not to say we must meet every request made by students. Situations arise where we must "stay the course" and students won't always agree with our decisions. However, if we want to be perceived as trustworthy, students should be made fully aware of the rationale behind our decisions and why we cannot comply—that our pedagogical approaches and convictions are born not out of egomania but of deeply considered methodologies (Brookfield, 1995).

- Solicit students' feedback regularly. Teachers commonly rely on end-of-course evaluations for students' feedback. Yet soliciting earlier and more frequent feedback throughout the course provides greater benefits. First, it encourages current students to critique our teaching—and our responding to their feedback demonstrates we are receptive and trustworthy (Brookfield, 1995). Second, maintaining an awareness of the classroom "temperature" enables us to address concerns before they arise. Third, if students are afforded opportunities to voice their perspectives and concerns, they are less likely to act out or hold resentment (Vanderbilt University, 2004).

   There are several methods to collect feedback at the end of each class session. For example, an open-ended approach enables students simply to share a reflection about the respective session. Student reflections can be as long or short as they like and can include anything the students wish to discuss, such as the most interesting or challenging moments or how the session contributes to their progress. In contrast, a more structured approach involves the teacher asking students specific questions. These can remain the same each week or evolve based on the type of feedback you would like about the course, your pedagogy, or other insights. For example, questions could include: "At what point(s) during class were you most engaged (or disengaged)?", "What material was most helpful or unhelpful?", and "What questions still linger for you?" Regardless of its structure, all submitted feedback (via hardcopy or digital formats) should be anonymous to increase the likelihood of receiving honest feedback, to maintain a safe environment in which students feel free from repercussion, and to promote trust.

   When you collect and analyze students' feedback, look for recurring themes. Are there any widespread problems, concerns, or ambiguity? Does anything need further clarification? Are the issues that are being expressed due to the material itself or to how it was presented? These themes can then be addressed by either using them to launch the next class session, emailing students a summary of the key themes with your response(s), or verbally reporting the themes and allocating time for comments and discussion at the start of the subsequent class. "Just as you owe it to your students to give them feedback on their graded work, you owe it to them to acknowledge their feedback on your teaching" (Harvard University Derek Bok Center for Teaching and Learning [HUBC], n.d., n.p.).

There will be times when particular issues cannot be adequately addressed because they lie beyond our control as teachers (e.g. school policies). Other issues may arise when students feel intellectually or creatively challenged by our pedagogy, curricular structure, or course material. We may feel some of these issues are nonnegotiable due to our knowledge and experience as designers and educators—as mentioned, we see the benefits of "staying the course." Also, some of these issues already may be explicated in our syllabi. In every instance, it is essential to discuss students' feedback and then explain or reemphasize why some areas can't be negotiated or eliminated.

Establishing trust in the design classroom offers vast benefits, for individuals and community alike. For instance, when students share their insights with teachers, they discover what might have been a purely personal, private reaction is one that is shared among their peers and therefore legitimate (Brookfield, 1995). Such discoveries can decrease imposter syndrome, improve transparency, alleviate student frustrations and anxieties, and subvert negative hierarchies. Consequently, through established trust, we can better understand how to strategically advance our teaching and students' holistic development.

## Conflict in the Design Classroom

Conflict is a part of human existence and thus inevitable in design classrooms. Feldmann (2001) describes classroom incivility as "any action that interferes with a harmonious and cooperative learning atmosphere in the classroom" (p. 137). Unlike disputes (which are short-term disagreements), conflicts are disagreements that go unresolved or become escalated. Their causes can include grades, vague course expectations, poor interpersonal conduct, differing values, and inappropriate behavior—all of which can arise spontaneously or be a persistent issue. At its worst, conflict can derail coursework, damage teacher-student/student-student relationships, and decrease the overall learning opportunity for students (Gallo, 2017). Persistent conflict often takes an emotional toll on all parties involved and, when chronic, can cause health problems such as insomnia, excessive eating, irregular heartbeat, and even strokes (Whalen, 2015).

*Strategies to Prevent Conflict*

Although conflict is inherent in any relationship, there are steps we can take to reduce or prevent it from occurring in our design classrooms. These practices include:

1 <u>Demonstrating warm interpersonal sensitivity.</u> Body language, eye contact, posture, smiling, and the use of questions are effective methods to convey your interest in and care for students. These simple acts, in turn, increase students' affinity toward you as their instructor and toward the course material (McCroskey & Richmond, 1992).
2 <u>Collaboratively develop a course framework.</u> Inviting students to co-develop your syllabus' agenda—including learning materials, design briefs, and weekly schedules—increases students' learning while reducing the potential for conflict. This collaboration enables students to understand why specific course materials are relevant and important. It also allows for all participants to obtain clarity around course expectations. Finally, it enables students to perceive you, their instructor, as caring, approachable, and receptive due to your collaborative disposition.
3 <u>Nurture community.</u> Throughout the semester, it is imperative that you cultivate a positive classroom community. One approach is by facilitating cooperative learning activities (e.g. group discussions and peer-to-peer tutoring). These and similar group activities promote students' learning, empathy, and mutual respect—thus engendering positive peer-to-peer connections and preventing conflict. In fact, "more than 375 published studies indicated that student participation in cooperative learning is associated with increased amounts of interpersonal caring, liking, commitment, and support among students" (Johnson et al., 1991, as cited in Meyers, 2003, p. 96).

*Strategies to Manage Conflict*

When conflict does occur, it is critical to demonstrate an awareness of the classroom's dynamics, the goal of promoting learning amid the struggle, and the care for students' well-being (HUBC, n.d.). The following select strategies can address and manage conflict productively:

- **Monitor your emotions and remain calm**
  Staying aware of your emotions is key to ensuring they remain in-check and preventing them from driving your responses in all

situations, particularly those that are emotionally charged. Simple mental practices can heighten your awareness of your emotions and restore your ability to think clearly when in an emotional situation. These practices include taking deep breaths in sequence to reduce adrenaline rushes, deliberately focusing your attention on the environment around you in order to shift focus off the physical signs of panic and ground yourself, literally slowing the rate at which you speak, and repeating a mantra internally, such as "Go to neutral" (Gallo, 2017; HUBC, n.d.). As a role model for students, it is essential that we maintain our calm, respectful demeanor even during times of conflict.

- **View the situation from above**
  Move from the "dance floor" to the "balcony" to understand and assess the situation more accurately (Heifetz & Linsky, 2002). What is *actually* being said? Is there an underlying cause or context to the conflict? By pivoting mentally, you are able to distinguish the issues from the emotions, thus enabling you to think more clearly, communicate more effectively, and create optimal solutions.

- **Consider students' perspectives**
  Empathy elevates our awareness and the potential for positive outcomes: we are better able to understand students' positions, remain sensitive to their needs, and propose or facilitate mutually beneficial solutions when we are empathetic toward our students. It is always beneficial to ask students about their perceptions of a problem—and then verbally paraphrase these perceptions and feelings back to them periodically both to verify you understand them correctly and to demonstrate to them that you understand their perspectives (Meyers, 2003). This technique promotes active listening, stronger communication, and mutual respect.

- **Pause and reflect**
  When things get "heated" in the classroom, ask everyone to pause for a few minutes and write their personal response to the situation. This break allows students to express their emotions, rather than keeping them bottled up inside. This period of reflection provides the distance required for tempers to de-escalate so that the conversation can resume in a more respectful, productive manner. Enabling design students (who are typically visual learners) to *see* their thoughts can be especially beneficial to the process; visualization helps them to better digest, organize, and clarify their thoughts and feelings so they may reenter the conversation more constructively.

  In other situations, it may be prudent to create space around the conflict. One way to do this is to say that you would like to give the situation some thought, and inform the student(s) that you will follow up at a later time. This allows all parties to decompress,

understand the situation more objectively, and brainstorm solutions before reengaging. This approach also conveys that you take the situation seriously. If you promise the student(s) that you will follow up, *always* carry through on that promise. Failure to do so results in a loss of credibility for you and decreased trust from students.
- **Address—do not avoid—conflict**
Responding to and addressing conflict as soon as it arises prevents it from unnecessarily negatively impacting both the students and the overall classroom climate—and its potential spillover into the broader institution. Our response as educators sets precedent: when teachers ignore conflict, "[s]tudents learn that such behavior is OK and that they are not protected from it. They miss the opportunity to learn about their own behavior and its consequences. And they miss the opportunity to have a more open classroom in which a wider range of ideas can be explored" (Warren, 2006, p. 3). Conflict should be addressed promptly to prevent it from intensifying and becoming unmanageable.

### *Strategies that Promote Conflict Resolution*

To resolve conflict positively and constructively, verbal and non-verbal interpersonal techniques can be practiced by ourselves and by our counterpart(s). These include:

1 **Permit venting**
When feelings of anger or frustration are high, do not interrupt, talk over, or tell your counterpart to "calm down"—these actions typically exacerbate conflict. Refrain from speaking while your counterpart is speaking and remain calm so your counterpart may express their emotions. Convey your attention by maintaining eye contact, nodding occasionally, and expressing statements like, "I understand." If the outburst occurs during class and the student loses their composure, acknowledge it and ask if they'd like to stay in the room or leave momentarily. When class ends, approach the student and ask if you can be of any assistance.
2 **Demonstrate active listening**
Active listening is vital to the conflict resolution process. In fact, one study found "when asked to describe their preferred outcome, relatively few students stated that they would have preferred a grade change. Rather, the outcomes that were most preferred by almost one third were more feedback and greater listening" on the part of their teachers (Tantleff-Dunn et al., 2002, p. 200).

Techniques for active listening include paraphrasing your counterpart's statements to verify you understand what they are saying, maintaining comfortable levels of eye contact, and probing for information and feelings. It is also beneficial to ascertain periodically your counterpart's level of active listing. Expressing phrases like, "I'd like to hear your thoughts on what I just shared," or "Do you seen any errors in my logic?" ensure you are heard accurately and the conversation is not one sided.

3 **Verbally acknowledge emotions**
Expressions that acknowledge emotions (e.g. "You sound angry," and "I understand this is a challenging situation for you") convey care and empathy for our counterpart. Acknowledging feelings also helps us to separate emotions from the issues at stake and to think more clearly.

4 **Adopt a "learning stance"**
To promote a positive, beneficial conflict resolution process, adopt a "learning stance" during the discussion. This mental state allows us to gain a more accurate understanding of the situation and remain sensitive to different perspectives. Various open-ended questions (Gallo, 2017) can be asked in this stance, such as:

- "Can you tell me more about that?";
- "What about this situation is most troubling for you?";
- "What would you like to see happen?";
- "How do you suggest we resolve this?"; and
- "Do you have ideas that would meet both our needs?"

When we pose questions—rather than make statements—we demonstrate our genuine receptiveness to dialog. When statements are used, they can be expressed from a personal perspective rather than hard fact ("In my opinion ...," "I feel ...," "From my perspective, I sense ..."). Statements conveyed in this manner demonstrate a willingness to hear opposing views and engage more openly.

5 **Monitor body language and personal space**
During conversations, monitor your body language and the overall message it exudes. Your posture, eyes, hands, voice, feet, legs, and face all communicate your level of receptivity to what is being said. Also monitor your counterpart's body language for signs of anger, frustration, disengagement, or other bodily signals that may contradict what they are saying. Throughout the interaction, especially during heated moments, try to remain at least four feet away from the student so they can protect their personal space and feel unthreatened. (See Chapter 16 for full descriptions of non-verbal communication and interpersonal distances.)

6 **Encourage a collaborative resolution process**
The aim of conflict resolution is not to determine right or wrong. Rather, it is to reach a solution that is mutually agreeable. This necessitates a collaborative process that can begin by asking ourselves and

our students, "What are my/your core needs?" and "Why are these needs important?" This should also include asking ourselves, "What do I want the students to learn?" As Warren (2006) asserts, help students "to learn something substantive from the experience—about themselves, about others, about possible positions, about the topic as a whole, and about how to voice their thoughts so that they can be heard, even by those who disagree. These conversations can save a student and keep them coming to class with an open and learning mind" (p. 3).

Once needs are identified, brainstorm for possible solutions. Refrain from critiquing ideas during this stage; rather than determining right or wrong, the goal of this work is to generate as many different ideas as possible. Empower students by helping them discover alternatives, combine ideas, evaluate consequences, and create beneficial solutions. As teachers, we can consider what alterations can be made to resolve the issues (e.g. project parameters, course schedule, etc.). It is essential for everyone to focus on the future and not get stuck in the emotions that ignited the conflict. Instead, objectively review and discuss each proposal to create a mutually agreeable solution.

The ultimate goal of this process is to reach an outcome that satisfies as many interests as possible, is fair and reasonable, and keeps the relationship intact (Gallo, 2017). Once achieved, plan follow-up actions to determine how the students are doing. Private office hours, a class-wide meeting, or an email can be used to convey your feelings of care and support while reducing the likelihood of similar situations arising in the future. In some circumstances, you may need to enlist a third party (e.g. a student's advisor) or be willing to simply agree to disagree—and then move on.

At the heart of conflict resolution is our attitude and behavior. By regularly expressing care toward students, communicating respectfully, showing sensitivity, and maintaining a warm, engaged presence, we can prevent and resolve conflict. When these practices are combined with feelings of trust, the students' likelihood of being committed to the conflict resolution process is increased (Meyers, 2003).

## Conclusion

Classroom dynamics inherently shape both teacher-student and student-student relationships as well as students' holistic academic experiences. These dynamics and consequential relationships are not completely natural situations; as design educators, rather than simply "hoping for the best," we need to pro-actively plan and employ thoughtful, strategic practices that engender a positive learning environment—one in which all students feel comfortable communicating and interacting with each other and you, the teacher. While there are numerous practices that can be used to foster this type of environment, building trust and resolving conflict in the classroom are vital. Trust is an antecedent to effective, high-functioning relationships, and artful conflict resolution ensures these relationships are sustained. As design educators, our concerted attention to classroom dynamics is essential given the fact that students frequently look to teachers for mentorship. In doing so, students come to understand not only what it means to be a professional designer but also what it means to be an adult in the world (HUBC, n.d.).

## References

Bain, K. (2004). *What the best college teachers do.* Harvard University Press.
Boice, R. (2000). *Advice for new faculty: Nihil nimus.* Pearson.
Brookfield, S. (1995). *Becoming a critically reflective teacher.* Jossey-Bass.
Brookfield, S. (2013). *Powerful techniques for teaching adults.* Jossey-Bass.
Feldmann, L. (2001). Classroom civility is another of our instructor responsibilities. *College Teaching*, 49(4), 137–140.
Gallo, A. (2017). *HBR guide to dealing with conflict.* Harvard Business Review.
Gallup-Purdue University. (2014). *The 2014 Gallup-Purdue index report: Great jobs, great lives.* https://www.gallup.com/services/176768/2014-gallup-purdue-index-report.aspx
Harvard University Derek Bok Center for Teaching and Learning (HUBC). (n.d.). *Online resources.* https://bokcenter.harvard.edu/online-resources
Heifetz, R., & Linsky, M. (2002). *Leadership on the line: Staying alive through the dangers of leading.* Harvard Business Review.
Johnson, D. W., Johnson, R. T., & Smith, K. A. (1991). *Active learning: Cooperation in the college classroom.* Interaction Book Company.
Kearney, P., & Plax, T. (1992). *Power in the classroom.* Erlbaum.
McCroskey, J. C., & Richmond, V. P. (1992). Increasing teacher influence through immediacy. In V. P. Richmond, & J. C. McCroskey (Eds.), *Power in the classroom: Communication, control, and concern* (pp. 101–119). Erlbaum.
Meyers, S. (2003). Strategies to prevent and reduce conflict in college classrooms. *College Teaching*, 51(3), 94–98.
Tantleff-Dunn, S., Dunn, M. E., & Gokee, J. L. (2002). Understanding faculty-student conflict: Student perceptions of precipitating events and faculty responses. *Teaching of Psychology*, 29(3), 197–202.
Vanderbilt University. (2004, November). Managing classroom conflict. *Center for Teaching Excellence*, 22. https://cdn.vanderbilt.edu/vu-wp0/wp-content/uploads/sites/59/2017/03/01130813/Managing_Classroom_Conflict-Center_for_Faculty_Excellence-UNC_Chapel_Hill.pdf
Warren, L. (2006). Managing hot moments in the classroom. *Harvard University Derek Bok Center for Teaching and Learning.* https://www.elon.edu/u/academics/catl/wp-content/uploads/sites/126/2017/04/Managing-Hot-Moments-in-the-Classroom-Harvard_University.pdf

Whalen, J. (2015, March 23). Angry outbursts really do hurt your health, doctors find. *Wall Street Journal.* https://www.wsj.com/articles/angry-outbursts-really-do-hurt-your-health-doctors-find-1427150596#:~:text=Medical%20researchers%20increasingly%20are%20finding%20just%20how%20toxic%20outbursts%20of,irregular%20heartbeat%2C%20other%20research%20shows

Zenger, J., & Folkman, J. (2019, February 5). The 3 elements of trust. *Harvard Business Review.* https://hbr.org/2019/02/the-3-elements-of-trust?utm_source=facebook&utm_campaign=hbr&utm_medium=social#

# 18 Motivation and Design Students

The importance of motivation in the process of learning cannot be overstated. As college students undertake greater responsibilities for their lives and choose what, when, and how they study and learn, motivation plays a pivotal role in directing and sustaining accompanying behaviors (Ambrose et al., 2010). Motivation—the reason(s) why somebody acts or behaves in a particular way—influences the intensity, persistence, and quality of the student's engagement in learning behaviors (Ambrose et al., 2010; Oxford Learner's Dictionary, n.d., n.p.). Highly motivated students "are agentic and inspired, striving to learn; extend themselves; master new skills; and apply their talents responsibly" (Ryan & Deci, 2000, p. 68). Peaked motivation in students leads them into a state of "flow": absorption, engagement, and fulfillment with an activity during which temporary matters (e.g. time, ego-self, food) are ignored (Csikszentmihalyi, 1990) (Figure 18.1).

The high value ascribed to motivation lies in the fact that it *produces* something on the part of the individual (Ryan & Deci, 2000). Motivation is therefore a great concern and common issue among design educators who regularly rally their design students to perform their best. However, because motivation is not something we *do* to people, but, rather, something individuals must *choose* to do themselves, it is important that design educators are able to determine how best to encourage students' motivation and achieve the optimal learning (Carucci, 2018).

## Understanding Motivation

There are two forms of motivation that influence a student's level of engagement in learning and the value they intend to derive from it.

***Intrinsic motivation*** is motivation that is driven by the individual's need to satisfy their own need for internal reward. It manifests as an inherent tendency on the part of the individual to explore, seek challenges and novelty, gain mastery, and exercise capacities (Ryan & Deci, 2000). Intrinsic motivation is typically more sustainable than extrinsic motivation, as the individual is willingly engaging in the task and working to

DOI: 10.4324/9781003049166-22

230  *Design Classrooms*

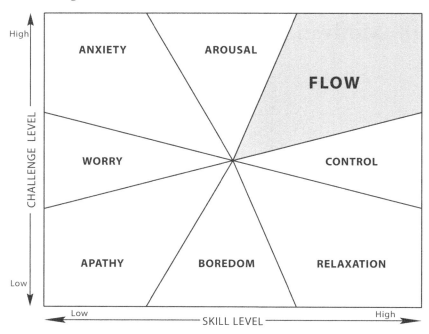

*Figure 18.1* Flow model.
Source: Adapted from Csikszentmihalyi (1990).

improve their competencies. Thus, intrinsic motivation focuses more on the *learning* rather than the *performance* (Lavoie, 2007).

Intrinsic motivation is bolstered in students by social and environmental factors. These factors include: feeling autonomous and having appropriate control over their learning; believing goals can be achieved with the necessary support (self-efficacy); acting from self-developed interest and not as a need to meet the demands of external pressures; and seeking to gain knowledge or competency and not outward rewards or recognitions (e.g. good grades) (Ryan & Deci, 2000). In fact, research shows external motivators and rewards—such as a prize for best portfolio—can diminish intrinsic motivation (Ryan & Deci, 2000). External rewards distract attention from the learning associated with the task itself; this can result in students being more likely to perceive the design project (or other learning opportunity) as a short-term goal rather than part of their long-term commitment to gaining mastery (Lavoie, 2007).

**Extrinsic motivation** is driven by external factors that influence the student's motivation, performance, and perceptions of value in the task. Rather than performing an activity for the inherent enjoyment in the activity itself, the student acts to attain a separable outcome (Ryan & Deci, 2000). External motivators can include influential individuals (e.g. parents, teachers, mentors), tangible earnings (e.g. design awards, potential salary in the chosen design field), and academic achievement (e.g. grades).

External rewards often result in negative consequences. Research shows "the more students are externally regulated the less they showed interest, value, and effort toward achievement and the more they tended to disown responsibility for negative outcomes, blaming others such as the teacher" (Ryan & Deci, 2000, p. 73). External rewards lead students to depend on teachers' assessments rather than self-assessment and this, in turn, undermines students' autonomy, ownership, and ultimately their sense of agency (Bain, 2004). The potential for such negative consequences is heightened by the prevalence of social media, which focuses on the external self. In this virtual world, students face extreme pressures to achieve and publicly display signs of success. This is in stark contrast to the individual driven by internal motivation, who is focused on achieving internal goals such as self-understanding (Brzycki & Brzycki, 2016). Consequently, unprecedented numbers of undergraduates are experiencing anxiety and depression due, in part, to the fact that the feeling of control they have over their lives is significantly undermined by external forces, including social media (see Chapter 11).

## What Influences Motivation?

Contemporary science cites numerous universal factors that influence motivation. They include the following four key factors:

1 **The Zone of Proximal Development (ZPD)**
Conceived by psychologist Lev Vygotsky (1896–1934), the ZPD (Figure 18.2) is "the distance between the actual developmental level as determined by independent problem solving and the level of potential development as determined through problem-solving under adult guidance, or in collaboration with more capable peers" (Vygotsky, 1978, p. 86).

If the student's competency is low and the challenge is too difficult, they are likely to experience anxiety, frustration, and immobilization. If the student's competency is high and the challenge is too easy, they may experience boredom, apathy, and disengagement. Learning and teaching within the ZPD ensures students' motivation is sustained through attainable challenges that increase competence.

2 **The environment**
Negative environments and attendant stressors can impair cognition and motivation in many ways. Chronic stress activates the brain's amygdala that then overproduces the stress hormone cortisol. Excessive cortisol levels shrink and functionally impair the prefrontal cortex—the region of the brain responsible for planning, problem solving, managing emotions, and related tasks—which can

232  *Design Classrooms*

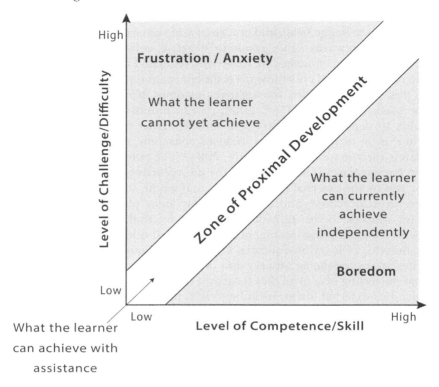

*Figure 18.2* The Zone of Proximal Development.
Source: Adapted from Vygotsky (1978).

result in student underachievement. For optimal learning to occur, students must feel emotional safety, trust, relatedness, empathy, and autonomy, and they must experience positive social interactions. The supporting or thwarting of these psychological needs can facilitate or forestall cognition and the cultivation of intrinsic motivation (Ryan & Deci, 2000).

3 **Fixed mindset and growth mindset**
What students think of themselves, their level of intellectual development, and many of their other capabilities lead them to approach learning through two distinct mindsets, fixed and growth (Dweck, 2000).

*Fixed mindset*—termed "entity theory"—leads students to view their abilities as a finite, fixed state that will not increase no matter how hard they work ("I'm just no good at drawing") (Dweck, 2000). As a result, they choose easily achievable targets over riskier intellectual challenges that may offer higher levels of learning (Dweck, 2000). Fixed mindset has negative repercussions for students: because failure may happen, it affirms the student's inherent negative bias, and this can lead them to "readily pass up valuable learning opportunities if these opportunities might reveal inadequacies or entail errors—and [students with a fixed mindset] readily disengage from tasks that pose obstacles, even if they were pursuing them successfully shortly before" (Dweck, 2000, p. 3). Students with a fixed mindset prioritize looking "smart" above all else, and how they are viewed in the eyes of others is of paramount importance to them.

*Growth mindset*—or "incremental theory"—is a more dynamic state in which students view their intelligence as a quality that can increase with effort and guidance (Dweck, 2000). Students with growth mindset thrive when engaging in challenging tasks, stretching their abilities, and working in collaborative environments. The student's goal, then, becomes their learning rather than their performance ("It's more important I learn how to use this design software than it is to get the best grade"). As Dweck (2000) notes, "[growth mindset] makes them want to learn. After all, if your intelligence can be increased why not do that? Why waste time worrying about looking smart or dumb, when you could be becoming smarter?" (p. 3).

4 Rewards

Rewards for motivation fall into two categories, namely intrinsic and extrinsic. Intrinsic rewards (e.g. intellectual stimulation and the pleasure of designing) and extrinsic rewards (e.g. grades and prizes) affect students' motivation in different ways. Research studies frequently debunk common misperceptions that extrinsic rewards work well with students. Instead of benefiting students, they unintentionally undermine intrinsic motivation due to the inherent "if/then" scenario that thwarts autonomy ("*If* you submit five design proposals, *then* I'll give you an 'A'") (Pink, 2009). This makes the destination—and not the journey—the more pressing issue for students (Pink, 2009). Consequently, students develop a limited, narrow focus. They may then experience future difficulty looking beyond the periphery of the narrow scope of an assignment—a trait that is essential for developing creativity and design innovation (Pink, 2009).

Although extrinsic rewards may prove beneficial in some instances—specifically, they provide focus for achieving quick goals—they ultimately transmute the students' joy of learning for learning's sake into the drudgery of work. The effect can negatively impact design students' development since creative processes require boundless, self-directed "tinkering," exploration, and freedom that run contrary to more controlling extrinsic motivation/rewards (Amabile, 1996).

## Methods That Motivate Students

Part of our role as design educators is to understand our students' distinct needs, interests, goals, and learning styles. Professor and author Paul Baker underscores this necessity when asserting, "My strongest feeling about teaching is that you must begin with the student. As a teacher you do not begin to teach, thinking of your own ego and what you know …. The moments of the class must belong to the student—*not the students*, but to the very undivided *student*. You don't teach a class. You teach a student" (Baker, 1972, as cited in Bain, 2004, p. 97). It is incumbent on design educators to implement the relevant motivational techniques so that each student may learn optimally and be their best.

Key motivational techniques include:

1 **Teach within the ZPD**
 When design assignments are either over- or under-challenging, students will likely disengage. If the work far exceeds students' abilities, frustration may ensue. If the work is too easy, students may view the work as unbeneficial and subsequently not worth their time. Assignments must therefore strike a balance between challenging students to learn and grow while providing opportunities for them to hone their current abilities. Teaching within this balanced area—the ZPD—elevates students' confidence, sustains motivation, and advances learning over time.

 To ensure your syllabi, assignments, and pedagogy keep students' learning within the ZPD:

 - Conduct a diagnostic design exercise. During the first class session, conduct a short design activity to assess your students' abilities accurately. This diagnostic includes reviewing preceding syllabi (particularly if your course is within a sequence) to ascertain prior learning. The first one to two weeks of your course should serve as a review of the previous semester's materials. This review period—which provides *further* assessment of students' skillsets—establishes a strong foundation to advance higher learning.
 - Identify appropriate challenges. Following these assessments, consider where readjustments can be made in your syllabus so that each student's ZPD is optimized; what challenged last semester's cohort of students cannot be presumed to challenge the current. Revise areas that will under- or over-challenge your current students and ensure students are given appropriate autonomy (see next section, below) over their learning.
 - Leverage the ZPD throughout the course. Develop challenging-yet-attainable assignments to specifically target each student's unique level. While the same design brief might be given to all students, subtle changes in the process of delivery, and even the final project outcome, may remain flexible and individually customizable. The goal is to ensure students build confidence, feel encouraged, and attain a sense of accomplishment—while being sufficiently challenged.

- <u>Provide small successes early and often.</u> If students are to remain engaged and motivated, they must feel they can succeed in your course, are making progress, and are improving. When small successes are offered early in the course, students form a positive view of the material and believe they will succeed. Small successes provided throughout the course help instill in students a sense of self-efficacy. Research suggests periods of advancement (versus periods of setback) increase students' intrinsic motivation. As a result, they tend to form more positive perceptions of the course, their classmates, the teacher, and the institution (Amabile & Kramer, 2011).

2 **Provide autonomy**
Autonomy "refers not to being independent, detached, or selfish but rather to the feeling of volition that can accompany any act, whether dependent or independent, collectivist or individualist" (Ryan & Deci, 2000, p. 74). Students who feel in charge of their decision to learn are more likely to feel greater intrinsic motivation, ownership and responsibility of their work, control, curiosity, desire for challenge, and enjoyment in their learning (Bain, 2004; Ryan & Deci, 2000). They ultimately achieve at higher levels and feel less burnout than those who experience less autonomy (Pink, 2009). Conversely, a controlling teaching style causes students to lose initiative and learn less effectively—particularly when learning conceptual, creative processing like design that requires freedom from control in order to engage in exploration and experimentation (Ryan & Deci, 2000).

This does not require the teacher to capitulate authority but simply to provide students with a sense of independent control and flexibility over their own learning. For instance, when we offer students a range of options that equally fulfill learning goals, they are free to select those that are most consistent with their interests, values, and goals. Other suggestions include:

- Offer three readings that address a shared theme (e.g. The future of design production and automation) from which students select one for class-wide discussion;
- Set the project's due date and allow students to fill out their own weekly schedules to meet the target;
- Provide flexibility to students for how they choose to demonstrate knowledge in a way that best meets their personal goals.

The provision of choice may also include portions of course content, topics for design assignments, questions for class discussion, and a final project deliverable.

3 **Develop community and interdependence**
A central factor in students' creativity and academic performance is their perception of the learning environment. Amabile and

Kramer (2011) note how happy people feel when working in a connected community; the quality of the community influences how positively they view an organization, their peers, their work, and themselves. Similarly, students must feel cared for and connected to others in the academic environment—a state of relatedness in which they feel unified as a collective. This requires teachers to attune their pedagogy to students' feelings about the classroom experience via informal conversation, students' written reflections, and personal intuition.

Optimal motivation arises when students feel they are contributing to something greater than themselves. These feelings are essential since "[t]his sense of connectedness with one's job has a predictive, positive effect on well-being and resilience and can decrease stress and anxiety" (David, 2019, p. 3). Conversely, research reveals a lack of connectedness to one's work results in burnout; this can erode people's relationships at school, work, and home (David, 2019).

Examples of how to instill community and relatedness among students include:

- Facilitate activities that allow students to learn about peers' values, goals, personal lives, worries, and fears—not *just* their design projects;
- Ask students how they *feel* about an assigned project, and evolving your pedagogy and syllabi accordingly;
- Encourage students to express their values, and, as their guide, articulate how shared values can foster greater connectedness with their coursework and peers;
- Invite students to discuss how and why the positive impact of their work extends well beyond classroom walls;
- Strength classroom community by regularly placing students in small groups to discuss peers' work and share suggestions in order to cultivate empathy and increase motivation among students;
- Relate coursework to things students care about most and/or their desired goals. Before each class, ask yourself, "What will make students care about this more?" and "How can I connect this work to the 'real world' and students' professional goals?" (This is especially important for the emergent design student generation that experienced the Great Recession and thus prioritizes their tangible employability over esoteric theory.)

As Ambrose et al. (2010) note, "if students do not find the content of the course interesting or relevant, they may see little or no value in mastering it and may fail to engage in the behaviors required for deep learning" (p. 69).

4   **Cultivate the teacher-student relationship**
    Theodore Roosevelt famously declared, "People don't care how much you know until they know how much you care." Within design education, a positive teacher-student relationship is fundamental for students' academic success—and their motivation. This relationship develops in part from a concerted effort by teachers to learn what drives each individual student and customizing their teaching to accommodate those drives.

    There are many informal ways to build this relationship and increase students' motivation. They include:

    - <u>Require each student to schedule at least one office-hour visit before midterm.</u> Use this opportunity to learn about your students' backgrounds, what they hope to gain from you and your course, the challenges and fears they may have, their current and future goals, how they learn best, and other relevant information they wish to share. Acquiring a better understanding of each student will enable you to develop a more meaningful, targeted, and appropriate learning experience for them. This is also an opportunity for them to learn about *you* in a more comfortable, less formal environment.

        During this meeting, it is important for you, the teacher, to establish an upbeat, supportive rapport with the student to ensure the student feels you are personable and approachable. This will help them feel comfortable both making future appointments with you throughout the term and coming to you for guidance when needed.

    - <u>Build caring relationships in your classroom.</u> Best practices include:
        i   Arrive to every class early and prepare the room before students arrive;
        ii  As students enter the classroom, welcome them with a warm tone of voice, smile and make eye contact, and use their preferred names;
        iii Mingle around the studio and ask students how they are doing, how they spent their weekends/free time, and how their other courses are going;
        iv  In the event of an absence, privately inquire about their health and well-being during the next class they attend;
        v   Throughout class—even during lectures—circulate throughout the room so students may feel your "side-by-side" presence rather than a literal and figurative disconnection from them by staying strictly at the front of the room;
        vi  Frequently acknowledge individual effort and improvement;
        vii Always address sensitive concerns (e.g. disruptive behavior) in private and in a tone that conveys concern, support, and care;

viii Regularly ask questions so students can sense your strong interest in hearing their viewpoints. This can include questions about their emotions around projects, in addition to the projects themselves (e.g. "How did it feel to experience that challenge in your project this week?");

ix As problems arise, ask students to propose solutions; resist the inclination to always provide answers. For example, if a student falls behind in an assignment or exhibits inappropriate behavior during class, consider asking, "How do you think we should proceed?" or "If you were in my place, as your teacher, what would you do?" This gives the student agency and opportunity to propose a self-determined outcome. Consequently, the likelihood for successful follow-through is increased.

Teaching, at its best, is a *relationship* and not merely a transaction of knowledge between teacher and student. By utilizing these and other techniques, you can cultivate your relationships with your students and subsequently increase your students' motivation.

5 **The importance of your enthusiasm**

Teachers set the tone and climate of their classrooms. As Lavoie (2007) posits, "if the teacher is enthusiastic, lively, and animated, the students are more likely to mirror this attitude" (p. 126). Yet, our enthusiasm does more than just excite students: it conveys that what we are teaching is important and worth learning. It is therefore imperative for teachers to be consciously aware of their overall affect in every teacher-student engagement. While Chapter 16 thoroughly examines this topic, select strategies for how to generate enthusiasm that effectively motivates students are provided below. Various research studies (e.g. Lavoie, 2007) reveal that enthusiastic teachers:

- Display passion for the discipline that raises students' curiosity;
- Speak in an upbeat manner, with animated vocal delivery;
- Employ demonstrative, dramatic physical gestures where appropriate;
- Vary body language when circulating around the room and when standing in place;
- Use rich vocabularies and adjectives throughout discussions;
- Show animated facial expressions when listening to students' suggestions, ideas, and questions;
- Maintain a high degree of energy and exuberance;
- Avoid monotone and monosyllabic dialog;
- Radiate positivity and acceptance.

Ideally, you should be able to incorporate some or all of the above consistently into your interactions with students. Doing so does not mean you adopt a false persona, however—it simply means incorporating these elements into your own style, in your own way.

6 **Promote students' growth mindsets and "grit"**
Some of the hallmarks of successful students are that they enjoy the learning process, they cherish effort, and they persist in the face of difficulties (Dweck, 2000). This growth mindset, coupled with "grit"—the perseverance, effort, and passion the student expends in spite of failure and adversity—is essential for optimal achievement (Duckworth & Eskreis-Winkler, 2013). It is therefore imperative that we educators promote these traits in our students. To facilitate this process, we can:

- Listen for students' fixed mindset internal "voice" that may inhibit their perseverance and resultant learning (e.g. "I tried 'Rhino' software last week, but I got confused and quit.");
- Remind students that challenges are not roadblocks but, rather, opportunities to stretch themselves;
- Frequently use the language of "growth" (e.g. "Keep up the hard work. You'll master it with time and effort, soon enough!");
- Replace extrinsic motivators, such as design awards, with intrinsic ones, such as self-satisfaction and creative stimulation;
- Encourage students' broader goals (e.g. becoming a design director) that carry more substantial value than narrow, specific goals (e.g. getting an "A" on a design assignment). Broader goals help sustain students' motivation over time;
- Remind students that acquiring mastery—through sustained engagement—is not merely a destination, but rather a persistent mindset. "It requires the capacity to see your abilities not as finite, but as infinitely improvable .... [It] is an asymptote: It's impossible to fully realize, which makes it simultaneously frustrating and alluring" (Pink, 2009, p. 208);
- Designate opportunities for students to reflect on their learning. Self-awareness of their own abilities ("metacognition") greatly supports academic success; reflection (e.g. written exercises) allows students to position more effectively or revise their cognitive processes when needed (Harvard University Derek Bok Center for Teaching and Learning, n.d.). Guided questions (e.g. "What did you learn from this design project?" or "How does this assignment support your goals?") will provide structure and enable students to see the work's value;
- Regularly solicit feedback (anonymous or named) to understand students' perceptions about class sessions, assignments, and the course. This will allow you to address potential concerns before they become significant problems.

7 Offer feedback and praise appropriately

How we offer feedback and praise to students plays a critical role in how they perceive themselves and experience motivation. When students receive praise of their "person" ("You're such a creative designer!") rather than their actions, they are more likely to believe what we praise is fixed rather than expandable through perseverance (Bain, 2004). When we praise the person ("person-praise"), we seemingly pass judgment about their worth as human beings (Lavoie, 2007). In doing so, we fail to deliver constructive feedback for learning. Person-praise also increases the student's dependence on the teacher for external assessment and validation; it undermines self-development and agency. Subsequently, this promotes a fixed mindset.

A more beneficial form of praise is that of "effort-praise," when we provide encouragement and demonstrate interest and enthusiasm over the efforts of the person, rather than judging the person themselves. This promotes a growth mindset because it focuses the student to accept praise for their effort, grit, improvement, risk-taking, and strategies for overcoming obstacles (Dweck, 2000; Lavoie, 2007). Additionally, this nonjudgmental feedback promotes a safe learning environment in which students are willing to step out of their comfort zones, make mistakes, try again, and overcome failure—all of which are necessary conditions for achieving design innovation. When we encourage and praise the *effort*, rather than the *person*, the student focuses more on personal goals and progress than on grades. Consequently, the student feels valued (rather than evaluated), independent and motivated, and more willing to explore diverse solutions to assigned tasks (Lavoie, 2007). Over time, a more collaborative teacher-student relationship develops.

Researchers (e.g. Bain, 2004; Dweck, 2000; Lavoie, 2007) cite best practices for offering effective praise. They include:

- Provide regular, targeted feedback. Feedback is most effective and powerful when it is given immediately following (or shortly after) a situation. The more specific the feedback, the greater the meaning and resonance it has for the student. For instance, telling a student "Your color application is effective because it strengthens the compositional flow and distributes your diagram's visual 'weight'" is far more valuable feedback for them than a generalization such as, "Effective composition.";
- Praise should be sincere, selective, and deliberate. Undergraduates easily recognize insincere praise. Utilizing insincere praise will undermine your credibility and the trust between you and your students. Also, be sensible about how much and how often you praise, or it will become disingenuous and desensitize students, thus rendering your techniques ineffective;

- Spotlight effort and improvement. Frequently address the *process* of learning—during both successes and failures—in order to underscore the importance of sustained learning, growth, and perseverance (e.g. "I see you really struggled with your garment pattern this week, but you've improved since our first project. Your patterns are well-balanced, seams are aligned, and now you need to reshape the armhole for better fit.");
- Use effective body language. The vast majority of our interpersonal communications come from nonverbal cues. This emphasizes the need for us to monitor our physical actions when delivering praise and ensuring they are in harmony with our words. Effective body language involves facing the student, making eye contact, smiling, and using a warm, expressive tone of voice to deepen the positive impact of your encouragement. Your words and body language should closely align with one another in order to achieve the intended effect on the student. If they are misaligned, your message will likely appear disingenuous and you subsequently will lose credibility.

## Conclusion

Motivation plays a pivotal role in students' learning. By understanding the distinct attributes of motivation—and the universal factors that influence them—design teachers will be better prepared to implement research-based motivational techniques that can elevate their students' engagement, perseverance, agency, and subsequent learning. For these techniques to be effective, concerted attention must be given to each student's distinct needs, interests, goals, and learning styles. Additionally, a strong classroom community and teacher-student connections must be cultivated. By adopting this holistic approach, design educators may positively impact their students' learning both during and beyond their design studies.

## References

Amabile, T. (1996). *Creativity in context*. Westview Press.
Amabile, T., & Kramer, S. (2011). The power of small wins. *Harvard Business Review*. https://hbr.org/2011/05/the-power-of-small-wins
Ambrose, S., Bridge, M., DiPietro, M., Lovett, M., & Norman, M. (2010). *How learning works: 7 Research-based principles for smart teaching*. Jossey-Bass.
Bain, K. (2004). *What the best college teachers do*. Harvard Press.
Baker, K. (1972). *Integration of abilities: Exercises for creative growth*. Trinity University Press.
Brzycki, E., & Brzycki, H. (2016). *Student success in higher education: Developing the whole person through high-impact practices*. The Brzycki Group.

Carucci, R. (2018, July 16). What not to do when you're trying to motivate your team. *Harvard Business Review*. https://hbr.org/2018/07/what-not-to-do-when-youre-trying-to-motivate-your-team

Csikszentmihalyi, M. (1990). *Flow: The psychology of optimal experience*. Harper & Row.

David, S. (2019). Why motivation is a manager's job. In S. David (Ed.), *HBR guide to motivating people* (pp. 1–8). Harvard Business Review.

Duckworth, A., & Eskreis-Winkler, L. (2013). True grit. *The Observer*, 26(4), 1–3.

Dweck, C. (2000). *Self-theories: Their role in motivation, personality, and development*. Taylor and Francis/Psychology Press.

Harvard University Derek Bok Center for Teaching and Learning (n.d.). *Motivation and metacognition*. https://bokcenter.harvard.edu/motivation-and-metacognition

Lavoie, R. (2007). *The motivation breakthrough: 6 Secrets to turning on the tuned-out child*. Simon & Schuster.

Oxford Learner's Dictionary. (n.d.). *Motivation*. Oxford University Press. https://www.oxfordlearnersdictionaries.com/us/definition/english/motivation

Pink, D. (2009). *Drive: The surprising truth about what motivates us*. Riverhead Books.

Ryan, M., & Deci, E. (2000). Self-determination theory and the facilitation of intrinsic motivation, social development, and well-being. *American Psychology*, 55(1), 68–78.

Vygotsky, L. (1978). *Mind in society: The development of higher psychological processes*. Harvard University Press.

# 19 The Inclusive Design Classroom

The pioneering psychologist Abraham Maslow (1908–1970) postulated over fifty years ago that an individual could not learn, function, or achieve their full potential unless and until their need for safety was met (Lavoie, 2007). Unless students feel safe in our design classrooms, their abilities to function successfully, remain motivated, and reach their fullest potential will be undermined. When a student feels safe—a state largely dependent upon whether or not the student feels *included* in the community—their focus shifts from their security and well-being to connecting with others, taking risks, exploring the unknown and unfamiliar, and consequently, their learning (Lavoie, 2007; Safir, 2016).

Design students' sense of inclusion is especially vital to their creativity and abilities to innovate design. One study noted "the single most important factor contributing to innovation … was 'psychological safety,' a sense of confidence that members of a group will not be embarrassed, rejected, punished, or ridiculed for speaking up" (Tavanger, 2017, n.p.). As design educators, if we are to support students' holistic development, we must *first* cultivate a safe and inclusive environment in which "[s]tudents … have equitable opportunities for learning, regardless of their race, ethnicity, sexual orientation, gender, religion, linguistic or socioeconomic background, ability, and more" (Harvard University Derek Bok Center for Teaching and Learning [HUBC], n.d., n.p.). This environment supports and develops each student's sense of belonging and distinct identity (including the respective student's values, goals, history, culture, and socioeconomic class) within the community (Lavoie, 2007). Adopting this approach enables design schools to raise the levels of engagement, authenticity, and respect between students and among the student body and faculty.

## What Is an "Inclusive Classroom"?

An inclusive classroom is one in which teachers and students work collaboratively to develop and sustain a climate where everyone feels "safe, supported, and encouraged to express [their] views and concerns"

DOI: 10.4324/9781003049166-23

(Saunders & Kardia, 1997, n.p.). It enables "all students [to] feel supported intellectually and academically, and [all students] are extended a sense of belonging in the classroom regardless of identity, learning preferences, or education" (Yale University Poorvu Center for Teaching and Learning [YUPC], n.d., n.p.).

Research literature on teaching in higher education (e.g. Greer, 2014) frequently points to two critical components of executing a program that is inclusive:

1 **Student belonging.** Students, in their design classrooms and within the broader school culture, must feel a sense of belonging if they are to engage fully in learning experiences. For instance, students who perceive themselves as members of minority and/or less privileged groups and those "whose past experiences have produced legitimate fears about how they will be treated in an academic culture may hold back [and] may elect for silence" as to avoid embarrassment (Fassinger, 1995, as cited in Brookfield, 1995, p. 12).

   Conversely, students' strong sense of belonging can bolster and enhance their holistic development: students who feel as if they belong "are more motivated to take control of their learning in classroom climates that recognize them, draw relevant connections to their lives, and respond to their unique concerns" (Ambrose et al., 2010, as cited in YUPC, n.d., n.p.). Moreover, studies show students who experience positive diverse interactions among community members have less social anxiety and feel they are a valued, contributing part of the wider campus community (e.g. Greer, 2014).

2 **Stereotype threat.** Stereotype threat refers to "the [learner's] fear of confirming a negative stereotype about their respective in-group, a fear that can create [a] high[-stress] cognitive load and [thus] reduce academic focus and performance" (Steele & Aronson, 1995, as cited in Greer, 2014, n.p.). This is partially due to the fact that when the human brain perceives a strong social threat—such as a stereotype threat—the amygdala (the brain's emotional response center) becomes overstimulated. This overstimulation draws resources away from cognition and into "fight, flight, or freeze" responses, which subsequently hinder the critical executive function skills (e.g. organization, time management, planning, self-monitoring, and working memory) that occur in the prefrontal cortex. Thus, rather than focusing on and retaining concepts and ideas effectively, the learner becomes distracted as they are biologically driven to attempt to grapple with the perceived threat first in order to restore their sense of safety. Subsequently, these students retain less information, engage in less self-reflection, and broadly are less able to access the full education they are attempting to receive.

## Cultivating an Inclusive Design Classroom

There are numerous ways to develop an inclusive design classroom. These practices commonly utilize a mixture of ongoing review of curriculum, new research and knowledge around inclusive practices, and inter- and intrapersonal awareness. We can begin this work by considering the following:

- the ways students' identities, values, experiences, and backgrounds influence their levels of engagement;
- why some students seem to learn more easily than others;
- why some students participate or disengage more frequently; and
- how course design and pedagogical approaches include or exclude students (YUPC, n.d.).

This reflection prepares design educators to enact the following strategies:

1 **Content approach**
   Several actions can be undertaken during the course design phase to create a more equitable and inclusive classroom. Key questions include, "What are you using to teach?" and "Do your course readings, visual/audio content, and examples used in your design classroom represent and respect multiple identities and communities as legitimate sources of critique or knowledge?" (HUBC, n.d.).

   A critical question to ask yourself if your content is homogenous is, "How/Where can inclusive material be incorporated so that it better conveys how people and perspectives from diverse backgrounds have a place in my course and the profession?" For example, if all the authors/designers of your materials:

   - are male (rather than female, transgendered, or non-binary),
   - white (rather than from another racial group), and
   - liberal (rather than of another political orientation),

   your teaching will send "a message about the voices that are valued and will be devaluing the scholarship of others who have written or created materials on the topic" (Saunders & Kardia, 1997, n.p.). Also, materials must be presented in ways that do not marginalize or trivialize the individuals' or groups' experiences.

   When choosing course content, consider your students and their histories. Wherever possible, ensure the material represents all your students' diverse experiences, values, backgrounds, identities, and perspectives in meaningful ways (Tavanger, 2017). The customization of content extends far beyond the design examples and readings mentioned above. It includes in-class activities, discussions, assignments, and other learning content that can reflect the community's diversity. Doing so may help all students to imagine themselves actively participating within various learning scenarios, cultural contexts, professional environments, and more (YUPC, n.d.).

You can also incorporate a diversity statement in your syllabus. By addressing diversity issues explicitly in writing in the syllabus—and orally during the first class of the semester—you can invite students to examine and discuss best practices for creating and sustaining an inclusive classroom (YUPC, n.d.). The statement could include:

- classroom protocols that engender respectful learning environments;
- materials about active listening and appropriate manners of response;
- statements/research about the importance, value, and benefits of diversity and inclusion in learning;
- your teaching philosophy (and how it relates to inclusive pedagogy); and
- an acknowledgment of your commitment to providing a safe, inclusive environment for every student (YUPC, n.d.).

2 **Inclusive pedagogical methods**
In the context of the inclusive classroom, there are numerous pedagogical methods we can employ, from those we practice alone to those practiced community-wide. These methods (e.g. HUBC, n.d.; YUPC, n.d.) include but are not limited to:

- <u>Diversify your teaching styles to reach</u> <u>all</u> <u>students.</u> The diversity of design students' identities mirrors the diversity of their preferred learning styles. Common learning styles include visual/spatial, aural/auditory, verbal/linguistic, physical/kinesthetic, logical/mathematical, social/interpersonal, and solitary/intrapersonal. Therefore, to support *all* students, we must understand and incorporate a broad repertoire of learning styles into our teaching methods to effectively target those styles (Brookfield, 1995).

    To achieve this, one approach involves structuring each class session into thirds and, during each third, targeting a different learning style. For example, when teaching textile dying, a class-wide **verbal** discussion of assigned texts could lead into a **visual** presentation about diverse cross-cultural approaches to textile dying, that is then followed by **physical** lab work. The approaches to the specific learning style should also be diverse. For example, visual/spatial approaches might include board work, slides, videos, and demonstrations. Aural/auditory approaches could include podcasts and class-wide or small-group discussions. Additionally, offering students heterogeneous opportunities to engage with you and classmates (e.g. in-class discussions, online

message boards, written reflections, and office hours) will support their preferred styles of learning.
- <u>Ensure positive group dynamics.</u> When facilitating collaborative learning, we must give concerted attention to group dynamics: if a group is dominated by more assertive students, particularly ones whose behavior may exclude others from full participation, we must intervene to guarantee we receive feedback from *all* students. This will ensure a sense of inclusion and of belonging throughout the complete class. Additionally, if patterns of seating arrangements are tied to patterns of nonparticipation, assign different seating arrangements or cluster small groups (YUPC, n.d.).
- <u>Allow learning to be demonstrated in multiple ways.</u> Not everyone shows their grasp of material in the same way. Some students excel during large, class-wide discussions while others shine during individual meetings or online discussions. Among design students, it is particularly common to see preferences for either 2D or 3D creative practices. While we should encourage our students to develop across multiple areas of expression (after all, big challenges often yield meaningful breakthroughs), we also must express our understanding of and openness to diverse forms of demonstrated learning (HUBC, n.d.). In doing so, we convey to students our acceptance of their learning styles and thus promote inclusivity.
- <u>Explain your teaching methods</u>. Your approach to and rationale for specific pedagogies may not be apparent to all students. You can include students in the pedagogical conversation by explicitly articulating to students both what your teaching methods are and that they are designed do three things: challenge and support student growth; promote equity and diversity in the classroom; and elevate students' feelings of belonging. Discussions that explicitly state the "why" behind your teaching methods allow students to understand and connect better with the broader learning experience.

    Conversations can also include offering students choices of teaching methods. For example, students could help decide how to structure a class session and/or choose from several activities that equally achieve a predetermined learning goal. By explaining your pedagogy and offering choices, students come to understand that our approach to teaching is not what we do *to* students, but rather, *with* them. As a result, a "side-by-side" teacher-student relationship develops while also deepening students' greater sense of belonging and inclusivity.
- <u>Encourage equitable participation.</u> Establishing ground rules for appropriate, courteous behavior (e.g. respectful studio critiques, civil debate) early in the course will help to promote

an effective, inclusive learning environment. These guidelines should describe the need for equitable participation and the use of best practices. For example, the protocol "Three Before Me" requires students who have spoken to wait for at least three peers to speak or participate before they contribute again. The gentle reminder "Watch Your Airtime" prevents dominant students from monopolizing discussions. An agreed upon time limit per student's contribution (e.g. three minutes) during class-wide discussions is another way to foster equitable participation. To achieve student buy-in to these tools, invite them to help create and maintain participation protocols.

Equitable participation also requires actively inviting *all* students into discussions. For instance, certain students should not be forced to serve as the spokesperson for their group; nor should an assumption be made that a student knows everything about issues related to their group or that students from their group feel the same way about an issue (YUPC, n.d.). By including all students in the discussion, we abandon exclusionary practices that enable the "alpha" personalities in the group to dominate the subject, direction, and tone of class discussions. Every student has an independent voice and valuable contributions, both of which should be called upon with regular frequency in any group discussion.

- Model inclusive language. Our words directly impact the tone of our environment. When modeled on inclusive language, these words can foster respectful, inclusive environments. This is especially true in education, where students look to teachers to establish and maintain the culture of the classroom. By modeling our communications on inclusive language, we can help create and foster an inclusive culture. Examples of utilizing inclusive language include:

    – using gender-neutral language instead of gender-specific pronouns (e.g. "Hi, everyone!" instead of "Hi, guys!");
    – using American idioms (e.g. "It's a piece of cake!") carefully; always explain them for the benefit of non-native English speakers; and
    – putting people first in your sentence structure (e.g. "A woman who is blind" rather than "A blind woman") to keep the individual as the focus of the statement.

- Proactively identify and address difficult topics and situations. In our design classrooms, difficult topics, situations, and conversations can arise. For example, our various design disciplines may have unbalanced representations of genders and Black, Indigenous, and people of color (BIPOC) communities, environmentally harmful practices, unbalanced power dynamics, and a lack of diversity in perspectives.

Although some may find it easier to ignore these situations, it is incumbent upon us design educators to acknowledge that these topics and situations exist—and how they may impact classroom dynamics and students' well-being. How much time is dedicated to discussing these is, ultimately, guided by the teacher. Providing even a short, organized opportunity for everyone to acknowledge and discuss the topic can be helpful and effective—especially if the topic or issue is then linked to whatever course content you might be covering (HUBC, n.d.).

3  **Self-development**
Ongoing self-reflection and responsive self-development are fundamental to creating and sustaining authentically inclusive classrooms. The following items present some critical areas you should examine during self-reflection:

- identifying our own biases, assumptions, and partialities;
- probing how we form stereotypes and prejudices;
- questioning our creative/academic discipline's history and looking for new approaches;
- practicing critically reflective teaching (see Chapter 13, Part 3);
- reviewing texts, documentaries, and additional learning resources that address diversity and inclusion in education;
- practicing empathy and seeing things from others' perspectives; and
- refraining from quick, "knee-jerk" judgments (YUPC, n.d.).

Building our social justice vocabulary is also essential. Professor Howard Stevenson of the University of Pennsylvania asserts, "By practicing racial literacy, we can learn to not be so fearful and learn to problem-solve together, rather than run away from conversations about race" (Tavanger, 2017, n.p.).

4  **Cultivate relationships and community**
Creating moments to personally connect with each student and resultantly strengthen a sense of community among our students is a core technique for supporting students' feelings of belonging and inclusion. Simple acts like asking students what they hope to gain from the course, how they're doing in their other courses, and what hobbies or extracurricular interests they have will demonstrate your care and genuine concern for them. These practices also allow you to see students as individuals who possess distinct backgrounds, needs, goals, and learning styles. This is critical information you need in order to shape your teaching to be centered on inclusivity—and the importance of the individual—as opposed to exclusivity or bias.

As with all relationships, respectful communication is of paramount importance. This includes learning and correctly pronouncing students' preferred names, asking them for their preferred gender pronouns, avoiding gender binaries with pronouns (he/she) in favor of using the pronoun "their," using contemporary terms for specific group identities (e.g. LGBTQIA+), and other forms of considerate interactions that promote inclusivity.

Respectful rapport between students is also essential. Throughout the course, provide opportunities for students to interact with each other via formal and informal activities. These can include group projects, small discussion or work groups, new seating arrangements, mid-class seat-swaps, and "15-minute peer-tutorials" whereby students pair-off to share tips and tricks related to the coursework. Activities like these strengthen students' sense of being part of a team, understanding of one another, empathy, mutual respect, and peer support. These techniques help ensure class dynamics stay fresh, and students are afforded regular opportunities to get to know *every* classmate throughout the course's duration (HUBC, n.d.).

5   **Reduce stereotype threat**
To reduce stereotype threat, researchers (e.g. Fournier, n.d.; Greer, 2014; Stroessner & Good, n.d.) posit the following methods:

- Support a "growth mindset." Help students to see their skillsets, creativity, and intelligence not as "fixed" entities (e.g. "I just don't have a 'computer brain'") but as expandable entities, ones that grow through perseverance (e.g. "I'll master 'CLO' software if I keep practicing"). The feedback we provide students should explicitly affirm that learning is an incremental process, and therefore each student has the potential to achieve mastery. We must also ensure the demands we make in our courses are equal for every student, rather than imposing requirements or restrictions that are based in any sort of bias. Utilizing the "growth mindset" shows students you see each one of them, individually, as a capable learner.
- Spotlight positive role models. Sharing the personal and professional stories of notable designers who have overcome adversities—particularly if they are from historically or currently marginalized groups—helps students see actual models who have succeeded, thus enabling them to make the cognitive transference of, "If they were able to overcome what they did, I can overcome my hurdles." As Greer (2014) notes, "[p]ositive role models, who perform well in fields that typically invoke stereotype threat, can increase otherwise poor performance for stigmatized groups" (n.p.).
- Examine external cause(s) for difficulty. Helping students identify the external cause(s) of their worries may help to alleviate these anxieties. Additionally, studies note "instructors reduced

[students'] poor performance by suggesting that anxiety might actually help with test taking, without connecting the anxiety to any stereotype" (Greer, 2014, n.p.).
- <u>Promote and affirm the value of diverse personal identities.</u> Research (e.g. Cohen & Sherman, 2014) suggests that the power of stereotype threat can be destabilized by instilling in students the understanding that their identity is a valuable asset to themselves and to the world. This can be achieved through practices such as self-affirmation. Likewise, respectfully highlighting students' diversity in class (rather than ignoring it) can become a rich teaching resource and thus further emphasize the importance of diversity, both in the design practice and in life. Be cautious, however, of turning to specific students so consistently as to make them defacto "spokespeople" for their respective backgrounds.
- <u>Give agency and choice.</u> Whenever possible, provide students with opportunities for self-directed learning. Allow students to develop work that tells their own stories, on their own terms. Ask yourself critical questions, such as, "How can small conversational groups precede large, class-wide discussions so that students can first assess their readiness to be vulnerable?" (Safir, 2016). Facilitating opportunities that provide choice in how, when, and where students share information about their identities is essential to creating safe learning spaces and trust.

## Conclusion

A well-cultivated and sustained inclusive design classroom environment—a place where *all* students feel supported personally, creatively, intellectually, emotionally, and academically—is fundamental to students' well-being and to ensuring every student is given equal opportunities to succeed. Establishing and refining this environment requires us, as design educators, to adopt the following inclusive pedagogical practices:

- understanding what constitutes an "inclusive" classroom,
- ensuring breadth and diversity in course content,
- widening the range of our teaching methods,
- performing ongoing self-reflective practices for personal development and improvement,
- cultivating relationships and community in our classrooms, and
- exercising practices that can alleviate students' stereotype threat.

Incorporating these and additional inclusive practices will support students' feelings of psychological safety, belonging, and inclusivity in our design schools so they may, in turn, flourish academically, personally, and professionally.

# References

Ambrose, S. A., Bridges, M. W., DiPietro, M., & Lovett, M. C. (2010). *How learning works: Seven research-based principles for smart teaching*. Jossey-Bass.

Brookfield, S. (1995). *Becoming a critically reflective teacher*. Jossey-Bass.

Cohen, G. L., & Sherman, D. K. (2014). The psychology of change: Self-affirmation and social psychological intervention. *Annual Review of Psychology*, 65(1), 333–371.

Fassinger, P. A. (1995). Understanding classroom interaction: Students' and professors' contributions to students' silence. *Journal of Higher Education*, 66(1), 82–96.

Fournier, E. (n.d.). Reducing stereotype threat. *Washington University*. https://ctl.wustl.edu/resources/reducing-stereotype-threat/

Greer, A. (2014). Increasing inclusivity in the classroom. *Vanderbilt University Center for Teaching*. https://cft.vanderbilt.edu/guides-sub-pages/increasing-inclusivity-in-the-classroom/#why

Harvard University Derek Bok Center for Teaching and Learning (HUBC). (n.d.). *Inclusive teaching*. https://bokcenter.harvard.edu/inclusive-teaching

Lavoie, R. (2007). *The motivation breakthrough: 6 Secrets to turning on the tuned-out child*. Simon & Schuster.

Safir, S. (2016). Fostering identity safety in your classroom. *Edutopia*. https://www.edutopia.org/blog/fostering-identity-safety-in-classroom-shane-safir

Saunders, S., & Kardia, D. (1997). Creating inclusive college classrooms. *University of Michigan*. http://crlt.umich.edu/gsis/p3_1

Steele, C. M., & Aronson, J. (1995). Stereotype threat and the intellectual test performance of African Americans. *Journal of Personality and Social Psychology*, 69(5), 797–811.

Stroessner, S., & Good, C. (n.d.). Stereotype threat: An overview. *Reducing Stereotype Threat*. https://www.reducingstereotypethreat.org/home

Tavanger, H. (2017). Creating an inclusive classroom. *Edutopia*. https://www.edutopia.org/article/creating-inclusive-classroom

Yale University Poorvu Center for Teaching and Learning (YUPC). (n.d.). *Diversity and inclusion*. https://poorvucenter.yale.edu/FacultyResources/Diversity-Inclusion

# 20 Designing the Learning Experience
## The Syllabus

## Introduction

A good syllabus is a *designed* syllabus: it "communicates the overall pattern of the course so the course does not feel like disjointed assignments and activities, but instead an organized and meaningful journey" (Slattery & Carlson, 2005, p. 159). Rather than being a mere checklist of projects, policies, and procedures, an effective syllabus structures and communicates course expectations in support of students' learning and holistic development. Ultimately, a syllabus "is a promise that, as a result of our course, students will be able to do a number of things either for the first time or at least better than they could before" (Gannon, 2018, n.p.).

The syllabus is typically the first contact students will have with you and your course, and this will lead them to form opinions about you, your classroom environment, your general expectations for them in the course, and your course's tone. As such, it should ignite students' curiosity and interest in the course, convey your commitment toward their learning, suggest your interpersonal style and approachability, and serve as a foundation upon which to cultivate positive teacher-student rapport (Gannon, 2018; Harnish et al., 2011). It is therefore important to ask yourself throughout its design process, "What am I saying to my students?" (Gannon, 2018).

## The Primary Functions of a Syllabus

A syllabus has three functions (Slattery & Carlson, 2005):

1 **To give structure**. At its core, a syllabus describes the "what, when, and how" students will learn. It structures and organizes the course's vision that subsequently determines the "learning outcomes" (LOs)—what students should know, be able to do, or value following their completion of the course.
2 **To provide evidence.** In its final form, the syllabus is a permanent record that contains precise and comprehensive information about

the course. This information includes details about assignments, course and school policies, course calendar, assessment methods, course materials, and other responsibilities and expectations for both students and teachers. Transparency is key as syllabi are typically reviewed when issues arise, such as during grade disputes or issues surrounding due dates. Syllabi also play important evidentiary roles in faculty members' dossiers (e.g. when applying for promotions or other teaching positions) and programs' accreditation efforts.

3 **To motivate students.** A major goal of the syllabus is to excite and motivate students. We can achieve this goal by employing a warm, inviting tone when crafting our syllabus. It is also important that we describe the course's rationale and our teaching strategies, explain how to succeed in the course, highlight the common misconceptions and pitfalls experienced by past students and how to avoid them, communicate how the coursework connects to students' future design careers, and express our own passion for the subject (Massachusetts Institute of Technology Teaching and Learning Lab [MITTLL], n.d.).

Collectively, these three functions help foster a learner-centered environment, namely one in which students' experiences are the primary focus. They additionally serve as ways in which to spark students' interest in the course and subject matter, both at the start of the course and throughout its duration.

## The Components of an Effective Syllabus

What questions will students have about your course? When deciding what information to put in your syllabus, anticipating these questions can help create a guiding framework for your syllabus. A comprehensive syllabus is of paramount importance; as Gannon (2018) asserts, omitting essential components "is tantamount to showing students that you are absent-minded and unprofessional, or that you don't care about their success in class" (n.p.).

While there are numerous ways to design syllabi, the following sections consistently should be included:

- **Basic information**
  Provide the course name and number, meeting dates, times, and location, any prerequisites, and course website URL. Include a preamble that can inspire, excite, or challenge student-readers.
- **Instructor information**
  Include your name, biography, design/scholarly focus(es), contact information (including phone and email), office location, and office hours (in-person and/or online).

- **Teaching philosophy**
  "Why do you teach? What do you believe is your role as an educator? How do you define successful learning?" You can use these and similarly reflective questions to help develop a teaching philosophy statement. Use this statement, which is usually the length of a short paragraph, to convey to students how they will benefit from your pedagogy, the broader ideas behind your particular course goals, your passion for teaching the subject and working with students, and your personal demeanor (Gannon, 2018).
- **Course description**
  Students will likely have read the online course description during registration. Your syllabus provides you the opportunity to elaborate on the course's conceptual and thematic structures, type(s) of knowledge and skillsets that will be emphasized, materials that will be covered, how and why the course is sequenced the way it is, and its relationship to the wider design profession(s). This course description should explain the holistic "journey" students will undertake during your course; it should articulate the opportunities offered by the course and ultimate potential for domain area expertise upon completion of the course.
- **Learning outcomes**
  Learning outcomes (LOs) are "measurable statements that articulate ... what students should know, be able to do, or value as a result of taking [the] course" (Cornell University Center for Teaching Innovation [CUCTI], n.d., n.p.). In other words, LOs are what your students will take away from the course. The identification and articulation of LOs benefits both teachers and students. For teachers, LOs help guide and determine what course content to include or omit, which pedagogical approaches to employ, and ways to assess students' learning accurately and effectively (CUCTI, n.d.). For students, LOs clearly indicate how they will be assessed, help them evaluate if the course meets their academic and personal goals, guide their focus throughout the semester so they may succeed in the course, and specify the knowledge and skills they will gain from the course (MITTLL, n.d.). (Later in this chapter, the section "Syllabus Design Strategies" details how to craft effective LOs.)
- **Teaching methods**
  What types of teaching and learning experiences can students expect? Discuss your chosen methods—such as individual and group projects, lectures, readings, field work, off-site meetings, class discussions, and written assignments—to clarify your pedagogical approach and each method's intent.
- **Course requirements**
  This section contains all the details of the project briefs, papers, and other formal (graded) assignments, along with their attendant

requirements (e.g. word-count ranges for papers, amounts of images/articles for design research, or quantities of iterative sketches for design development).

Providing rationale for each requirement is necessary because "[c]larifying how a particular assignment aligns with the subject's goals can help students better understand why they are doing the work they are assigned and can help them reflect on their learning as they complete assignments" (MITTLL, n.d., n.p.). For each assignment and requirement, ask yourself, "Why am I asking students to do [X]?"

- **Course calendar**
  The course calendar lists the class sessions' themes and topics, due dates for weekly assignments and final critiques/exams, off-site visits, guest speakers, and other relevant information so that students can prepare properly for each session. By creating a session-by-session breakdown, you are able to plan your lessons accordingly, with greater insight into the overall connections between classes. This breakdown also allows you to determine how to distribute students' workload evenly throughout the term.

- **Course materials**
  What materials, readings, technologies, and other supplies will students need? Where can these be acquired? Which materials are required, suggested, and optional? Whatever you are using in your course (e.g. materials, readings, and technologies) should be discussed, along with *why* they were chosen for your course.

- **Assessment and grading**
  How will work be assessed and graded? What values guide these evaluations? Making these processes explicit and transparent will mitigate the potential for confusion, conflict, or complaints (Gannon, 2018). Evaluation criteria should discuss policies and percentages allocated to assignments and other measurable areas of learning (e.g. class participation). Additionally, assessment rubrics can be incorporated into the syllabus to guide students' evaluations and promote transparency in the grading process.

- **Policies**
  This section features both "boiler-plate" program and school policies and those that are unique to your course. Course policies around attendance, late work, requests for extensions, academic integrity, guidelines for classroom conduct, and use of technology during class are just some that are commonly articulated in a strong syllabus. When crafting your policies, keep in mind that policies can sometimes come across to some students as adversarial rather than supportive and constructive. To foster a positive, supportive tone, explain the rationales behind your polices rather than simply creating a bullet list of rules and consequences.

- **Student success**
  How can students succeed in your course? What advice can you offer them for meeting the course goals, managing time, approaching design briefs, and studying? Regardless of their prior experience, all students will benefit from your advice on how to succeed in your unique course.
- **Inclusivity, diversity, and accessibility**
  An inclusive and welcoming learning environment is essential, both pedagogically and institutionally (Gannon, 2018). Including an *explicit* statement about your commitment to creating and sustaining this type of environment in the syllabus will clearly communicate to students that they will be supported fully and be given equal opportunities in your design classroom. (See Chapter 19 for full information.)
- **Campus resources and services**
  List your institution's resources and support services, such as design technology labs, writing and tutoring centers, advising and counseling offices, career services, international student affairs, mental health services, and other facilities that support students academically and personally.

## Syllabus Design Strategies

Designing a syllabus is a highly creative yet methodical and analytical process. Employ the following strategies as you develop your syllabus to ensure complex variables are considered, effective choices are made, and the course dynamically supports students' learning and holistic development.

### *Course Context*

When designing your syllabus, consider how your course contributes to your department or program, its relationship to other courses, and how it prepares students for advanced learning. If it is a preexisting course, review past syllabi and, if possible, discuss the course with the previous teacher(s). Researching online syllabi from similar disciplines can also provide additional insights and aid your iterative process. Always remember: "Know your audience." Who are your students? What knowledge and skills do they possess upon entering your course? This particular context is especially necessary for elective courses that often contain students who have diverse design backgrounds and goals.

### *"Backward Design"*

Backward design involves starting with your end goals (LOs) and then working backward to create the learning experiences (course content) that can meet these goals. This occurs as part of a three-step process:

1 **Identify LOs.** As described, LOs are measurable objectives of things that students should know or be able to do upon successful completion of your course. To begin, first identify the key areas of learning you want students to develop by asking yourself, "What are the most important things a student should know (cognitive), be able to do (skills), and value (affective) after completing this course?" (CUCTI, n.d., n.p.). A course typically lists three to six LOs to ensure the outcomes are focused and realistic. Reviewing different learning models, including Bloom's Taxonomy or Fink's Taxonomy, can be extremely useful for conceiving and articulating appropriate LOs. LOs often take this form: "By the end of this course, you will be able to: (verb) (learning statement)." For example, if one of your course goals is to provide an introduction to textiles manufacturing, an LO might be, "By the end of this course, you will be able to: Identify different fibers, weaves, finishes, and key properties of fabrics commonly used in apparel design."

   Next, evaluate each LO to ensure it is measurable and specific. If it is unmeasurable, you will be unable to evaluate students' progress effectively and know if your course achieved its goals. LOs must be specific so they clarify students' goals and provide you with focus when proceeding to the second step, "Define Assessments" (MITTLL, n.d.). Finally, it is of critical importance that LOs need to be achievable for every student within the course's timeframe. If you fail to ensure this, you set up both the students and yourself for failure.

2 **Define assessments.** How will students demonstrate they have achieved the LOs? What types of acceptable evidence—such as projects, papers, and assignments—will enable you to measure and determine the levels of students' learning? Assessment formats should align with the predetermined LOs and will vary, from formal, graded projects to less formal situations such as class discussions and in-class activities. Once the assessments are defined, determine your grading framework and weigh the assignments appropriately.

3 **Develop and incorporate diverse learning experiences.** Consider how students will learn via lectures, readings, screenings, in-class activities, and other teaching and learning strategies. Prioritize which experiences and materials are essential, recommended, and supplemental. Resist the temptation to overload your syllabus with too many experiences, as this can overwhelm students and subsequently undermine their ability to succeed. As mentioned above, contextualize the chosen materials by expressing why you have selected them and how they help students achieve the LOs.

Once you have completed this preliminary three-step process, you are ready to put the syllabus together.

## Course Contextualization

Why should students take your course? Even if it is a required course, explain its context and rationale to heighten students' interest and passion for the subject, convey your own excitement for the material, and articulate how the course and the assignments contribute to students' academic and professional goals. For example, a contextualized rationale for group work could state:

> Group projects are extremely beneficial in helping you become a more effective and prepared designer. The team-based nature of group projects will enable you to learn different perspectives and skillsets from classmates, accomplish more than you could alone, and experience versatility in aesthetic "vocabulary." In the design professions, effective teamwork is crucial for success, and this project will give you an opportunity to practice this skill for your professional development.

## Structured Yet Flexible Framework

A structured syllabus allows everyone to stay on schedule, prepare for each session, and successfully engage in strategically sequenced learning experiences. Simultaneously, this structure should be flexible and adaptable for numerous reasons. Your current students may learn at a faster or slower rate than previous cohorts. You might decide certain topics deserve more or less time for this particular group of students. Unexpected events could upset your intended plans. A syllabus should be a thoughtful guide that can, when necessary, adjust to meet students' experiences and needs.

At the same time, your students rely on your syllabus to plan their time effectively. Thus, while having flexibility in your syllabus' content is important, it is also important to avoid frequent changes that might cause students frustration or lead them to view you as disorganized and incompetent, as that only serves to weaken teacher-student relationships.

## A Learner-Centered Focus

A learner-centered syllabus shifts the focus of instruction from the teacher's needs to the students'. It places emphasis on cultivating classroom community, promoting the balance of power and control between teacher and students, and making transparent the connections between evaluation and the LOs (Cullen & Harris, 2009). This type of syllabus can be crafted in numerous ways, such as by inviting students to determine certain areas of the syllabus (e.g. classroom discussions, readings, and projects' timelines) (see below, "Balance of Power"). Additionally, incorporating supportive language, a teaching philosophy statement, and explanations for what you believe are your personal responsibilities to the course, as well as the students' responsibilities, within the syllabus will further promote a learner-centered environment.

For example, consider these two approaches to the same interior design project brief:

1 **Teacher-centered focus**
   Students will be required to design five restaurant seating plans for dissimilar floor plans and customers. They will then be asked to fabricate a model of one of the five plans.
2 **Learner-centered focus**
   Restaurant Seating (LOs 1, 3, and 5): This assignment will challenge your creativity as an interior designer by applying the concepts we've learned thus far about space, traffic flow, and scale. Deep consideration of how these design elements coalesce will support your future professional practice and abilities to solve a design brief aesthetically and practically. To begin, you will be asked to design five distinct seating plans for dissimilar floor plans and customer demographics. Then, you will select one of your plans to create a fully articulated 3-D model. This assignment builds upon our previous assignment's exploration of design fundamentals by introducing targeted client briefs, the primary focus in our upcoming assignment, "Nantucket Beach House."

While these design briefs may accomplish the same basic task, namely providing students with the parameters of their assignment, the learner-centered approach uses a more inviting tone, is written *to* students rather than *at* them, ties the learning to specific LOs, makes connections to professional practice, and rationalizes the learning sequence.

## Warm Tone

Learner-centered syllabi often employ a warm-tone; they encourage and motivate the reader, discuss expectations in a friendly fashion, and point out that learning experiences are *collaborations* between the teacher and students. Harnish et al. (2011) provide six strategies for creating a warm syllabus:

1 Use friendly, inviting language (e.g. "I welcome you to reach out to me throughout the semester");
2 Offer rationale for all work (e.g. "This video screening supports your professional development as urban planners because it

uncovers the complex relationships between select cityscapes and their waterways");
3  Share appropriate personal experiences, particularly those related to your own academic and professional background;
4  Incorporate humor, which can be used simultaneously to show students that you do not take yourself too seriously and also to draw students' attention to key concepts and areas of your course;
5  Express compassion (e.g. "While I strongly encourage you to attend every session because it will allow you to learn optimally, I also understand that unforeseen life events happen to everyone. Please contact me if situations are affecting your attendance so I can assist you");
6  Convey your enthusiasm for teaching, the subject, and working with students. This is important, as the level of teachers' enthusiasm often correlates with students' own levels of engagement in learning.

These and similar strategies can produce positive results. For example, research shows students are more likely to seek help and resolve their academic struggles after reading statements that explicitly offer assistance than when they simply are given verbal offers from teachers (Perrine et al., 1995).

Avoid a negative, punitive tone (particularly when describing course policies) since "[s]tudents who read less-friendly syllabi may believe their professor does not expect them to be successful, which can create a self-fulfilling prophecy" (Slattery & Carlson, 2005, p. 160). It is therefore critical that you also read your syllabus from the *student's* perspective to ensure it uses warm, inviting language that articulates policies and prohibitions and how they promote students' success.

*Effective Formatting*

A visually stimulating, user-friendly syllabus positively impacts students' perceptions of a course and their motivation to engage with the teacher (e.g. Ludy et al., 2016). Syllabi should be user-friendly and provide easy-to-access references. They should have clear section headers, graphics, and layouts that highlight and guide readers through key information. Moreover, as the syllabus often makes the first impression on students of both your course and your level of professionalism, it is essential that you avoid sloppy editing (e.g. misspellings, incorrect dates, poor formatting, typos, and similar blunders) as any message you are trying to communicate to students about the importance of being detailed-oriented will be significantly undermined.

When designing a syllabus, how long should it be? Do lengthy formats deter students? Contrary to common assumptions, longer, more detailed syllabi are rated more positively by students. Researchers (e.g. Harrington & Gabert-Quillen, 2015; Saville et al., 2010) assert students who receive detailed syllabi typically perceive their teachers as more caring, helpful, and possessing higher levels of master-teacher behaviors (e.g. creativity, approachability and personableness, enthusiasm, and reliability). Additionally, students gain numerous benefits from detailed, learner-centered syllabi: they remember more of its elements, experience higher levels of empowerment and motivation in the course, and believe their course and teacher are more receptive, reliable, and fair (Richmond, 2016; Richmond et al., 2016; Wilson & Ryan, 2013).

Ultimately, a detailed syllabus provides clear, explicit expectations to help students succeed, mitigate misunderstandings, and increase students' willingness to engage with their teacher (Harrington & Gabert-Quillen, 2015; Ramsden, 2003). Conversely, a less detailed syllabus may lead students to feel the teacher is less concerned about them and their learning—and that the instructor may be underprepared for teaching the course (Saville et al., 2010).

When preparing a syllabus, remember: while readers benefit from an appealing format, a visually attractive syllabus can *never* be used to mask underdeveloped content. If you do not have the content to back up the syllabus, students will identify this quickly, and you stand a strong chance of losing credibility in the eyes of your students.

### *Balance of Power*

Sharing ownership of classroom experiences elevates students' investment of their time and energy in your course. Within the syllabus, you can achieve a collaborative tone by expressing a sense of common purpose, frequently using the pronoun "We," as in "We will explore ..." or "We will come to understand ...." During the first class, ask students to co-create select portions of the syllabus, such as course policies, classroom norms, and degree of flexibility in due dates.

Another way to promote balanced classroom dynamics is by inviting students to teach mini-lessons. With this technique, each student chooses a class session in which they teach new content or a new skill for a short amount of time (usually between five and ten minutes). In providing them with this opportunity, you enable students to support one another and build community while simultaneously determining learning content (see Chapters 17 and 19 for further details).

Once you have completed your syllabus' sections—namely teaching philosophy, LOs, course calendar, assessment and grading methods, course and program policies, and campus resources and services—you are ready to share it with students and begin the course.

# Next Steps

## Before Classes Begins

Before your course begins, it is necessary to complete various administrative tasks. These include such things as:

- Scheduling anything that may require advance planning, such as guest speakers, off-site visits, and special equipment;
- Visiting your classroom before the first meeting to ensure that it is appropriate for your course, the room's technology operates, and there is adequate seating;
- Printing your roster;
- Determining which supplies you will need for the first session (e.g. chalk/dry-erase markers); and
- Reviewing all policies pertaining to your program and your institution as a whole.

## How to Motivate Students to Read the Syllabus

Given the aforementioned benefits offered by well-designed syllabi, it behooves students to read and access them regularly—but they do not always do that. Motivational strategies you can use to encourage them to do so include:

- Creating an ice-breaker questionnaire. During your first class session, pair students and ask them to complete a questionnaire together as they review the syllabus. For example, the form might include questions such as: "Where is my office located, and when are office hours?"; "What is the policy for submitting late work?"; and "How does this course relate to your own professional goals?" This activity fosters classroom community and affords time to students to understand better the goals of your course, your expectations, what resources are available to them, and more, all while learning the syllabus more intimately.
- Using live polling. Live polling platforms (e.g. Kahoot!, iClickers, Poll Everywhere) can be used during class to shift the syllabus' review process from one that is onerous and staid to one that is lighthearted and fun. The process will also reveal if students closely read and understand the syllabus—and if you need to devote more time to its review.
- Co-developing content. As suggested, inviting students to co-create portions of the syllabus content will increase their overall engagement with the course. It also helps students understand the powerful control they have over their own learning and success.

- Explicitly offering help. Students are more likely to say they would be willing to use a syllabus in which teachers explicitly offer help (Perrine et al., 1995). For instance, stating, "I encourage you to see me for office hours at any point to discuss further your work, general progress, and/or professional goals," or "I believe my primary role as an educator is to support your learning and unique goals. Please contact me throughout the semester so I may support you best!" will likely leave positive impressions on students and encourage them to seek your assistance.
- Frequently mentioning your syllabus. For example, at the end of every class, present to the students the course calendar and discuss the upcoming session(s). This simple act reminds students that the syllabus is a useful, practical tool they can use when planning their week. Additionally, an occasional reminder of where the syllabus can be easily accessed online can prove beneficial, particularly for students who feel reluctant to ask.

## Conclusion: The Syllabus Is a Living, Changing Document

The syllabus is a living, changing document that is constantly evolving over the semester to meet student needs most effectively. The syllabus itself is never fully finalized until your work on that course is completely finished.

You may find at the start of the course that some initial plans are overly ambitious and revisions are necessary. Ideally, the revision process will involve students, particularly if these adjustments stem from something they have identified as a challenge. Whenever you make revisions, post the updated syllabus online, ensuring you note the revisions and email it to your students. Although revisions can be advantageous, it is important to use them *infrequently*; early on in the term, students have finalized their schedules and budgets and thus require a degree of consistency in the course calendar and required course materials. Subjecting them to significant unexpected changes, particularly if costs are involved (such as the case with materials needed), introduces additional stress into student life that is unnecessary.

When the course ends, but before too much time has passed, reflect on your syllabus' design. What have you learned about your syllabus during this particular term? What insights and ideas can be gleaned from students' course evaluations? A syllabus is never perfect, so discern what worked well and where improvements can be made in the sequencing of classes, assignments, selected readings, class demonstrations and activities, and overall structure. Also consider where students struggled most in their understanding of the course content and reflect on how and where your pedagogy can improve. In this reflective mode, you must ask yourself, "Did the challenges that students experienced over the term result from the syllabus' content or from how I taught the material?" Let your answers inform both your syllabus' revisions for the next term in which you teach it and your overall pedagogy.

Lastly, once you have finalized the syllabus, you should use it as the foundation document for the next time the class is taught. Bearing this in mind, incorporate any updated or new policies for the upcoming semester into the next iteration of the syllabus.

A host of factors require our syllabi to remain a living thing: the evolving nature of design practices, fluctuations in new student populations, and updated institutional directives require us, as design educators, to reflect and respond to these factors constantly. It is by incorporating a responsive, adaptive, and malleable approach to syllabi design that we ensure our courses remain relevant to our students, schools, and design practices.

# References

Cornell University Center for Teaching Innovation. (n.d.). Writing a syllabus. *Cornell University.* https://teaching.cornell.edu/teaching-resources/designing-your-course/writing-syllabus

Cullen, R., & Harris, M. (2009). Assessing learner-centredness through course syllabi. *Assessment & Evaluation in Higher Education, 34*(1), 115–125.

Gannon, K. (2018, September 12). How to create a syllabus. *The Chronicle of Higher Education.* https://www.chronicle.com/article/how-to-create-a-syllabus/?cid=wcontentgrid_7_1a

Harnish, R., McElwee, R., Slattery, J., Frantz, S., Haney, M. R., Shore, C. M., & Penley, J. (2011, July 11). Creating the foundation for a warm classroom climate: Best practices in syllabus tone. *Association for Psychological Science.* https://www.psychologicalscience.org/observer/creating-the-foundation-for-a-warm-classroom-climate

Harrington, C. M., & Gabert-Quillen, C. A. (2015). Syllabus length and use of images: An empirical investigation of student perceptions. *Scholarship of Teaching and Learning in Psychology, 1*(3), 235–243.

Ludy, M., Brackenbury, T., Folkins, J. W., Peet, S. H., & Langendorfer, S. J. (2016). Student impressions of syllabus design: Engaging versus contractual syllabus. *International Journal for the Scholarship of Teaching and Learning, 10*(2), 1–23.

Massachusetts Institute of Technology Teaching and Learning Lab (MITTLL) (n.d.). Design a course. *Massachusetts Institute of Technology.* https://tll.mit.edu/teaching-resources/course-design/

Perrine, R. M., Lisle, J., & Tucker, D. L. (1995). Effects of a syllabus offer of help, student age, and class size on college students' willingness to seek support from faculty. *Journal of Experimental Education, 64*(1), 41–52.

Ramsden, P. (2003). *Learning to teach in higher education.* Routledge.

Richmond, A. S. (2016, September). Constructing a learner-centered syllabus: One professor's journey. *IDEA Paper 60.* https://files.eric.ed.gov/fulltext/ED573642.pdf

Richmond, A. S., Slattery, J. M., Mitchell, N., Morgan, R. K., & Becknell, J. (2016). Can a learner-centered syllabus change students' perceptions of student-professor rapport and master teacher behaviors? *Scholarship of Teaching and Learning in Psychology*, 2(3), 159–168.

Saville, B. K., Zinn, T., Brown, A., & Marchuk, K. (2010). Syllabus detail and students' perceptions of teacher effectiveness. *Teaching of Psychology*, 37(3), 186–189.

Slattery, J. M., & Carlson, J. F. (2005). Preparing an effective syllabus: Current best practices. *College Teaching*, 53(4), 159–164.

Wilson, J. H., & Ryan, R. G. (2013). Professor-student rapport scale: Six items predict student outcomes. *Teaching of Psychology*, 40(2), 130–133.

# 21 Assessment as Learning

*Mariah Doren*
Rhode Island School of Design

In art and design practice, success is determined through a mix of aesthetics, efficacy, originality, and innovation. The ideal of creating something new, better, or unexpected means that what is produced is, by definition, unknowable in advance. This expectation of the discipline that "outcomes emerge, often unexpected, from the process of inquiry and cannot be known at the start" (McNiff, 2019, p. xii) makes determining success complex. This is due to the cognition involved, which culminates from a synthesis of ideas and processes learned along the way.

In traditional academic contexts, assessment is understood to measure success, but in doing so it must also define characteristics of success and determination of value. The *process* of assessing requires defining this criteria and measuring the extent to which they are evidenced in the outcomes of student work. Having a process that is linear and clear supports the expectation of assessment as fair, impartial, and objective.

However, the indeterminate nature of outcomes that is central to art and design simply does not fit into the traditional practice of assessment. This misalignment, between outcomes that are predetermined and those that are emergent, creates skepticism about the value of assessment within the art and design community. So, while engaging in assessment is a necessary condition for being part of academic institutions, the discomfort felt by art and design faculty and students alike is often palpable. This is most clearly evident in the "end-of-project critique," the signature pedagogy in art and design. The critique is reflective by nature, looking back at completed work with the goal of determining value, but done in the absence of predetermined criteria. The result is that goals, outcomes, and expectations are often ill-defined. Engaging assessments in a more direct manner, and then shifting expectations to value the ambiguous and malleable nature of the discipline, is an opportunity to serve art and design students better. It also affords an opportunity to broaden horizons within assessment practices more generally.

There is a distinction between the process of making in art and design and the objects produced from that process. If teaching is focused on outputs, often called "content knowledge" in academic disciplines, and that

DOI: 10.4324/9781003049166-25

content is unknowable in advance, then, logically, the discipline would be unteachable. Recognizing this predicament, many art and design faculty "know all too well that they can communicate only rules and conventions" (de Duve, 2005, p. 25) and are frustrated because they also know what is prized as truly successful work "overthrows, displaces, abandons or subverts rules and conventions" (de Duve, 2005, p. 25).

Turning to other models of progressive education, the approach to this kind of learning is embodied in the methodologies utilized, namely ones that focus on developing students' interests, proclivities, and approaches to making. However, if the process of assessment itself were framed as "learning," the critique is an opportunity to develop dialogue where meaning and new understandings emerge. In this way, assessment becomes embedded in teaching; learning happens through dialogue, with a community that has understanding of context for the project.

## The Three Pillars of Assessment

At its core, assessment requires picking a point at which to stop, look back, and take stock of work that either has been or is in the process of being completed. Assessment is looking back at completed work, often in dialogue with other people, and understanding the extent to which the project meets stated learning goals. Assessment is usually an ongoing activity. Every time you check to see if your students "get it," you are conducting an assessment.

There are three basic kinds of assessment: formative, summative, and developmental (Hickman, 2007). These three have different goals, occur at different points in time, and often evaluate different aspects of a given assignment or project.

- **Formative assessment** is offering feedback and advice in the middle of the project. This assessment is meant to be actionable, since students are working and developing ideas. It assesses a student's engagement with their own thinking and checks to see if their internal ideation process is evident in the sketches, prototypes, or drafts. The subject of formative assessment is the work in progress, an opening of possibilities presented by what is there so far.
- **Summative assessment** is given at the end of a project, often in the form of grades, a judgment on completed work. This assessment functions as closure, marking an end point for the project. The subject of summative assessment is the final product, assessed against the criteria inherent in the project.
- **Developmental assessment** is offered iteratively as a way to recognize an individual student's growth. The subject of this assessment is personal growth and not the objects the student produced. It is a way of evaluating improvement that is measured according to a student's

prior performance. Conducting a developmental assessment, recognizing growth, requires you to expand your thinking, looking horizontally at a given project and longitudinally, backward in time at each student's performance.

Formative and summative assessments are listed separately. However, the line between them is permeable: one completed project can also be a key point on the larger trajectory of a student's education. Successful educational environments offer students a balance of the three different forms of assessment.

The ultimate goal of design education is to produce graduates who can recognize quality in their own work, know when to make improvements, engage with a community to articulate value, and look for emergent understandings as components of their professional practice. Developing strong self-assessment skills is essential for success in a discipline where being innovative and thinking creatively are critical skills.

In art and design schools, "assessment" and "critique" are essentially synonymous. The critique is a summative assessment, located at the end of a project. Students often describe the experience of using critiques as assessment as complex and charged, highly subjective, and painfully public. Simultaneously, there is an educational expectation that the critique is a learning experience, not simply the final judgment of quality.

## Where Assessments Fall Short

In schools of art and design, there are three key places where these three pillars of assessment intertwine in ways that cause faculty and students to mistrust the pillars' usefulness. The first place is the critique. During this summative assessment, feedback offered addresses the finalized project. For students, receiving feedback at the end of a project, when it is no longer specifically actionable, can be uncomfortable (Elkins, 2001). The second misalignment is the use of feedback offered during desk critiques, which are one-on-one meetings between students and faculty to discuss in-progress work. During these sessions, formative assessment is often utilized. When not framed as assessment, however, there is no explicit expectation of learning outcomes or deliverables. The third incongruence is the approach to developmental assessment, which is often conducted informally and not explicitly part of a student's grades.

The incongruencies between traditional assessment practices and the studio critique can result in environments that are not supportive of students' growth and learning. The absence of developmental assessment means there are no designated moments (within the process of creation) where individual progress or themes engaged over time are discussed. This omission stifles dialogue about socially complex themes such as race, discrimination, and identity politics. A powerful examination of critiques was made by Eloise Sherrid (2016) in the film *The Room of Silence* that includes interviews with students who described what is taboo and not open for discussion during a typical critique. If used more explicitly, developmental assessment can create opportunities for discussion of thematic issues with individual students that can be tracked at multiple stages of progress across multiple projects.

## Assessment and Success

In the traditional context of assessment, it is important to establish goals and criteria for assessment in advance. This is considered the basis for establishing fair and impartial evaluation. **Objectivity** defines the "what" of assessment, which is clearly separated from the "who," or person whose work is being assessed. Objectivity is the process of creating mental distance from the subject of assessment. **Subjectivity**—your opinions, mood, and preferences—stand in stark contrast to the objective approach. The idea of creating mental distance is to move away from the subject of assessment so that your evaluation is not influenced by your subjective opinions, mood, or preference. This pivot (from the subjective to the objective) is a stumbling block in art and design exactly because success in any given project is indeterminate, not known in advance.

Success is often measured by the originality of a given solution, making it difficult to articulate parameters for success in advance. Expertise in design fields and in academia are understood differently due to the complexity of framing problems in practice-based situations (Schön, 1990). "Reflection-in-action" is the term assigned by Schön to describe a kind of puzzle-solving strategy that is context specific; each new situation requires a response based on experience and dynamic improvisation and invention and is inherently unknowable in advance. Sinapius (2018) points out that the "detours and bottlenecks" (p. 39), which are integral to learning and normal parts of a productive design process, might be understood as failures when framed by traditional academic assessment.

The critique of objectivity in assessment extends beyond schools of art and design. bell hooks, an educator who writes about transgressive teaching, also questions the assumption that objectivity is simply the creation of mental distance in order to assess something. She describes the fallacy of believing that distance equals neutrality and points out that creating mental distance, or objectivity, makes our thinking static and is an impediment to seeing or imagining alternative viewpoints (hooks, 2003) that are at the center of art and design practice. hooks suggests challenging the status quo and advocates for more dialogue and stronger community as the needed basis for effective learning and teaching (hooks, 1994), believing that exploration through dialogue—developed and sustained over time, within a group that has established trust, mutual respect, and caring—creates space for art as social critique or subjective assessment as valuable to students' growth.

## Reflective Practice

Reflective practice is the continuous process of thoughtful consideration of one's own experiences as a way of checking and monitoring how to proceed. When teaching students about reflective practice, the goal is for them to develop internal mechanisms for understanding their own approach to projects, problem-solving, and growth. Reflective practice develops processes that check if what the individual was attempting to convey is being received and understood by others as intended, and how to adjust one's approach when it is not. This practice is dependent on input and assistance from others; after all, it is problems that stimulate dialogue and that serve as a continual source of engagement (Brookfield, 1995).

However, reflective practice does not fit comfortably into summative assessment, as the process is ongoing and cyclical—examining assumptions and practices as a way of acting and reflecting in order to act again. During a typical critique, students present their projects. Discussion is framed around efficacy of communicating what was intended through what was made—the assessment is of the relationship between the individual's ideas and their execution. Reframing the critique to be more conceptual, engaging open-ended subjects like the connection between reception and address and how it is changeable over time and understood differently by different people, might better serve student learning. This practice would stretch beyond the simplistic idea of being able to talk about one's work and ask students to engage in dialogue where knowledge comes into being through the conversation, and not just an explanation of a priori ideas.

At the formative stage of a project, the importance of dialogue around ideas and utilizing dialogue to avoid problems cannot be overstated. Lev Vygotsky (1978) described the ways one can use an ongoing practice of reflection as a way to look back and synthesize information in order to create clarity and integrate new understandings. There is a socio-cognitive "conflict" inherent in the perception of differing points of view that is uncovered through dialogue. When our students negotiate these moments of discord they stimulate learning and capacity for reasoning. Reflective practice might include "the process of describing one's own experience [in a manner such that it] increases opportunities for communication and collaboration" (Osterman, 1990, p. 149). Talking through an idea is a valid way of seeking discovery and constructing new knowledge. Knowing is best developed as learning through the social context of dialogue (Vygotsky, 1978).

## 272  Design Classrooms

By creating an opening for subjective responses, we create opportunities to explore the unknowable in art and design practice. This understanding of success—that it is an engagement with the idea that knowledge is changeable, malleable, and temporal—does not preclude the idea of learning as an incremental process with steps, benchmarks, and progression.

### Bloom's Learning Objectives

The educational psychologist Benjamin Bloom (Anderson & Bloom, 2001) developed a taxonomy of learning objectives as part of his methodology for understanding learning. The taxonomy's pyramid shape (Figure 21.1) places lower order thinking, simple tasks of repeating or applying knowledge received from instruction, at the bottom. The pyramid builds upward with more complex, higher order thinking, like analysis and synthesis, as the pyramid narrows toward creating and innovation that reside at the pinnacle.

Articulating these progressive steps in art and design assessment requires building a rubric that includes this progression from lower to higher order thinking. This is with the goal of moving through the progressively higher steps of cognition that lead to developing the capacity for generative or creative thinking. Lower order thinking might be

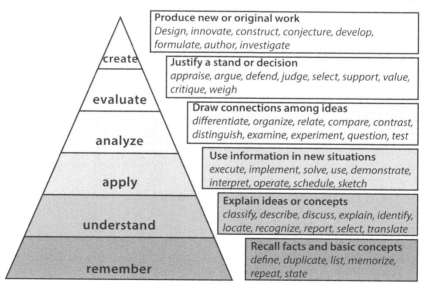

*Figure 21.1* Bloom's Taxonomy Pyramid.

accurately reproducing something by rote following assignment parameters. From lower order thinking, students must move into higher order thinking in order to achieve creative thinking. To achieve this, one should choose the best approach across multiple possible solutions and testing combinations of different approaches to achieve a desired solution.

## The Learning Assessment Rubric

As Bloom writes about the cognitive aspects of learning, he shows how it is the *process* of progression, the moving through the steps, that prepares students for generative thinking and innovative responses (Anderson & Bloom, 2001). Using a rubric shifts the focus of the assessment to the process and progression rather than the completed object. Many of the ideas described as unteachable in art and design can be framed as higher order thinking skills. When teaching progresses incrementally, in steps through the development of a project that aligns with how cognition works, students are able to reflect and make explicit connections along the way. As a result, the rigidity of the "unknowable" in art and design assessment is undone. The rubric functions as a progressive checklist: demonstrate you understand, then execute and check again through analysis, and then you are ready for posing new solutions.

- **Each criterion** in a rubric is distinct, allowing students to clearly see areas of strength and places where they need to grow. For example, three very different projects might all receive a "B" grade evaluation, but without the clear articulation of difference, grading can look random and arbitrary. When looking at these three distinct projects through the lens of a rubric, one could see that one had a great concept but a poorly constructed model, another had the inverse, and the third was not well-executed but represented a huge leap for this particular student. Taken a step further, a class might develop the criteria for assessment, or an individual might offer a counter argument for feedback in a specific area. This provides an opening for students to have more control of their own development: specifically, their work, process, and growth. Activating students in the assessment process engenders in them a sense of agency, displacing some of the authority usually held by the professor.
- **Communicating criteria** for establishing value and assigning grades is still an entrenched part of the educational system. Judgments that emerge from clear expectations and criteria are valuable. One must ensure the criteria, at the higher levels of thinking, is not static but instead is malleable and context-sensitive. Utilizing this criterion, one could start to shift the focus of learning to the process, an engagement through dialogue about the work. This would allow

for assessment's changeable and ambiguous nature not only to be tolerated but celebrated. Developmental assessment must be emphasized as another important moment that focuses on individual students and the themes that guide and frame their thinking. This might include something like risk-taking that is assessed as progress and evaluated in parallel with their ability to innovate.

What keeps ambiguity and openness from becoming rampant relativism is the sense of responsibility constructed within an engaged community. Ernesto Pujol (2009) writes about engagement with a community as the grounding element that provides useful context for innovation without overly focusing on originality. For example, a critique might be simply a conversation that bridges themes and material manifestations in the work being reviewed. The philosopher Maxine Greene (1978) writes about subjectivity as allowing us to see reality as full of variety and alternative interpretations, changeable based on our perceptions. She describes how the imaginative subjectivity of these moments fosters a sense of agency and possibility in a student's education. In maintaining the binary opposition between objectivity as neutral and subjectivity as biased or relativistic, we lose the sense of purposefulness that embracing a contextually bound understanding of art and design might bring.

Reengaging and reassembling the three pillars of assessment to pull apart the binaries of predetermined and indeterminate, subjective and objective, begins with a project brief that articulates clear expectations and lists criteria that will be used during assessment. As students begin to work through ideas, feedback and advice are offered at key moments during project development so that the student may integrate any useful insights provided. Interwoven throughout are opportunities for a shared dialogue about ideas that helps build a strong classroom community. This phase is aligned with the formative assessment.

At the end of the project, the evaluation consists of two distinct parts. The first is a summative assessment in the form of a rubric which mirrors the project brief's list of criteria as developed through the rubric. This enables the evaluation of the criteria separately and the progression of student development from lower to higher order thinking is clear. This part of the assessment is shared between student and faculty privately, not as part of a public exchange. The second part is the critique, a community dialogue that is an open-ended conversation where meaning emerges. This meaning results from a collective discovery process through both the comparison of themes developed and nurtured and the material form or shape of the work produced. In this way, there is a shift from assessment *of* learning to assessment *as* learning—thoroughly and thoughtfully embedded in the classroom experience and project development.

## Improving Critiques

Building critiques around changeable understandings of learning reframes the dialogue to function as opportunities for recalibration of our expectations and assessments. However, measurement against changeable circumstances is impossible within the academic construct of objectivity's supremacy. Pitting the subjective experience of our current understanding against the objective task of measurement with static standards is a mistake. Instead, assessment can be understood as an incremental process wherein we check and adjust and then recheck, not as verification of the object of our inquiry but to calibrate, to see how the standard or measurement has changed.

This process goes beyond an approach to looking at completed works of art and design and starts to question the overall approach to assessment. Foregrounding dialogue as the place where meaning is constructed creates a sense of agency among participants as they watch and see themselves form and build knowledge through this communal engagement. Assessment could be about:

- the nature of our dialogue,
- the value of our selected criteria,
- the process of selecting itself, or
- how participants are changed through this engagement.

By decoupling assessment from an objective measurement of success and instead seeing it as part of the iterative process of developing understanding, the experience is transformed. In taking this approach, the critique experience can become a lively, dynamic conversation about ambiguity and uncertainty—and their value in our disciplines.

## References

Anderson, L. W., & Bloom, B. S. (2001). *A taxonomy for learning, teaching, and assessing: A revision of Bloom's taxonomy of educational objectives.* Longman.
Brookfield, S. (1995). *Becoming a critically reflective teacher.* Jossey-Bass.
de Duve, T. (2005). When form has become attitude—And beyond. In Z. Kocur, & S. Leung (Eds.), *Theories in contemporary art since 1985* (pp. 19–31). Blackwell Publishing.
Elkins, J. (2001). *Why art cannot be taught: A handbook for art students.* University of Illinois Press.
Greene, M. (1978). *Landscapes of learning.* Teachers College Press.
Hickman, R. (2007). (In defense of) whippet-fancying and other vices: Re-evaluating assessment in art and design. In T. Rayment (Ed.), *The problem of assessment in art & design* (pp. 77–88). Intellect Books.
hooks, b. (1994). *Teaching to transgress: Education as the practice of freedom.* Routledge.

hooks, b. (2003). *Teaching community: A pedagogy of hope*. Routledge.
McNiff, S. (2019). Foreword. In M. R. Prior (Ed.), *Using art as research in learning and teaching: Multidisciplinary approaches across the arts* (pp. xi–xvi). Intellect Books Ltd.
Osterman, K. (1990). Reflective practice: A new agenda for education. *Education and Urban Society*, 22(2), 133–151.
Pujol, E. (2009). On the ground: Practical observations for regenerating art education. In E. Madoff (Ed.), *Art school: (Propositions for the 21st century)* (pp. 1–13). MIT Press.
Schön, D. (1990). *Educating the reflective practitioner: Toward a new design for teaching and learning in the professions*. Jossey-Bass.
Sherrid, E. (2016). *The room of silence* [Video]. Rhode Island School of Design. https://digitalcommons.risd.edu/archives_activism_racialjustice/18
Sinapius, P. (2018). Not sure': The didactics of elusive knowledge. In R. W. Prior (Ed.), *Using art as research in learning and teaching: Multidisciplinary approaches across the arts* (pp. 31–41). Intellect Books Ltd.
Vygotsky, L. (1978). Interaction between learning and development. In M. Cole, V. John-Steiner, S. Scribner, & E. Souberman (Eds.), *Mind and society: The development of higher psychological processes* (pp. 79–91). Harvard University Press.

# 22 Faculty Mentorship

Mentorship is an essential component to achieving success as a design educator. Faculty members bring a tremendous amount of professional design experience and knowledge to their students and schools, but they cannot be expected to learn and grow as academic professionals in isolation. Therefore, while the previous chapters in this Section presented extensive methods for self-developing and strengthening one's pedagogical skillsets in design higher education, this final chapter serves to underscore the imperative that we cannot and should not do it alone. It is with this guiding ethos that best practices for establishing and developing mentorship programs for design educators are examined.

## Introduction to Mentorship

Mentorship, in its simplest form, is taking an active interest in your coworkers, providing practical guidance, and sharing your knowledge and networks (Harvard University [HU], 2016). It is about collaborating with and learning from one another to develop as professionals. As the American politician John Crosby famously stated, "Mentoring is a brain to pick, an ear to listen, and a push in the right direction."

In the mentoring relationship, a **mentor** is someone who goes beyond the obligatory or conventional supervision or engagement: mentors demonstrate a genuine, concerted interest in overseeing and nurturing another person's development. Effective mentors advise, coach, and support. They "have an understanding of the organization's values, culture and norms so they can pass these along to mentees. The mentor should be sensitive to the mentee's needs and wishes, and enhance the mentee's career potential, while simultaneously looking for ways the mentee's potential can benefit the organization" (The Wharton School, University of Pennsylvania [WS], 2007, n.p.).

The **mentee** is someone who desires to learn and gain from someone else's knowledge and experience—professionally and/or personally through a period of guidance and support (University of California, Davis [UCD], n.d.). Effective mentees take ownership of their learning

DOI: 10.4324/9781003049166-26

and developmental needs, are proactive in requesting feedback, and drive the mentor-mentee relationship forward. This requires them to establish and maintain contact with their mentor, arrange meetings, create agendas with objectives, maintain accurate meeting notes, and record their progress throughout the mentoring relationship.

### Common Functions, Responsibilities, and Activities of Mentorship

Kram (1985) posits two key functions of mentorship: to support career development and to provide psychosocial support. Career-oriented functions "are those aspects of the relationship that enhance learning the ropes and preparing for advancement in an organization" (p. 22). These functions encourage work productivity. Psychosocial-oriented functions "are those aspects of the relationship that enhance a sense of competence, clarity of identity, and effectiveness in a professional role" (p. 22). These functions enhance work satisfaction. Through mentoring, psychosocial development is fostered by the close interpersonal relationship that engenders mutual trust and increasing intimacy (Kram, 1985). Although these two functions are defined separately, they are complementary and need to be practiced together during the mentorship. As Bland et al. (2009) note, "[i]t is common for mentors to focus quickly on the career development activities of mentoring, but effective mentoring attends to both components of the mentoring process. Doing so optimizes the likelihood of productive, satisfied faculty remaining at an institution" (p. 6) (Figure 22.1).

To develop these two functions, a scope of general responsibilities and activities are undertaken by both the mentor and the mentee. These include:

- getting to know each other genuinely as people, scholars, and teachers;
- cultivating a trusting relationship;
- meeting, at minimum, once per semester;
- establishing a multi-year plan for the mentee that lists appropriate goals, expectations, deliverables, and measures of progress, along with a longer term career vision;
- finding ways for the relationship to be mutually beneficial; and
- maintaining the confidentiality of the relationship (e.g. Bland et al., 2009; Columbia University [CU], 2016).

Mentors must also *socialize* their mentees into the organization, particularly if a mentee is new to the profession and/or organization. Socialization is "a mechanism through which new members learn the [unwritten] values, norms, knowledge, beliefs, and the interpersonal and

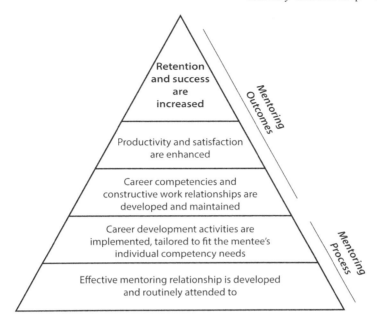

**Components and Outcomes of Effective Mentoring**

*Figure 22.1* The Model of Effective Mentoring.
Source: Adapted from Bland et al. (2009).

other skills that facilitate role performance and further group goals" (Mortimer & Simmons, 1978, p. 423). The process of socialization schools the mentee in the organization's particular language and ideology that help guide the member's everyday experiences, namely "models for social etiquette and demeanor, certain customs and rituals suggestive of how members are to relate to colleagues, subordinates, superiors, and outsiders, and a sort of residual category of some rather plain 'horse sense' regarding what is appropriate and 'smart' behavior within the organization and what is not" (Van Maanen & Schein, 1979, p. 210).

Socialization is especially necessary for new design teachers who are long-term design industry professionals and unfamiliar with academia. For these mentees, socialization illuminates not only those areas discussed above, but also the ways to navigate successfully and fulfill the three areas of their work as design educators—teaching, research and/or creative practice, and service—that are reviewed during annual evaluations and typically determine promotions. Accordingly, through socialization, the design educator is positioned for achieving success in the design Academy. When performed successfully, socialization of the individual facilitates effective performance, develops deep commitment to the work, stimulates motivation, and bolsters productivity and achievement throughout their career (Clark & Corcoran, 1986).

Specific mentoring responsibilities and activities commonly practiced in each of the three areas of work can include but are not limited to those presented in Table 22.1 (e.g. CU, 2016; HU, 2016).

### Guiding Principles and Characteristics of Mentorship

To support and guide these responsibilities and activities throughout the mentor-mentee relationship, specific principles and characteristics are practiced (e.g. Bland et al., 2009; CU, 2016; UCD, n.d.; WS, 2007). These include:

- **Collaboration**. Mentoring is a reciprocal, collaborative partnership that, in the traditional model, relies on the expertise of experienced faculty as mentors and the dedication of mentees to grow and improve their professional abilities (Bland et al., 2009).
- **Commitment**. Mentorship requires dedicated engagement by each participant. Mentors and mentees need to invest their time and effort in the process while also bringing high levels of enthusiasm and willingness to the partnership. This includes always fulfilling expectations and requirements in a timely manner.
- **Purpose**. Participants need to adhere to a defined purpose that is guided by structured, deliberate, and goal-oriented interactions. Meeting agendas, trajectories for development, recorded meetings (e.g. note taking), and reflective practice bolster this shared sense of purpose.
- **Evolution**. The mentor-mentee collaboration is not static but evolutionary; it can range in focus for the mentee depending on where they are in their career, what their professional goals are, and how much guidance they need. "Thus, [mentorships] may be enduring, long-term relationships that evolve over time into collegial rather than mentoring relationships, or they may be more transient relationships focused on specific areas of guidance at key career points" (CU, 2016, p. 7).
- **Trust**. The mentoring relationship flourishes best within a trusting, safe, and supportive environment—not an evaluative one. The relationship must be one in which the mentee feels free from judgment yet is able to receive thoughtful, constructive, and accurate feedback (HU, 2016; UCD, n.d.). The relationship is about "having a sounding board and a place where it's safe to be vulnerable and get career advice. It's a relationship where one can let one's guard down, a place where one can get honest feedback, and a place, ideally, where one can get psychological and social support in handling stressful situations" (Klein, as quoted in WS, 2007, n.p.).
- **Benefits**. The mentor-mentee partnership offers a myriad of formal and informal benefits. These include enhanced teaching skills, scholarly

Table 22.1 Examples of specific responsibilities and activities commonly practiced in faculty mentorship

| Teaching | Research and creative practice | Service |
| --- | --- | --- |
| • Observing each other's classes and offering helpful feedback afterward.<br>• Showing past syllabi and reviewing those in development.<br>• Discussing effective pedagogical methods along with those that are less successful.<br>• Offering support for advising and working with students.<br>• Sharing relevant course materials and organizational tips.<br>• Co-teaching a course or designated session(s) or creating other collaborative teaching opportunities.<br>• Reviewing current teaching assignments and strategizing future courses; this can also include developing new courses.<br>• Providing helpful resources about teaching and student development, such as books, articles, and websites.<br>• Reading students' course evaluations and discussing ideas for pedagogical improvements and revisions for the next term. | • Advising the development of academic and/or creative outputs across short- and long-term trajectories.<br>• Discussing each other's work and giving constructive feedback.<br>• Offering advice about approaching publishers for works in preparation.<br>• Helping connect mentees with potential journals, galleries, and similar networking opportunities for disseminating their output.<br>• Providing insights into internal and external funding sources, professional groups, and academic organizations.<br>• Reviewing grant proposals and discussing those that have been successful as a learning tool.<br>• Advising on the output types viewed favorably by the institution that are beneficial for advancement and promotion. (This is especially important for tenure-track mentees.)<br>• Sharing tips for balancing the research and/or creative practice workload with other institutional responsibilities and demands. | • Strategizing and answering questions about service commitments—both service to the institution and service to the field.<br>• Providing advice about what to expect from service commitments, such as committees and leadership appointments.<br>• Explaining how to navigate the institutional and departmental structure(s), culture(s), and governance.<br>• Discussing the numerous ways mentees can increase their visibility and impact at the institution and in the field.<br>• Reviewing service to the field and focusing on those that offer substantial value for academic and professional growth.<br>• Offering ideas for performing service to the field, such as serving on editorial boards and design organizations, performing peer reviews for publishing houses, sitting on juries and external committees, and conducting program reviews at peer institutions. |

independence, internal and external networks, and preparation for professional advancement. Mentoring is about cultivating agency and independence in the mentee. It is also about preparing the mentee to become a highly skilled mentor at the institution in the future.
- **Accessibility.** Mentorship must be made available to *all* levels of faculty, and not limited to new, junior-level faculty. While the aims of the mentoring partnership may differ depending on the individual's professional experience and unique goals, everyone can—and should—benefit from mentoring.

## Developing a Mentor-Mentee Relationship

While there is no "right" way to develop a mentor-mentee relationship, there are best practices and select models that participants should consider before deciding which specific approach(s) will suit their personal goals and needs best. The first step is to decide if the approach to mentorship should be formal or informal.

*Formal mentoring* is often organized and driven by the school; it adheres to certain institutional structures and provides direct guidance on how to initiate and work in the mentoring relationship (Galanek & Campbell, 2019). In this model, mentors are typically provided training so they can follow institutional guidelines and expectations. An example of formal mentoring is a senior-level faculty member who works with a junior-level colleague as they prepare for tenure review. During the specified timeframe, the mentor provides standardized information and guidance about the dossier's components, submission guidelines, crafting an effective personal statement, and key deadlines.

*Informal mentoring* fosters a more organic connection between colleagues. It might even look and feel like a somewhat casual friendship (Galanek & Campbell, 2019). In this sense, the partnership typically offers additional psychosocial support and longer-term career guidance. An example of informal mentoring includes peer faculty sharing best practices for teaching, writing syllabi, advancing within the institution, and developing and disseminating research and/or creative practice in the field.

Whichever approach is adopted, mentoring partnerships can be formed by assigning pairs or small groups, allowing participants to self-select, or a combination of the two. However, research suggests the relationship is often more successful when both persons are afforded choice—though institutions may also consider the colleagues' scholarship/creative practices for mentorship pairings (CU, 2016).

### *Mentorship Models: Traditional, Peer, and Group*

Once the general approach to mentoring has been determined, the faculty member(s) need to consider which mentorship model will provide the mentee(s) with the appropriate support. There are three common mentorship models: traditional, peer, and group mentoring.

- **Traditional mentoring**, the most common model, involves a senior colleague (or a senior-level team) working with a less experienced faculty member. While this is the most hierarchical of the three models, it allows mentees to gain the wide-ranging knowledge, organizational insight, contacts, and experience that come from working with senior colleagues (Bland et al., 2009). One possible drawback, however, is the perpetuation of the status quo if the senior colleague chooses to keep things "just as they are" (Bland et al., 2009). It is best for mentees to avoid mentors who are their direct supervisors, or a conflict of interest could arise.
- **Group mentoring** is a more collaborative model wherein one or more facilitators (usually seniors) assemble a small cohort of faculty (of similar or near rank) for professional development. Group formats can be especially useful and efficient under two conditions: when providing general guidance and when the information needs to be made transparent and standardized (such as the institution's set procedures for a tenure review). Group mentoring can also facilitate valuable networking opportunities and a stronger sense of community among faculty; the feeling that "we are all in this together" is promoted through group members' mutual sharing of experiences, challenges, questions, and ideas for solving problems.
- **Peer mentoring** involves a pair or trio of faculty at similar career stages who convene for professional development and support. Kram and Isabella (1985) note the relationship is based not on a senior-junior dynamic, but rather a peer-to-peer construct whereby the absence of steep hierarchies among participants can make communication, mutual support, and collaboration easier to establish. Accordingly, this model fosters a safe environment for each colleague to discuss their challenges candidly, gain different perspectives, achieve expertise, and build networks without the possible scrutiny or judgment of more senior faculty (Bland et al., 2009). Moreover, this model often provides a beneficial sense of equality and empathy among the participants, which can sometimes be absent from the other models (e.g. Kram & Isabella, 1985).

Although these three models are presented separately from one another, there are several areas of overlap and they are highly adaptable; multiple models can be employed during the mentoring period to address the diverse needs, goals, and contexts of the mentee(s). Engaging across modalities may also reduce the strain of mentoring on individual senior faculty, as well as junior faculty's reliance on a single mentoring relationship (CU, 2016). Working with more than one mentor can be particularly beneficial for mentees, given the extensive roles faculty play that, in turn, result in the need for different types of expertise and guidance from each respective mentor.

*Establishing the Mentoring Relationship*

When faculty begin mentorship, it is necessary to establish key principles and practices that will ensure their mentor-mentee relationship is well grounded, clear, and meets everyone's needs. These include:

- **Setting a time commitment**
  When and how often will meetings occur? What will be the length of each meeting? Is there an end-date, or a time when assessments will be made about continuing the mentorship? Extensive sources about faculty mentorship (e.g. CU, 2016; HU, 2016) affirm regular, structured meetings yield the most productive engagement with lasting impact. Meetings should occur as frequently as once a month, and no less than once a semester. An "open-door" policy should also be established so that the mentee can contact their mentor at any time with questions or concerns.

  Over time, the frequency of these set meetings may change to reflect the mentee's growth and evolving needs. And while the typical length of mentoring relationships last 3.3 years and averages four hours of talking time per month (Olivet Nazarene University [ONU], 2019), these frequencies can change to meet participants' needs and schedules. Regardless of the time commitment, it is critical that the mentorship include an annual comprehensive review that assesses the mentee's overall progress and future plans.

- **Determining the scope of the mentorship**
  No matter which mentorship model is chosen—traditional, group, or peer—it is necessary to determine the overall scope of the mentorship. Will the focus be pedagogy, scholarship/creative practice, institutional service, holistic career development, or a combination of these? To answer these questions and subsequently define the scope, the mentee must first reflect on *why* they need a mentor, what can be realistically accomplished within the specified timeframe, and the type of guidance the mentor can actually provide.

  Another effective method to determine this scope is for the mentee to create a career plan that envisions what they would like to accomplish within the next three to five years. The plan could, for example, outline the mentee's "overarching vision of the impact on a field they wish to have, the specific areas (mission) in which they will work to realize that vision, and then the specific goals (strategic goals) with timelines for accomplishments that will mark progress within their field" (CU, 2016, p. 18). This plan will then reveal the types of competencies the mentee will need to acquire and/or strengthen, along with the "benchmarks" that need to be achieved to show progress. Over time and with the mentor's counsel, the mentee's plan may change, but this initial iteration constructs the necessary preliminary framework that grounds and strategizes future conversations and actions.

Additionally, when determining the mentoring scope, it is advisable to set boundaries for what will and will not be discussed. Are there any topics that might be off-limits or derail the relationship's focus? These topics should be clearly articulated to avoid potentially undermining the mentorship experience, set timeframe, and pre-established goals.

- **Recording the meetings**
  Throughout the mentoring process, both mentor and mentee need to maintain written records ("meeting minutes") of their conversations. The ongoing minutes' format and level of specificity or generalization should be mutually decided. However, the ultimate goal of these notes is to serve as a beneficial tool for visualizing and remembering thoughts and ideas, actionable items, and designated commitments. They also afford ample opportunities for reflection and assessment, particularly during annual reviews when the minutes are read by both partners to better understand the mentee's holistic progress.

## The Benefits of Mentorship

Extensive research reveals high-quality mentoring produces substantial benefits and positive outcomes for the mentee, the mentor, and the institution itself (e.g. Allen et al., 2004; Bland et al., 2009; CU, 2016).

The mentoring relationship enables **mentees** to acquire different approaches to work, build contacts for psychosocial support, and come to understand better the broader institution's operations and inherent culture. Consequently, they are better equipped to overcome professional challenges; feel more confidence and vitality toward their work; determine a vision for their career path; establish short-, mid-, and long-term goals; and learn strategies for meeting these goals. Thus, mentees commonly experience higher levels of socialization in the academic profession, productivity of research and/or creative practice, teaching effectiveness, and job satisfaction and commitment. A study of approximately 8,000 full- and part-time workers across the US found that over 90% of employees who had a mentor at work were satisfied with their jobs, including 57% who noted their job satisfaction as "very satisfied" (Wronski & Cohen, 2019). The same study noted "[a]mong those who don't have a mentor, each of those numbers drop by double digits" (n.p.). Moreover, studies reveal mentored employees have less stress, feel happier at their jobs, earn more money, and get promoted more rapidly than non-mentored employees (Melicher, 2000; ONU, 2019; WS, 2007). Mentees are also more likely than those without mentors to state they are well paid (79% versus 69%, respectively) and to feel their work is valued by their colleagues (89% versus 75%, respectively) (Wronski & Cohen, 2019).

**Mentors**, too, receive substantial benefits from the mentoring relationship. They gain personal satisfaction by helping colleagues advance, experiencing career rejuvenation and intellectual stimulation, recognition of and perspective on their leadership role, new friendships, broader networks at the institution and in the field, and credit for strengthening the institution through faculty development (e.g. CU, 2016; HU, 2016; UCD, n.d.). Mentors are provided other positive outcomes from the work, including career advancement and financial reward. For example, a study of more than 1,000 employees over a five-year period revealed mentors participating in a mentorship program were promoted six times more frequently than those not in the program, and 25% had a salary change as opposed to just 5% in the control group (Holincheck, 2006, as cited in WS, 2007).

For the **institution**, mentoring programs serve as a central mechanism for promoting long-term, sustainable success. Mentored employees are more knowledgeable, productive, satisfied, and committed to their work—and the institution itself. These attributes, in turn, directly affect institutional performance and its finances. For instance, in a survey of forty-five organizational leaders in the private sector who engage in formal mentoring, "71% said they were certain that company performance had improved as a result. Strong majorities reported that they were making better decisions (69%) and more capably fulfilling stakeholder expectations (76%). More than anything else, these [leaders] credited mentors with helping them avoid costly mistakes and become proficient in their roles faster (84%)" (de Janasz & Peiperl, 2015, n.p.).

Furthermore, effective mentoring positively impacts faculty retention. In the aforementioned five-year study, mentees (72%) and mentors (69%) had much higher retention rates than employees who did not participate in the mentoring program (49%) (Holincheck, 2006, as cited in WS, 2007). And in another study of 8,000 employees, more than 40% of respondents who did not have a mentor said they had considered resigning in the last three months, compared to 25% of those who were being mentored (Wronski & Cohen, 2019).

In design higher education, significant negative financial implications can arise from high faculty turnover and the consequential need to recruit replacements. Recruitment and start-up costs (e.g. travel, interviews, meals, and associated events) for a university can surpass $100,000 US (e.g. Demmy et al., 2002; Wingard et al., 2004). Institutional expenses also rise from hiring new faculty who often command a higher salary: for example, a new assistant professor may require an additional $10,000 US per year to replace a departing assistant professor (Hobbs et al., 2005). Financial implications like these can be especially pronounced in the private sector where mentoring can save a firm $10 million US annually from the cost of recruiting and training new employees (Boyle, 2005, as cited in Bland et al., 2009). Thus, while the cost of mentorship is free, its positive impact and benefits on all those involved—including the design school itself—are exponential.

## Conclusion

At its core, mentorship is about sharing human capital (HU, 2016). It is about encouraging the exchange of ideas, stimulating each other's professional development, advancing our work, and strengthening the institution. It is about creating a highly positive, collegial work environment. It is, in sum, about empowering everyone engaged in the process so that they can do their very best work in a supportive environment.

Mentorship is particularly essential for new design faculty who are typically highly experienced design practitioners and are, understandably, unfamiliar with how the design Academy operates. Mentoring affords them the necessary emotional support, community, and assurances that they are not alone in their challenges. In time, these mentees gain confidence, autonomy, motivation, agency, self-direction, and connectedness to the institution, all of which are necessary for them to achieve optimal success in their teaching careers. As evidenced through extensive research, mentoring positively impacts the following outcomes for faculty-mentees: scholarly output (e.g. research studies, design projects, and publications), promotions, career satisfaction, feeling valued and supported by the institution, networking, and self-efficacy related to attaining career goals (e.g. Bonilha et al., 2019). While mentorship is imperative for new design faculty, those representing all levels of experience in the Academy can benefit equally from mentoring relationships.

Together, with their mentors, faculty-mentees grow into more talented, productive, knowledgeable, and contributing colleagues, school citizens, educators, leaders, and even future mentors—both at the institution and in their respective fields.

## References

Allen, T. D., Eby, L. T., Poteet, M. L., Lentz, E., & Lima, L. (2004). Career benefits associated with mentoring for protégés: A meta-analysis. *Journal of Applied Psychology*, 89(1), 127–136.

Bland, C. J., Taylor, A. L., Shollen, S. L., Weber-Main, A. M., & Mulcahy, P. A. (2009). *Faculty success through mentoring: A guide for mentors, mentees, and leaders*. Rowman & Littlefield.

Bonilha, H., Hyer, M., Krug, E., Mauldin, M., Edlund, B., Martin-Harris, B., Halushka, P., McGinty, J., Sullivan, J., Brady, K., Ranwala, D., Hermayer, K., Harvey, J., Paranal, R., Gough, J., Silvestri, G., & Chimowitz, M. (2019). An institution-wide faculty mentoring program at an academic health center with 6-year prospective outcome data. *Journal of Clinical and Translational Science*, 3(6), 308–315.

Boyle, M. (2005). Most mentoring programs stink—But yours doesn't have to. *Training*, 22(8), 12–15.

Clark, S. M., & Corcoran, M. (1986). Perspectives on the professional socialization of women faculty. *Journal of Higher Education*, 57(1), 20–43.

Columbia University (CU). (2016). Guide to best practices in faculty mentoring. *Office of the Provost*. https://provost.columbia.edu/sites/default/files/content/Best%20Practices%20in%20Faculty%20Mentoring.pdf

de Janasz, S., & Peiperl, M. (2015). CEOs need mentors too. *Harvard Business Review*. https://hbr.org/2015/04/ceos-need-mentors-too

Demmy, T. L., Kivlahan, C., & Stone, T. T. (2002). Physicians' perceptions of institutional and leadership factors influencing their job satisfaction at one academic medical center. *Academic Medicine*, 77, 1235–1240.

Galanek, J., & Campbell, S. (2019, August 5). Types of mentoring: Pick one that works for you. *Educause*. https://www.educause.edu/ecar/research-publications/mentoring-in-higher-education-it/2019/types-of-mentoring-pick-the-one-that-works-for-you

Harvard University (HU). (2016). *Guide to faculty mentoring in the Faculty of Arts and Sciences*. https://facultyresources.fas.harvard.edu/files/facultyresources/files/mentoring_guide_to_departments_2016_10_18.pdf

Hobbs, B. K., Weeks, H. S., & Finch, J. H. (2005). Estimating the mark-to-market premium required to fill vacant business school faculty lines: The case of finance. *Journal of Education for Business*, 80(5), 253–258.

Holincheck, J. (2006, October 27). Case study: Workforce analytics at Sun. *Gartner*. https://www.gartner.com/en/documents/497507/case-study-workforce-analytics-at-sun

Kram, K. E. (1985). *Mentoring at work: Developmental relationships in organizational life*. Scott Foresman and Company.

Kram, K. E., & Isabella, L. A. (1985). Mentoring alternatives: The role of peer relationships in career development. *Academy of Management Journal*, 28(1), 110–132.

Melicher, R. (2000). The perceived value of research and teaching mentoring by finance academicians. *Financial Practice and Education*, 10, 166–174.

Mortimer, J. T., & Simmons, R. G. (1978). Adult socialization. *Annual Review of Sociology*, 4, 421–454.

Olivet Nazarene University (ONU). (2019). *Study explores professional mentor-mentee relationships in 2019*. https://online.olivet.edu/research-statistics-on-professional-mentors

The Wharton School, University of Pennsylvania (WS). (2007, May 16). *Workplace loyalties change, but the value of mentoring doesn't*. https://knowledge.wharton.upenn.edu/article/workplace-loyalties-change-but-the-value-of-mentoring-doesnt/

University of California, Davis (UCD). (n.d.). *The mentoring relationship*. https://hr.ucdavis.edu/departments/learning-dev/toolkits/mentoring/relationship

Van Maanen, J., & Schein, E. H. (1979). Toward a theory of organizational socialization. *Research Organizational Behavior*, *1*, 209–264.

Wingard, D. L., Garman, K. A., & Reznik, V. (2004). Facilitating faculty success: Outcomes and cost benefits of the UCSD National Center of Leadership in Academic Medicine. *Academic Medicine*, 79(10 Suppl), S9–S11.

Wronski, L., & Cohen, J. (2019, July 16). Nine in 10 workers who have a career mentor say they are happy in their jobs. *CNBC*. https://www.cnbc.com/2019/07/16/nine-in-10-workers-who-have-a-mentor-say-they-are-happy-in-their-jobs.html

# Conclusion

"Don't worry, you'll figure it out."

I begin both the Preface and the Conclusion of this book with the above statement, "bookending" the text, so to speak, for two distinct reasons. The first, in the Preface, is to highlight that we, as design educators and academic leaders, must stop this practice. The Academy cannot thrive by leaving its design educators to "figure out" how to teach on their own, whether they are recent hires, junior-level colleagues, or well-seasoned master educators. Each of this book's chapters have brightly illuminated that there is just too much at stake in design higher education and, indeed, our world, to continue with this broken model. Rather, we must emphasize the importance of our design pedagogy and elevate it by recognizing its intricacies; we must promote a more publicly active culture of pedagogical discourse across institutions of design higher education. The second reason, here in the Conclusion, is to offer assurance to the reader. This book provides a tremendous amount of information that may, at first, feel daunting. Yet, with time—and through a synthesis of personal interpretation, practice, and dedication—you will "figure out" how to customize, apply, and evolve this knowledge in your own teaching contexts, in your own way.

Pedagogy, as this book has shown, is remarkably complex. It has substantial short- and long-term impacts on our students, colleagues, and institutions. If we do not have a strong supply of highly trained educators, other things (e.g. our curricula) will be ineffective. While course syllabi are vital to our institutions' success in many ways, these documents are, in fact, pages of content that must be communicated to students through thoughtful, strategic, and artful pedagogy. Without an educator's high-quality, nimble pedagogical skills that facilitate learning effectively and meaningfully, all the syllabi and content knowledge in the world mean little. It is precisely through multifaceted teaching practices that students' cognitive and emotional development are advanced. Educators contribute to the *holistic* pedagogical ecosystem wherein stellar pedagogy leads to highly motivated and knowledgeable students who are prepared for success in the design industries. These alumni, in turn,

DOI: 10.4324/9781003049166-27

help bolster and elevate our institutions' reputations that then attracts and helps retain top students.

This pedagogical ecosystem extends well beyond the design school. Each year, our design graduates enter the traditional design industries (e.g. fashion, interiors, graphics, and architecture) along with an increasingly diverse array of other sectors that are investing heavily in design thinking (e.g. healthcare, finance, and technology). This growing number of professional options enables design-trained graduates to go forward and share the values, approaches, beliefs, skills, and "ways of being" in the world that were imparted to them through our signature design pedagogies. In this respect, our pedagogy (via our graduates) helps shape the characteristics of these professions (whether they are in traditional design or in "other" markets) themselves. A robust pedagogical ecosystem can produce a sea change across not only US design education and its attendant industries, but also our nation's overall financial well-being as well as global economies.

Accordingly, the academic pendulum of design higher education will swing in a direction that responds to and is pulled by the current and forecasted financial, social, and political climates, as was the case with The Bauhaus. This is a time when we must ask ourselves critical questions about the future of design higher education. For example, should design curricula become more business-oriented or should it remain conceptually based? Should we train students to become deep-knowledge specialists or broad-thinking interdisciplinary practitioners? The Academy's academic direction must stay fluid since design education prepares students for the world as it *is* and as it *will become*. And yet, no matter its direction and associated discourse, the critical necessity of developing and sustaining talented educators will be—*must be*—forever constant. Faculty development (e.g. workshops, mentorship, and certificate programs) heightens teachers' sense of preparedness, self-efficacy, job satisfaction, retention, and overall success in their respective institutions. Pedagogical training improves the students' academic experience and, more specifically, promotes more meaningful teacher-student relationships—a particularly essential skillset when working with the emergent student generation that is experiencing unprecedented challenges. While the traditional "teacher as content provider" model may have succeeded with past generations, it is the advanced "teacher-mentor" role that is needed most to educate and support the current generation.

We must also sustain our growth as educators. This never-ending process (a "pedagogical mobius strip") requires us to be steadfast in our ongoing questioning, experimenting, learning, and reflecting, no matter our level of teaching experience. It is only by doing so that we can successfully navigate and adapt to the continuous evolutions of our students, schools, and design fields. In short, we must be perpetual learners who are never fully satisfied with all we have learned or achieved. An integral part of this ongoing development is that our teaching methods must always remain "live"—that is, always evolving and changing as the experience of teaching advances—and not static by succumbing to a mechanized, prescribed script we follow. Moreover, by consistently examining and improving our pedagogical skillsets, we help elevate teaching from simply a career to an innovative, dynamic, and rewarding art form that catapults students' learning and, consequently, the potential for the future of the design industries.

It is my ardent wish that this book—through its extensive provision of theory, research, and practical applications in design education—has shown both the *power* of our design pedagogy and that the impact of this power *must never be underestimated*. In every interaction we have with a student, we intellectually, creatively, and emotionally develop them for success—or failure. Be a positive contributor. Embrace your influential role and delve deeper into your pedagogy through a process of continuous improvement. As educators, we help shape society itself—as well as our future world. Therefore, it is imperative that you craft the most effective pedagogy possible for yourself: not only for the benefit of your students but also, ultimately, for the benefit of the world itself.

# Index

Note: Page references in *italics* denote figures, and in **bold** tables.

accessibility: and mentorship 282; and syllabus 257
active listening 224–225
Adidas 22
adolescence: drivers for prolonging 134; prolonging and young adults 133–135; *see also* design students; students
Agreement on Textiles and Clothing (ATC) 14
AIR-INK 34
Alabama Chanin 21
Albers, J. 75
Alessi 103
Amabile, T. 235–236
American College Health Association 61–62
ancillary services 63
apparel industry: employees in *15*; importation 14–17; rise of 12–14; *see also* fashion industry
apprenticeships 68–70
AR (augmented reality) 47
Argentina: and design education 93–97; design graduates 95; economic models 93–94; gross domestic product (GDP) 94; identity and tradition 96; signature designers 95; teaching design perspectives 96; technology and production approaches 96
Arket 36
artificial intelligence (AI) studios 79–80
assessment: backward design 258; Bloom's learning objectives 272–273; developmental 268–269; falling short 269–270; formative 268; improving critiques 275; as learning 267–275; learning assessment rubric 273–274; reflective practice 271–272; and success 270–271; summative 268; syllabus 256; three pillars of 268–269
Association of Independent Colleges of Art and Design (AICAD) schools 62
attendant stressors 128–131
autobiographical reflection 171
automated manufacturing 30
automation (sewbots) 16, 22
autonomy 48, 104, 118, 124, 166, 172, 233–235

backward design 257–259; assessments 258; diverse learning experiences 258–259; identify LOs 258; *see also* design
Baker, P. 233
banking pedagogy 79
basic information, and syllabus 254
Bauhaus principles 71–75, 140
behaviorism 118
behaviorist pedagogy 118
belonging, and sense of community 156
Bialetti 103
*bildung* 166–167
bio-fabricated materials 21
Black Lives Matter movement 126
Bland, C. J. 278
Bloom, B. 272, 273
Bloom's Taxonomy 258, 272
*Blown Away* 29

body language 225; arms and hands 211–212; face 210–211; legs and feet 212–213; stance 209–210; teaching performance 209–213
body scanning 22
Bok, D. 55
Boles, K. C. 153, 175–180
Boston's Museum of Fine Arts (MFAB) 29
Breuer, M. 74
Brookfield, S. 157, 170, 171, 219

Cai Yuanpei 97
campus resources and services 257
career: and design students 126–128; and young adult development 126–128
Cashin, B. 13
Central Academy of Arts and Crafts (CAAC) 98
Chanin, N. 21
Charbit, C. 38
China: design education in 97–101; geographic proximity with US 16; labor costs in 16; Mao Zedong era 98; modern design education 98–99; and offshore manufacturing 15
Chinese design industries: and design graduates 100; future prospects 101; modern 99–101; phases of growth in 99; *see also* design industries
Chochinov, A. 9
classrooms *see* design classrooms
classroom community 159, 236, 241, 263, 274; creating 155–156; cultivating 159; positive 222
classroom dynamics 217–227; conflict in design classroom 221–226; defined 217; trust in design classroom 218–221
classroom management 161, 163, 167, 168, 207
Coach 32
cognition: and multitasking lifestyle 131–132; and young adult development 131–132
cognitive development: of first-year design students 142–148; student-centered approach to 167
collaboration, and mentorship 280
collaborative resolution process 225–226

college: and design students 126–128; and young adult development 126–128
commitment: mentorship 280; in relativism 143
communication *see* nonverbal communication
community: cultivating 249–250; design students 235–236; developing 235–236; inclusive design classroom 249–250; nurturing 222
competent pedagogy 152–181; critically reflective teaching 169–174; effective educator 175–181; Finland 164–167; Singapore 160–162; South Korea 162–164; and teachers 153–159; *see also* pedagogy
conflict 217; in design classroom 221–226; socio-cognitive 271; strategies to manage 222–224; strategies to prevent 222
conflict management: addressing conflict 224; monitoring emotions and remain calm 222–223; pause and reflect 223–224; strategies for 222–224; and students' perspectives 223
conflict resolution: and body language 225; and collaborative resolution process 225–226; demonstrate active listening 224–225; learning stance, adopting 225; permit venting 224; and personal space 225; strategies promoting 224–226; verbally acknowledging emotions 225
connection, and sense of community 156
consistency and trust 218
constructivist pedagogy 118
consumerism/consumer behavior 9, 28, 31, 33, 37, 95
content: effective teaching 177; knowledge 177, 267, 290
corporate transparency 33–36
Council of Fashion Designers of America (CFDA) 17
course calendar, and syllabus 256
course description 255
course materials 256
course requirements 255–256
COVID-19 pandemic 36, 80; and design schools 81; emergence of 126; impact of 85; and lifestyles

## Index 295

89; post, and design schools 82–83; and use of digital network 81; and virtual learning experience 90–91
craft guilds 68–70
Creative Attributes Framework (CAF) (UAL) 108
Creative Computing Institute 109
critically reflective teaching 169–174; autobiographical reflection 171; fundamental tenets of 170–171; peer mentorship 172; promoting 171–173; scholarly literature 172; students' perspectives 171–172
critically reflective teaching practice 153, 169–174
critique ("crit") 121–122
Crosby, J. 277
crypto currencies 80
Cultural Revolution 98
culture: Argentine religious 96; Chinese pop 45; Confucian 160; of design 93; and designers 45; Finnish 165; institutional 168–169; lifetime milestones in US 133; modern industrial, in Italy 103; and personal space 213; shock 146
customized design 33

Darling-Hammond, L. 7, 191
*Das Englische Haus* 72
Davis, M. 8, 187
Decolonizing Art Institute 109
democratic design classroom 219–220
design: culture of 93; dexterity 76; emerging obsession with 28–29; ethos of 93; as immaterial agent 111–112; as knowledge-producing activity 111; marketplace, consumption and production in 29–31; massification of "high" 29; as national identity 111; pedagogy 122–123; practice 38–40; signature pedagogies of 120–122; skills 45; as social responsibility 111
"Design Against Crime" initiative 107
design classrooms 187–191; conflict in 221–226; conflict management strategies 222–224; conflict prevention strategies 222; and conflict resolution strategies 224–226; democratic 219–220; trust in 218–221

design education: academic models/design programs for 87–88; attributes/characteristics of US 85–87; challenges for 49, 88–90; in China 97–101; contemporary, in the US 75–76; future of 85–92; growth in 58–59; implications for 38–40; in Italy 102–106; modern, in China 98–99; pre-college (US) 144–145; unique approaches to 93–112; in United Kingdom 106–110
design educators: effective 175–181; Matthew Kressy's advice for 50–51; and shift in designer's role 39–40; Tim Marshall's advice for 91–92
design entrepreneurs 27–41; creating emotional value 31–33; Designer-As-Social Scientist 38–40; social justice 36–38; sustainability and corporate transparency 33–36
Designer-As-Social Scientist 38–40
designers: -as-auteur 27; Matthew Kressy on 50; traits important for 49
design faculty: development 63; and Tim Marshall 92
design industries: Argentina 95; attributes/characteristics of US 44–45; challenges for 49; emerging paradigm in 31–38; future of 44–51; growing 3–5; modern, in China 99–101; role and responsibility 5–6; uncertainty in 7–9; United Kingdom 106–107
design learning opportunities 156–157
design schools 56–57; apprenticeships 68–70; craft guilds 68–70; École des Beaux-Arts 70–71; experience 68–76; public and private, in Italy 105; Staatliches Bauhaus 71, 71–75; structure, future 78–83; students' transition from high school to 140–151; supporting student's transition into 148–150; and virtual learning experience 90–91
design school undergraduates *see* design students
design students 125–135; and autonomy 235; cognitive development of 142–148; commitment in relativism 143; community and interdependence 235–236; curricular gap

between academic levels 145–147; dualism 143; emotional development of 142–148; and enthusiasm 238–239; feedback and praising 240–241; growth mindsets and "grit" 239; motivational techniques for 233–241; multiplicity 143; personal development of 147–148; practical guide to teaching new 192–205; practical teaching strategies for **193–204**; pre-college experiences 144–145; relativism 143; teacher-student relationship 237–238; teaching within ZPD 234–235; transition into design school 148–150, **149–150**; two discordant worlds 140–142; *see also* students
design systems 6
design thinking 4, 11
Devalle, V. 94–95
developmental assessment 268–269
Dewey, J. 3, 170
*Die Brücke* 72
digital natives 128
digital networks 81
digital technology 21; and design students 128–131; and young adult development 128–131; *see also* technology
diverse learning experiences: developing 258–259; incorporating 258–259
diversity 62, 126, 257; of design students 246; of educational models 68; of opportunities 91; and syllabus 257
Domus Academy 105
DonorsChoose 37
dualism 143
Dweck, C. 233

Eames, C. 9
École des Beaux-Arts 70–71
education *see* design education
educators *see* design educators
effective teaching: content 177; pedagogy 177–179; relationships 179–180; three ingredients of 176–180
"e-flow" technology 22
Eileen Fisher 35
*Ellen's Next Great Designer* 29
*Emile* (Rousseau) 154

emotional development 154; of first-year design students 142–148; student-centered approach to 167
emotional intelligence 188
emotional value: of design creations 27, 28, 31–33; instilling 32
emotional well-being 61, *129*
employment: and design industries 4; growth prediction of US 5
empowerment, and sense of community 156
enthusiasm: design students 238–239; importance of 238–239
"entity theory" 232
entrepreneurs *see* design entrepreneurs
environment, and motivation 231–232
equitable participation 247–248
Escobar, A. 81
ethos of design 93
external rewards 231
extrinsic motivation 230–231

face-to-face social interaction 130
facilitated learning 157–158
faculty mentorship 277–287; benefits of 280, 282, 285–287; establishing 284–285; peer-to-peer 163–164, 172, 283; responsibilities and activities practiced in **281**; types of 282–284; *see also* mentorship
fashion industry: apparel importation 14–17; contemporary US 17–20; education 11–12; as model of widespread systemic change 11–23; offshore manufacturing 14–17; sustainable fashion practice 18–20; US apparel industry, rise of 12–14; *see also* apparel industry
The Fashion Pact (TFP) 35
fast fashion 18–19, 21, 30
feedback 240–241
Feldmann, L. 221
Fiat 500 102
Fink's Taxonomy 258
Finland 164–167
"Five Educations" model 97
"Five Honors" principle 97
fixed mindset 232–233
"Flow" concept *230*
Folkman, J. 218
formal mentoring 282
formative assessment 268

Freire, P. 119, 153
French Revolution 69
frictionless service 47
*Full Bloom* 29
"Futures Cone" 78

"G2" technology 21–22
Gannon, K. 254
Gates, B. 78
Generation Z 20, 33
Giacosa, D. 102
Global Climate Strike 20
global economies of scale 30
globalization 140
Goh Chok Tong 160
Google's Teachable Machine 80
grading, and syllabus 256
graduate demographics, profiles, etc
grants 17, 56; federal 60
Graves, M. 28
Great Recession (2008) 126
Greene, M. 274
Greer, A. 250
Gropius, W. 72–73, 73, 74
group mentoring 283
"groupthink" 173
growth mindset 233, 250
Gucci 36
guiding principles and characteristics of mentorship 280–282
guilds: craft 68–70; defined 69; function of 69

Hackers & Designers 82
hand gestures 211–212
Harnish, R. 260
Harvard University Graduate School of Design (HGSD) 58
Hasso Plattner Institute of Design 57
HCD (Human Centered Design) 46, 49
"Heavenly Bodies: Fashion and the Catholic Imagination" exhibition 29
Hennes & Mauritz (H&M) 18, 19, 28, 30
higher education (US): challenges 55–56; costs of 59–62; degrees, and student enrollment 57–58, 58; global best practices for design 167–169; growth of institutions 57–58, 58; historical and contemporary contexts of 55–64; negative effects on student experience 61–62; overview 55–56; strategies for improving affordability of 62–64; success of 56–59
hooks, b. 270
Hu, A. 168
Huang, L. 168
Human Centered Design (HCD) 44

IBM 4
IKEA 34
inclusion/inclusivity 126, 257
inclusive design classroom 243–251; content approach 245–246; cultivate relationships and community 249–250; cultivating 245–251; inclusive classroom 243–244; inclusive pedagogical methods 246–249; reduce stereotype threat 250–251; self-development 249; stereotype threat 244; student belonging 244
inclusive pedagogy 246–249
incremental theory 233
informal mentoring 282
institutional culture, and TPD 168–169
institutions 286; and culture 168–169; growth of 57–58, 58
Integrated Design & Management (IDM) Program (MIT) 44, 46
interdependence: design students 235–236; developing 235–236
interdisciplinary design 6
interpersonal sensitivity 222
intimate space 213, *214*
intrinsic motivation 229–230
Isabella, L. A. 283
"Italian economic miracle" (1958–1963) 103
Italy: design education in 102–106; link between industry and design 103; Made in Italy concept 103–104; and motorization 103; origin of Italian design 102–103; public and private design schools in 105

Jeanologia 21, 22
Juana de Arco 95
Julier, G. 93

Karl Lagerfeld 28
Kartell 103
Kenneth Cole 37
Kirp, D. 62

knowledge-based economy 140
Kosacoff, B. 94
Kram, K. E. 278, 283
Kramer, S. 235–236
Kressy, M. 44–51

La Londe, P. 162
Lanvin 28
Lavoie, R. 238
learner-centered syllabus 259–260; learner-centered focus 260; teacher-centered focus 260; and warm-tone 260–261
learning: assessment as 267–275; facilitated 157–158; holistic view of 168; instilling love of 158; through practice, theory, and research 168
learning assessment rubric 273–274
learning outcomes (LOs) 255; backward design 258; identify 258
learning stance 225
Lee Kuan Yew 160
Lego Group 32
Levi Strauss & Co. 22
liberationism pedagogy 119
Liew, W. 162
Loughran, J. J. 170
Lubbock, J. 158

machine learning 47–49
Made in Italy concept 103–104
manufacturing 48; automated 30; -focused design practices 11; innovations in 21; offshore 14–17; and sustainable practice 21; textiles 258; and US apparel industry 11–12
Marangoni 105
Marcia, J. 125
Marshall, T. 85–92
Maslow, A. 243
Maslow's Hierarchy of Needs 31, 32
material waste 21
Matthews, L. 76
McCardell, C. 13
McKinney, J. 156
meetings, recording of 285
mentees 277, 285; relationship with mentor 282–285
mentoring: formal 282; group 283; informal 282; peer 283; relationship 284–285; traditional 283
mentors 277, 286; -mentee relationship 282–285

mentorship: accessibility 282; benefits of 280, 282, 285–287; characteristics of 280–282; collaboration 280; commitment 280; common functions 278–280; determining scope of 284–285; evolution 280; guiding principles of 280–282; introduction to 277–282; mentor-mentee relationship, developing 282–285; models 282–284; purpose 280; responsibilities and activities of 278–280; trust 280
Metaverse 79–80
#MeToo movement 126
Metropolitan Museum of Art's (MMA) 29
Meyer, H. 74
Michelin 34
Mies van der Rohe, L. 74–75
Minerva 89–90
model inclusive language 248
Model of Effective Mentoring 279
Moholy-Nagy, L. 73, 75
Moore, N. 36
motivation: and design students 229–241; environment 231–232; extrinsic 230–231; factors influencing 231–233; fixed mindset 232–233; growth mindset 233; intrinsic 229–230; methods that motivate students 233–241; rewards for 233; students and syllabus 254; understanding 229–231; Zone of Proximal Development (ZPD) 231, 232
multiplicity 143
multitasking lifestyle, and cognition 131–132
Museum of Modern Art (New York City) 29
Muthesius, H. 72

Nanyang Technological University, Singapore 161
national identity, design as 111
National Institute of Education (NIE), Singapore 161
national mental health crisis 132–133
*Neue Sachlichkeit* 72
New York City Economic Development Corporation 17
New York Economic Development Corporation (NYCEDC) 17

New York Fashion Week (NYFW) 17–18
Nike 32
non-fungible tokens (NFTs) 80
nonverbal communication 213; autonomic 206; idiosyncratic 206; negative 211; pervasiveness of 206
Norell, N. 13
Norman, D. 76
North American Free Trade Agreement (NAFTA) 14
Nø School Nevers 82
Novembre, F. 106

objectivity 270
offshore manufacturing: and China 15; and fashion industry 14–17; *see also* manufacturing
Ogilvie, S. 69
Olivetti 103
online education 63–64
operant conditioning 118
optimal motivation 236
Organisation for Economic Co-operation and Development (OECD) 57, 162–163

Pandora 34
Parsons School of Design 57
participation: equitable 247–248; and sense of community 156
Patagonia 35
Pavlov, I. 118
Pease, A. 211, 214
Pease, B. 211, 214
"pedagogical ecosystem" 188, *189*
pedagogical methods: evolving 158–159; improving 158–159; questioning 158–159
pedagogy: "banking system" of 153; behaviorist 118; constructivist 118; critique ("crit") 121–122; defined 117; design 122–123; effective teaching 177–179; effect on student development 188–190; experimental 165; key approaches to 118–119; and learning environment 117; liberationism 119; overview 117–118; personalized 195; social constructivism 118–119; targeted 195
*Pedagogy of the Oppressed* (Freire) 119
peer mentoring 283

peer mentorship 172
Pendoley, R. 189
permit venting 224
Perry, W. 142, 144
Perry's Theory of Intellectual and Ethical Development *142*, 142–144
personal space 213, *214*, 225
Piaget, J. 118
Pink, D. 31
pluriversality 81
policies, and syllabus 256
Politecnico di Milano 104
positive relationships 218
practical teaching strategies for the new generation of design school undergraduates **193–204**
praise 240–241
pre-college experiences 144–145
presence, teaching performance 207–208
progressive teaching style 118
*Project Runway* 29
psychological distance 219
psychological safety 243
public space 213, *214*
Pujol, E. 274
purpose, and mentorship 280

Qing Dynasty 97

Ramirez, P. 96
Reagan, R. 15
RealReal 34
reengineered materials 21
reflective practice 169–174, 271–272
"reflective thought" 170
"RefScale" methodology 36
relationships: with colleagues 179; cultivating 249–250; effective teaching 179–180; inclusive design classroom 249–250; positive 218; with students 179
relativism 143
reshoring/nearshoring: apparel manufacturing 15–17; defined 15
rewards: external 231; for motivation 233
Rhode Island School of Design (RISD) 4
Rocco Design Group (RDG) 100
Roosevelt, T. 237
Rotman School of Management 86
Rousseau, J.-J. 154
Runway machine learning 80

300  *Index*

Saavedra, J. 166
safety: psychological 243; and sense of community 156
salary stagnation 55–56, 60
Savannah College of Art and Design (SCAD) 58
Save the Garment Center initiative 16
Schleicher, A. 165
scholarly literature 172
Schön, D. 270
School of Architecture and Planning 57
schools *see* design schools
Schools for Africa program 36–37
School SOS 82
Seletti 103
self-development 249
Sherrid, E. 270
Shulman, L. 120
signature designers 95
signature pedagogies 119; deep structure 120; defined 120; of design 120–122; implicit structure 120–121; surface structure 120; *see also* pedagogy
Simon Crawford Company 12–14
Sinapius, P. 270
Singapore 160–162
Skinner, B.F. 118
smartphones: addiction 192, **195**; use 128–131, 133
smart textiles 21
social constructivism pedagogy 118–119
Social Design Institute 109
socialization 279
social justice 36–38, 126
social media 129–131, 231; emotional well-being *129*; hashtags on 125; undergraduates on 129
social responsibility 6, 111
social space 213, *214*
socio-cognitive conflict 271
Socratic questioning 158
soft skills 187
Somerson, R. 4
South Korea 162–164
spatial relationships 213–215
Staatliches Bauhaus *71*, 71–75
stereotype threat: defined 244; inclusive design classroom 244, 250–251; reducing 250–251
Stevenson, H. 249
stressors *see* attendant stressors
structural inequality 108–109
students: belonging 244; cultivate relationships with 155; motivating, to read syllabus 263–264; relationships with 179; success, and syllabus 257; transition from high school to design school 140–151; *see also* design students
subjectivity 270
success: and assessment 270–271; of students, and syllabus 257
summative assessment 268
support, and sense of community 156
sustainability 33–36; and fashion practice 18–23; and virtual sampling 40
syllabus: assessment and grading 256; basic information 254; campus resources and services 257; before classes 263; components of 254–257; course calendar 256; course description 255; course materials 256; course requirements 255–256; inclusivity, diversity, and accessibility 257; instructor information 254; learning outcomes 255; as living and changing document 264–265; motivating students 254; motivating students to read 263–264; policies 256; primary functions of 253–254; providing evidence 253–254; structure 253; student success 257; syllabus design strategies 257–262; teaching methods 255; teaching philosophy 255
syllabus design strategies 257–262; backward design 257–259; balance of power 262; course context 257; course contextualization 259; effective formatting 261–262; learner-centered syllabus 259–260; structured yet flexible framework 259; warm-tone 260–261
"systems-before-artifacts" design process 6
systems-oriented design 6–7

Target 28
teachers 153–159; education and subject knowledge 167–168; effective attributes 175–180; preparation 152, 161; -student relationship 237–238; training 168, 188

## Index  301

teachers professional development (TPD) 168–169
teacher-student mentorship model: create classroom community 155–156; design learning opportunities 156–157; educating/developing whole person 154–155; facilitating learning 157–158; pedagogical methods 158–159; relationships with students 155
teaching: candidate's aptitude for 167; critically reflective 169–174; evaluating and rewarding effective 169; holistic view of 168; methods 218–219, 247, 255; as performance 206–215; philosophy 255; through practice, theory, and research 168; within the ZPD 234–235
teaching performance 206–215; arms and hands 211–212; body language 209–213; competitive seating position 215, *215*; components of 207–215; face 210–211; legs and feet 212–213; L-shaped seating position 214, *215*; presence 207–208; side-by-side seating position 214–215, *215*; spatial relationships 213–215, *214*; stance 209–210; voice 208–209
technology: advancements in 8–9; approaches to 96; and design education 109; digital 21, 128–131; "e-flow" 22; "G2" 21; machine learning 79–80; simplification of 47–49
*The Room of Silence* 270
Thorndike, E. 118
three-year bachelor's degrees 62–63
"Tied with Pride" advertising campaign 37
time, and mentoring relationship 284
Toms 36
*Top Design* 29
traditional mentoring 283
Troen, V. 179
trust 217; consistency 218; democratic design classroom 219–220; in design classroom 218–221; group interactions 219; high expertise and good judgment 218; mentorship 280; pedagogy, discussing 219; positive relationships 218; students' feedback 220–221

Uniqlo 18
United Kingdom: design education in 106–110; design industries 106–107; design pedagogies 107–108; speculations 108–110
United Nations: Alliance for Sustainable Fashion 20; Sustainable Development Goals (SDGs) 35
United States-Mexico-Canada Agreement (USMCA) 14
University of the Arts (UAL) 106–108; Creative Attributes Framework (CAF) 108
US Bureau of Labor Statistics (USBLS) 14
US economy: arts and design industries 3–4; and fashion design industry 18

Versace 28
Vespa scooter 102
Vestiaire Collective 34
Villarreal, C. 155
virtual learning experience: and COVID-19 pandemic 90–91; and design schools 90–91
virtual sampling 40
voice, and teaching performance 208–209
*Vorkurs* 72–74
Voros, J. 78
Vygotsky, L. 118–119, 231, 271

Warby Parker 37
Ward, William Arthur 154
warm-tone 260–261
Warren, L. 226
waste reduction 22
World Food Program 38

young adult development: and career 126–128; and cognition 131–132; and college 126–128; and digital technology 128–131; and diversity 126; emergent generation of design students 125–135; and inclusion 126; national mental health crisis 132–133; overview 124–125; prolonging adolescence 133–135; and social justice 126

Zara 18, 19, 21
Zenger, J. 218
Zone of Proximal Development (ZPD) 231, 232, 234–235